Flair Donglai Shi, Gareth Guangming Tan
(eds.)

WORLD LITERATURE IN MOTION

Institution, Recognition, Location

STUDIES IN WORLD LITERATURE

The book series STUDIES IN WORLD LITERATURE is devoted to the analysis of global literature, and the multiple, sometimes contradictory, tendencies it accommodates. Its field of enquiry is the 'new' world literature, a category currently emerging through multiple changes from the old Romantic concept of *Weltliteratur*, attuned to the challenges posed by postcolonialism and multiculturalism, the increasing globalisation of literature (but also its reverse trend, regionalisation), and the diversification of the market place. STUDIES IN WORLD LITERATURE encourages research which celebrates and critically assesses a phenomenon that can be understood, as Pheng Cheah points out, as the 'literature of the world—imaginings and stories [...] that track and account for contemporary globalization as well as older historical narratives of worldhood'.

World literature can be brought into dialogue with postcolonial writing through scrutiny of how it is written, read, circulated, and received transnationally within the contemporary circuit of global cultural capital. The series also responds to the need to examine the inherent contradictions in the concept of a world literature and dependence on a hegemonic (often English-centred) literary and critical discourse.

The series seeks to address these tensions, and consequently welcomes:

1) volumes which debate such matters theoretically (including definitions of what counts as 'world literature' and the place of postcolonial literary production within this larger category);
2) comparative studies of texts and genres from different countries and cultures under common headings or concepts such as memory, ethics, and human rights.

Volumes on national literatures, when these are set in a world/comparative or generic context, will also be considered, and the series will include discussions of other complementary aspects of discourse, narratology, and media. While writing by 'canonical' authors will be covered, the series will additionally propose wider cultural and intellectual genealogies for 'minor' or occluded writers. A key aim of this series is to redeploy the familiar rhetoric of postcolonial theory and discourse in relation to concepts relevant to world literature by introducing arguments that will be integrated with the evidence of individual literary practice. This emphasis on contesting definitions of 'diasporic' or 'postcolonial' writing, 'transnational' or 'transcultural' literatures and 'world' literature as used by writers, critics and thinkers may lead to a reconsideration of the boundaries that divide and intersections that link these related fields.

Recent volumes:

3 *Bruce King*
From New National to World Literature
Essays and Reviews
ISBN 978-3-8382-0856-5

4 *Gareth Griffiths, Philip Mead (eds.)*
The Social Work of Narrative
Human Rights and the Cultural Imaginary
ISBN 978-3-8382-0858-9

5 *Johanna Emeney*
The Rise of Autobiographical Medical Poetry and the Medical Humanities
ISBN 978-3-8382-0938-8

6 *Gerri Kimber, Janet Wilson*
Re-forming World Literature
Katherine Mansfield and the Modernist Short Story
ISBN 978-3-8382-1163-3

Flair Donglai Shi, Gareth Guangming Tan (eds.)

WORLD LITERATURE IN MOTION

Institution, Recognition, Location

Bibliographic information published by the Deutsche Nationalbibliothek
Die Deutsche Nationalbibliothek lists this publication in the Deutsche Nationalbibliografie; detailed bibliographic data are available in the Internet at http://dnb.d-nb.de.

Bibliografische Information der Deutschen Nationalbibliothek
Die Deutsche Nationalbibliothek verzeichnet diese Publikation in der Deutschen Nationalbibliografie; detaillierte bibliografische Daten sind im Internet über http://dnb.d-nb.de abrufbar.

ISBN-13: 978-3-8382-1163-3

Printed in the United States of America

Table of contents

Foreword

Peter D. McDonald and Michelle Kelly

That Flair Donglai Shi and Gareth Guangming Tan have elected to frame their first collective research publication as a manifesto for and example of a "critical world literary studies" is a source of particular pride to us, as co-teachers of the course in which the seeds of this wonderful collection of essays were sown. With impressive insight into the approaches, canons, and methods currently operating under the sign of "world literature", Shi's Introduction cuts through the various polemics to identify one of the fundamental questions for students and scholars of the field: what does one study when one studies *world literature*? Building on the injunction articulated by Stefan Helgesson and Pieter Vermeulen that world literature should be "investigated in its actuality", Shi and Tan have assembled a group of early career and established scholars from around the world who offer various accounts of how literature emerges to prominence as *world* literature, and what is at stake in the scholarly framing of it as such. By focusing on the materiality of the object of study, in its full linguistic and institutional complexity, they reflect both the methodological necessity of giving definition to the emphasis on circulation by many of the field's leading proponents and the institutional context from which Shi and Tan's crucial questions first emerged. It seems in keeping with the self-reflexivity at the heart of this collection to sketch that context.

Many of the essays collected in this volume developed initially from Oxford University's Master of Studies (M.St.) in World Literature in English, specifically the so-called "B-Course" that we have been co-teaching since 2013. While the programme's "A-Course" offers students a grounding in some of the prevailing debates in world and postcolonial literature, the "B-Course" encourages them to approach these debates from a different perspective. With its origins in the scholarly traditions of early modern European humanism, this part of the masters programme reflects Oxford's longstanding commitment to manuscript studies, editing and bibliography, though it is now officially billed as "Research Skills (Bibliography, Palaeography, Transcription, Book History etc.)".

For us that "etc" has always been reassuring. For one thing, it creates space to think with and beyond the founding assumptions of the course, its European origins, and its established methods. For another, it gives us room to encourage students from all over the world to reflect on their own diverse experiences of literary studies, to develop new skills, questions and methods, and ultimately to produce new kinds of writing.

This is why we begin the seminar series on world book history with two, seemingly straightforward questions. How, we ask, did your academic training so far construe your primary object of study? And how did it expect you to engage with it?

About the first question, there is usually a debate. Some students point out that their courses, though primarily literary, included options on film and other visual media or advertising and other language-related cultural phenomena. The discussion does not last long, however. After a few minutes, a consensus begins to emerge: broadly speaking, their previous degrees privileged the text, specifically, the linguistic text, as the object of study. The approach or activity? Again, there is some debate because most of their courses required them to think about various critical methods and traditions. But, as with the first question, they soon agree that some or other version of "close reading" was always paramount.

Bearing in mind that we have students from a diverse range of countries and regions with very different linguistic and cultural backgrounds, the conclusion is surprising, perhaps even dismaying. At the start of the 21st century, no matter if you are studying in Africa, Asia, Oceania, Europe, or the Americas, it appears that you spend most of your undergraduate years as a student of literature analysing texts up close. The "B course", we then explain, does something different. In fact, it actively encourages students to question the guiding assumptions of their undergraduate courses, first by re-imagining the objects of study, and second by re-construing the basic protocols of critical enquiry.

If the centrality of the "B-Course" to Oxford's masters programmes is in part an accident of institutional history, it has nonetheless converged with the challenge that has emerged in some articulations of world literature studies to give greater definition to the material realities of world literature. In this regard, Shi's manifesto for a critical world literature studies, following Helgesson and Vermeulen, is to some extent building on the legacy of Pascale Casanova's (2005) efforts to chart the contours of a "world literary space". In "Literature as a World" she postulates "a mediating space [. . .] between literature and the world", one that is "relatively autonomous" of politics and economics (as well as "relatively dependent" on them), and therefore a space in which "questions, debates, inventions of a specifically literary nature" and "struggles of all sorts—political, social, national, gender, ethnic—come to be refracted, diluted, deformed or transformed according to a literary logic, and in literary forms" (71–72, 85). While her *World Republic of Letters* offers one map through this space, and has been critiqued for its Eurocentricity among other things, she insists in the later essay that the world literary space she imagines "is no more than a tool that should be tested by concrete research, an instrument that might provide an account of the logic and history of literature, without falling into the trap of total autonomy" (72).

The collection of essays gathered here by Shi and Tan offers new routes through this world literary space, emphasising the ways in which its texts, forms and scholarly debates are shaped by "Postcolonial Institutions", "Recognition through Prizes", "Minor Locations", and "Translations beyond the Anglophone". Its objects of study are literary texts, archival resources, and paratextual and translational materials, and its methods are primarily bibliographic, book historical, and sociological—exactly the kind of "concrete research" that can test the textures and limits of Casanova's world literary space.

This too reflects the aspirations of the Oxford "B" course, which we deliberately start outside the seminar room. In the first term of teaching, students are introduced to manuscript materials, rare books, artefacts and printed ephemera at the Bodleian's Weston Library. The world book history seminars then begin with a morning in the archives of Oxford University Press, followed by an afternoon at Oxford Brookes University, which has among its collections the complete records of the Booker Prize. While these visits allow the students to develop their research skills in a practical, hands-on way, they also give them the chance to experience the pleasures of discovery, to see how theoretical and archival enquiry ideally inform each other, to consider the acts of curation shaping the various collections they encounter, and, perhaps most importantly, to get a feel for the creative possibilities the "B-Course" affords. The methods and materials of the course enable students to rethink the theoretical assumptions of their subject, whether the emphasis falls on the postcolonial or the world. Moreover, the dynamic processes of circulation and translation that we engage with put particular pressure on the idea of a world literature *in English*.

This wonderful volume of essays demonstrates the productivity of this line of critical inquiry. As it shows, once you lift your eyes from the screen or page, there are essentially no limits to the questions you can ask about the workings of a literary culture, its shaping power and your own place in it. All the expressive media come into view—gestural, oral, scribal, print and digital—as do the many ways in which texts of all kinds are created, published, sponsored, circulated, translated, read and prized. Even the category of "World Literature", the academic field of "World Literary Studies" and the presumed anglocentricity of both come under scrutiny, since they are themselves caught up in these processes, rather than safely outside or above them.

Casanova begins "Literature as a World" with a key question: "Is it possible to re-establish the lost bond between literature, history and the world, while still maintaining a full sense of the irreducible singularity of literary texts?" (2005, 71). As her own work shows, she has been better at answering the first part. As this volume makes clear, however, much remains to be done when it comes to the second. How much room does critical world literary studies have for innovative literary writing and the worlds it creates? And how might a more sustained engagement with this encourage us to re-imagine, not once but repeatedly, the bonds between literature, history and the world that are never secure, always in the making? Moving deftly and self-reflexively across continents, institutions, languages, and media, the essays in this volume testify to the energy, ingenuity and creativity with which the exceptional group of students and colleagues with whom we have been lucky to work over the past five years have begun to address these questions. They have taught us, and now they can teach you.

Works Cited

Casanova, Pascale. 2005. "Literature as a World." *New Left Review* 31 (Jan-Feb): 71–90.

Introduction: A Manifesto for Critical World Literature Studies

Flair Donglai Shi

When Franco Moretti (2000) declares that "world literature is not an object, it's a problem" (55) in his now classic article "Conjectures on World Literature", he is nonetheless envisioning a field of inquiry where "world literature" as such constitutes the primary object of study for his proposed method of "distant reading", a mode of reading that produces "graphs, maps, and trees" of patterns, tropes, and other connections of form in literary works produced all over the world (1). However, a more pertinent and relatable way to conceive of "world literature" as a "problem" in the more mundane sense may come through imagining what "world literature" as a subject of study entails, for the average student or researcher identifying it as their primary discipline. This is especially relevant in the context of social settings where a certain level of existential anxiety is consistently evoked around self-reflective (and often self-deconstructive) questions of disciplinary boundaries, methodologies, efficacies and purposes. For example, in the most common scenario of academic socialising, where simple introductory questions such as "what do you study?" and "what is your research about?" come up, the answer "World Literature", compared to more conventional terms like "English Literature" and "German Politics", or even relatively new ones like "Neuroscience" and "Cybersecurity", can immediately provoke presumptuous, even contemptuous, reactions: "What is that? Do you mean all of the literatures in the world? How many language classes do you have to do?" Each of these questions presents a unique set of challenges to the very legitimacy of "world literature" as an organising concept. While we may find it hard to give any succinct and definitive answer to the first question (even David Damrosch's [2003] book-length effort, *What is World Literature?*, has generated more questions and contentions than easy answers, after all), it is equally difficult for us to summon the arrogance necessary to say yes to the second question. As for the last question, regarding linguistic competence, we are, first and foremost, obliged to admit that we rely on translations (especially *into* or *from* the English language), to the point that, in Susan Bassnett's (2016) words, "we cannot conceive of World Literature without translation" (312). At the same time, we are also impelled to clear ourselves of the tacit sense of shame (for the implied lack of expertise in specific languages) associated with such reliance by arguing, à la David Damrosch, that translations afford an "expansion in depth" for literary texts and thus constitute independently productive and creative sites of scholarly investigation (2003, 289).

What such common social scenarios reveal is the high degree of self-reflexivity wired into the very ontological and conceptual foundation of "world literature". To mitigate the confusion induced by this self-reflexivity, it is necessary to separate, rather than conflate, individual examples of "world literature" as objects of study (i.e. a set of literary texts and events to be analysed) and "World Literature" as a subject of study (i.e. a set of academic discourses and methodological debates). Understandably, such a separation can be difficult to envision or maintain because the latter is a meta-language in relation to the former, the conceptual boundaries of which in turn depend on this very meta-language. One solution to this "problem" of tautological tendencies, this volume contends, is to triangulate, and in effect clarify and affirm, this separation between "world literature" and "World Literature" with what Stefan Helgesson and Pieter Vermeulen (2016) call "critical world literature studies". Helgesson and Vermeulen have proposed this term in their edited book, *Institutions of World Literature*, to highlight that world literature does not need to "be 'defended,' but [. . .] should be investigated in its actuality", and the editors of this current volume believe that "critical world literature studies" as a discursive coinage can realise its full theoretical potential when it is applied to the investigation of the academic discourses of "World Literature" as well (2). That is to say, a *critical* approach to world literature studies takes as its object of study the very subject of

World Literature itself, and more importantly, this critical gesture should be seen as a highlighted *continuation* of, rather than radical breakaway from, the self-reflective qualities of the subject. As Haun Saussy (2017) puts it, "the question has never been, 'What is world literature?', but 'Whence comes this fantasy, and what is the hold it still has on us?'" (403). Utilising primary data such as literary texts, archival resources, and paratextual and translational materials, critical world literature studies reflects on the disciplinary motivations, theoretical validities, and discursive effects of the various academic discussions on world literature, rather than simply taking sides in the ongoing debate. In essence, critical world literature studies emphasises the materially-grounded specificity of socio-historical contexts, and it participates in the current debate on world literature with a sustained sense of meta-academic suspicion, especially with regards to the tautological, totalising, and reductive tendencies in the many theories of World Literature. As an alternative response to the aforementioned question of "What do you study?", "critical world literature studies" may be a more complicated answer, yet it also more effectively pre-empts judgmental assumptions associated with "world literature" writ large, and allows the student or scholar in conversation to demonstrate the self-reflective and investigative power of what he or she actually does—"I study how certain literary texts come to be regarded as world literature" or "I study how people define and debate world literature as such".

This introductory chapter presents a summative explanation of how critical world literature studies works. It is divided into four main sections to outline the different schools of thought in the ongoing debate in World Literature and synthesise them into the particular analytical angles and literary events this volume seeks to emphasise, including colonial institutions, global book prizes, and comparative translation studies. The first section identifies four major schools of thought in the post-millennial revival of world literature as a theoretical concept, including the idea of circulation proposed by David Damrosch (2003), the focus on international recognition found in the works of Pascale Casanova (2004) and Shu-mei Shih (2004), the prioritisation of politico-economic systems by Franco Moretti (2000), Mads Rosendahl Thomsen (2008), Alexander Beecroft (2015), and Warwick Research Collective (2015), and lastly, the philosophical shift towards "literary worlds" championed by Eric Hayot (2012) and Pheng Cheah (2016). To set up the opposition camp for these different propositions of world literature, the second section then presents three major responses from different disciplines, which argue against the notion of world literature and question the validity and desirability of many of the proposed methods of doing World Literature. They are the postcolonial response from Peter Hitchcock (2010), Magdi Youssef (2015), and Elleke Boehmer (2015), the comparatist response from Haun Saussy (2011) and Matthew Reynolds et al. (2015), and the provocative response from Emily Apter (2013) and Tim Parks (2015) from the vantage point of untranslatability. Situated in this more or less antagonistic structure of definitional, and sometimes ideological, contention, the third section singles out the sociological approach to world literature inspired by Robert Darnton's (1982) "communication circuit" and Pierre Bourdieu's (1986) theories on cultural capital. Highlighting the *situatedness* and analytical productivity of this particular approach, the current volume is closely associated with the pioneering research of scholars like Graham Huggan (2001), Sarah Brouillette (2007) and Peter McDonald (2016). Finally, the last section of this introduction identifies four key issues in the creation of world literature made more visible by the sociological approach and argues that they constitute a set of specific literary phenomena particularly germane to critical world literature studies. These four key issues serve as organising agendas corresponding to the four sections of this volume—"Postcolonial Institutions", "Recognition through Prizes", "Minor Locations", and "Translations beyond the Anglophone"—and together they demonstrate both the inclusionary and the exclusionary power of world literature (as well as "World Literature") as institutions and discourses.

What is World Literature? Circulation, Recognition, Systems, and Worlds

David Damrosch's *What is World Literature?* is widely cited and regarded as *the* academic monograph that reactivated World Literature as a field of inquiry in the post-millennial age of intensified globalization, even though many of the primary texts used in this book have been, or at least could have been, studied in a range of pre-existing disciplines such as Classics, Modern Languages, and Comparative Literature. According to Damrosch, "world literature" is a useful organising concept for literary studies in so far as it allows us to see how much the process of circulation constitutes *literature* as such. For him, world literature refers to "all literary works that circulate beyond their culture of origin", and when he states that "world literature is writing that gains in translation" (as a specific kind of circulation), the implicit emphasis is put upon the creative quality of literary texts as opposed to other more utilitarian forms of writing such as legal documents (2003, 4 and 281). In accordance to the meta-analytic spirit of critical world literature studies, this circulational mode of world literature can be applied to the so-called origin of the idea of world literature itself: the German writer Johann Wolfgang von Goethe's notion of *Weltliteratur*, as recorded by his disciple Johann Peter Eckermann, was inspired by his reading of a contemporary Chinese novel (in translation, of course) and thus the product of literary circulation *par excellence*. However, as Jing Tsu (2011) has noted, this circulation was only possible because of the western missionaries based in the southern province of Canton—a geopolitical situation foreshadowing the rise of European imperialism in China. Like the Chinese novel read by Goethe, all literary circulations take place under specific conditions influenced by a set of political, economic, and cultural structures, and the problem with Damrosch's definition of world literature, as Harish Trivedi (2013) rightly points out, is that "it need involve no more than what we are reading anyhow because it is already in circulation" (22). In other words, when critically examined, Damrosch's idea of circulation has served as a productive point of departure for different interpretations of world literature exactly because it is overtly generic and has to be challenged by specific case studies. Since all texts can be said to be circulating in one way or another and the idea of "culture of origin" can only be as vague or clear as it is discursively (and subjectively) constructed (Thornber 2016, 108), it makes sense that, in following or refuting Damrosch's definitions, many schools of thought have focused on the aforementioned structural factors shaping literary circulations instead.

This structural focus is most prominent in the theoretical approaches taken by a range of world literature scholars, who can be divided into two related schools of thought based on the different emphases in their methodologies and primary arguments. Firstly, Pascale Casanova's *La République Mondiale des Lettres* and Shu-mei Shih's proposition of "technologies of recognition" focus on the fixed range of mechanisms and structures of international recognition as the *problématique* of world literature (Shih uses the term "global literature" instead, but in this case the difference is only nominal). Informed by Pierre Bourdieu's theories, Casanova's "world republic of letters" is organised by the unequal distribution of literary capital, which results in a dichotomy between the international literary space, which she regards as the "autonomous pole" of world literature, and the national literary space, pertaining to the "politico-literary pole" of the same structure (2004, 105). In Casanova's paradigm, Paris serves as the centre of world literature, followed by New York and London, because these places hold strong economic advantages, and more importantly, power of consecration, over the literary output of other regions and nations. With a much stronger anti-hegemonic stance, Shu-mei Shih's article highlights four specific "technologies of recognition" employed by "the West" to secure its dominant position as "the agent of recognition" vis-à-vis "the rest" as "the object of recognition", including "the systematic", "the allegorical", "global multiculturalism" and "the exceptional particular" (2004, 17). Notably, both Casanova and Shih cite the Chinese-French Nobel laureate Gao Xingjian as a prime example of the importance of western recognition for a writer's mobility and reputation; Casanova even goes so far as to say that it is "owing to his knowledge of French" that Gao is able to make use of "Western literary innovations and techniques and [. . .] the aesthetic norms of the literary present" and become "the incarnation" of an international writer (2004, 152). However, this heavy emphasis on the power of western recognition has also been criticised by many scholars, who argue that such a lopsided emphasis on literary capital may perpetuate the "French (or Western) hegemony" of such oppressive structures as it neglects writers' agency to negotiate their own (non-)recognition by different circles (Graham et al 2012, 467; Fang 2018, 7).

Secondly, another diverse group of scholars is also interested in structural inequalities, but their theoretical agenda differs from the recognition school in that they seek to describe or picture the overarching system(s) by which literary texts and their circulations are governed. Following the recent development of digital humanities, Franco Moretti's method of distant reading testifies to his ideas on centres and peripheries borrowed from Immanuel Wallerstein's world-system theory. Much like Wallerstein's division of the world into dominant centres and dominated peripheries based on political and socioeconomic analyses, "world literature", especially in the form of the modern novel, follows certain "law(s) of literary evolution" and consists of different combinations of "European literary forms" and "local (i.e. non-European) materials" (2000, 58 and 60). In relation to Casanova and Shih's claims, such systemic descriptions of world literature can explain why "the west" holds the power of recognition in the first place. Taking this focus on the systemic further, the Warwick Research Collective (WReC) insists on "a *single* world-literary system" governed by "*capitalism as a world-system*" (2015, 8 and 14; original emphases). Guided by Fredric Jameson's idea of a singular modernity and the Marxist interpretation of world literature as a result of the expansion of bourgeois capital, the WReC rejects the totalising division between the west and the rest and regards world literature as "the literature of the modern capitalist world-system" (15): literary texts that register the reality of capitalist modernity formally and thematically to various degrees. More recently, some scholars closely associated with the WReC, such as Sharae Deckard and Stephen Shapiro (2019), have sought to further extend this line of critique to examine the dynamics between neoliberalism and world cultures in more generic terms. Differing from the political inclinations of these paradigms, Mads Rosendahl Thomsen (2008) and Alexander Beecroft (2015) treat world literature as a more loosely connected kind of system. For Thomsen, it is made up of thematic constellations of literary texts that are "far apart in time and place" but nonetheless connected by what Ludwig Wittgenstein calls "family resemblances" (4); for Beecroft, it is a set of "empirically derived [...] ecologies", which trace the development of literary texts in different historical periods in a non-evolutionary manner (2015, 27). Notably, for both of them, these systems and categories of "world literature" do not possess any essential meaning and only become meaningful when employed as modes of reading that serve to bring together a diverse range of texts and enable collaborative scholarly investigations. As such, they echo Damrosch's original proposition that "world literature is not a set canon of texts but a mode of reading: a form of detached engagement with worlds beyond our own place and time" (2003, 281).

Dissatisfied with the privileging of "literature" over "world" in these interpretations of world literature as circulational or structural, a more recent addition to the definition debate can be found in the works by Eric Hayot (2012) and Pheng Cheah (2016). Informed by the philosophies of Mikhail Bakhtin and Martin Heidegger, they regard world literature not as mere material objects that exist and circulate in the physical world but as creative activities with world-constructive capabilities. For Hayot, literature generates and interacts with different "chronotopes", or time-space formations, and its "resistance to the social and the normative locates itself precisely at this level of ungeneralisability" (2012, 16). Cheah's book, *What Is a World?* (2016), draws on Edward Said's discussion on "worldliness" and also emphasises the temporal dimension of world literature. For him, world literature as a temporal category possesses "an active power in the making of worlds that is both a site of processes of worlding and an agent that participates and intervenes in these processes" (2). Moreover, this philosophical shift to the internal power of literature warrants a distinction between this creative world literature and what Cheah, à la Jacques Derrida, regards as literatures of "the globe"—texts produced by the WReC's singular system of global capitalism. On the one hand, this conceptual distinction is useful as it enables this philosophical school of world literature studies to align itself with the anti-global politics of scholars like Gayatri Spivak (2010), Duncan Chesney (2017), and Jaouad El Habbouch (2019) and at the same time affirms the interventionist agency of literature at global levels. On the other hand, as Karolina Watroba (2017) has argued, the contrast between such theoretical affirmation and promotion for "creative world literature" and the sometimes more-than-subtle scholarly disdain against global "popular literature" reveals an ironic tendency of certain academic discourses to fall back on "the tradition of Eurocentric elitism", with their value judgements against the "low-brow" now packaged in a quasi-geopolitical language characterised by an increasingly moralistic tone (57).

Against World Literature: The Postcolonial, the Comparative, and the Untranslatable

As much as the definition of world literature remains in contention, there have also been many scholarly responses against the idea of world literature. Firstly, despite, or perhaps because of, the significant overlap in the range of contemporary literary texts they address, postcolonialism and world literature tend to encounter each other in conflict. For example, Peter Hitchcock (2010) is of the opinion that "world literature [. . .] allows one to consume postcolonialism without that nasty taste of social struggle in which a reader's own cosmopolitanism may be at stake" (5). Focusing on the pedagogical effects of the discourse of world literature, Magdi Youssef (2015) has called for a decolonisation of world literature in order to prevent the field from being reduced to "the dominant and generally recognised

European–US literary canon" (125). Similarly, Elleke Boehmer (2014) has expressed the worry that the "convergence of the postcolonial and the world" may usher in a kind of "post-postcolonial world literary studies" that in practice involve "the overwriting of the specificity of the former by the universal cultural values implied by the latter" (304–05). However, scholars like Helgesson (2014) and Cheah (2016) have sought to reconcile postcolonialism and world literature from different angles, and this effort is followed by 2019 special issues on this exact topic in the *Journal of World Literature* (Volume 4, Issues 3–4), edited by Bhavya Tiwari and David Damrosch. In a contribution that echoes Cheah's emphasis on postcolonial creativity and literature as world-making activities, Helgesson notes that "because of their heightened awareness of the rift between subjective experience and institutionally sustained literary language, writers from colonies and postcolonies have been at the vanguard of world literature" (2014, 498). More indicatively, Boehmer has also moved towards this reconciliatory stance in her latest monograph, *Postcolonial Poetics* (2018), and affirms that

> if world literary studies were to take on board radical postcolonial energies, this could produce a more mobile, expansive, and genuinely horizontal conception of the world than previously existed in the former domain, and, as a corollary, a constructive interrogation of still-definitive Eurocentric paradigms in both fields. (165)

As the chapters in the first section of this current volume demonstrate, these eclectic views are shared by many of our contributors.

Secondly, some Comparative Literature scholars have also expressed concerns for the intellectual rigour and institutional implications of World Literature as a disciplinary force. In a published conversation with David Damrosch, Haun Saussy contends that World Literature "may aid in a long-standing project of academic administrators, the reduction of all language and literature departments to subsets of the English department" (2016, 662). Not only has he called for the abandonment of "the use of 'world literature' to designate an international Winner's Circle" (2011, 290), but Saussy is also worried that World Literature is "reining in [. . .] the wild interdisciplinarity of the founders (of Comparative Literature)" (2016, 662). Similarly, Matthew Reynolds et al. (2015) have declared that "the point of comparative criticism is to be a thorn in the side of 'world literature'" as it gives "more opportunity for the texts at issue to challenge the critical categories that are brought to bear on them" (148 and 157). Finally, with regards to World Literature's reliance on translated texts for many of the systemic statements in the field, Emily Apter (2013) argues that "incommensurability and what has been called the Untranslatable are insufficiently built into the literary heuristic" (3). Together with Tim Parks (2015), Apter has cautioned against World Literature's tendency to homogenise and erase the linguistic and cultural specificities of literary texts which are brought into comparison or simply grouped together. Ironically but perhaps unsurprisingly, this abstract evocation of "the Untranslatable" has been criticised by scholars in Translation Studies, such as Lawrence Venuti (2016, 202) and Susan Bassnet (2019), as a "dubious" way of "side-stepping investigation into the actual processes of translation and the ideological frames within which translations happen" (6). Notwithstanding the polemical complexity of much of these disagreements, the editors of this volume acknowledge that the method of comparative criticism actualises the self-reflective and meta-academic spirit of critical world literature studies. To be specific, we believe that the analytical act of cross-cultural, and more importantly, cross-linguistic, comparison, when grounded in solid primary data from specific locations, makes clear the structural mechanisms and limitations of world literature in whichever definition mentioned so far. This method, explicitly or implicitly, can be found in all of the chapters collected in this volume (but most notably in those in the final two sections).

Creating World Literature: The Sociological Approach

As the two previous sections have summarised, the post-millennial debate on the idea of world literature has focused on the power of literary creativity vis-à-vis political, economic, and cultural structures, and much of it is driven by a predetermined set of ideologies and philosophical positions always already in conflict with one another. While we agree with Matthew Reynolds et al. that ideological reductionism is hard to avoid and "any critical or scholarly event (and theory, really) is necessarily to some extent hegemonic" (2015, 157), the editors of this volume believe that there is a need for a more ideologically neutral, materially grounded, and self-reflective way to study world literature (as well as the academic field of World Literature). As such, the very concept of world literature employed throughout this volume is "at best only a means, a way of pointing to the many worlds it both inhabits and creates" (McDonald 2019, 32). Applying Pierre Bourdieu's theories on cultural capital to Book History as an interdisciplinary "field", we follow Helgesson and Vermeulen's advocacy of a sociological approach to world literature. Differing from the polemical efforts to determine what world literature *is* or *should be*, the sociological approach highlights the various processes in which world literatures are *created as such*—"an interrelated set of social phenomena" including "production, circulation, distribution and consumption", and at the same time it allows literary works to manifest, via distant or close readings, as "disruptive acts of institution in their own right" (Helgesson and Vermeulen 2016, 12 and 14).

In his field-defining essay "What Is the History of Books?" (1982), Robert Darnton proposes "the Communication Circuit" to demonstrate that "the life of a book" is much more than its textual content and readership and requires an interdisciplinary approach from historians, sociologists, economists, and literary scholars to be fruitfully examined in full detail (81). He includes "publisher", "printers", "shippers", "booksellers" and even "binder" and "ink" as important agents or factors in the making of a book, which interacts with an intersecting force of "intellectual influences", "political and legal sanctions" and "economic and social conjuncture" (68). With the post-Cold War acceleration of global capitalism, recent scholarship in Book History has paid much more attention to the marketisation of the international book industry aided by a series of institutional publicities, such as book cover designs, academic endorsements, and book fairs and prizes. Taking the "global literary marketplace" as a field where different "forms of capital" circulate and intermingle, the editors and contributors of this volume seek to join this effort as we believe that these particular institutions offer valuable entry points towards a more grounded and productive critical world literature studies (Brouillette 2007, 44; Bourdieu 1986, 47).

This volume considers the sociological approach to be particularly germane to a more *critical* mode of world literature studies in relation to both its analytical features and methodological specificity. Firstly, it is more descriptive than prescriptive of literary texts and events and can be combined with other political and theoretical readings, which should facilitate, rather than dictate, the interpretation and analysis of the sociological observations and descriptions at hand. Secondly, it is inherently self-reflective in its awareness of both the constructive effects of academic meta-discourses and their limited capacities to "change the fundamental structuring realities that dictate which works are taught and read" (Brouillette et al. 2017, xxix). Indeed, as Raphael Dalleo's (2016) edited volume, *Bourdieu and Postcolonial Studies*, shows, there has been a sociological turn in Postcolonial Studies that reflects upon "the neoliberal context of its own emergence" (2). Graham Huggan's monograph, *The Postcolonial Exotic* (2001), has convincingly argued that the commercialisation of postcoloniality (often as thematic concerns regarding authenticity and identity) is now "integral to [. . .] the postcolonial field of cultural production—a field in which 'commercial' and 'academic' products intermingle" (121). Sarah Brouillette carries this claim further and uses her close reading of a range of popular or consecrated postcolonial writers to argue that this "marketability of postcolonial self-consciousness" has also come to be integrated into the textual content of much literature marketed as "postcolonial" or "global". As these postcolonial critics' scholarship has shown, not only has the rise of postcolonialism resulted in a kind of "strategic exoticism" that performs postcolonial identities for the global literary marketplace dominated by Euro-American institutions, but this "strategic exoticism" also keeps updating itself with heightened awareness of the political force of postcolonial critique in response to the reader's "exoticising tendencies" (Brouillette 2007, 7). Similarly, sociological meta-analyses of the institutionalisation of "world literature" as a marketing/consecrating strategy and more importantly, as "a literary act" of intervention, can reveal both the "internal" and "external" forces that shape this "field of cultural production" (McDonald 2016, 42 and 51). This edited volume exerts and effectuates this institutional focus in many forms, including archival research on the founding of a particular book series (Katelyn Edwards), the observation on the evolution of book covers of a consecrated postcolonial classic (Carmen Thong), the successes and failures of multilingual book prizes in a specific location (Rashi Rohatgi), the rediscovery of socialist literary connections beyond the Western world (Yan Jia) and many more. The archival and comparative work underpinning all these projects guarantees that their critical reflections on the current debate on world literature are both original and grounded.

As Kelly Yin Nga Tse (2018) comments in her combined book review for the recent major publications in World Literature, despite the diverse views and agendas expressed by all the different schools of thought mentioned, their accounts of world literature are better viewed "as complementary rather than competing or conflicting" (452). The sociological approach to critical world literature studies, we want to stress, is an indispensable addition to the constellation of theories and methodologies in literary studies broadly conceived. Its materialist (but not necessarily a priori Marxist) mode of critique can both assist scholarship conducted from particular theoretical and ideological angles and re-evaluate their validities and effects, especially when "world literature" as such is prone to generic and totalising claims. Through the consistent emphasis on the agency of the primary data and contexts in question, we hope that the flexible and holistic qualities of this critical approach can offset the sense of fragmented territorialisation in the ever-expanding field of World Literature.

World Literature in Motion: Key Issues and Chapter Outlines

As the title of this volume suggests, critical world literature studies regard world literature as *dynamic* processes shaped and mediated by certain conceptual and institutional forces, which materialise in physical and organisational forms that can be taken as sociological evidence for scholars. The meaning of the thematic keyword "motion" in the title of our book, which brings all of the chapters together, is twofold. First, it refers to movement, mediation, and mobility and serves to emphasise the very dynamism of world literature. No matter whether it is taken as material circulation, institutional recognition, comparative or systemic modes of reading and interpretation, the creative acts of translation, or a combination of any or all of these different aspects of literary engagement, world literature is always already shaped by (inter-)textual movements. As an organising concept, it cannot intervene meaningfully in the global literary marketplace or in our current system of reading and critique without the mobility and flexibility to travel across different socioeconomic, politico-cultural, and intellectual contexts. Second, "motion" can also mean "proposal" and "discussion", especially in the context of a debate, and the phrase "in motion" as employed in the title of our volume is to highlight the self-reflective nature of critical world literature studies. As mentioned in the opening section of this introduction, World Literature as an academic discipline can be confusing for "outsiders" and inconvenient for "insiders" because it conflates the object and subject of study. As long as this field of research keeps using the haughty modifier that is "(the) world" as one of its defining signifiers, meta-academic (self-)reflections are needed to keep the discipline in motion/check. What are the pragmatic gains of framing or defining world literature in a certain way, and for whom? As such, critical world literature studies may not make it any easier to pinpoint what world literature is, but it certainly makes clear *what it is not*: isolated and static.

With the characteristics of the sociological approach in mind, we propose the following four *motions*, each of which actively leads to a productive principle or original point of departure for research in critical world literature studies:

1. Postcolonial Studies is constructive of, rather than in conflict with, critical world literature studies, and the combination of the former's attentiveness to colonial legacies and neo-colonial power structures and the latter's grounded analysis of the institutional structures of a given literary activity can yield illuminating discoveries on the bigger picture of the political, economic, and cultural developments in the world today.

2. The literary prize, as the most important form of institutional recognition and consecration for authors and publishers, provides a particularly productive site of research for cases studies on the creation of world literature.

3. The discourse of world literature and its institutionalisation in the literary marketplace and academia can deliver pragmatic benefits by increasing the visibility and accentuating the importance of minor literatures in these fields.

4. Translations beyond the Anglophone, that is, between different languages that are not English (or at least between different contexts where English is not the primary linguistic medium), have been one of the blind spots in the current discussion in World Literature; however, combined with comparative criticism, they can be the most indicative object of research for world

literature and complicate our understanding of how literary centres and margins work in practice.

The four sections of this volume are guided by these motions respectively, but the chapters in each section also use archival resources and/or multilingual close reading to testify to and reflect on the connections between them. The first section, "Postcolonial Institutions", not only shows that both postcolonialism and world literature are disruptive of the neat divisions in national literatures but also highlights the continued relevance of colonial histories and repercussions in the institutionalisation of world literature in the postcolonial era. The four chapters in this section focus on the decolonisation period of the 1960s–70s and discuss how the state apparatus, publishers or literary events managed to fulfil their own ideological agendas through their interactions with and promotion of postcolonial texts as world literature. Rivkah Brown's paper on the Zimbabwe International Book Fair examines UNESCO's developmental agenda that lies behind the Fair, linking the intricate relations between its economic and social aspects to earlier colonial perceptions of the book as an economic tool. Similarly, Katelyn Edwards's discussion of Oxford University Press and the career of Athol Fugard points out a new paradigm of exploitation of African textbook markets by using the "regional" label. Such exploitation of (post-)colonial connections also constitutes the central concern of Meleesha Bardolia's and Gareth Tan's archival research on the British company Penguin and the British Information Research Department respectively. Bardolia's analysis of the correspondence between Penguin, Longmans Publishing and the South African editors of *The Penguin Book of South African Verse* (1968) reveals the way in which the book was modified to get through the censorship system in South Africa for commercial and political reasons. Rather than providing a univocal account of how external and global institutional pressures shape a national text, her chapter adds complexity to the story of the intersections between world literature and anthologies by highlighting the internal national complexity of this case study in apartheid South Africa. Offering a broader viewpoint, Tan's paper shows that in the context of the anti-Soviet "Cultural Cold War", the domestic publishing industry of the UK retained significant power over the ideological developments in the newly independent post-colonies. Together, these chapters constitute a holistic effort to bridge the gap between "the astuteness of postcolonialism as a symptomology of the contemporary world and the broader (but distinctly literary) comparative concerns of world literature" (Helgesson 2014, 498).

Taking this effort further and in more concrete forms, the second section, "Recognition through Literary Prizes", moves from the ideological exploitation of books during periods of decolonisation to the politics of recognition of books in the contemporary era. The chapters in this section offer four different case studies on prominent international book prizes and their engagements with non-western writers. Drawing on a wide range of letters, media reports and paratextual materials such as book covers, Carmen Thong's study of V.S. Naipaul's 1971 award of the Booker Prize for *In a Free State* provides fresh insights into the many institutional contingencies of literary categories as well as the writer's negotiation between institutional forces and their own creative agency. Her analysis reveals the process of adaptation the judges and coordinators of the prize had to undergo in order to capitalise on Naipaul's unconventional "novel". She also observes that as Naipaul accrues more cultural capital in his career, he is more willing to compromise his sense of agency. This forms a nice comparison with Lubabah Chowdhury's chapter, which focuses on Arundhati Roy's dealings with a forced notion of authenticity after receiving her Booker Prize in 1997. With particular attention to the management of the Booker's public relations, Chowdhury argues that the compulsory marketing of Roy's literary identity as a life writer is indicative of a wider problematic of postcolonial sexism in the international literary space. Moving from these two prominent postcolonial writers from the Caribbean and India, Sana Goyal's study on The Caine Prize for African Writing shifts the focus to regimes of literary recognition related to the vast continent of Africa and problematises the very concept of

"African Writing" itself. Engaging with Sarah Brouillette's theories, she demonstrates the different struggles faced by African authors on their journey to literary authenticity and singularity. Finally, my own chapter on the Man Asian Literary Prize as an interesting phenomenon of institutional failure points to the partial agency of top-down recognition regimes in today's neoliberalised global literary market. I seek to provide concrete examples of the practical difficulties of overcoming the ideologically entrenched expectations on non-western writers and literatures in a world literature space still dominated by American and European institutions. The four chapters in this section create intersecting critical dialogues as they all point towards the hierarchical power structures within the cultural domain in which the postcolonial marketplace and the space of world literature overlap. Moreover, all of them engage with James English's (2005) discussion on the "economy of prestige" in relation to "the agency of the cultural prize" and demonstrate the need for a more nuanced understanding of this agency as a process of negotiation and compromise between the different institutional forces shaping the "international literary space" (320).

The third section, "Minor Locations", shifts the institutional focus from recognition to location, and explores how texts may or may not transcend sociocultural boundaries in small island countries and regions. In accordance with Deleuze and Guattari's (1986) concept of "minor literature", this section addresses literary texts and events that originate in marginal geopolitical locations but operate in dominant European languages as efforts "to counter the hegemony of the majors" (D'haen 2016, 37). Rashi Rohatgi's chapter offers a continuation of, as well as transition from, the previous section as it discusses the failure of two important local literary prizes in Francophone Mauritius. Rohatgi shows that the contradictory ideological forces behind these two prizes have contributed to the same nationalistic pretension of internationalism that fails to make Mauritius the centre of any literary worlds. In contrast, Daniele Nunziata uses the literary bifurcation in the island nation of Cyprus as a case study to show how international translations may provide a means by which writers of minor literature can escape divisive local politics and its multilingual oppressions. His chapter offers a compelling analysis of Cypriot writers' constant negotiation with the Greek and Turkish hegemonies on the island and the balance they have managed to achieve by entering the anglophone markets. Lastly, Lucy Steeds's chapter calls for a more inclusive view of (post-)colonial literary history by investigating the role played by multiple media forms in the making of anglophone Caribbean literature. The archival research in her chapter brings due attention to the role BBC radio programs played in the creation and dissemination of a particular kind of Caribbean aesthetic, which functioned as a unique aural design of marketing strategies and enabled a select group of writers to move from minor locations to being included in one of the major postcolonial canons in world literature. On the one hand, the three chapters in this section come together to emphasise that world literature is indeed "always necessarily located" and it is this geopolitical *situatedness* and sociocultural specificity that makes minor literatures particularly indicative of the larger institutional forces that govern the international circulation and recognition of world literature (Orsini et al 2018, 4). On the other hand, the very concept of "minor" is employed differently in each chapter and always discussed in relation to the structural influence exerted by certain larger systems—it is "a fungible attribute dependent on a comparative perspective and shifting cultural networks" (Bachner 2017,155). As long as there is "no getting away from major/minor questions" in World Literature (D'haen 2016, 37), it is our belief that to improve the visibility of minor literatures (especially those written in minor or indigenous languages not yet covered by this section) and to assert their value will continue to be important pragmatic tasks of critical world literature studies. After all, the sheer breadth of an interdisciplinary formation like critical world literature studies can at least create an enabling condition for us to embrace and highlight the contribution of such (ultra-)minor languages and literatures, which tend to be marginalized or ignored in the existing fields of academic research based on large geopolitical divisions (the Area Studies model) or Eurocentric theoretical frameworks (i.e. the different *-isms* in literary and cultural studies developed in Europe and North America).

Following the trans-regional and trans-lingual approach advocated by Karen Thornber (2009), Waïl Hassan (2013), Helgesson and Kullburg (2018), and Banerjee and Fritzsche (2018), the final section, "Translations beyond the Anglophone", deepens the discussion on location through a series of specially solicited chapters on under-explored translational directions of regional literatures written by multilingual scholars. Yan Jia's and Galina Rousseva-Sokolova's case studies offer unique insights on literary exchanges outside of the Anglophone and Francophone spheres focussed on by most existing research in World Literature. Yan Jia's study on the representation of Indian literature in the Chinese journal *Yiwen/Shijie Wenxue* uncovers the forgotten history of anti-Eurocentric literary relations guided by the dominant socialist ambitions during the Cold War. He contends that the journal constitutes an alternative "world of literary relations" without the west, which was constructed through a great deal of curatorial work, including the selection and interpretation of texts, the (re)framing of authors' literary and political identities, and the strategic use of editorial devices. His analysis of this constructive process not only reveals but also reflects on this particular vision of world literature mediated by the diplomatic politics between India and China before their "rise" in the later game of global capitalism. In a more informative manner, Rousseva-Sokolova's chapter provides a comprehensive overview of how the Bulgarian literary market is adapting to the change of socio-political environment after the Cold War and negotiates with the rising tide of translated literature from Asia, a form of (inter-)national and centripetal literary engagement beyond the postcolonial paradigm. As her chapter shows, the use of Russian and English translations in these inter-regional engagements has been diminishing but will not disappear soon due to practical considerations of the literary market and structural constraints imposed by the residual but still strong geopolitical power of Russia in East Europe and the global cultural hegemony of the English language.

Taking the relationship between translation and trans-location further, Wen-chin Ouyang's and Yeogeun Kim's papers offer comparative analyses of different translations of classical Asian texts into different languages. Ouyang's comparative close reading of the English and Chinese translations of *The Arabian Nights* challenges the assumed effects of "Orientalism by proxy"—the migration of "western orientalism" into the Chinese view of the Islamic Middle East. Focusing on the particular editorial changes made to the plots and tropes in these different translations, she observes that in the process of such cross-cultural communication, literary norms and aesthetic traditions matter as much as the political and cultural structures surrounding the context of translation. Similarly, in the final chapter of this volume, Kim uses *Kuunmong* (*Cloud Dream of the Nine*), one of the most important classical Chinese texts from Korea, as an indicative case study for the translational circulation of world literature from a minor location. It covers *Kuunmong*'s centrifugal transnational afterlives in multiple East Asian and European languages, including modern Chinese, Japanese, Korean, Russian, German, Italian, Spanish, English and French, and offers a great terminal link between the multilingual trans-regionalism of this section and the concerns on the major/minor division of the previous one. Reflecting on the institutional (mal)functioning of the Literature Translation Institute of Korea (LTI Korea), an outreach project established by the South Korean government, Kim puts doubt on the efficacy of such top-down approaches to promoting literary circulation and notes that cultural appropriations of *Kuunmong* take place in both textual and visual forms despite the interventionist agendas of the government and publishers.

The editors of this volume consider the final section to be a particularly enriching contribution of this book to the field of World Literature for two reasons. First, even though postcolonialism and world literature can be fruitfully reconciled via the sociological approach highlighted in the first two sections, the current discussion on world literature has indeed been affected by the linguistic limitations of the former. As much as we see this book as an elaborate companion to Helgesson and Vermeulen's *Institutions of World Literature* (2016), ours is also an attempt to overcome its conflation of postcolonial literature and world literature by bringing more languages to the table than the four dominant European languages (English, French, Spanish and Portuguese) to which their volume is limited. Notably, in a more recent publication that has emerged from the ongoing research program "Cosmopolitan and Vernacular Dynamics in World Literatures", Stefan Helgesson (2018) and his colleagues in Sweden have started to emphasise the multiplicities of language, register, and genre within literary texts to further caution against the "equation between world literature and the global anglophone market for literary publishing" (6). Continuing this effort, this volume, especially in the last two sections, includes chapters on translation activities and book industries that operate through a more diverse range of languages (English, Bengali, Punjabi, Bulgarian, Italian, Japanese, German, Russian, Spanish, Chinese, Hindi, French, Arabic, Korean and Greek), involving regional circulations in East Asia, South Asia, the Middle East, Eastern Europe and Africa, in ways that are not necessarily mediated by postcolonial conditions. Through this wide coverage, these two sections illustrate our emphasis that the "world" in world literature is much more than the Anglo-sphere or the postcolonial world. Second, the trans-regional and trans-lingual focus of the final section demands significant revisions of Franco Moretti's systemic claim that "movement from one periphery to another (without passing through the centre) is almost unheard of" (2003, 75). While all of the chapters in this section do reveal that English does operate as a "vanishing mediator" across the world's disparate cultural–linguistic spaces and thus still exerts a significant amount of influence on the creation and circulation of world literature as such (Mufti 2016, 16), they also caution against the tautological and totalising application of Moretti's model (with "centre" readily defined as the institutional or cultural space that "peripheries" have to pass through) and gesture towards a more democratic cartography of world literature that is fundamentally constitutive of its own multilingual, multi-directional development. Opposite to Moretti's deterministic vision fixated on the hegemonic centre, we hope that the observations and arguments presented in this section can challenge literary scholars to at least imagine the very significance of "the translation of literature from one small peripheral language to another small peripheral language" in reshaping our ideas about the world and the operation of its cultural flows (Leppänen 2018, 97).

As a collection of theoretically informed, materially grounded case studies, this volume seeks to demonstrate how critical world literature studies can be practiced in the most concrete ways. However, as trained literary scholars, we are also highly aware of the irreducibility of literary texts and contexts and the analytical and performative nature of academic discourses. Indeed, texts, contexts, and (academic) meta-texts, much like world literature, are always in motion, as the boundaries and characteristics of "(the) world(s)" will always be different when examined through different perspectives or methods. In this sense, my amateur art piece featured on the cover of this book is to be taken as a visual representation of world literature, or rather, an abstract manifesto for critical world literature studies. Named "浮想 (floating ideas)", it is a picture of kaleidoscopic motion with detectable traces of patterns or directions of various movements, and yet, upon closer look, there are always details that escape the rule and stand out. A constant flux of floating ideas, it implies, is what critical world literature studies consists of.

Bibliography

Apter, Emily. 2013. *Against World Literature: On the Politics of Untranslatability*. New York: Verso.

Bachner, Andrea. 2017. "At the Margins of the Minor: Rethinking Scalarity, Relationality, and Translation." *Journal of World Literature* 2 (2): 139–57.

Banerjee, Anindita and Sonja Fritzsche, eds. 2018. *Science Fiction Circuits of the South and East*. Oxford: Peter Lang.

Bassnett, Susan. 2016. "The Figure of the Translator." *Journal of World Literature* 1 (3): 299–315.

—. 2019. "Introduction: The Rocky Relationship between Translation Studies and World Literature." In *Translation and World Literature*, edited by Susan Bassnett, 1–14. London: Routledge.

Beecroft, Alexander. 2015. *An Ecology of World Literature: From Antiquity to the Present Day*. London: Verso.

Boehmer, Elleke. 2014. "The World and the Postcolonial." *European Review* 22 (2): 299–308.

—. 2018. *Postcolonial Poetics: 21st-Century Critical Readings*. London: Palgrave Macmillan.

Bourdieu, Pierre. 1986. "The Forms of Capital." In *Handbook of Theory and Research for the Sociology of Education*, edited by J. G. Richardson, 46–58. New York: Greenwood.

Brouillette, Sarah. 2007. *Postcolonial Writers in the Global Literary Marketplace*. New York: Palgrave Macmillan.

Brouillette, Sarah et al. 2017. "Introduction." In *Literature and the Global Contemporary*, edited by J. G. Richardson, xv–xxxviii. Cham, Switzerland: Palgrave Macmillan.

Casanova, Pascale. 2004. *The World Republic of Letters*. Trans. M. B. Debevoise. Cambridge, MA: Harvard University Press.

Cheah, Pheng. 2016. *What Is a World? On Postcolonial Literature as World Literature*. Durham, NC: Duke University Press.

Chesney, Duncan McColl. 2017. "An Essay against Global Literature: Literature and the Global Public." *Concentric: Literary and*

Cultural Studies 43 (20): 251–274.

Dalleo, Raphael. 2016. "Introduction." In *Bourdieu and Postcolonial Studies*, edited by Raphael Dalleo, 1–16. Liverpool: Liverpool University Press.

Damrosch, David. 2003. *What is World Literature?* Princeton, NJ: Princeton University Press.

Darnton, Robert. 1982. "What Is the History of Books?" *Daedalus* 111 (3): 65–83.

Deckard, Sharae and Shapiro, Stephen, eds. 2019. *World Literature, Neoliberalism, and the Culture of Discontent*. Cham, Switzerland: Palgrave Macmillan.

Deleuze, Gilles, and Félix Guattari. 1986. *Kafka: Toward a Minor Literature*. Translated by Dana Polan. Minneapolis, MN: University of Minnesota Press.

D'haen, Theo. 2016. "Major/Minor in World Literature." *Journal of World Literature* 1 (1): 29–38.

El Habbouch, Jaouad. 2019. "Decentering Globalization: World Literature, Terror, and the Postcolonial." *Interventions* 21 (1): 1-34.

English, James. 2008. *The Economy of Prestige: Prizes, Awards, and the Circulation of Cultural Value*. Cambridge, MA: Harvard University Press.

Fang, Weigui. 2018. "Introduction: What is World Literature?" In *Tensions in World Literature: Between the Local and the Universal*, edited by Fang Weigui, 1–65. Singapore: Palgrave Macmillan.

Graham, James, et al. 2012. "Postcolonial Studies and World Literature." *Journal of Postcolonial Writing* 48 (5): 465–71.

Hassan, Waïl. 2013. "Which Languages?" *Comparative Literature* 65 (1): 5–14.

Hayot, Eric. 2012. *On Literary Worlds*. New York: Oxford University Press.

Helgesson, Stefan. 2014. "Postcolonialism and World Literature." *Interventions* 16 (4): 483–500.

— 2018. "General Introduction: The Cosmopolitan and the Vernacular in Interaction." In *World Literatures: Exploring the Cosmopolitan-*

Vernacular Exchange, edited by Stefan Helgesson et al., 1–14. Stockholm: Stockholm University Press.

Helgesson, Stefan and Pieter Vermeulen. 2016. "Introduction: World Literature in the Making." In *Institutions of World Literature: Writing, Translation, Markets,* edited by Stefan Helgesson and Pieter Vermeulen, 1–20. London: Routledge.

Helgesson, Stefan and Christina Kullberg. 2018. "Translingual Events: World Literature and the Making of Language." *Journal of World Literature* 3 (3): 136–52.

Hitchcock, Peter. 2010. *The Long Space: Transnationalism and Postcolonial Form.* Stanford, CA: Stanford University Press.

Huggan, Graham. 2001. *The Postcolonial Exotic: Marketing the Margins.* London: Routledge.

Leppänen, Katarina. 2018. "Reflections on Gender and Small Languages in World Literature Scholarship: Methods of Inclusions and Exclusions." In *World Literatures: Exploring the Cosmopolitan-Vernacular Exchange,* edited by Stefan Helgesson et al., 89–102. Stockholm: Stockholm University Press.

McDonald, Peter D. 2016. "Instituting (World) Literature." In *Institutions of World Literature: Writing, Translation, Markets,* edited by Stefan Helgesson and Pieter Vermeulen, 39–52. London: Routledge.

—. 2019. "See Through the *Concept* of World Literature." *Journal of World Literature* 4 (1): 13–34.

Moretti, Franco. 2000. "Conjectures on World Literature." *New Left Review* 1 (Jan-Feb): 54–68.

—. 2003. "More Conjectures." *New Left Review* 20 (Mar-Apr): 73–81.

Mufti, Aamir. 2016. *Forget English! Orientalisms and World Literatures.* Cambridge, MA: Harvard University Press.

Orsini, Francesca et al. 2018. "Multilingual Locals and Significant Geographies: For a Ground-up and Located Approach to World Literature." *Modern Languages Open* 1 (article 19): 1–8.

Parks, Tim. 2015. *Where I'm Reading from: The Changing World of Books.* New York: New York Review of Books.

Reynolds, Matthew, et al. 2015. "Guest Editors' Introduction."

Comparative Critical Studies 12 (2): 147–59.

Saussy, Haun. 2011. "The Dimensionality of World Literature." *Neohelicon* 38 (2): 289–94.

—. 2017. "The Three Futures of World Literature." *Canadian Review of Comparative Literature* 44 (3): 397–406.

Saussy, Haun et al. 2016. "Trying to Make It Real: An Exchange between Haun Saussy and David Damrosch." *Comparative Literature Studies* 53 (4): 660–93.

Shih, Shu-mei. 2004. "Global Literature and the Technologies of Recognition." *PMLA* 119 (1): 16–30.

Spivak, Gayatri Chakravorty. 2010. "Translating in a World of Languages." *Profession* 1: 35–43.

Thomsen, Mads Rosendahl. 2008. *Mapping World Literature: International Canonization and Transnational Literatures.* New York: Continuum.

Thornber, Karen. 2009. *Empire of Texts in Motion: Chinese, Korean, and Taiwanese Transculturations of Japanese Literature.* Cambridge, MA: Harvard University Press.

—. 2016. "Why (Not) World Literature: Challenges and Opportunities for the Twenty-First Century." *Journal of World Literature* 1 (1): 107–118.

Trivedi, Harish. 2013. "Comparative Literature, World Literature and Indian Literature: Concepts and Models." In *Interdisciplinary Alternatives in Comparative Literature,* edited by E.V. Ramakrishnan, 17–34. New Delhi: Sage Publications.

Tse, Kelly Yin Nga. 2018. "WHITHER THE WORLD? The Discourse of World Literature." *Interventions,* 20 (3): 446–52.

Tsu, Jing. 2001. "World Literature and National Literature(s)." In *The Routledge Companion to World Literature,* edited by David Damrosch et al., 158–68. New York: Routledge.

Venuti, Lawrence. 2016. "Hijacking Translation: How Comp Lit Continues to Suppress Translated Texts." *boundary2,* 43 (2): 179–204.

Warwick Research Collective. 2015. *Combined and Uneven Development: Towards a New Theory of World-Literature.*

Liverpool: Liverpool University Press.

Watroba, Karolina. 2017. "World Literature and Literary Value: Is 'Global' The New 'Lowbrow?'" *Cambridge Journal of Postcolonial Literary Inquiry* 5 (1): 53–68.

Youssef, Magdi. 2015. "Decolonizing World Literature." In *Major versus Minor? Languages and Literatures in a Globalized World,* edited by Theo D'haen, Iannis Goerlandt, and Roger D. Sell, 125–40. Amsterdam and Philadelphia: John Benjamin's Publishing Company.

Section 1:
Postcolonial Institutions

The Zimbabwe International Book Fair and the Idea of Book Development

Rivkah Brown

In 1965, UNESCO's Department of Mass Information employee Julian Behrstock (who, after 28 years of service, won an award "for outstanding services to the cause of books" [UNESCO n.d., n.p.]) declared books "basic to the achievement of almost all of the Organization's objectives"; as such, he said, they "permeate the whole of Unesco's programme" (1965, 21). Indeed, UNESCO's commitment to "the conservation and protection of the world's inheritance of books" (UNESCO 1945, n.p.), realised in 1948 as the Collection of Representative Works, configured the book as a unique form of national-mascot-cum-historical-artefact. More pertinent to this investigation is how the UN agency constitutionally tasked with "advancing, through the educational and scientific and cultural relations of the peoples of the world, the objectives of international peace and of the common welfare of mankind" (UNESCO 1945, n.p.) configured the book as "a technology [. . .] of development" (Slaughter 2007, 272).

As Sarah Brouillette (2014) points out, the agency has "since its founding [. . .] gathered a considerable mass of statistics about the global book trades" (33), and found the production of books in a number of (almost universally non-western) countries wanting (33). In fact, UNESCO was so appalled by the inequalities of global book production that it declared "book hunger", "inscrib[ing] the global 'crisis' of illiteracy within the same moral, humanitarian economy that motivates people to give their old clothes and unused canned goods to the poor" (Slaughter 2007, 282). So persuasive was book hunger as a developmentalist metaphor that it remains axiomatic: "Everyone," wrote Hans Zell in 1992, "has heard of food famine in Africa. [. . .] What must happen to alert the international community to the tragedy of bookless countries in Africa?" (75). Its suggestive power was threefold: first, that books were as indispensible as food; second, that those countries that suffered from this figurative hunger were the same as those afflicted by actual hunger; and by inference third, that those countries were underdeveloped *because* of their lack of books—in other words that books were "an aspect and means, not merely an index, of modernization" (Slaughter 2007, 272). At this point, UNESCO's constitutional commitments to the "promot[ion of] the free flow of ideas by word and image" (UNESCO 1945, n.p.) and to "[granting] the people of all countries access to [. . .] printed and published materials produced by any of them" (n.p.) begin to fall into place. As capital was to the New World Economic Order, so were books to the New World Information Order. UNESCO was instrumentalizing the book in the name of rectifying the global imbalances of power instigated by colonialism and escalated by capitalism. Just as missionaries had converted barbaric unbelievers into People of the Book, UNESCO's attempt to bring "the developing, 'book hung[ry]'" countries of the global south in line with "the industrialized, book-sated nations" of the north enacted an "intellectual bipolarization" that "divided the world into readers and nonreaders [. . .] modern reading nation-states [. . .] and premodern, illiterate huddled masses" (Slaughter 2007, 279–82).

The many conferences convened by UNESCO in the 1960s and 70s to devise a solution to book hunger concluded that this "immense gap" in global book wealth was "to be bridged" only by "increased local book production and consumption" (UNESCO 1969, 23)—a process it would dub "book development". Conference delegates considered a number of ways of stimulating consumption, including "book philanthropy"—the supplying of books from First World Countries to Third as one might "old clothes and unused canned goods". Production, however, was a trickier issue to address, and involved investing in infrastructure and engaging in trade. One of the primary recommendations of a UNESCO-sponsored conference in Ife, Nigeria in 1973 was "that publishers' associations sponsor book fairs in their own countries" (UNESCO 1975, 12). With the wave of decolonization still sweeping the continent, "[i]t was decided that at this point it would be impractical to organize an all-African book fair, but this desirable development should be kept in mind for the future" (12). Exactly ten years later, however, "this desirable development" came to pass with the establishment in 1983 of the Zimbabwe International Book Fair (ZIBF). Described by UNESCO as "the most significant literary event in Africa south of the Sahara" (ZIBF 1991, n.p.), the Fair was intended to kick-start both the production and consumption of books in Zimbabwe and Africa as a commercial trade fair and a public celebration of books and reading.

This chapter will examine the way in which UNESCO's mandate of "book development" was taken up by ZIBF both implicitly through its programming choices and promotional materials, and explicitly through the public Indaba (Xhosa/Zulu for "conference") that formed the Fair's centerpiece, and where ideas of book development were discussed and contested. Its primary evidential basis will be archival material drawn from the Paul Hamlyn Collection on Publishing in Africa housed at Oxford Brookes University, supplemented by interviews with individuals who attended, organized, exhibited at or were otherwise linked to the Fair. It will begin by thinking about the manifold and often contradictory ways in which ZIBF interpreted "book development", in particular through its attempt to cultivate a national and continental "reading culture", a concept deeply embedded in Benedict Anderson's notion of "imagined communities" (1983). It will suggest that in positing a teleology of the book from economic product to educational tool to enactor of spiritual enlightenment, ZIBF demonstrated that the developmentalist concept of the book was fundamentally the product of colonialism and its missionary presses. It will end by situating these discussions within the context of Robert Darnton's communications circuit, arguing that Darnton's "Economic and Social Conjecture" is less a pivot than a lacuna; that in understanding books as a good *per se*, the Darntonian circuit precludes any question of how books had come to be seen an "essential technology" (Slaughter 2007, 275). Nga Tse's (2018) observations about the Warwick Research Collective's understanding of world literature are instructive here. Just as WReC "registers the combined and uneven contours of the world system", yet "does not imbue such literature with an inherent criticality against modern capitalism (Nga Tse 2018, 449-50), so too does the idea of book development conceived of by UNESCO and espoused at ZIBF challenge the unevenness of global book production without critiquing the culturally-specific motivations of that challenge. UNESCO and ZIBF, in turn, declared that Africa must read, without interrogating *why*.

Reading Maketh a Man: How ZIBF Mediated the UNESCO Doctrine of Book Development

Though UNESCO's special relationship with the book was apparent from its earliest days, it was formalized by its designation of 1972 the Year of the Book, and concomitant publication of the Charter of the Book. The Charter illuminated the Constitution by pinpointing how books were to enact the Constitution's ill-defined "modernization": by "promoting individual fulfillment, social and economic progress, international understanding and peace" (UNESCO 1972b, 238), a wide-ranging statement that moves between quantitative ("economic progress") and qualitative outcomes ("individual fulfilment", "international understanding"). It soon becomes apparent that this oscillation is not arbitrary but a binary sustained across the Charter, distinguishing the book as pure commodity, a unit of economic value, from the book as a "unique category of commodity" (Brouillette 2014, 33), a privileged form of cultural production. Article IV takes up the first position: "A sound publishing industry is essential to national development" (UNESCO 1972b, 239). It talks in technical terms about the need for a publishing "infrastructure", "economic and social planning" and "low interest financing" (239). Articles V to IX continue in this vein, concatenating the practicalities of building a national publishing "infrastructure": "Book manufacturing facilities" will need to be constructed, "Booksellers" and "Libraries" opened (240). These Articles paint books as an "industry" like any other. Indeed, at a conference on African book development sponsored by UNESCO and held in Ife, Nigeria in the year following the Charter's publication,

Julian Behrstock (1975) spoke of book production in economic terms analogous to per capita income: "It was estimated that [. . .] no more than one-thirtieth of a book was available per person per year" (79). The Charter is sandwiched, however, by Articles that assume the second position, stressing the qualitative benefits conferred by the content of books: Article I, "Everyone has a right to read" (UNESCO 1972b, 239), Article II, "Books are essential to education" (239), and Article X, "Books serve international understanding and peaceful co-operation" (241). Later in the Ife conference, Chinua Achebe (1975) underscored this ambiguity: "When we speak of the *book trade* we blur the difference between merchandising and a very delicate process of bringing one human mind into communion with the minds of his [sic] fellows" (41). The idea of the book set in motion by UNESCO in the early 1970s was as "a technological bridge between material and immaterial development" (Slaughter 2007, 272).

Into this crossfire entered the ZIBF, whose organizers wished "to combine the function of a commercially viable trade fair with a public celebration of books and reading" (Gibbs and Mapanje 1999, 350)—to stimulate, in other words, both economic development through the "trade" of books, and social development through their "reading". The Fair's billing as "Africa's foremost and fastest-growing book-trade and literary event" (ZIBF 1994a, 1) bespeaks these bipartite aims, with "foremost" laying claim to the social prestige of a "literary event", and "fastest-growing" the economic stimulus resulting from increased "book-trade". At times ZIBF appears to have privileged trade: the Zimbabwe International Book Fair Trust (ZIBFT) established in 1989 to administer the Fair stated that its "overriding aim" was "to make the Fair a truly commercial trade fair for the publishing industry" (Shamuyarir 1992, n.p.). Two years later, ZIBFT relocated the Fair from the Harare Gardens, the city's largest public park and a popular local hangout, to the Harare International Conference Centre, in a bid to establish the Fair's "corporate identity" (ZIBF 1993, 2). Yet despite the desire in some quarters of the book industry that the Fair be strictly a trade event, it was by popular demand also a cultural event. The move to the Conference Centre move lasted only a year, and in 1992 ZIBF moved once again to the more relaxed environs of the National Gallery Sculpture Garden (it has since resumed residency at the Harare Gardens). That year, 32,000 members of the public attended. Far from the easy coalition implied by the polysyndetic "book-trade and literary event", "books and reading", the Fair struggled to mediate the push-and-pull between its public and commercial aspects, a tension it attempted to resolve in 1995 by introducing "two Traders-Only" and three public days (ZIBF 1995b, 2). ZIBF bore out the difficulty of realizing UNESCO's dream of stimulating book production and consumption.

The Fair also demonstrated that UNESCO's bifocal vision for book development was in fact varifocal. Just as UNESCO's Charter of the Book divided book development into economic and social categories, so too did it subdivide social book development (i.e. reading) into its quantitative and qualitative impacts, as a source of "information and knowledge" and "wisdom and beauty" respectively (UNESCO 1972b, 240). This distinction was particularly apparent at the 1992 Fair, which held a "Creative Writers' Workshop" for "Zimbabwe's literary community" (Anon 1992, n.p.) alongside a "Three Day Practical Workshop" on "Writing for the Environment", during which participants visited an Agritex agricultural machinery factory to learn about "improving Soil Conservation and yields" (ZIBF 1992b, 1). When Trish Mbanga, ZIBF's Director from 1990 to 2000, addressed book hunger in a press release for the Fair that year, she referenced the "technical know-how" with which this practical workshop was attempting to equip writers. Books, said Mbanga, were not only "as essential as food", but could instruct readers how to grow it, and so "climb out of the morass of mass starvation" (ZIBF 1992c, 1). The Fair promoted textbooks in the hope of realizing the economic benefits books could confer not directly as a light industry, but indirectly through the "information and knowledge" they would impart to readers, empowered by their book learning to sate their actual as well as figurative hunger. Yet such workshops were inevitably overshadowed by sections of the programme that sought to privilege fiction. The Fair sought to boost its literary credentials by attracting high-profile literary figures—poet Benjamin Zephaniah was heralded the "major attraction" at ZIBF93 (Maruziva 1993, n.p.), while Africa's two Nobel laureates Wole Soyinka and Nadine Gordimer were among "the all-star line-up of international writers" at ZIBF95 (ZIBF 1995b, 3)—and bestowing literary prizes. The Noma Award for Publishing in Africa (ZIBF 1994b, n.p.), a prize that sought to encourage autonomous, indigenous book publishing was reportedly founded as "an allied literary/cultural event", and the Zimbabwe Book Publishers' Association (ZBPA)'s Literary Awards, were purpose-built for the Fair and described as "a major feature" of it (Maruziva 1994, n.p.). One testament to how strongly ZIBF came to consider itself a continental arbiter of literary tastes was its publication of *Africa's 100 Best Books of the 20th Century* (ZIBFT and ABC 2002) to mark the millennium. Though such prizes and lists included categories for non-fiction, their stated aim was, as Davison Maruziva pointed out, "to encourage local publishers [. . .] to publish creative writings" (1994, n.p.). The inaugural Noma Award went to Senegalese author Mariama Bâ for her novel *Une si longue letter*; 71 of *Africa's 100 Best Books* fell under "Creative Writing", and only 25 under "Scholarship/Non-Fiction" (ZIBFT and ABC 2002). If the tournament of values staged at ZIBF was between fictional and non-fictional books (see Moeran, 2010), the former came out on top.

Yet, as stated in a report on the 1992 Fair and restated by Mbanga (2016) in a recent interview, "ZIBF's long term object" was not to champion a specific type of book but rather, as the Fair put it, "to foster an interest in books and a love of reading on the part of the public at large" (ZIBF 1992c, 3). According to its organizers, fiction and non-fiction coexisted rather than competed at the Fair. A central component of the Fair's discourse on book development belies this contention, however: the idea of reading for pleasure. "We want to promote literacy in our country", announced Mbanga in a 1992 press release, "but more than just literacy per se: we want to encourage, through general exposure to books, the idea of reading for pleasure" (quoted in Enochs 1992, 2). Mbanga's statement invites us to consider the difference between taking pleasure *in* books and reading *for* pleasure. Whilst the former stresses only the reader's enjoyment and is uninterested in the choice of reading material, the latter suggests the deriving of entertainment rather than information. The link between pleasure and literature implicit in Chinua Achebe's (1972) complaint in that "Africans [. . .] did not go in search of *literary pleasure*" (547; emphasis mine) was made explicit at ZIBF96, where Zimbabwe's Minister of Education, Sport and Culture, Gabriel Machinga stated the government's intention to "ensure [that] reading for pleasure is addressed in the curriculum and that trainee teachers [. . .] encourage *reading literature for pleasure*" (ZIBF 1995a, emphasis mine).

ZIBF's privileging of the fictional book can be traced directly to UNESCO. In the opening address of the Ife conference, Chief Eke (1975), the Nigerian Federal Commissioner for Education, started by defining books as practical tools for cultivating the "trained manpower and technical know-how of which Africa is in short supply" (348). However, Eke's encomium begins to fall apart as he attempts to broaden his definition to comprehend books' intangible value: "the demand for trained manpower is not only a demand for quantity but also for quality. It is a demand for manpower trained in the new skills and techniques needed for rapid material and spiritual development" (349). The reason Eke's rhetoric struggles to comprehend the "material and spiritual" may be that he is referring not only to two different types of reading, but to two different types of book entirely: fiction and non-fiction. Slaughter (2007) strengthens our suspicion that Eke's distinction may be categorical: "Reading and writing are valorized both as tools for acquiring the knowledge necessary for socioeconomic advancement and as the primary media of modern transcendental personal fulfillment through the imaginative extension of the individual into the world" (272). Here, "imaginative extension" suggests that while "socioeconomic advancement" ("material [. . .] development") might be derived from the "knowledge" of "new skills and techniques" imparted by non-fiction, fiction alone can provide "transcendental personal fulfillment" (Eke's "spiritual development"). With "transcendental", Eke makes clear that

UNESCO's notion of book development is implicitly hierarchical, with "wisdom and beauty" transcending "information and knowledge". What UNESCO created was not a singular concept but rather a *teleology* of book development, one that began with textbooks and culminated in fiction.

In his report on ZIBF96 for the US Peace Corps magazine *WorldView*, and in a radical departure from the Fair's insistence on fiction and non-fiction as equal partners in book development, Charles R. Larson (1996) places fiction at the end of a book developmental timeline: he observes that "the entire concept of reading for pleasure has yet to take hold of most African readers. [. . .] Creative works are the last to be purchased, after technical works, self-help books, and textbooks" (64). Indeed, there has long been concern about this within the Zimbabwean publishing community: a 2011 reading survey by the non-profit organization Zimbabwe Reads reported "minimal interest in books other than textbooks, set texts, and books for exam preparations", and concluded that "textbooks are not enough" for a "culture of reading" (Zimbabwe Reads, 2011, n.p.); more recently, publisher Irene Staunton (2016) expressed her concern that Zimbabweans read solely "to pass exams" (n.p.). ZIBF promoted the fictional over the non-fictional book, then, in an attempt to move the country and indeed the continent further along the journey to full book development as set out by UNESCO: ZBPA's Literary Awards were established to "encourage local publishers, who are sometimes tempted to concentrate on educational textbooks [. . .] to publish creative writings" (Maruziva 1994, n.p.), while at the 1995 awards ceremony, Guest of Honour and Zimbabwean Minister of Higher Education, Dr Ignatius Chombo, remarked that "it was imperative that schools instill the habit of reading into pupils not only to enable them to pass examinations, but also to enjoy themselves" (Maruziva 1995, n.p.). Professor of African History Diane Jeater (2011) has blogged that "the problem in Zimbabwe is not that books are dying out as objects made of paper, but that they are dying out as a genre"—the notion that Zimbabwe *is* reading, but that it is simply reading the wrong things, is a persistent one.

Yet fiction's placement in a developmental teleology generates an internal hierarchy within the category itself. At the 1996 ZIBF Writers' Workshop, Nadine Gordimer asserted, "comic-book literacy does not mean an ability to read a story, poem or novel that has more than a vocabulary that consists largely of grunts and explanatory syllables" (quoted in Larson 1996, 64). Just as Wendy Griswold discounts "self-help books, or tracts on business or management" from a Nigerian reading culture (Fraser 2008, 166), so too does Gordimer differentiate "comic-book literacy" from the "ability to read a story, poem or novel". As Paul Zeleza (1996) made clear at the 1996 Indaba, fiction *per se* is insufficient for spiritual development:

> Only a voracious and discriminating reading public can ensure that Africa produces not only more books, but *good books*, books that enlighten and enrich our lives, rather than debasing our sensibilities. The privileged few can, and ought, to do more than simply buy and read books. (1996, 19, emphasis mine)

Zeleza's analysis implicitly denigrates Gordimer's "comic-book literacy", or what what Mwesiga Baregu would at the 2001 Indaba call "trivial and family literature [. . .] designed to appeal to the [. . .] basic instinct but never to the intellect" (2001, 63), his term "basic" cognate with Zeleza's "debasing". This distinction between the casual reading of "trivial" books and the serious reading of "good books" can similarly be heard in Ronald Barker and Roger Escarpit's UNESCO-sponsored pamphlet *The Book Hunger* (1973), in which they argue that casual reading is intellectually unstimulating: "The term 'pastime' is probably the most suitable [for casual reading], indicating an activity undertaken to fill in time, like taking a drink, filling in an easy crossword puzzle or vaguely watching the first programme one finds on television" (120–21). Ironically, then, book hunger as projected by UNESCO was to be sated not by "ravish[ing books] as one devours food" (Larson 1996, 63), but by a "discriminating reading public" selecting tomes that "enrich [their] lives" and heighten their "sensibilities". Indeed, this idea of social refinement enacted through the consumption of carefully selectedworks of literature was tacit in A.D.H. Leishman's (1983) praise for ZIBF's "spacious, dignified air" (179), as well as in Terence Ranger's (1994) description of the Fair as "a popular, not to say populist event" (1). Together, Barker and Escarpit, Gordimer, Zeleza and Baregu typify what the Brazilian educator Paulo Freire (Freire and Macedo 1987) termed "The Academic Approach to Reading", "the acquisition of predefined forms of knowledge [. . .] organized around [. . .] the mastery of the great classical works", rather than "The Romantic Approach" that "greatly emphasizes the affective and sees reading as the fulfillment of self and a joyful experience" (146). What Zeleza and Achebe refer to when they speak of "good literature" and "discriminating" taste is a canon, a corpus of "great classical works" agreed upon by a literary elite and exemplified by *Africa's 100 Best Books.* The very concept of canonicity rests not on *enjoyment*, but on a specific body of *knowledge*; seen in this light, "all reading is utilitarian, it is purposeful" (Zeleza 1996, 15). Claims of reading for pleasure here begin to fall apart: it is not, as Escarpit (1966) wrote, "unpracticality" which defines "the literary book", but an emphasis on personal development subtler than that of the textbook, though just as serious. It was this fundamental utilitarianism to literary reading that Ronald C. Benge (1970) pinpointed when in *Libraries & Cultural Change* he wrote that "the disinterested pursuit of knowledge, truth, beauty or goodness [. . .] is always mixed up with other motivations" (99).

Though neither Larson nor Eke directly link spiritual development and fiction, the way in which the higher order benefits of books are described by UNESCO and subsequently at the Fair unmistakably references fiction, with Dr Chombo's desire to "broaden their horizons" being an obvious example. In his message for International Book Year in 1972, UNESCO Director-General René Maheu (1972) described the ultimate goal of book development thus:

> The problem is not only one of quantity [c.f. Eke]. [. . .] It is equally or more important that the book—the unparalleled instrument for setting down man's wisdom and knowledge—promote individual fulfillment and social progress; that it give all persons a chance to appreciate the best that the human mind has to offer the world over; and that it serve to create a better understanding between peoples as a necessary step towards a true and lasting peace. (3–4)

Though at first Maheu appears to mediate between non-fiction and fiction, amalgamating the Charter's "wisdom and beauty" and "information and knowledge" in the hybrid "wisdom and knowledge", he spotlights the fictional book by referencing two qualities commonly attributed to it: an emphasis on individual genius ("the best that the human mind has to offer"), and the creation of humanistic fellow-feeling ("a better understanding between peoples"). Similarly, the mission statement of "Books for All" (1972a), a UNESCO campaign initiated in International Book Year, speaks of a book as "a passport to the world [. . .] breaking through the barriers of time and space, proffering the joy of fulfillment. It can be a faithful companion, a spinner of dreams, or a source of wisdom" (27), avoiding naming fiction by referring instead to ideas associated with it: the traversing of space-time, the conjuring of dreams. The concomitance of literature and spirituality was cemented, however, at the Literary Awards held at ZIBF93, where Zimbabwean Minister of Education Dr Stan Mudenge commented: "I need not belabour the importance of books and literature. [. . .] A nation without a literature or a literary tradition is a nation without a soul" (Anon 1993, n.p.), making a critical distinction between "books" and "literature". What UNESCO implicitly and ZIBF more explicitly communicates is that the pinnacle of book development is a spiritual dimension accessible only through fiction; what Achebe calls the "spiritual bond [that] exists between the true artist and his community" (1975, 43).

The "individual fulfillment" provided by the creative book is in turn credited with "social progress", and the production of enlightened citizens (citizenship being inherent in the metaphor of books as a "passport to the world") capable of upholding a "true and lasting peace". This link between literary fiction and citizenship, first suggested by UNESCO (recall Bhely-Quenum's [1972] comment that "books can help the individual to understand his own culture and to integrate in his own community as well as the international community") emerged at the Fair in 2000, where Gerald McCullough (2000) spoke at the Indaba of the African book industry's "overemphasis on developing textbooks" meaning that "our professionals [. . .] are not lovers of literature and ideas" (175); we hear once more the suggestion that spiritual development, the love of "ideas", is concomitant with "literature" alone. At the 2001 Indaba, Irene Staunton enlarged upon the nebulous process of literature's spiritual development, reinforcing its connection with civil society:

> By identifying with characters in many different situations we learn about values, and the complexity of experience. We learn tolerance and understanding [. . .]. Reading is one's extension of one's mind, knowledge, imagination [. . .]. A reading society forms the basis of a more democratic, liberal and thoughtful society. (Staunton 2001, 225–26)

The unique "complexity" and robust empathy ("identifying with characters in many different situations") required by literary fiction humanistically enlarges the "mind, knowledge [and] imagination", argues Staunton, echoing Slaughter's "imaginative extension". Staunton's logic, that literary fiction instills civic qualities, derives from Barker and Escarpit's (1973) discussion in *The Book Hunger* of the difference between reading textbooks and literature:

> The stronger and more determining the constraints, the more 'functional' is the text and the less the margin left to the reader's initiative: as, for example, in didactic, technical or scientific works. The more latitude the reader is given to

> exercise his predispositions, the more 'literary' is the text. (104)

Contrast this with the comments made by Baregu (2001), that due to an overreliance on textbooks, "[Tanzanians] have become gullible consumers and knowledge and regurgitators of received wisdom", rather than "active, vibrant participants" in cultural production (64–65). While Baregu's suggestion is that prescribed reading material restricts independence of thought, Barker and Escarpit propose that the "initiative" required specifically from the reader of "literary" fiction engenders the autonomy necessary for citizenship.

Indeed, it is not only the citizen but also the state itself that is brought into being by fiction. Peter Weidhass (1993), a guest speaker at the 1993 Indaba, announced that

> the maintenance of a nation's perspectives requires upholding the process of cultural proliferation. The book industry [. . .] is vital to the cultural process. Without books, written and published locally, a nation is facing the danger of loss of her national identity. I would even go as far as saying without [. . .] books being written and published locally, there will be neither development nor democracy. (3)

That Weidhass's subtext is literary fiction is apparent not only from the coded terms "cultural proliferation" and "cultural process", but from his idea that books canonically communicate "a nation's perspectives". Yet while literary fiction may be tacit in Weidhass's remarks, the conclusion he arrives at is quite clear: by empowering citizens to express and exchange values, literature is essential to the formation of the sovereign citizen subject and by extension the democratic nation-state. The social development with which the book was credited, then, was far more specific than was set out in UNESCO's Constitution or Charter. Books created a specific type of subject, under a particular form of governance, that in turn placed a particular kind of premium on books; a 1992 press release from the Fair spoke of the "winds of democracy blowing through Africa" sparking "an explosion of creativity", a "modern-day renaissance" (ZIBF 1992a, 2), directly modeling the concomitant spread of literature and national identity on a European example.

Following the claims made about books at ZIBF to their furthest possible extension—the point at which a national canon engenders the democratic nation-state—demonstrates that the social aspect of book development conceived by UNESCO and percolated through the Fair derives directly from the colonial enterprise of forming enlightened states in the colonizer's image, the divinely-mandated creation of Peoples of the Book. The predominant literary manifestation of colonialism was the missionary press, whose workings are blueprinted by Christian literacy worker Margaret Wrong (1934) in *Africa and the Making of Books: Being a Survey of Africa's Need of Literature*. There, Wrong outlines what she calls the three "stages of demand" for literature in Africa. First are "Books about Christianity"; second, "General Knowledge and Text-books" (6); finally, "the third stage in the demand of the African for books is for general reading" (9). "They will need good literature both in the vernaculars and in European languages", she says; books "with serious purpose. [. . .] If they cannot get good literature they will read bad" (9). Note Wrong's vacillation between descriptive and normative statements, observing the "demand of the African for books" and prescribing the books with which Africa ought to be supplied ("They will need . . ."). Note, too, how the "general reading" in which her teleology culminates is not popular fiction but "good literature"; "they will read bad" signaling a devolution to the "grunts" and "explanatory syllables" cited by Gordimer. Crucially, Wrong's teleology bears a remarkable resemblance not only to that threaded through ZIBF—a progression from from the Bible to textbooks to leisure reading to "good literature"—but to the colonial enterprise itself, religious evangelism followed by the creation of infrastructure and finally gentrification, culminating in the birth of an enlightened nation-state.

Chairman of ZIBFT John Manyarara (2001) channels precisely this colonial ethos in his welcome message in the ZIBF2001 Catalogue: "we intend to build on our efforts to cover the whole of the African books industry in furthering a culture of reading, thereby enlightening the nations" (2). However, perhaps the best synthesis of colonial thought the Fair witnessed—enlightenment, high literature, development, self-fulfillment and nation-building—was that of Ghanaian publisher Kwesi Annoh (2001), who at the Indaba that same year recited his original poem:

> Reading maketh a man
> Reading good books brings enlightenment
> A nation whose people do not read
> Wallow in darkness and poverty.
> Books bring knowledge and wisdom
> And through books
> We build nations. (129–30)

From the idea of a man of letters to that of a heart of "darkness", Annoh's poem is deeply informed by the colonial wisdom of bringing books to Africa to "enlighten the nations". As Slaughter puts it, "literacy is [. . .] a crucial component in an Enlightenment-liberative view of modernity [. . .] a primary means to enlightenment itself" that enables "all persons to participate in a free society" (2007, 272–73). Like Fraser's use of the term "custom", Slaughter's silent shift from upper-to lower-case "enlightenment" indicates a paradigm imported from a Euro-American context and forcibly indigenized in an African one; a paradigm whose simplest form is "literacy", and its most advanced literary fiction. Ironically, the genres that remain most popular in Zimbabwe, but are now deemed insufficient for "enlightenment"—"exemplary lives, conversion narratives, didactic poetry [cf. Annoh's own], self-help manuals, and ethnographic accounts"—were themselves "literary genres encouraged by missionary presses" (van der Vlies 2013, 516). Champions of book development such as Annoh advocate finishing what the missionary press began, building on its evangelical and educational foundations with the literary fiction envisaged as its crowning glory.

Read Africa! Reading for its Own Sake

Parallel to this discourse of book development as "enlightenment" runs another that has actively, though less vocally, resisted it. At the 1973 Ife conference, some delegates felt "that both publisher and librarian had a moral obligation to provide literature of a high calibre". Note the term "moral obligation", recalling the "cultural mission" of ABC and by extension the missionary press itself. Others wanted libraries "to stock indigenous 'ephemeral' literature of the Onitsha chap-book variety—high standards notwithstanding" (Behrstock 1975, 6). To this latter group, "the important thing is to stimulate people to read, regardless of what they read, and this type of [market] literature has provided to be very popular among new literates throughout the continent" (6). The model of "stimulat[ing] people to read, regardless of what they read" returns us to the Fair's stated aim of "foster[ing] an interest in books and a love of reading on the part of the public at large" rather than cultivating literary refinement among a "privileged few".

This discourse, having been dormant for many years at the Fair, was revived by Head of the South African Centre for the Book, Elizabeth Anderson (2001), who at the 2001 Indaba circled back to a recommendation made by the Ife conference almost three decades earlier:

> How do we hook readers? Popular books! Take the Onitsha market in Nigeria, the Kano market, those pamphlets sold like hot cakes, produced on the ground by people in the communities, sold in the market place, they could not make enough. Why are we not producing that sort of thing?
>
> Comic books! In Africa there is a tendency to say, 'Uh! Comics! We won't learn English or French the right way. Our language will not develop.' Reading comics develops an

> interest in reading for its own sake. [. . .] Publishers should be producing that kind of literature and librarians and teachers should be pushing what their potential markets want. (223)

Anderson's argument openly contests Gordimer's, though not on the same terms; rather than claiming any spiritual development for comics, she shifts the measure of "value" from utility ("learn[ing] English or French") back to "reading for its own sake". Yet Anderson's interest in readers' preferences is not philanthropic. Rather, she argues quite pragmatically that intervening at the "Economic and Social Conjuncture" of Darnton's (1990) communications circuit, shoehorning a "cultural mission" that stipulates the sort of books Zimbabwe requires, inhibits the circuit's functioning, since supply must always exist in a symbiotic (rather than prescriptive) relationship with demand. As Dr Chombo had tentatively suggested at the 1995 Literary Awards, in terms borrowed from Darnton, "the communication circuit can only be complete when there is a readership" (quoted in Maruziva 1995, n.p.). Interestingly, this idea can be heard in *The Book Hunger*, where Barker and Escarpit recognize that the "solution" they propose "will be ineffective unless the flow of information is two-way, book producers being informed of readers' needs" (1973, 123). In a lesser-known UNESCO publication, *The Book Today in Africa*, S.I.A. Kotei (1981) so far extends Barker and Escarpit's caveat as to conceptually undermine "book hunger":

> book provision in Africa could be planned more systematically if reading needs, and habits, were better known. It has to be so as books are unique commodities to be provided for the right person at the right time and place. They are not vital consumer items needed by all persons at all times for the sustenance of life or personal well-being, like food and drugs. (147)

Kotei anticipates Brouillette by highlighting that "books are unique commodities", yet not in order to privilege them, but to underscore their cultural specificity; the fact that to many books are, as Caine Prize Director Lizzy Attree points out, "an old-fashioned product" (2016). "Not all readers", says Gaston-Pierre Coly (2001), adding his voice to the growing chorus against deterministic book development at the 2001 Indaba, "have the same tastes in reading materials or have the same expectations in pursuit of this activity (295). Kotei calls for a book industry responsive to "reading needs, and habits" of readers, a call ZIBF appears latterly to have answered: the first of the "Objectives" currently listed on the Fair's website is "to uphold the right of the peoples of Africa to have full access to books, which are culturally and materially relevant to their reading needs" (ZIBF 2016, n.p.). This statement marks a significant departure from UNESCO's Charter of the Book: its nuancing of the "right to read" as "the right [. . .] to have full access to books" insists less upon reading as essential than upon the autonomy of "the peoples of Africa" to draw on literary resources as they are "culturally and materially relevant to their reading needs".

Yet Anderson does not simply urge publishers' awareness of what their *readers* want, but of "what their *potential markets* want" (emphasis mine). She therefore *does* gesture to a motive beyond "reading for its own sake": profit. Whatever is "very popular" must necessarily be very profitable: market literature, she says, sells "like hot cakes"; City Press's "sales have soared" after their publication of "a comic strip about soccer" (Anderson 2001, 223). Anderson is just as concerned by the failure of transplanting "conservative" Euro-American "value" of "literature" with a "serious message" to "develop real readers" as she is by the economic illogic of this tactic (219), a concern shared by Elieshi Lema of the Tanzanian NGO Code which supports the development of publishing and libraries: "Unless publishers capture the market of the rural majority, their business will never prosper" (Anon 1996, n.p.). What we return to is the notion of books as an economic product. The collateral result of allowing Darnton's communications circuit to function organically, Lema and Anderson argue, is the stimulation the book industry. As development discourse begins to distance itself from a social project whose ambitions have become muddied with those of neocolonialism, economic prosperity has become the recognized global measure of book development. Though this still places "developing countries" such as Zimbabwe in a game of catch-up with the "developed world", it at least frees Zimbabwe from "menacing interventions" to autonomously determine how to develop its book industries (Brouillette 2014, 36). More than this, by surrendering book development to market forces, Zimbabwe devolves power to readers as consumers, reinvesting meaning in the Fair's motto, "books belong to everybody in the community" (ZIBF 1996b, 6).

Yet this persistent focalization of the book in the discourse of development substantiates a claim made by Brian Cummings (2013) that "[e]ven as the book is demystified and deconsecrated in the modern world, its symbolic value endures" (96). We might extend this by suggesting that time has dangerously divorced the book from its historical origins, thus presenting its "symbolic value" as axiomatic. Recent scholarship on Africa's rich precolonial scribal history should not obscure the fact that the transmission of the book—indeed the Book—to Africa was integral to the colonial project (see Krätli and Lydon, 2010). Christian missionaries arrived on the continent with just that: a clearly-defined mission to standardize knowledge production, disseminate religious orthodoxy and so bring light to Africa's heart of darkness through a specifically European Christian "technology of the intellect" (Goody 1975, 10). Yet in the two centuries since those missionaries' arrival, the book as an instrument of colonial reform has been subordinated to an understanding of the book as "an ostensibly politically neutral and expedient resource" (Brouillette 2014, 50) and indisputable technology of global betterment (a shift that has perhaps prompted corrective research into Africa's indigenous book history, since Africa, we insist, must always have comprised book societies). Yet while it may be increasingly for Zimbabweans to decide how to answer it, the call to read is as strong as ever it was.

Bibliography

Achebe, Chinua. 1972. "What Do African Intellectuals Read?". *The Times Literary Supplement*, May 12: 547.

—. 1975. "Publishing in Africa: A Writer's View." In *Publishing in Africa in the Seventies: Proceedings of an International Conference on Publishing and Book Development Held at the University of Ife, Ile-Ife, Nigeria, 16–20 December 1973*, edited by Edwina Oluwasanmi, Eva McLean, and Hans M. Zell, 41–46. Ile-Ife, Nigeria: University of Ife Press.

Anderson, Elizabeth. 2001. "Strategies for Targeting Readers: The Rewards of Reading". In *Indaba 2001: Changing Lives Promoting a Reading Culture in Africa Harare, Zimbabwe, 4–5 August 2001*, 219–24. Harare: Zimbabwe International Book Fair Trust.

Annoh, Kwesi. 2001. "Modernity and Tradition in Africa: Culture and Reading—Who Determines the Priorities? An Anglophone Perspective." In *Indaba 2001: Changing Lives Promoting a Reading Culture in Africa Harare, Zimbabwe, 4-5 August 2001*, 127–30. Harare: Zimbabwe International Book Fair Trust.

Anon. 1992. "ZIBF Offering Variety of Regional Publications." *The Weekend Gazette*, July 31. ZIBF92 Box. Paul Hamlyn Foundation/CODE Europe Special Collection on Publishing in Africa, Oxford Brookes University, Headington, Oxford. Accessed January 26, 2016.

—. 1993. "Minister Commends Writers at Literary Awards Ceremony." *The Herald*, August 9. Zimbabwe International Book Fair, 1993 and 1994: Press cuttings, press releases and photographs. Paul Hamlyn Foundation/CODE Europe Special Collection on Publishing in Africa, Oxford Brookes University, Headington, Oxford. Accessed 16 January 2016.

—. 1996. "Writers, Publishers Ignore Needs of Rural People." *The Herald*, July 30. Zimbabwe International Book Fair, 1995 and 1996: Press cuttings, press releases and photographs. Paul Hamlyn Foundation/CODE Europe Special Collection on

Publishing in Africa, Oxford Brookes University, Headington, Oxford. Accessed January 26, 2016.

Attree, Lizzy. 2016. Personal Interview, February 29.

Baregu, Mwesiga. 2001. "Knowledge Production and Dissemination: The North/South Divide: Who Decides What Is Read? An Anglophone Perspective." In *Indaba 2001: Changing Lives Promoting a Reading Culture in Africa Harare, Zimbabwe, 4–5 August 2001*, 63–72. Harare: Zimbabwe International Book Fair Trust.

Barker, Ronald E., and Robert Escarpit, eds. 1973. *The Book Hunger.* Paris: UNESCO.

Behrstock, Julian. 1965. "UNESCO and the World of Books." *The UNESCO Courier*, September.

—. 1975. "National Book Development Councils in Africa: A Report by UNESCO Secretariat." In *Publishing in Africa in the Seventies: Proceedings of an International Conference on Publishing and Book Development Held at the University of Ife, Ile-Ife, Nigeria, 16–20 December 1973*, edited by Edwina Oluwasanmi, Eva McLean, and Hans M. Zell, 78–88. Ile-Ife, Nigeria: University of Ife Press.

Bhely-Quenum, Olympe. 1972. "Africa and International Book Year." *UNESCO Chronicle* 18 (8–9): 323–26.

Benge, Ronald C. 1970. *Libraries and Cultural Change.* London: Clive Bingley.

Brouillette, Sarah. 2014. "UNESCO and the Book in the Developing World." *Representations* 127 (1): 33–54.

Coly, Gaston-Pierre. 2001. "The Government's Role in Reading Promotion." In *Indaba 2001: Changing Lives Promoting a Reading Culture in Africa Harare, Zimbabwe, 4–5 August 2001*, 292–98. Harare: Zimbabwe International Book Fair Trust.

Eke, Chief A. Y. 1975. "Official Opening Address." In *Publishing in Africa in the Seventies: Proceedings of an International Conference on Publishing and Book Development Held at the University of Ife, Ile-Ife, Nigeria, 16–20 December 1973*, edited by Edwina Oluwasanmi, Eva McLean, and Hans M. Zell, 347–51. Ile-Ife, Nigeria: University of Ife Press.

Enochs, Liz. 1992. "Press Release: Zimbabwe Bookfair Addresses Environmental Issues." February 20. ZIBF92 Box. Paul Hamlyn Foundation/CODE Europe Special Collection on Publishing in Africa, Oxford Brookes University, Headington, Oxford. Accessed January 26, 2016.

Freire, Paulo, and Donaldo P. Macedo. 1987. *Literacy: Reading the Word and the World*. London: Routledge and Kegan Paul.

Fraser, Robert. 2008. *Book History through Postcolonial Eyes: Rewriting the Script*. London: Routledge.

Gibbs, James, and Jack Mapanje, eds. 1999. *The African Writers' Handbook*. Oxford: African Books Collective.

Goody, Jack. 1975. *Literacy in Traditional Societies*. Cambridge: Cambridge University Press.

Jeater, Diana. 2011. "Zimbabwe's Crisis of Creativity and Creativity in the Crisis: What Is the Point of Books?" *African Arguments*, July 15. http://africanarguments.org/2011/07/15/the-crisis-of-creativity-and-creativity-in-the-crisis-what-is-the-point-of-books-in-zimbabwe-by-diana-jeater/

Kotei, S.I.A. 1981. *The Book Today in Africa*. Paris: Books about Books.

Larson, Charles R. 1996. "Enthusiasm for the Word: Africa's Publishers Gather in Zimbabwe Every Year to Debate the High Cost of Paper, the Power of the Government Censor." *WorldView: The National Peace Corps Association's Quarterly Magazine of Developing-World News and Opinion* 9 (October). Zimbabwe International Book Fair, 1995 and 1996: Press cuttings, press releases and photographs. Paul Hamlyn Foundation/CODE Europe Special Collection on Publishing in Africa, Oxford Brookes University, Headington, Oxford. Accessed January 29, 2016.

Leishman, A.D.H. 1983. "The First Zimbabwe International Book Fair." *The African Book Publishing Record* 9 (4): 179–81.

Maheu, René. 1972. "Books for All: Director-General's Message for International Book Year 1972." *UNESCO Chronicle* 18 (1): 3–4.

Manyarara, John. 2001. "Welcome." In *Catalogue of the Zimbabwe*

International Book Fair 2001. ZIBF2001 Box. Paul Hamlyn Foundation/CODE Europe Special Collection on Publishing in Africa, Oxford Brookes University, Headington, Oxford. Accessed February 5, 2016.

Maruziva, Davison, 1993. "Writers' Workshop Will Be an Open Forum This Year." *The Herald*, July 26. Paul Hamlyn Foundation/CODE Europe Special Collection on Publishing in Africa, Oxford Brookes University, Headington, Oxford. Accessed January 29, 2016.

—. 1994. "New Format Literary Awards to Be Presented Tomorrow." *The Herald*, August 1. Zimbabwe International Book Fair, 1993 and 1994: Press cuttings, press releases and photographs. Paul Hamlyn Foundation/CODE Europe Special Collection on Publishing in Africa, Oxford Brookes University, Headington, Oxford. Accessed January 29, 2016.

—. 1995. "Read More Books, Urges Minister." *The Herald*, August 5. Zimbabwe International Book Fair, 1995 and 1996: Press cuttings, press releases and photographs. Paul Hamlyn Foundation/CODE Europe Special Collection on Publishing in Africa, Oxford Brookes University, Headington, Oxford. Accessed January 29, 2016.

Mbanga, Trish. 2016. Personal Interview, March 11.

McCullough, Gerald. 2000. "The Book Chain: The Weak Link." In *Indaba 2000: Millennium Marketplace: Harare, Zimbabwe, 31 July–1 August 2000*, 175–76. Harare: ZIBF Trust.

Moeran, Brian. 2010. "The Book Fair as a Tournament of Values." *Journal of the Royal Anthropological Institute* 16 (1): 138–54.

Ranger, Terence. 1994. "Books, Science, and Technology in Africa." *Bellagio Publishing Network Newsletter: An Occasional Publication Concerning Publishing and Book Development in the Third World* 10: 1–2.

Shamuyarir, Nathan. 1992. "Speech by the Honourable Dr Nathan Shamuyarir, Minister of Foreign Affairs, on the Occasion of the Ambassador's Luncheon in the Book Garden." May 29. ZIBF92 Box. Paul Hamlyn Foundation/CODE Europe Special Collection on Publishing in Africa, Oxford Brookes University, Headington, Oxford. Accessed 5 February 2016.

Slaughter, Joseph R. "*Clefs à Roman*: Reading, Writing and International Humanitarianism." In *Human Rights, Inc.*, 270–316. New York: Fordham University Press.

Staunton, Irene. 2001. "Strategies for Targeting Readers: What Can Publishers Do to Promote a Reading Culture?" In *Indaba 2001: Changing Lives Promoting a Reading Culture in Africa Harare, Zimbabwe, 4-5 August 2001*, 225–31. Harare: Zimbabwe International Book Fair Trust.

—. 2016. "Re: Weaver Press: Graduate Project." Personal e-mail, February 22.

UNESCO. 1945. *UNESCO Constitution*. http://portal.unesco.org/en/ev.php-URL_ID=15244&URL_DO=DO_TOPIC&URL_SECTION=201.html. Accessed 8 February 2016.

—. 1969. *Book Development in Africa: Problems and Perspectives*. Reports and Papers on Mass Communication 56. Paris.

—. 1972a. *Books for All: A Programme of Action*. Paris.

—. 1972b. "Charter of the Book." *Unesco Bulletin for Libraries* 26 (5): 238–41.

—. n.d. "Behrstock, Julian." *UNESCO Archives AtoM Catalogue*. http://atom.archives.unesco.org/julian-behrstock. Accessed February 28, 2016.

van der Vlies, Andrew. 2013. "Sub-Saharan Africa." In *The Book: A Global History*, edited by Michael F. Suarez and H. R. Woudhuysen, 512–23. Oxford: Oxford University Press.

Wrong, Margaret. 1934. *Africa and the Making of Books: Being a Survey of Africa's Need of Literature*. New York: Friendship Press for the Africa Committee of the Foreign Missions Conference of North America.

Zeleza, Paul Tiyambe. 1996. "A Social Contract for Books." In *National Book Policies for Africa: The Key to Long-Term Development: Proceedings of the Zimbabwe International Book Fair Indaba 96, Harare, Zimbabwe, 26-27 July*, edited by Murray McCartney, 12–20. Harare: Zimbabwe International Book Fair Trust.

ZIBF. 1992a. "Proposal for Ford Foundation Regional Fund." ZIBF92

Box. Paul Hamlyn Foundation/CODE Europe Special Collection on Publishing in Africa, Oxford Brookes University, Headington, Oxford. Accessed February 5, 2016.

—. 1992b. "Report on Writing for the Environment: A Three Day Practical Workshop." ZIBF92 Box. Paul Hamlyn Foundation/ CODE Europe Special Collection on Publishing in Africa, Oxford Brookes University, Headington, Oxford. Accessed February 5, 2016.

—. 1992c. "Feature: For Immediate Release." ZIBF92 Box. Paul Hamlyn Foundation/CODE Europe Special Collection on Publishing in Africa, Oxford Brookes University, Headington, Oxford.

—. 1993. "Press Release." October 11. ZIBF93 Box. Paul Hamlyn Foundation/CODE Europe Special Collection on Publishing in Africa, Oxford Brookes University, Headington, Oxford. Accessed February 5, 2016.

—. 1994a. "Information and Application Forms, 1994." ZIBF94 Box. Paul Hamlyn Foundation/CODE Europe Special Collection on Publishing in Africa, Oxford Brookes University, Headington, Oxford.

—. 1994b. "In the Beginning..." *Bookworm* 1 (2). Zimbabwe International Book Fair Bulletins. Paul Hamlyn Foundation/ CODE Europe Special Collection on Publishing in Africa, Oxford Brookes University, Headington, Oxford. Accessed 5 February 2016.

—. 1995a. "Enabling Policy for Sustainable Readership Needed." *Bookworm* 1 (6) August 8. Zimbabwe International Book Fair Bulletins. Paul Hamlyn Foundation/CODE Europe Special Collection on Publishing in Africa, Oxford Brookes University, Headington, Oxford. Accessed 5 February 2016.

—. 1995b. "Press Release." ZIBF95 Box. Paul Hamlyn Foundation/ CODE Europe Special Collection on Publishing in Africa, Oxford Brookes University, Headington, Oxford. Accessed 5 February 2016.

—. 1996b. *National Book Policies for Africa: The Key to Long-Term Development: Proceedings of the Zimbabwe International Book*

Fair Indaba 96, Harare, Zimbabwe, 26-27 July. Edited by Murray McCartney. Harare: Zimbabwe International Book Fair Trust.

—. 2016. "Objectives: Zimbabwe International Book Fair." http://www.zibfa.org.zw/index.php/about-zibfa/objectives. Accessed 27 March 2016.

Zimbabwe International Book Fair Trust (ZIBFT) and African Books Collective (ABC). 2002. *Africa's 100 Best Books of the 20th Century: Bibliographic and Acquistions Details*. Harare: Zimbabwe International Book Fair Trust.

Zimbabwe Reads. 2011. "Is Zimbabwe Reading? The 2011 Reading Survey." *Zimbabwe Reads*. http://zimbabwereads.org/how-we-help/is-zimbabwe-reading-the-2011-reading-survey/#GBS.

Athol Fugard as "Regional Writer": Oxford University Press, Three Crowns, and *Three Port Elizabeth Plays*

Katelyn Edwards

Athol Fugard is touted as "South Africa's most important and prolific playwright" (Walder 1984, 1). Constellating the playwright's "long and celebrated career" amidst the field of postcolonial literary production,[1] critic Dennis Walder points to how Fugard "has helped create a kind of drama that has established South African theatre as an arena in which audiences around the world have seen the emergence of a unique cultural form, drawn from the multiple traditions of Africa and Europe" (Walder 1984, 1). The first playwright of South African birth to enjoy an international reputation, Fugard is also among the first to be anointed with the Oxford imprint. After being initially published within the Three Crowns Series in the early 1970s, "Fugard's preferred British publisher" became Oxford University Press (OUP). As "the main publisher to exploit its legal advantage and seek British territorial rights for Fugard's texts", OUP had, by 1983, twelve of Fugard's major plays in publication, which "proved to be of [such] enduring financial value for the Press" that they are still in print today (Davis 2013a, 162).

While it is hardly surprising, then, that Fugard would be the subject of extensive biographical scholarship (see Gray [1982], Benson [1983], Walder [1984], Read [1991] and Wertheim [2000]), more surprising is the relative scarcity of scholarship on Fugard's publishing history. Catherine Davis's (2013a) *Creating Postcolonial Literature: African Writers and British Publishers* and Gail Low's (2011) *Publishing the Postcolonial: Anglophone West African and Caribbean Writers in the UK 1948–1968* (2011) make compelling—though, I argue, incomplete—interventions as they "foreground the

---

1 For a chronology of Fugard's career, see Appendix 1.

impact of the globalized publishing industry on literature and authorship", drawing attention to the distinct role of the UK publisher in the commodification of postcolonial literature (Davis 2013a, 4). By way of case study, Fugard enters into their respective examinations of how value was negotiated in relation to the changing "educational and/or literary character" of the Three Crowns Series, as they describe the troubling moments in which OUP editors came to terms with "what was new and distinctively local and authentic about African writing" (Low 2011, 28). Together, Davis and Low read Fugard's publishing into the wider academic debate animating the 1960s and 1970s around defining an aesthetic value system for African literature, though each critic charts a distinct editorial track: one political, the other geographical.

Central to OUP's packaging and promoting of Fugard, Davis argues, was the question of politicization: "Was he a political, anti-apartheid dramatist or a writer of universal truths?" (2013a, 164) The question of Fugard's political transcendence was equally raised, and hotly contested, by critics. Davis notes a number of examples:

> Stephen Gray (1982: 26) wrote of the 'universalism' of Fugard, and suggested that: 'It is a kind of critical injustice [. . .] to deal with Fugard's plays exclusively in terms of the political issues they dramatise'. [. . .] Dennis Walder in 1984 argued that Fugard's plays were undeniably about the 'inhuman facts of apartheid' and that such interpretations of him as 'universal' were simply attempts to make Fugard institutionally acceptable. [. . .] Albert Wertheim (2000) insisted that Fugard's universalist themes extended 'well beyond the borders of his homeland'. Harry Garuba (2001) positions *The Island* within the 'writing back' dimension 'of postcolonial discourse', in which 'issues of colonialism, of race and color, of political disenfranchisement and tyranny come to the fore'. (163)

Davis's enquiry into OUP's editorial strategies glosses Fugard as "a 'universal' writer who transcended immediate social and political situations" (164). Such a supposition, however, begs the question of "universal for whom?" in a global situation wherein metropolitan, predominantly anglophone publishing dominated (and still dominates). And while Fugard's universalism was of concern for OUP, as my enquiry will illustrate, there is a danger in giving too much weight to the tendency to polarize editorial processes, bifurcating them into the political and universal. It is an oversimplification of OUP's editorial strategy.

Complementing questions of political positioning, the question of Fugard's placedness equally animates the Press's archives. Was Fugard to be a kind of local literary figure, since he himself commented that "virtually all my plays are rooted in the specifics of one place and time: that little corner of South Africa centered round Port Elizabeth" (Fugard 1983, 172)? An African or South African spokesperson? Or something in between? Pushing at the political poles Davis assembles, Low articulates the "politics of postcolonial publishing" with a geographical inflection, casting OUP's concerns as a "Question of the 'Local'". The Press was ultimately published and controlled from London. Given the different cultural and aesthetic traditions between centre and margin, questions of how to judge the script—such as whether European standards of dramatic performance applied, or whether local experts were "expert" enough to pass judgment—represented real moments of anxiety in the early editorial correspondence of the archives (Low 2011, 37).

Low's scholarship teases out some arresting questions concerning Fugard's geographic positioning, but she, like Davis, flattens this arrangement to a set of binaries. What was "local", according to Low, begged the question of whether "authenticity was itself simply a product of difference from 'Western' or metropolitan norms" (2011, 37). In their rush to pigeonhole the symbolic production of Fugard's work as either essentially political or universal, local or western, book-historians like Davis and Low collapse the complex set of exchanges between playwright and publisher that ultimately packaged and positioned him as a "Regional Writer"—which "unlike all the other labels", according to Fugard, "has the virtue of being completely accurate" (1974b, v).

In what follows, I consider how the postwar scramble in the 1960s and 1970s for the (South) African textbook market—an impulse facilitated by Anglo-American trade agreements and policed by the political conditions of apartheid—resulted in the symbolic production of the "regional", a quality that proved "profitable and politically expedient" for British publishers and African authors.[2] I am interested in the discursive development of the "regional" as an editorial label and an authorial role as it gained momentum early on in Fugard's publishing career with OUP. The value of Fugard's regionality, I argue, lies in its ability to contain and diffuse an array of forces: balancing the competing editorial demands for "western standards" of literariness, but also for the "authentic" and "local colour", while bending to accommodate internal editorial pressures for economic profitability and external expectations for a certain degree of "the political". Crucial for the Press was the perception of Fugard as being political *enough*, so as not to be publically perceived as complicit in an apartheid agenda, but not *too* political so as to catch the attention of apartheid censors. In essence, the "regional" represented an elusive site at the critical juncture of intersecting political, economic, and literary fields. How progressively important this position became can be gauged in comparing the paratexts fringing Fugard's *Hello and Goodbye*, which increase in number, editorial sophistication, and regional pronunciation across subsequent editions—first as published within the Three Crowns series in 1973, then as part of the hardcover trilogy *Three Port Elizabeth Plays* in 1974.

Given that the bulk of Fugard scholarship centers on his dramas as performative or linguistic texts, this essay will instead read the editions of *Hello and Goodbye* as institutional things to be filtered

2 Minutes of Meeting between Jon Stallworthy, Richard Brain, Ron Heapy and Jonathan Crowther, April 24, 1976. Three Crowns General File LG29/222, Oxford University Press Archives (OUPA).

through Gérard Genette's paratextual apparatus. Advancing Genette's methodologies, I will also engage with Sarah Brouillette's (2007) assertion that "author's careers are key paratexts for reception and reproduction" (3), to unpack how both OUP as publisher and Fugard as author engaged in acts of authorial construction. Most apparent in Fugard's introduction to *Three Port Elizabeth Plays,* this methodological approach represents yet another critical intervention in the scholarly corpus on Fugard's publishing history, which tends to diminish the agency of the author in focusing primarily on the publisher and its processes. My larger aim, then, is to use the publication of *Hello and Goodbye*—principally for being a work deemed "not directly about race" by an African author officially classified as "white"—to reflect on the negotiations between, and the roles assumed by, British publishers and African authors, and on the influence of transnational cultural and economic relations on the postcolonial constitution of an African literary canon (Wertheim 2000, 33).

Working with OUP's archival materials, including editorial correspondence, readers' reports, and critical reviews, my chapter will be structured by Genette's paratextual taxonomy into two sections. The first section will begin by examining the implicit contexts and public epitexts that frame Fugard's *Hello and Goodbye* to open up the complex problems confronting the playwright, Press, and publishing sphere at large during the postwar period. Responding to and resolving these concerns, the second section will chart the editorial evolution of the private epitexts and peritexts[3] across the Three Crowns and *Three Port Elizabeth Plays* editions of *H&G,* wherein the "regional" becomes, for Fugard, "the one label I'm happy to have tied around my big toe when I lie in the morgue" (2000, 1). While one cannot expect there to be a single, smooth teleological evolution

3 In Gerard Genette's (1997) terminology, peritexts include prefaces, blurbs, tables of contexts, etc., while epitexts are "any paratextual element not materially appended to the text within the same volume" (344) such as interviews, book reviews, letters to editors, or private correspondence.

running through the playwright's publishing career, especially as it is represented by several editions of a singular text (which is itself an admittedly limited procedure), one *can* see how an increasing consciousness of the playwright's positionality opened up new means of symbolic production and value creation in the postcolonial publishing sphere. In being rooted in the regional, Fugard's reputation and his dramatic works were thus enabled, in Wertheim's (2000) words, to extend "well beyond the borders of his homeland" (xi).

The Problems of Postcolonial Publishing: Implicit Contexts and Public Epitexts

Following World War II, the creation of new anglophone export markets for educational texts "fostered cultural connections at a time when political independence might have spelt the dissolution of colonial ties" (Low 2011, xiv). Yet this scramble for the African textbook trade, particularly for the Press, was not a straightforward manoeuvre. By the late 1960s, OUP's Three Crowns series, a series "of cheap paper backs for the African market [. . .] by Africans themselves",[4] was caught in the midst of conflicting internal demands and external expectations. As Davis explains:

> On the one hand, the series carried a certain cultural kudos—it represented the Press's literary engagement with postcolonial Africa and its attempt to create a new canon of African literature. On the other hand, as part of OUP's mass educational publishing strategy in Africa, the series was expected to deliver profits to the centre. (2013a, 164)

The intention of this initial section is to represent the manifold problems British publishers encountered in an effort to maintain cultural dominance over anglophone African literature beyond the end of formal colonization and in parallel to South Africa's

4 Collings to Neale, June 26, 1962. Three Crowns General File, LG29/221, OUPA.

burgeoning censorship bureaucracy, as these issues are borne out in the publishing processes of Fugard's *Hello and Goodbye* as a Three Crowns series paperback. Considering the implicit contexts surrounding *Hello and Goodbye's* provenance and publication—"facts of contextual affiliation [that] to a greater or lesser degree, clarify or modify its significance" (Genette 1997, 7)—I describe OUP and Fugard's mutual interest in including *Hello and Goodbye* within the Three Crowns series to determine what kind of epitextual value Fugard's works accrued in either being performed or published. In particular, I seek to establishthe value of being published by a certain British publisher in a certain series, and to understand how these published works were evaluated by a similar set of criteria deployed by British publishers and South African censors to underscore their shared roles as "literary guardians".

First Impressions and Previous Publications

Fugard's *Hello and Goodbye* was first recommended to Jon Stallworthy, then the Three Crowns series editor, in 1968 by Charles Lewis of the Oxford Nairobi office. Lewis had sought the advice of the academic Bob Green, from University College, Dar es Salaam, who enthusiastically encouraged the idea: "As you know I am a Fugard fan and I think it would be a marvelous idea if *Hello and Goodbye* were to come out in your 'Three Crowns' list" (Davis 2013a, 164).[5] Enlisting the help of David Philip in Cape Town to negotiate with Fugard over British territorial rights, it emerged that OUP was not the first to recognize Fugard's potential. *Hello and Goodbye* had already been published by A.A. Balkema in 1966.[6]

---

5 Green to Lewis, June 25, 1968. Fugard: Hello and Goodbye, OP2005/15115, OUPA (cited hereafter as H&G).

6 The copyright page of the Three Crowns edition falsely credits the original rights to Buren Publishers–a curious editorial mistake but not surprising given the generally poor craftsmanship of the Three Crowns edition. Buren did initially publish *Boesman and Lena*. See Brain to Gracie, March 1972. Fugard: Boesman and Lena, OP2001/15136, AOUP. For photo of cover, see Appendix 2.

The Dutch publisher, whom Brain refers to as "cunning old Balkema",[7] was so well known for his "off-beat book selection" that it "became a minor tradition in South Africa that Balkema would publish books which more established publishers had turned down" (Breytenbach 1999, 442). Despite "fierce and venomous criticism", Balkema published in 1958 what Kerneels Breytenbach considers "the first Afrikaans anti-apartheid novel" (442), Jan Rabie's *Ons, die Afgod*. Published just six years later, Fugard's *Hello and Goodbye* was, in effect, aligned with such an anti-apartheid agenda under the Balkema brand, although any indication of Fugard's political affiliation is absent from *Hello and Goodbye*'s paratexts. Balkema's paratexts pale in comparison to the "accompanying productions" (Genette 1997, 1) constituting OUP's later editions of Fugard's work. Lacking dust jacket, front or back blurb, introduction or preface, Balkema's edition does little to "meditate the world of publishing and the world of the text" (xvii). The copyright page of Balkema's 1966 edition, however, does point to an interesting critical direction: noting that "the first public performance of this play was given at the Library Theatre, Johannesburg on 26th October 1965", it gestures towards the performative dimension of Fugard's dramas.

Public Peritexts, Performance, and Publication

Deliberation on the performance of Fugard's dramas as public epitexts is especially indicative of the high stakes of postcolonial publishing. Genette defines an epitext as "any paratextual element not materially appended to the text within the same volume but circulating, as it were, freely, in a virtually limitless physical and social space. The location of the epitext is anywhere outside of the book" (1997, 344) and, in Fugard's case, anywhere on stage. In distinguishing between public and private epitexts, Genette describes the former in juxtaposing performative and published modalities, noting than when an author "chooses to present his work by way of

7 Brain to Sheil, April 4, 1972. Fugard: Hello and Goodbye, OP2005/15116, AOUP.

an interview rather than a preface, he no doubt has a reason for making such a choice" (344). Genette here asserts a distinction between the authorial intention to perform, and the authorial decision to publish - and draws attention to the motivation behind the conscious act to choose one over the other. In his introduction to the trilogy *Statements*, Fugard reasons that "I have always regarded the completed text as being only a half-way stage to my ultimate objective–the living performance and its particular definition of space and silence" (1974, vii). In a later interview, Fugard observes again that his interest was in the play as performance, rather than as a static textual product: "The thing for me is, a play is not so many words on paper; a play is an experience in a theatre. I have absolutely no reverence for words on paper, texts" (quoted in Davis 2013b, 114). Given Fugard's "distinct contrast in attitude towards his plays as performances and as texts" (see Davis 2013b , 8–10), one could make Genette's epitextual arrangement work in the opposite direction, to question why Fugard chose to present *Hello and Goodbye* by way of a publication in addition to a performance, and to ask what were the effects? And conversely, why did OUP choose to publish the play in light of the implicit contexts moderating the late 1960s literary space?

I contend that OUP's publication of Fugard opened up new opportunities for both publisher and playwright to exploit the other's cultural capital and implicit economic value. The archival evidence supports this contention. Fugard may have had little "reverence for words on paper", but correspondence between Fugard's New York agent, the William Morris Agency, and Richard Brain, indicates that he *did* hold the Oxford imprint in high regard. Quoting Fugard, Brain restates, "The playwright has written to us, 'If OUP wants to publish for the UK and Commonwealth Markets, I would obviously be only too happy to say yes'".[8] Fugard's response registers an astute awareness of the wider international trade agreements governing the international publishing sphere, of which the Traditional Market Agreement (TMA) may have been the most influential.

8 Brain to Lois Wallace, 9 December 1970. Fugard: H&G, OP2005/15116, AOUP.

In the Traditional Markets Agreement (TMA), which was signed in 1947, Britain and the United States divided "the increasingly competitive anglophone 'world market' into a series of protected trading zones", giving British publishers exclusive selling rights in South Africa (McDonald 2009, 132). Thus, Oxford publication would confer on Fugard a degree of symbolic capital, aligning him with the likes of West African playwrights Wole Soyinka, John Pepper Clark, and Obi Egbuna, and with South African writers Lewis Nkosi and Oswald Mtshali. The Press's imprint would also grant the author access to a more "universal" audience in a way that South African publishers like A.A. Balkema, who was prevented by the TMA from entering the "world market", could not. Such international exposure would add further momentum to Fugard's increasing popularity as playwright and producer—a reputation OUP was eager to add to its Three Crowns list as it was considerably constrained within South Africa, given an intensification in political tensions and draconian censorship laws.

Noting the latter's increasingly dire effects in a journal entry dated June 1963, Fugard writes that, "For so many, life seems no longer possible here in S.A. Even those who have not yet had banning orders issued against them or been put under house arrest, cannot see themselves continuing" (1983, 83). Following in the wake of Sharpeville, the late 1960s and early 1970s bore witness, as Fugard does, to a litany of legislative crackdowns: the Terrorism Act of 1967 authorized the imprisonment of suspects without trial; oppositional organizations were banned in 1968; the Black Homeland Citizenship Act of 1970 reclassified non-white South Africans into citizens of Bantustans, culminating in the enforced resettlement of nearly 400,000 non-white South Africans. The international publishing industry was equally inculpated by the censorship bureaucracy affecting relations between British publishers and South African writers. While the Customs Act of 1955 strictly controlled the import of material that was deemed to be "objectionable", the Publications and Entertainments Act of 1963 would "serve as the cornerstone of the apartheid censorship bureaucracy" for, as McDonald explains,

"The Act broke new ground by making the publication, printing, or distribution of 'undesirable' materials [. . .] produced both locally and abroad a statutory offence, punishable by severe fines and prison sentences"—marking a seminal moment in Fugard's career as playwright (McDonald 2009, 32–33).

Henceforth, his plays would be performed before segregated audiences (Fugard 1983, xvii). Following the BBC's airing of *The Blood Knot* in 1965, his passport was revoked and he was informed by "the special branch that they could arrange a one-way ticket, an exit permit, for me" (Fugard 2000, 9). It is on this basis "which I now live as a man and function as a writer" that Fugard describes his assumption of an authorial role: "My decision to throw in my lot 'here and now', to *witness*" (Fugard 1983, 161). In a "period when, for the first time, my work was receiving a lot of attention abroad", the "witnessing" of a new kind of censorship bureaucracy reinforced Fugard's now desperate interest in international publication provided that performance, like South African life in general, "seems no longer possible".

Implicit Contexts, Criteria of "Desirability", and "Guardians of the Literary"

Peter D. McDonald's (2009) *The Literature Police*, as its subtitle suggests, examines "apartheid censorship and its cultural consequences", paying particular attention to the paradoxical functionalities of apartheid censors,

> who were, first and foremost, agents of the government's repressive anxieties about the medium of print [. . .] who were formally charged with the task of protecting the apartheid order from seditious, obscene, and blasphemous representations, [and] were at the same time, officially certified guardians of the literary. (11)

McDonald looks in great detail "at the censors' often copious reports, many of which read more like exercises in literary criticism than legalistic judgments", and many of which read like the readers' reports commissioned by OUP (17).

Though they report on two different texts of Fugard's that address two different themes and topics, it is worth placing Press editor Carol Buckroyd's report of Fugard's *Hello and Goodbye* alongside apartheid censor E.G. Malan's 1977 report on Fugard's *Statements: Three Plays* (1974), [9] in order to underscore the resemblances in their criteria of desirability. Such a cross-examination suggests that the cultural and political sanction of Fugard's dramas depended on estimations of literary value (i.e. composition and language use) and educational value. Though these evaluations were often made for different reasons, both publisher and censor function as institutionalized, so-called guardians of the literary.

In the main, *Hello and Goodbye* was well received by Buckroyd, but the Press editor does qualify her generally positive evaluation with "some random points". Buckroyd's first point regards the work's educational, and thus potential profit, value. "The fact that there are only 2 characters make it slightly unsuitable for schools, as usually more than 2 characters want a part", Buckroyd notes.[10] Her attention to the drama's educational value signposts OUP's keen commercial interest in exploiting the earlier Bantu Education Act of 1953, which had created a homogenous market of centrally-prescribed texts that was, as David Philip describes, "ripe for

---

9 To quote a personal email received from McDonald: "I am fairly confident that this [*Statements*] is the only Fugard book ever to have got into the system". I thus resort to Malan's report on *Statements*, part of which is included in Appendix 3. In 1974, however, censorship legislation shifted, worsening the strictness of censors' criteria.

10 Buckroyd to Stallworthy, *c.* January 1969. Fugard: H&G, OP2005/15116, AOUP. Buckroyd was an editor in the House Books department, the general publishing department of OUP; Stallworthy, at this point, was the House Books editor.

expansion".[11] The rush towards the African textbook trade became all the more desperate given that the Clarendon Press and the paper mill operated at a loss for both 1971 and 1972. Likewise, profits for the London Business were pegged at 1.7 per cent in the year ending March 1971, and group profits as a whole fell by 75 per cent (Ovenden 1996, 310–12). As one arm of the Press worked to consolidate their market share in the African textbook trade, the other sought to distract the public gaze from perceptions that this might represent a residual colonial capitalization by looking to consecrate an African literary canon. The editorial underpinnings of this canon reflected this, as Burton's reference to assessing "local books [...] by local standards"[12] implies.

Buckroyd's second critique of Fugard subsequently articulates a concern for an "alleged lack of local colour and context", insofar as "there is nothing in the play specifically South African. Indeed, apart from occasional slang phrases and references to places and railways, anything that couldn't equally well have been written by an Englishman of England." [13] As Buckroyd links these "local standards" to the national, Stallworthy seconds her observation to assert that, "Fugard's Western treatment of a Western theme" did not hit the expected note required of a Three Crowns product. Low takes Stallworthy's comment to imply that, "the Three Crowns label represented [...] a signifier of 'Africanness'"[14]—further encompassing the continental within the series's "local standards" (2011, 38). This

11 David Philip, "Notes relating to meeting with the Delegates, the Publisher, E. Parnwell and D. Neale", August 30, 1957. Three Crowns General File, LG29/221, OUPA.

12 Neal Burton to "AM", February 8, 1963. Three Crowns General File, LG29/221, OUPA.

13 Buckroyd to Stallworthy, *c.* January 1969. Fugard: H&G, OP2005/15116, AOUP. Sarah Brouillette (2007, 115) identifies a similar vocabulary engaged in the censor's report on J.M. Coetzee's 1980 novel *Waiting for the Barbarians*.

14 Stallworthy to J.F. Bell, November 13, 1968. Fugard: *People Are Living There*, 015116/2005, AOUP.

signifier of "Africanness" extended well beyond the works within the series to implicate the writers themselves.

Questions regarding Fugard's "Africanness" punctuated early editorial correspondence in weighing up whether the series could accommodate a white writer. Although several non-fiction white authors were included within the Three Crowns, Davis notes that "all the literary authors had been Black Africans" (2013a, 165). Responding to Stallworthy's enquiries into Fugard's ethnicity, Philip replies, "Fugard is as white [. . .] as most white people in this country, and is officially classified as such".[15] For the Press, this was both good and bad news. Philip's response evinces an understanding that Fugard's official classification as "white" would decrease the probability of his work being banned, but functioning paratextually, this "white" authorial identity would further reinforce the perceived westernness imbuing his work.

Interestingly, estimations of educational value, according to Malan's report, work in the opposite direction to indeed privilege "Fugard's Western treatment of a Western theme". For South Africa's "literature police", the playwright's "educational value" is judged by his "international" reputation and in terms of of "recognition" "for his positive contribution towards the development of new dramatic forms in the theatre" (McDonald 2009, 17).[16] Malan evidences such an evaluation in observing that "this book is prescribed for the Open University Drama course in Britain".[17]

Buckroyd's report concludes with a passing remark on *Hello and Goodbye*'s literary value: "Without being good at analyzing why a play is good, I feel that this one certainly has considerable merit. It is gripping—in that one wants to read on—and it is memorable".[18] In

---

15 Philip to Stallworthy, November 26, 1968, Fugard: H&G, OP2005/15116, AOUP.

16 E.G. Malan, 'Application for a Decision/Review', August 17, 1977. Western Cape Provincial Archives and Records (WCPAR).

17 Ibid.

18 Buckroyd to Stallworthy, *c.* January 1969. Fugard: H&G, OP2005/15116, AOUP.

contrast, Malan's report deliberates more deeply on the "undoubted literary value" of *Statements*, looking to previous verdicts of desirability: "As stated in the decision in Case 23 (op. cit): 'With a serious novel or a book having literary value the South African community would be more tolerant towards the use in it of unsavory language or the portrayal of violence'".[19] Evident in both reader's and censor's reports is a careful attention to Fugard's word choice as a crucial determinant of value. While Buckroyd considers the "occasional slang phrases and references to places and railways" to be an integral element contributing to the work's authentic "Africanness" and ultimate literary and educational value,[20] Fugard's "unsavory language" detracts from the censor's estimation of his "literariness", although this is quickly qualified when he concludes that these "unsavory expressions are not abused in this book".[21]

Comparing the reports commissioned by publisher and censorship board suggests the interconnectedness of criteria for defining conceptions of literature, a complex and highly politicized matter, particularly in view of OUP's aim to consecrate an African literary canon. Even if Philip does deny OUP's collusion with apartheid state censors, insisting "to my knowledge [. . .] we never submitted anything to the censorship board",[22] the traffic between publisher's and censor's reports on educational and literary value broadly gestures to their analogous roles as "guardians of the literary". It also more narrowly points to the Press's consciousness of the contexts problematizing Fugard's authorial identity and the position of his works, an awareness that would translate into the production of *Hello amd Goodbye*'s paratexts.

19 E.G. Malan, 'Application for a Decision/Review', August 17, 1977. WCPAR.

20 Buckroyd to Stallworthy, *c.* January 1969. Fugard: H&G, OP2005/15116, AOUP.

21 E.G. Malan, 'Application for a Decision/Review', August 17, 1977. WCPAR.

22 Interview with David and Marie Philip by Caroline Davis, April 5, 2007. Cape Town.

Locating a Solution: Peritexts and Private Epitexts

Seeing that Fugard's dramas had to work alongside these institutional literary authorities, and work through the aforementioned implicit contexts problematizing the sphere of postwar publishing, the aim of this section is to describe how the regional functioned and evolved as an editorial solution and authorial role. I will first analyze the peritexts of the Three Crowns Series to examine: what the regional represented; how it was shaped by the previously described criteria for "desirability"; what immediate effect the regional label had on Fugard's paratextual production; and more broadly, how it influenced both his insertion into a western-consecrated African literary canon and his definition of an increasingly precise authorial role as "witness". Against the backdrop of changing censorship legislation, I then look to the private epitexts and peritexts of *Three Port Elizabeth Plays* which further emphasize the editorial attention fixated on Fugard's positionality and exhibit how Fugard is given a more immediate role in the paratextual production of his work. I argue that *Three Port Elizabeth Plays*'s engagement with a plethora of paratextual forms illustrates how important Fugard's geographic orientation became in refining his authorial role as a *regional* witness in response to the political demands of his new international readership.

Defining the "Regional": Peritexts of the Three Crowns Series

By 1971, OUP's cultural and commercial capital in South Africa had declined. Now primarily producing and selling prescribed educational texts for segregated schools, the Press's Cape Town branch so actively avoided oppositional publications as to achieve what critics considered "the state's purpose through [. . .] blatant act[s] of self-censorship" (Merrett 1994, 63). The particular "act of self-censorship" to which Christopher Merrett refers relates to the publication of the second volume of Monica Wilson and Leonard Thompson's *Oxford History of South Africa* (1971), wherein Leo Kuper's chapter "African

Nationalism in South Africa, 1910–1964" was replaced in South Africa's edition with 52 blank pages—a slipshod editorial strategy that publically revealed too much of the Press' profit motives. Whereas OUP's status was slipping, Fugard's reputation was on the rise and on its way towards the regional.

Fugard made headlines, for instance, following the return of his passport after public petition; this, in turn, enabled him to direct *Boesman and Lena* for the Theatre Upstairs in London. Fundamental to my enquiry, however, is his 1971 interview with London's *Ink*, where Fugard identifies for the first time as a regional writer. Nuancing critical assertions of his work's universality, Fugard opines:

> I think there are writers—maybe all writers—who work in the specifics of one time and place. And if they're any good as writers, then finally a few universals will emerge in the course of their writing about the specifics. (Fugard 1971, 27)

The "regional" here comes through in Fugard's allusion to authors operating in "the specifics of one time and place"—which is placed deliberately in contrast to the quality of the universal.

What emerges from a peritextual analysis of *Hello and Goodbye*'s Three Crowns edition is how these regional "specifics" simultaneously (a) bracket in several geographic sites, accommodating "western" labels of literariness and local signs of authenticity, but also (b) blur out a specific South African authorial identity. This identity is the one Fugard finds "the most irksome"—"[that of the] political playwright'" (Fugard 2000, v). Funneled through the regional apparatus, the playwright's works were paratextually rendered into what Sandra Ponzanesi (2014) calls "forms of bland multiculturalization of the canon" (151). The process Ponzanesi describes—which "involves granting access to postcolonial authors as remakers and respondents of an established and consolidated Western tradition (the rewriting of Western literary genres, the problem of intertextuality, the abrogation and appropriation of the English language)" —is clearly at work on *Hello and Goodbye*'s back cover blurb, which begins as follows:[23] "On its appearance in South Africa in 1966, this was the second play to be published by the writer whom the *Cape Times* has called 'the best English playwright this country has produced'" (Fugard 2014, 151). Written by Brain, the first line of the blurb references several cultural cartographies, orienting Fugard and his work amid the national ("South Africa"), regional ("*Cape Times*"), western ("best English playwright"), and national again ("this country"); the second line subsequently settles the plot into a regional setting, insofar as "Hester Smit, a prostitute, returns from Johannesburg to the house in Port Elizabeth". The blurb's geographic bent is shaped by the criteria set out in Buckroyd's reader's report.

Concerns over Fugard's "lack of [specifically South African] local colour and context" are mediated in mooring the plot to Port Elizabeth, while questions of *how* to judge the work by "local standards" and of *who* was "'expert' enough to pass judgment" are resolved in referencing the regional authority of the *Cape Times*. Interestingly, the *Cape Times* authorizes Fugard by western standards of dramatic performance in deeming him the "best English playwright this country has produced"—a status ultimately sanctioned by the Three Crowns imprint. The emphasis on Fugard's literariness, however, was fundamental not simply for his insertion into a western-consecrated canon of African literature. It also marks a strategic manoeuvre in guarding Fugard's work from South Africa's censorship bureaucracy, provided that "the censors' aestheticist commitments and entrenched scholasticism", as McDonald suggests, "informed their decisions to pass some works [. . .] which they recognized were potentially 'undesirable', because their literariness somehow de-emphasized or overwhelmed their political effectiveness" (2009, 165). Although in *Hello and Goodbye* Fugard has "temporarily put aside his examination of South Africa's racial tensions", Brain is still cautious in his deployment of sociopolitical labels such as "English" and "South African" (Green 1970, 140).

---

23 For a photo of the back cover, see Appendix 4.

What is evident in *Hello and Goodbye*'s blurb is that the editorial emphasis rests not on Fugard as an individual (his name goes entirely unmentioned), but on his *authorial identity.* A paratext in the sense of the term used by Sarah Brouillette, for whom an author's career is a "key paratext for reception and reproduction" (2007, 3), Fugard's identity is not straightforwardly sanctioned as a "South African playwright"—at that time, "a politically questionable literary role"—but is instead implicitly positioned as that of a playwright of South African birth. While the play's "appearance" is explicitly linked to South Africa, Fugard as "the best English playwright" is only implicitly connected to South Africa when it is described as "this country" (McDonald 2009, 108). What, then, should be made of Fugard's self-proclaimed literary role of bearing "witness" to "the inhumanity of racial politics and laws in South Africa"—an authorial function that many critics point to in evidencing their position on Fugard's politicality (Davis 2013a, 167)? How can this be accommodated by OUP's editorial strategy?

The answer lies in Fugard's *Notebooks,* where he specifies in more geographically precise terms what it is he bears witness to. In an entry dated August 1968, the playwright suggests that his authorial role is "to witness as truthfully as I could, the nameless and destitute (desperate) of *this little corner of the world*", known as Port Elizabeth (1974, 172; emphasis added). Narrowing the scope of his witnessing to the "specifics of one time and place", Fugard can give a publicly compelling but not politically incriminating testimony of South African life as represented by Port Elizabeth. The "regional", then, becomes a fundamental element in the constitution of Fugard's authorial role as a specific kind of witness—a redemptive quality OUP's image desperately needed and, given Fugard's burgeoning popularity, one that OUP sought to further develop in *Three Port Elizabeth Plays.*

Refining the "Regional": Private Epitexts and Peritexts of *Three Port Elizabeth Plays*

Having become "too big for Three Crowns", Fugard's works were quickly ushered out of that paperback series into an out-of-series hardback trilogy issued primarily for the UK market—either a serendipitous or strategic shift in readership given the changes to South African censorship legislation in 1974. Having secured the hardback rights for the trilogy's works in 1971,[24] Brain as literary editor in London's General Division began work on *Three Port Elizabeth Plays*'s publication soon after the Three Crowns edition was produced. The early editorial correspondence regarding the trilogy's title emphasizes the continued attention OUP paid to "geographically locating the playwright". In a letter dated 8 May 1972, Brain writes of Fugard:

> He's replied, "I completely agree with your objections to some of the titles suggested. The one I personally like most [. . .] is Three Port Elizabeth Plays. That strange, little ugly town has been so decisive in my work so far that I couldn't think of a more accurate and honest title for a book containing the three plays which I have written out of my response to it..." [. . .] I too think Three Port Elizabeth Plays a good title [. . .] *memorable and geographically locating the playwright and his dramas.*[25] (emphasis added)

Brain's attention to the positionality of "the playwright and his dramas" is fleshed out in *Three Port Elizabeth Plays*'s dust jacket blurb,[26] nearly half of which consists of an excerpt from Fugard's Introduction. This introduction is worth scrutinizing as it represents the first time in the playwright's publishing career with OUP that he is granted such a degree of immediate paratextual control. Brain's blurb belies the paratextual complexity in operation: in a triply paratextual

24 Brain to Sheil, October 22, 1974, Fugard: H&G, OP2005/15116, AOUP.

25 Brain to Teresa Egan. In ibid.

26 For a photo of the dust jacket, see Appendix 5.

exercise, Fugard utilizes (a) the peritextual form of the introduction as supported by (b) the private epitexts of "extracts from notebooks" describing (c) the implicit contexts framing the publication of his dramas, in order "*to ensure that the text is read properly*" (Genette 1997, 197; my emphasis). However, given the autobiographical nature of the introduction, such paratextual dynamism equally points to an anxiety that the *author* be read properly.

Fugard begins *Three Port Elizabeth Plays*'s introduction by listing, in rapid succession, his place of birth, mother tongue, race, and socio-economic status:

> I was born in Middleburg, a small village in the semi-desert Karroo region of South Africa, on 11 June 1932. My mother is an Afrikaner, my father an English-speaking South African. [. . .] My parents owned a small general dealer's store in the village, but we sold this when I was about three years old and moved to Port Elizabeth, which has been my home ever since. (2000, vii)

As if anticipating the reader's question (like Stallworthy's) of his racial classification, Fugard qualifies his "authenticity" not by his skin color but by his almost immediate connection to the place of Port Elizabeth; "local colour" is cast in geographical terms. Authenticating himself as a regional expert, Fugard's paratextual message here has less to do with autobiographical documentation than with testimony. Fugard continues by describing his previous employment

> as a clerk in a Native Commissioner's Court. [. . .] Any violation of these [pass] endorsements is a statuary offense and is dealt with in a Native Commissioner's Court. [. . .] My time in the Fordsburg Court in Johannesburg was traumatic for me as a white South African. [. . .] I began to understand how my country functioned. (vii–viii)

Though identifying himself as the beneficiary of South Africa's system of separate development, Fugard's "witnessing" of the

Fordsburg Court is cast as an arresting moment when the playwright asks, as Elleke Boehmer (1989) does in her essay "Speaking from the Periphery", "what am I doing?". Boehmer continues, "White writing, in or of South Africa, is clearly a difficult endeavor. Behind the individual white liberal's question of 'what am I doing?' lies the more general, and trickier, 'what shall be done?'" (166). The latter question is framed as a one of authorial role.

Fugard's introduction provides answers. In its first sentences, the playwright describes Port Elizabeth as being both racially and socio-economically representative of South Africa:

> Port Elizabeth is an almost featureless industrial port on the Indian Ocean. [. . .] Close on half a million people live here—black, white, Indian, Chinese, and Colored. [. . .] It is also very representative of South Africa in the range of its social strata. [. . .] I cannot conceive of myself as separate from it. (Fugard 2000, i)

Since Fugard "cannot conceive of [himself] as separate from" Port Elizabeth, and as it represents South Africa, Fugard assumes the role of a regional spokesperson both representative of, but separate from, the South African nation. Once again engaging the process Ponzanesi describes earlier, both Press and playwright manipulate Fugard's authorial identity into "a cultural commodity of Postcolonialism, which glamorizes the exiled, cosmopolitan and diasporic authors as the best spokespersons for former colonial outposts which are still under the spell of exoticism and colonial nostalgia" (Ponzanesi 2014, 151). Brouillette elaborates on the demands of being "the best spokesperson" in the context of South Africa's political struggle, specifying that those like Fugard who enjoyed

> the special privilege of accessing markets outside of South Africa were, as a consequence of preeminence, particularly subject to the most virulent demands for political engagement and responsibility. They were thought to be

> responsible for expressing the political goals of the anti-apartheid movement, and for doing so in stark terms. (2007, 117)

Fugard, as a newly minted "Oxford author" writing for a "few 'literary' readers", instrumentalizes *Three Port Elizabeth Plays*'s introduction to nuance the working mechanism Brouillette points out, and subtly shirk demands for overt political activism (Davis 2013a, 177; Brouillette 2007, 117). As a "regional writer", Fugard is able to cater to the "global literary marketplace that sought insight into the local conditions of life in South Africa, a place with a literary output then typically defined in terms of apartheid political violence" (Brouillette 2007, 117). Pivoting the conventional angle of South Africa's "literary output", the playwright's introduction defines his work "in the specifics of one time and place" in foregrounding "the settings for all three plays" in Port Elizabeth and fading the "stark terms" of South Africa's political environment into the background (117). The political demands made by Fugard's UK audience were inseparable from the authors' access to them, but these demands were adroitly mediated and muddled by the regional apparatus, allowing Fugard as a specific spokesperson of Port Elizabeth to capitalize on OUP's international readership and evade incrimination by South Africa's "literature police".

Conclusion

It is nearly impossible to recapture fully the nature and meaning of the "regional" as it was understood by Fugard, his publishers, and his readers during the postwar period. My archival enquiry has sought to illustrate, if only superficially, the emergence and evolution of this editorial label and authorial role as represented and refined by the paratexts surrounding Fugard's work. Stretching Genette's methodological remit, the paratextual and archival materials with which I engage locate the regional at the intersection of previous book-historical scholarship on Fugard—a site sliding across political and geographical spectrums and flexing to internal editorial and external political demands. As my analysis of *Hello and Goodbye* has demonstrated, Fugard's work does not seek to "transcend the immediate circumstances of its making" to access the global literary space, as Walder would suggest. Rather, such access, as guarded by British publisher and South African censor, was grounded in the "specifics" of Port Elizabeth and granted by the role of the "Regional Writer".

Bibliography

Benson, Mary. 1997. "Keeping an Appointment with the Future: The Theatre of Athol Fugard." *Theatre Quarterly* 7 (28): 77–83.

Boehmer, Elleke. 1989. "Speaking from the Periphery." *Third World Quarterly* 11 (1): 161–66.

Breytenbach, Kerneels. 1999. *They Shaped Our Century: The Most Influential South Africans of the Twentieth Century.* Cape Town: Human & Rosseau.

Brouillette, Sarah. 2007. *Postcolonial Writers in the Global Literary Marketplace.* New York: Palgrave Macmillan.

Davis, Caroline. 2013a. *Creating Postcolonial Literature: African Writers and British Publishers.* Basingstoke: Palgrave Macmillan.

—. 2013b. "Publishing Anti-Apartheid Literature: Athol Fugard's Statements Plays." *The Journal of Commonwealth Literature* 48 (1): 113–29.

Fugard, Athol. 1966. *Hello and Goodbye.* Cape Town: A A Balkema.

—. 1969. *People Are Living There.* Cape Town: Buren Publishers.

—. 1970. *People Are Living There.* London: Oxford University Press.

—. 1971. "Athol Fugard [Interview with Naseem Khan]." *Ink* 9: 27.

—. 1973a. *Boesman and Lena: A Play in Two Acts.* London: Oxford University Press.

—. 1974a. *Statements: Three Plays.* London: Oxford University Press.

—. 1974b. *Three Port Elizabeth Plays.* London: Oxford University Press.

—. 1983. *Notebooks, 1960-1977.* Johannesburg: AdDonker.

—. 2000. *Port Elizabeth Plays.* Oxford: Oxford University Press.

Garuba, Harry. 2001. "The Island Writes Back: Discourse/Power and Marginality in Wole Soyinka's *The Swamp Dwellers,* Derek Walcott's *The Sea at Dauphin,* and Athol Fugard's *The Island.*" *Research in African Literatures* 32 (4): 61–76.

Genette, Gérard. 1997. *Paratexts: Thresholds of Interpretation.* Translated by Jane E. Lewin and Richard Macksey. Cambridge: Cambridge University Press.

Gray, Stephen. 1982. *Athol Fugard.* Johannesburg; New York: McGraw-

Hill.

Green, R. J. 1970. "Athol Fugard's *Hello and Goodbye*." *Modern Drama* 13 (2): 139–55.

Low, Gail Ching-Liang. 2011. *Publishing the Postcolonial: Anglophone West African and Caribbean Writing in the UK, 1948–1968*. New York and London: Routledge.

Malan, E.G. 1977. "Application for a Decision/Review." August 17. Western Cape Provincial Archives and Records (WCPAR).

McDonald, Peter D. 2009. *The Literature Police: Apartheid Censorship and Its Cultural Consequences*. Oxford; New York: Oxford University Press.

—. 2016. Fugard Materials. Feb. 10. E-mail.

Merrett, Christopher. 1994. *A Culture of Censorship: Secrecy and Intellectual Repression in South Africa*. Cape Town: David Philip.

Ovenden, Keith. 1996. *A Fighting Withdrawal: The Life of Dan Davin, Writer, Soldier, Publisher*. Oxford: Oxford University Press.

Ponzanesi, Sandra. 2014. *The Postcolonial Cultural Industry: Icons, Markets, Mythologies*. Basingstoke: Palgrave Macmillan.

Read, John. 1991. *Athol Fugard: A Bibliography*. Grahamstown, South Africa: National English Literary Museum.

Study Commission on U. S. Policy toward Southern Africa. 1981. *South Africa: Time Running out: The Report of the Study Commission on U.S. Policy Toward Southern Africa*. Berkeley, CA: University of California Press.

Walder, Dennis. 1984. *Athol Fugard*. Houndmills: Macmillan.

Wertheim, Albert. 2000. *The Dramatic Art of Athol Fugard: From South Africa to the World*. Bloomington, IN: Indiana University Press.

Wilson, Monica, and Leonard Thompson. 1971. *The Oxford History of South Africa Volume II: South Africa 1870 to 1966*. Oxford: Clarendon Press.

Appendices

Appendix 1: Biographical timeline of Fugard's career from 1932–1974

1960: London: turned down by Royal Court. With Sheila, joins Tone Brulin in the New Africa Group, which performs prize-winning try-for-white play, *A Kakamas Greek*, with Fugard in the lead role, at Festival of Avant-garde Theatre, Brussels. 21 March: Sharpeville massacre and five-month State of Emergency in South Africa, to which they return. Works on *Tsotsi, The Blood Knot* and begins notebooks.

1961: 3 September: *The Blood Knot* performed with Zakes Mokae at Dorkay House, Johannesburg. Reduced version tours for six months. South Africa becomes a republic, after expulsion from the British Commonwealth.

1962: Open letter to British playwrights leads to boycott of performances of their plays in segregated venues.

1963: *The Blood Knot* at the New Arts Theatre, Hampstead, LondonBegins association with the Serpent Players, directing adaptations of Machiavelli, Camus, Brecht, Beckett, Sophocles. Purchases house at Schoenmakerskop, outside Port Elizabeth.

1964: *The Blood Knot* at the Cricket Theatre, New York.

1965: First improvisations with the Serpent Players. 26 October: *Hello and Goodbye* opens at the Library Theatre, Johannesburg. Several Serpent Players arrested.

1966: Forms short-lived Ijinle Company, Hampstead Theatre Club, to perform *The Blood Knot* and Soyinka's *Trials of Brother Jero. The Coat* performed in Port Elizabeth. Dr Verwoerd assassinated, succeeded by B. J. Vorster.

1967: *The Blood Knot* produced for BBC TV; the day after transmission, Fugard's passport withdrawn.

1968: 13 March: *People Are Living There*, premiere, Close Theatre, Glasgow. *Mille Miglia* appears on BBC TV. Prohibition of Political Interfer-ence Act: extinction of Liberal Party.

1969: 14 June: *People Are Living There*, Cape Town. 10 July: *Boesman and Lena*, premiere, Rhodes University Theatre, Grahamstown.

1970: *Boesman and Lena* tours; New York premiere.

1971: 24 March: *Orestes*, Castlemarine Auditorium, Cape Town. Fugard's passport returned after public petition, to enable him to direct *Boesman and Lena* at the Royal Court Theatre Upstairs in London.

1972: 28 March: *Statements after an Arrest under the morality Act* opens at The Space Theatre, Cape Town, followed on 8 October by *Sizwe Banzi Is Dead* (This original spelling was altered to *Sizwe Bansi* for subsequent performances.)

1973: 2 July: *The Island*, also in collaboration with Kani and Ntshona, premieres as *Die Hodoshe Span*, The Space Theatre. *Boesman and Lena* filmed by Ross Devenish. Purchases house in Nieuw Bethesda. MS of *The Blood Knot* deposited at the National English Literary Museum, Grahamstown, thereafter main depository of Fugard's papers. From 12 December: 'South African Season' (including *Sizwe Bansi* and *The Island*) at the Royal Court.

1974: From 22 January: *Statements* joins *Sizwe Bansi* and *The Island* at the Royal Court. *Sizwe Bansi* and *The*

Island transfer to New York. Fugard changes view on playwrights' boycott. *No-Good Friday* and *Non-gogo* at Crucible Theatre, Sheffield. Builds house at Sardinia Bay, 'The Ashram'.

Source: Walder, Dennis. 1984. *Athol Fugard*. Houndmills, Basingstoke: Macmillan: ix-xii.

Appendix 2: Cover of A.A. Balkema's 1966 edition of *Hello & Goodbye*, courtesy of The National Library of South Africa, Cape Town Division.[27]

27 With some degree of difficulty I could only track down two copies of Balkema's edition in South African libraries: the first from the University of Cape Town, which as the librarian put it, "seems to be missing at the moment"; the second, of which I refer to and which is pictured above, from the National Library of South Africa, Cape Town Division.

Appendix 3: First page of the Republic of South Africa 1977 censor report on Fugard's *Statements: Three Plays*

DECISION: The publication STATEMENTS: Three Plays by Athol Fugard is not undesirable within the meaning of Sec. 47(2). This decision only applies to the written publication [illegible].

REPORT: 1. The book was first published by the Oxford University Press in 1974. This is the 1976 edition. It contains three plays: (a) "Sizwe Bansi is Dead", devised by Fugard, John Kani and Winston Ntshona; (b) "The Island", devised by the same three; and (c) "Statements After An Arrest Under The Immorality Act", by Fugard. In the Introduction Fugard explains three types of experiments with theatre he had tried. The first was having only the actors on the bare stage; the second was the process of improvising as the play went along; and the third, used in this book, which is a further development of the two former methods, in which the actual play is preceded during rehearsal by a great deal of improvisation, but the play itself is cast in a more or less permanent form for the actual production. Fugard describes his basic device as that of Challenge and Response, which seems to bear traces of the Greek theatre in its pre-Aeschylus years, and developed by the latter when he introduced a second actor on the stage, [illegible] the dialogue no longer consisted in exchanges between a single actor and the chorus. All this serves to explain why the first two plays were "devised" rather than written. Fugard is one of the greatest of contemporary English playwrights, who has placed [illegible] store by testing innovations in his theatre workshops, of which the Space Theatre in Cape Town was one.

2. The book was judged solely as a written publication. That is to say, it was judged as if the three plays were cast in the form of three short stories, without regard to whether they were intended for the stage. The desirability or otherwise of these plays as intended public performances is dealt with at a later stage. As a written production, intended for the ordinary reader with a healthy mind, the book has certain negative as well as positive characteristics when tested against the criteria of undesirability in Sec. 47(2).

3. Negative factors: Sec. 47(2)(a): Offensive language: Words appear in the plays which would not often be used in polite mixed company. "Shit" appears 20 times (13 times in "The Island"); "fuck" 12 times; "moer" three times; "bullshit" twice; "poes" four times, "moer" thrice, "bullshit" twice, and "cunt", "kak" and "balls" once each. This selective enumeration of objectionable words is, however, calculated to give an exaggerated view of their use in the book. They are mostly functional, more often than not used as "throw-away" expressions in passing, and, coming from the mouths of ordinary Black males talking to each other, in character. The nature, circumstances in which it is used, the manner in which it is used and the functional value of the unsavoury material are alleviating factors (Cf. Case 23: Marathon Hahn, p. 3). The words are not, despite the count above, so excessively or obtrusively used as to be repugnant. The reading of a book does not usually involve a third person or an audience, and is a private experience between the reader and the author, which the former can evaluate unemotionally.

4. Negative factors: Sec. 47(2)(a) - cont.: Indecent descriptions or scenes: On pp 70 and 71 two Robben Island prisoners, Winston and John, discuss the latter's pending release. Winston tries to picture for John's benefit, in earthy language, what the latter's first sexual encounter after his release will be like. In "Statements", from p. 81 onwards, the Coloured principal, Errol Philander, and the White librarian, Frieda Joubert, are naked on stage for a great deal of the play. Mostly the light is dim, except when police torches shine on them. They do not make love on stage and are mostly engaged in what can be called intelligent conversation. There are no specific descriptions which would be considered indecent under Sec. 47(2)(a). The nearest to this is at the bottom of p. 101. Reference to the nudity of the characters on pp. 96, 98, 100 and 101 are, in the book, only stage directions.

Source: Malan, E. G. 1977. Application for a Decision/Review. Western Cape Provincial Archives and Records.

Appendix 4: Back cover blurb of the 1973 Three Crowns edition of Fugard's *Hello and Goodbye*, courtesy of the Oxford University Press Library.

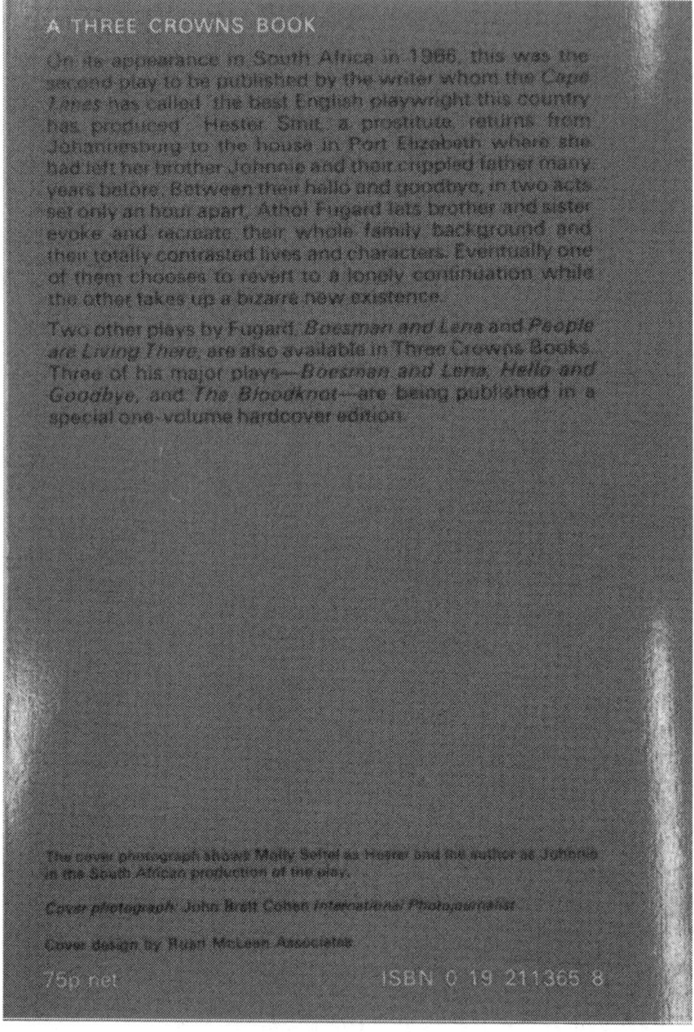

A THREE CROWNS BOOK

On its appearance in South Africa in 1966, this was the second play to be published by the writer whom the *Cape Times* has called 'the best English playwright this country has produced'. Hester Smit, a prostitute, returns from Johannesburg to the house in Port Elizabeth where she had left her brother Johnnie and their crippled father many years before. Between their hello and goodbye, in two acts set only an hour apart, Athol Fugard lets brother and sister evoke and recreate their whole family background and their totally contrasted lives and characters. Eventually one of them chooses to revert to a lonely continuation while the other takes up a bizarre new existence.

Two other plays by Fugard, *Boesman and Lena* and *People are Living There*, are also available in Three Crowns Books. Three of his major plays—*Boesman and Lena*, *Hello and Goodbye*, and *The Blood Knot*—are being published in a special one-volume hardcover edition.

The cover photograph shows Molly Seftel as Hester and the author as Johnnie in the South African production of the play.

Cover photograph: John Brett Cohen *International Photojournalist*

Cover design by Ruari McLean Associates

75p net ISBN 0 19 211365 8

Appendix 5: Dust Jacket Blurb of the 1974 Oxford edition of *Three Port Elizabeth Plays*, courtesy of the Oxford University Press Library.

In the Introduction specially written for this volume South Africa's leading playwright speaks of what has been his home town since he was about three years old:

> Port Elizabeth is an almost featureless industrial port on the Indian Ocean. It is assaulted throughout the year by strong north-westerly and easterly winds. Close on half a million people live here – black, white, Indian, Chinese, and Coloured (mixed-race). It is also very representative of South Africa in the range of its social strata, from total affluence on the white side to the extremest poverty on the non-white. I cannot conceive of myself as separate from it. It is the setting for all three plays in this book.

They are *The Blood Knot* (first produced in South Africa in 1961), *Hello and Goodbye* (1966), and *Boesman and Lena* (1968); all three have subsequently had acclaimed performances in Britain and the U.S.A., and *Boesman and Lena* has been filmed (1973). Each is effectively for two players; brother and brother, brother and sister, man and woman; but the emotional tension in *Hello and Goodbye* stems from Johnnie and Hester's relations with their father and mother, and Boesman and Lena's fierceness and pain are largely those of parents, so Athol Fugard has seen these plays as a trilogy that might have been called 'The Family'. His Introduction, including extracts from notebooks kept at the time, provides both a short autobiography and rare and valuable glimpses into the conscious and unconscious processes of playwriting.

Cover photograph from the film of Boesman and Lena, *with Athol Fugard and Yvonne Bryceland in the name parts, by courtesy of Contemporary Films Ltd.*

£2.75 net
IN UK

The Politics of Censorship: The Making of *The Penguin Book of South African Verse* (1968)

Meleesha Bardolia

The Penguin Book of South African Verse (Cope and Krige 1968) was one of the first multilingual books of poetry translated into English in South Africa that aimed to represent the linguistic desegregation of Afrikaans, English and Indigenous African poetry.[1] The successful publication of this racially inclusive anthology in South Africa during apartheid appears as an anomaly. The competing institutional pressures at work in the production of this text reveal the complexity underlying the story of British publishing and apartheid censorship in South Africa. This innovative anthology, edited by South African writers Jack Cope and Uys Krige, was commissioned by Penguin, a British publisher noted for its anti-apartheid position. It explicitly attempted to be an inclusive text with the particular aim of foregrounding black South African writing. The text included political and non-political poetry from white South Africans, black South

1 The expression 'Indigenous African poetry' will be used throughout this chapter to refer to the poems translated from isiZulu, isiXhosa, seSotho and Khoe and San languages into English in this anthology. While acknowledging the contention around the use of the term 'Indigenous' to refer to all of these language groups in contemporary South Africa, this imperfect, wide-ranging expression ('Indigenous African poetry') will be used to distinguish references to these poems in the anthology from the editors' and publishers' now outdated and demeaning references to poems in these African languages as "native verse"/"native poetry" throughout their correspondence from 1959-1968.

Africans and "Coloured"[2] South Africans in one volume. The book included poems in English as well as translations of poetry from Afrikaans, seSotho, isiXhosa, isiZulu and Khoe[3] and San languages into English.[4] Though the entirety of the exhaustive list cannot be stated here, it included a range of South African poets from different language and racial groups, including: poets writing in English such as Roy Campbell, Alan Paton, Guy Butler, Ruth Miller and Perseus Adams; poets writing in Afrikaans such as N.P. Van Wyk Louw, Olga Kirsch, and Ingrid Jonker; and poets writing in Indigenous African languages such as B.W Vilakazi, L.T. Manyase, A.Z Ngani and Demetrius Segooa. Jack Cope, the more prominent editor of the two, was a South African poet and writer for the left-wing *Guardian* magazine and the editor of *Contrast* magazine. His co-editor, Uys Krige, was a South African poet, translator and short-story writer known for bridging the gulf, both politically and linguistically, between Afrikaans and English. From 1961 to 1967, the translation process took place with Krige translating the Afrikaans poems, Dr. Dan Kunene and M.C. Mcanyangwa translating the seSotho and isiXhosa poems, and, Wits University helping with the isiZulu poetry translations into English for the work of B.W. Vilakazi.

An investigation into archival material of the editorial correspondence between Jack Cope, Uys Krige (the editors) and

2 The poet Adam Small, whose work appears in the text, is identified throughout the correspondence between the editors and Penguin as "Coloured". During the apartheid era, the term "Coloured" was an imposed category by the apartheid state for people of mixed parentage. Although there are many self-identifying "Coloured" communities in South Africa today, many people formerly classified as "Coloureds" prefer to interrogate this construction and choose their own individual and collective identity (Ruiters 2009, 127).

3 In the contents page of *The Penguin Book of South African Verse*, the editors use the term 'Hottentot' to refer to the people of this language group. This is a derogatory colonial term for speakers of Khoe languages.

4 Although Penguin originally intended the book to contain original verse next to translations for all languages in the book, this idea was dropped once the publisher realised the exorbitant cost involved in printing such a large text.

Penguin (the publisher) during the making of *The Penguin Book of South African Verse,* complicates current studies in world literature on the impact of the global market on the construction of national anthologies. In recent world literature debates about the function and role of national anthologies for global audiences, it has been argued that the production of anthologies published in English, a major former colonial language, "are almost inescapably inflected by economic and strategic interests of geographically distant agents" (Helgesson and Vermeulen 2016, 11). Institutional studies of world literature have been preoccupied by the ways in which the global market influences the formation of national literatures. An example of this can be found in James Currey's 2008 account of the Heinemann African Writers Series from 1962 to the 1980s. Currey's insights suggest that African authors writing in English were dependent on a transnational system of publication that was "pan-African or more broadly Commonwealth" (McDonald 2017, 392-393). Similarly, in *Creating Postcolonial Literature: African Writers and British Publishers*, book history scholar Caroline Davis (2013) interrogates the dominance of the transnational aspects of publishing in Africa through an analysis of Oxford University Press's Three Crowns series. Through archival research, Davis highlights the, at times, neo-colonial influence of British publishers on the commodification of African literature. Likewise, in *Minding Their Own Business: Penguin in Southern Africa*, Alistair McCleery (2018) demonstrates the influence of British publishers and editors on South African literature. McCleery's study demonstrates the significance of "transnational interchange in providing a means of publication to authors and texts that would otherwise have been censored in their own countries" (Davis et al. 2018, 381).

An analysis of the making of *The Penguin Book of South African Verse* both intervenes in and contributes to an understanding of the tensions between the global and the national in the study of world literature. Rather than providing a univocal account of how external, global institutional pressures shape a national text, I will add complexity to the story of the intersection between world literature and national anthologies by focusing on the internal, local complexity of this case study. In order not to attribute too much agency to British publishers regarding the commodification of South African literature, this chapter will demonstrate how *The Penguin Book of South African Verse* was formed by competing national and global institutional pressures. In line with Stefan Helgesson and Pieter Vermeulen's (2016) sociological approach to the study of world literature, I will highlight the various processes through which world literatures are created through "an interrelated set of social phenomena" which allows literary works to manifest as "disruptive acts of institution in their own right" (2016, 12 and 14). Highighting the agency literature has to disrupt external institutional forces, Helgesson argues that literature "cannot be understood exclusively in terms of political power and domination" but must also be understood "as a world of its own and an enabling alternative to other domains of power" (Helgesson 2014, 484). As I will argue, the making of *The Penguin Book of South African Verse,* and its reception by censors in South Africa, demonstrate how a literary work can simultaneously evade and adhere to institutional pressures in national and global literary marketplaces.

The text was shaped by Penguin's contradictory desires to gain economic power in Anglophone African publishing within South Africa and to maintain its popularity in the international market as an anti-apartheid publisher. A sociological critique of this text reveals how the competing institutional pressures of apartheid censorship (local) and the anti-apartheid stance of the global literary marketplace (international) shaped the construction of the text. More specifically, Penguin constructed itself as an anti-apartheid publishing house and, as one correspondence from Richard Newnham, commissioning editor of the *Penguin Book of South African Verse,* to Jack Cope reveals, Penguin was adamant on being seen as "the first British publisher who is not tailoring a book on South Africa to suit the public's preconceptions"[5] in the local market. Rather than pandering to the

---

5 See: University of Bristol Special Library Collections: Penguin Archive: Penguin Books Ltd. editorial files, Penguin African Library Series, The

apartheid censorship laws, Penguin's aim was "to give as fair allocation of space to all the poetry in the Union as possible" in order to be seen as restoring "justice" to South African literature.[6] However, Penguin also expressed anxiety about how it would be able to fulfil this editorial mission within the confines of apartheid censorship laws. More specifically, Penguin worried that pressure to conform to censorship laws to get the book published in South Africa might weaken the anti-apartheid stance of the text and affect its anti-apartheid reputation in the UK. As Richard Newnham stated:

> What worries us more than this overseas sales aspect is the effect of current events on our home market. [. . .] I know of course that what you both are doing in no way ties up with your Government's policies—quite the reverse—but people aren't to know this even given the Penguin imprint on the book.[7]

This statement suggests Penguin's ideological and commercial concerns about producing an anti-apartheid text for a global market. However, rather contradictorily, correspondence between Penguin and the editor also seems concerned with the chances of the book gaining educational prescription in South Africa through the strategic, political expurgation of the text. What is revealed in the correspondence between publisher and editors is a bifurcation between the institutional marketing pressures at play in the global market and the South African market. In addition to attempting to maintain its anti-apartheid reputation abroad, the editorial correspondence suggests that Penguin was concerned about how the racial and linguistic inclusivity of the book would be assessed by the censors in South Africa.

Penguin Book of South African Verse, DM1107/D109, Fol. 1 [Hereafter, referred to as Penguin, *PBSAV*, Fol 1.] Letter from Richard Newnham to Jack Cope, February 23, 1962.

6 *Ibid.*

7 Penguin Archive, *PBSAV*, Fol. I. Letter from Richard Newnham to Jack Cope, 30 August 1963.

The racial and linguistic inclusivity of this anthology in the 1960s was noticeable during a time when racial division had become the South African government's main objective after the policy of apartheid was introduced by the National Party in 1948. The 1960s represented "the decade of high apartheid" (Dubow 2014, 99) in which "apartheid ideology evolved from the pronouncement of white domination" to the implementation of "separate development" through the acceleration of the Bantustan policy by the National Party (Dubow 2014, 105). From 1966, many black writers were forced into exile and their work was banned in South Africa (Van der Vlies 2007, 13-14). As I will argue throughout this chapter, the making of the *Penguin Book of South African Verse*, which took place from 1959 to 1968, was shaped by sensitivities towards the stringent policies implemented as a result of the Publication and Entertainments Act of 1963. This Act reified many of the draconian recommendations from the Cronjé Report. In 1956, Geoffery Cronjé, a former sociology professor and head of the Cronjé Commission, "authored a report that recommended the formation of South Africa's Publications Control Board", which formed "the censorship arm of the state" (Decker 2016, 71). This "centralised apparatus" reviewed locally published and imported books (Sanders 2006, 104). Cronjé's report, which shaped censorship measures into the 1970s, created regulations that would "foster a national Afrikaner literature while eliminating the undesireable text" (Decker 2016, 71). Undesireable text was the phrase used for subversive literature classified as "offensive", "harmful", "indecent" and "blasphemous" to "the inhabitants of the Republic" (Section 5 (2), Publications and Entertainment Act of 1963).[8] Undesirable publications were texts that did not conform to the ideologies of apartheid. As Mark Sanders (2006) argues, "notions of undesirability" were "inextricably interwoven with the Commission's subscription to precepts and goals of racial separation and white guardianship over blacks" (Sanders 2006, 105). Writers

8 The Publications and Entertainments Act 1963 is cited from McDonald, *The Literature Police*. http://www.theliteraturepolice.com/documents/

whose work could be interpreted as seditious or subversive were at times punished through exile, imprisonment or death.

Despite the apparent inflexibility of the Act, Gerrit Dekker's appointment as the first chair of the new Board also enabled some "looseness" (McDonald 2009, 52) to be introduced into the system. As a respected Afrikaans literary critic, Dekker was able to put his "cultural credentials at the service of the government" (McDonald 2009, 38). Under Dekker's leadership, the new board, which consisted mostly of a cultural elite, came to define its role as "guardians of the literary" (McDonald 2009, 52). The idiosyncrasies that defined the Dekker Board of assessors can also be seen in the Kruger Board who assessed *The Penguin Book of South African Verse.* H. van der Merwe Scholtz, one of the censors who assessed the 1968 Penguin anthology, revealed in an interview with Peter D. McDonald in 2001 that one of the tacit principles governing the selection of texts was its literary quality rather than its political palatability.[9] This admission suggests that from the censors' point of view, from the inside, "censorship can appear to be coextensive with literature" (Darnton 2014, 234). Although the censors' self-appointed role as guardians of literature did not alleviate the repression of state censorship, it did introduce an element of unpredictability into the assessment of texts. The political nature of certain texts could be deemed permissible according to the censors' use of literary criteria in their adjudications. The censors' view of themselves as guardians and protectors of literature clashed with the way in which many literary publishers saw their rivalry with the censors as one predicated on a division between the high-minded and the oppressive.

In *Publishing South African Literature in English in the 1960s,* Walter Ehmeir (1995) appears to fall into the trap of simplifying the story of censorship in his romanticisation of Penguin as a heroic publisher during apartheid. Throughout his analysis, Ehmeir looks at the publication of South African texts by British and local publishing houses during the 1960s and discusses the ways in which many

9 H. van der Merwe Scholtz, personal interview with Peter McDonald, 22 Aug. 2001.

conceded to self-censoring their texts in order to get them passed by repressive censors. In his appraisal of the publishing landscape, Ehmeir isolates Penguin as an uncompromising publisher. In his beatifying review, he emphatically declares that "one of those publishing houses that stood firm and refused to give in to the demands of censorship was Penguin" (114). He cites Penguin's publication of *South African Writing Today* (Abrahams and Gordimer 1967), as one brave example. This anthology included many gagged writers and, as a result, was banned in South Africa. However, unnoted in Ehmeir's positive assessment of Penguin's provocative publishing genealogy is the publication of *The Penguin Book of South African Verse.*

The seemingly incongruous publication of this political anthology during apartheid suggests that the story of censorship in South Africa cannot be reduced to a monolithic narrative of an ideological duel between liberal writers/editors and an oppressive group of censors. As I will argue, during apartheid censorship, Penguin was not immune to the institutional pressures of the South African market. This inference is made from the discrepancy between the initial political intention of the book and the censors' assessment of the final publication as non-political. Highlighting the original intention of the racial inclusivity of the text, a commissioning editor at Penguin declared that the *Penguin Book of South African Verse* "actually makes the admission that our black brothers have a cultural heritage comparable to that of any race".[10] Seemingly at odds with what the book intended to represent, H. van der Merwe Scholtz, one of the censors who assessed the text, contended that the anthology could be passed because it was a "bona fide literary selection", which did not make the "race-problematic its starting point" (BCS 5/69).[11] Scholtz's assessment negates Penguin's original ideological positioning of the work. Spurred by the apparent disjunction between

10 Penguin Archive, *PBSAV*, Fol. 1, Letter from Richard Newnham to Jack Cope, August 30, 1963.

11 Censors's Report BCS 5/69. Original document translated by Peter McDonald.

the original intention of the work and its assessment by the censors, this chapter will interrogate the cycle of transmission of the text.

An investigation into previously unexamined archival material undermines Ehmeir's overriding conceptualisation of Penguin as a dauntless anti-apartheid publisher in the 1960s. The archives demonstrate the concessionary modifications Penguin made to its work to ensure publication in apartheid South Africa. An analysis of the correspondence between Jack Cope, Uys Krige, Penguin and Longmans[12] indicates the extent to which *The Penguin Book of South African Verse* was modified for commercial and political reasons to get through the censorship system in South Africa. The evidence here resonates with Robert Darnton's (2014) assertion that because "complicity, collaboration, and negotiation pervaded the way authors and censors operated… it would be misleading to characterize censorship simply as a contest between creation and oppression'" (234). Indeed, rather than the censors being oppressive in this particular case study, it was Penguin and Cope's totalising evocation of the South African censor as an oppressive bureaucrat which caused Penguin to dilute the political framework of the text in the making of the book. This point can be substantiated from letters between Cope and the commissioning editor of Penguin which illustrate Cope's hyperawareness of the censors' presence. More specifically, on September 10, 1968, an irate letter was sent from Cope in Cape Town to commissioning editor Nick Stangos in the Penguin office in London regarding the interception of a manuscript. After being chastised in an earlier letter for the lateness of the copy, Cope lamented:

> I can only surmise that they were intercepted by the Censorship and held for just under a fortnight. I will return the job by the thirteenth. If a new lot of proofs are on the

12 Unlike Penguin, Longmans, previously named Longmans Green, was primarily an educational publisher. In order to tap into this market, Penguin signed an agency agreement with Longmans Green. From 1 April 1959, Longmans represented Penguin in South Africa and the rest of Africa through Longmans Southern Africa Pty Ltd (McCleery 2018, 513).

> way, well, it may give the Censors another dose of light reading. They don't seem to mind, because they individually get a fat fee for every document they peruse, rather like paying the hangman for every head.[13]

Cope's reference to the censor as a literary "hangman" mythologises the South African censor as a malign figure whose objective is to decapitate seditious works and, in effect, kill literature. This negative imagining of the censor was not unique to Cope. Prominent South African author J.M. Coetzee (1996) caricatured the censor as "an intrusive reader, a reader who forces his way into the intimacy of the writing transaction, forces out the figure of the loved or courted reader" (38). Painting a picture of the censor as a trespasser of literature, Coetzee lampooned the censor during the Snyman regime as "the dark-suited, bald-headed censor, with his pursed lips and his red pen and his irritability" (Coetzee 1996 38). However, as Hermann Wittenberg (2008) astutely points out, "ironically [. . .] Coetzee's actual censors were not unimaginative, grey government bureaucrats, but intellectuals, writers and academics like himself, among them even colleagues at the University of Cape Town where he was teaching" (137).

Coetzee's and Cope's characterisation of the censor is one example of the way in which the censorship debate in South Africa typically descends into a crude set of binaries. In *Censors at Work: How States Shaped Literature,* Robert Darnton (2014) complicates the Manichean division between censors as oppressive and editors/publishers/authors as heroic by taking an ethnographic approach to the study of censorship in Bourbon France, India under the Raj and Communist East Germany.[14] Darnton's methodology humanises the figure of the censor by treating censorship holistically as "a system of control, which pervades institutions" and "colours

---

13 Penguin Archive, *PBSAV*, Fol 1. Letter from Jack Cope to Nick Stangos, Sept. 10, 1968.

14 This dichotomy has also been challenged by Nicole Moore (2012) in an Australian context.

human relations" (2014, 243). By applying this methodology to the study of censorship, "ethnographic history can do justice to the different ways that censorship operated in different societies" and can avoid reducing censorship to a "formula" (2014, 243). Darnton argues that studies of censorship that do not take into account the "complexities of experience" (2014, 243) of specific cultural systems end up caricaturing censors by "pitting the children of darkness against the children of light" (2014, 17) or, in this case, pitting the censor as literary hangman against the literary "heads" of the publishing industry including editors and writers.

Although the object of Darnton's analysis does not extend to South Africa, building on the work done in Peter D. McDonald's (2009) seminal text *The Literature Police: Apartheid Censorship and its Cultural Consequences*, Hermann Wittenberg's (2008) *The Taint of the Censor: J.M Coetzee and the* Making of *In the Heart of the Country,* and Andrew van der Vlies's (2012) *Print, Text and Book Cultures in South Africa*, this essay argues for a more nuanced analysis of the complexities of apartheid censorship and British publishing in South Africa.

My aim is to modulate the story of South African censorship to demonstrate how a univocal interpretation of editorial herosim or, equally, of a totalitarian censor, do not hold. I will complicate traditional narratives of a clash between a heroic publisher and an oppressive censor by taking a sociological approach to the study of archival material on *The Penguin Book of South African Verse.* By exploring the cultural contexts and "strains of humanity" (Darnton 2014, 15) that defined the publication of this book, I aim to challenge conventional readings of apartheid censorship by demonstrating how Penguin's concern with creating a text that worked in both the local and global literary marketplaces affected the formation of the text.

I will begin with an analysis of Penguin's presentation of its original intention in creating the work, then examine the volatile process of concessionary modifications and subversive modifications made to the text. I will investigate how these changes were made in light of the editors' and Penguin's dual concerns with getting the book passed by the censors in South Africa while maintaining its appeal to the global literary marketplace as an anti-apartheid publisher. Finally, I will examine the censors' report on the text and consider what its ambivalent, but ultimately positive assessment, of the work reveals about the inconsistencies and complexities of censorship in apartheid South Africa. By pinpointing the strains of humanity that defined the operation of censorship in South Africa, I hope to offer a more nuanced sense of the means by which Penguin sought to be sanctioned by a critical institutional fortress of South Africa's dominant political and cultural order while maintaining its anti-apartheid reputation abroad.

Local Sensitivities

During the editorial process, Penguin, Cope and Krige vacillated between a bifurcated editorial strategy of political defiance and political concessions in an attempt to conform to and challenge local sensitivities. This contradictory editorial strategy revealed Penguin's competing desires to maintain an anti-apartheid stance abroad while ensuring the palatable reception of the book by the censors in South Africa. Initially, Penguin's decision to publish a representative text of South African verse, during a time of censorship and racial segregation, was aggrandized by the commissioning editors at Penguin as a heroic political move aimed at increasing the representation of black writing in South Africa. *The Penguin Book of South African Verse* was initially imagined as a corrective to Penguin's *Modern Poetry from Africa* (1963). Before the idea for *The Penguin Book of South African Verse* took hold, Penguin was engaged in the publication of *Modern Poetry from Africa,* edited by Ulli Beier and Gerald Moore. This text was "a collection of poems by African writers". [15] Despite including black writing, this text privileged European languages and English over African languages. In a letter from Richard Newnham, commissioning editor of the *Penguin Book of*

15 University of Bristol Special Library Collection: Penguin Archive, Penguin African Library Series, Modern Poetry Series, DM1107/D109, Fol. 1. From Modern Poetry Series file, Memo, May 29, 1962.

South African Verse, to Ronald Segal, founder of the Penguin African Library, Newnham writes that black South African author Es'kia Mphahlele complained that, in Penguin's *Modern Poetry from Africa* (1963), "by leaving out all the native verse they were not reproducing a representative book." [16] According to Mphahlale, "apart from a volume by Roy MacNab which includes only a section of a long poem by Dhlomo [. . .] African writers have never been regarded as part of the literary world". [17] Significantly, Mphahlele suggests that this discrimination and literary gap will be ameliorated in the upcoming *Penguin Book of South African Verse.* [18] Mphahlale premptively aggrandizes Penguin's anti-apartheid undertaking in his assertion that "by including native African verse in translation you will have blazed a new trail in the field of anthology publication".[19] Penguin's self-aggrandizement of its mission to include English translations of poetry in seSotho, isiXhosa, isiZulu, and Khoe and San languages is evident in its assessment of the book as evidence of it being the "first British publisher", during the repressive period of apartheid publishing, "who is not tailoring a book on South Africa to suit the public's preconceptions".[20] At one point, Penguin even asserted that it wanted to place considerable emphasis on "native verse"[21] in the collection.

However, as concern with local politics grew, Penguin, Cope and Krige made more concessions and the significance of

---

16 Penguin Archive, *PBSAV*, Fol. 1. Letter from Richard Newnham to Ronald Segal, from May 29, 1962.

17 University of Bristol Special Library Collections, Penguin Archive: Penguin Books Ltd editorial files, Penguin African Library Series, The Penguin Book of South African Verse, DM1107/D109, Fol. 2 [Hereafter referred to as *PBSAV*, Fol. 2.] Letter from E. Mphalalae to Richard Newnham, May 19, 1961.

18 *Ibid.*

19 *PBSAV,* Fol 2. Letter from E. Mphalalae to Richard Newnham, May 19, 1961.

20 Penguin Archive, *PBSAV,* Fol. 1. Letter from Richard to Jack Cope, February 23, 1962.

21 Penguin Archive, *PBSAV*, Fol. 1. Letter from Richard Newnham to William Plomer, July 15, 1959.

foregrounding English translations of poetry in Indigenous African languages weakened. In the letters between Penguin and the editors, the need for caution regarding the book's reception in South Africa is revealed. Unlike its Australian, New Zealand and Canadian book of poetry counterparts, Penguin registered that its considerations for this *South African Book of Verse* would be different. After receiving news that "the general sales in the Union for such an anthology would be modest" and that "the book would not be prescribed widely unless its contents steered clear of political implications", Richard Newnham asserted that—unlike their approach to the other books of verse—"it does show the need for caution on our part".[22] Despite Penguin's initial wish to foreground English translations of poetry in seSotho, isiXhosa, isiZulu, and Khoe and San languages, in May 1961, Richard Newnham began the process of making the book palatable to the censors by reducing the space allotted to "African verse". Newnham decided that the allocation of space should be "half English poetry and one-quarter each for Afrikaans and native African verse".[23] Fearful of the impossibility of getting this "radical" book passed by the censors and gaining educational prescription, this structural suggestion was couched by Newnham as an "editorial diktat'" to the editors.[24]

Despite concern from Longmans that the selection of Krige and Cope, known to be radical intellectuals, might cause Penguin to run into trouble regarding the political nature of the book,[25] both Cope and Krige seemed to be attuned to the need for caution. In both the early and late stages of the book's development, Krige and Cope attempted to present their anthological "scheme" as purely literary and one unaffected by politics.[26] Krige defined the politics that shape anthological schemes as "cultural-historical nonsense". By using the

22 Penguin Archive, *PBSAV*, Fol. 1. Letter from Richard Newnham to Uys Krige, March 14, 1960.

23 Penguin Archive, *PBSAV*, Fol. 1. Letter from Richard Newnham to Jack Cope, May 19, 1961.

24 *Ibid.*

25 Penguin Archive, PBSV, Fol. 2, Memo from W.P. Kerr to Penguin, 1959.

26 Penguin Archive, *PBSAV*, Fol. I. Letter from Uys Krige to Richard Newnham, January 29, 1960.

phrase "cultural-historical nonsense", Krige was referring to the concept of selecting poems according to a "preconceived theory" regarding "the South African poet vis à vis the South African problem".[27] Unlike Penguin's Australian, Canadian and New Zealand Books of Verse, the *South African Book of Verse* was pitched by its editors as one that would be motivated simply by "considerations of intrinsic poetic merit", something which Krige considered "unexplored by previous anthologies".[28]

While it is true that the book did not foreground a specific thematic to encapsulate South African poetry, these statements of neutrality regarding what is euphemistically described as "the South African problem" are undermined by the way in which the South African problem of language and race governed the editors' ordering of the text. In 1961, it was decided that the book would begin with English poems, followed by translations of Afrikaans poetry and lastly, translations of poetry from Indigenous African languages into English. In a letter to one of Penguin's commissioning editors, Anthony Richardson, Cope provides some insight into the rationale behind the ordering of the text:

> The present order of the book is the most satisfactory—English first, followed by Afrikaans translations and then the indigenous languages in alphabetical order. This, as you say, gives an easier way into the book and also meets some of the sensitivities bound to be touched.[29]

By avoiding a chronological ordering of the text, the anthology appeared to be governed by local sensitivities about the politics of language and race in South Africa. Cope and Krige's implicit concern that beginning the book with translations of poetry from seSotho, isiXhosa, isiZulu, and Khoe and San languages into English

---

27 *Ibid.*

28 *Ibid.*

29 Penguin Archive, *PBSV*, Fol. 1. Letter from Jack Cope to Anthony Richardson, October 20, 1960.

might inflame the Nationalists reveals the influence of local political sensitivities on their anthology. In a letter to Richard Newnham, Cope lamented that "South Africa is such a quarrelsome country" that "to place oneself on absolutely safe ground in making a literary choice is virtually impossible".[30] Even the seeming neutrality of a chronological ordering of the text was dismissed by Penguin as too radical. In 1964, South African poet David Wright suggested to editor Anthony Richardson, in his response to Richardson's request for a review of the book, that "the anthology should begin with the Bushmen, Hottentot and native poems, continue with the Afrikaans, and end with the English".[31] According to Wright, "this is the order in which the races that now inhabit South Africa make their appearance there".[32] Despite Wright's suggestion that they adhere to a chronological order of South African history, which would, in fact, fulfill Penguin's original mission of foregrounding the significance of including English translations of poetry in Indigenous African languages, Penguin remained unmoved. The final text began with English poems followed by Afrikaans translations and the Indigenous languages translated in alphabetical order.

It is important to note here that while conforming to local sensitivities compromised the original, politically radical intention of the text, subversion of local sensitivities also informed the organization of the text. More specifically, the organisation of poets within the language divisions of the "contents" page challenged apartheid policies. In initial drafts of the book, the text was organized according to ethno-linguistic principles. In a society in which "no communication" is allowed "between the sections of a people carved up into categories of colour and language" (Gordimer 1994, 151), this was not surprising. However, in 1966, Cope disrupted the ethno-linguistic organization of the text by including Adam Small, a Coloured

30 Penguin Archive, *PBSAV*, Fol. I. Letter from Jack Cope to Richard Newnham, 16 February 1962.

31 Penguin Archive, *PBSV*, Fol. 1. Letter from David Wright to Anthony Richardson, September 21, 1964.

32 *Ibid.*

poet, in the Afrikaans section. In a letter to Anthony Richardson, Cope asserted that Adam Small's poem should go at the end of the Afrikaans section, after Ingrid Jonker. Cope's sensitivity towards the racism experienced by Small is evident in his assertion that:

> Small is a young coloured lecturer in philosophy at one of those revolting 'ethnic' universities set up by the Nationalists for Coloureds only and referred to by them as the 'Bush College'. Can you imagine Small's feelings about it?[33]

Cope's inclusion of Small in the Afrikaans section can be read as a subversive move to deracialise Afrikaans in the arrangement of the contents page. As the politically palatable ordering of language groups in the text and the politically subversive inclusion of Small in the Afrikaans section demonstrate, despite stating that they merely had literary concerns in the organization of this anthology, Cope and Krige's editorial policy was shaped by political concerns that were concessionary and subversive.

The tension between sensitivity toward local politics and the desire to produce an anti-apartheid representative book of verse intensified once the Publications and Entertainments Act of 1963 was implemented. After it took effect, Penguin expressed concern about the likelihood of getting the book published. As Richard Newnham asserts:

> The way things are going in your part of the world is naturally a factor that we must consider in planning to publish a book of South African verse. It seems likely that before long your authorities will get tough on importing books at all, let alone prescribing them in schools and colleges, and of course with a book like yours, that actually makes the admission that our black brothers have a cultural

33 Penguin Archive, PBSV, Fol. I. Letter from Jack Cope to Anthony Richardson, November 12, 1966.

> heritage comparable to that of any race, the problems will be even greater.[34]

Newnham concludes by asking whether "there is an earthly chance of the book getting into schools at the moment" and suggests that they expedite the book's publication before even more stringent laws are implemented. [35] In line with Penguin's desire to gain educational prescription, from 1963 to 1968, the archives reveal that Penguin began to expurgate the text and consider how to get the book passed by the censors. The first indication of Penguin's willingness to self-censor the book can be seen after Cope discovered that he had been placed on a banned persons list in 1965. On July 6, 1965, in a letter to Anthony Richardson, Cope suggests the impossibility of getting *The Penguin Book of South African Verse* published in South Africa. He laments that owing to a new law recently passed, "either my name or my work [*sic*] must come out of the book", if it is the intention to have it on sale in South Africa, or "the book goes ahead as planned and is banned to [*sic*] the country of origin". Rather grimly, Cope concedes that "a third option would be to drop the whole project".[36]

As I will proceed to argue, Anthony Richardson's response prompted a new scheme aimed at ensuring the publication of the book in South Africa. Claiming that he does not see how Penguin "can do the book and not attempt to sell it in South Africa", Richardson suggested that they "may have to exercise some kind of voluntary censorship, or at least disguise". [37] By mentioning "voluntary censorship", Richardson was referring to the self-censorship practiced by many overseas publications that wanted to get their books published in South Africa. In response to Richardson, Cope mentions the possibility

34 Penguin Archive, *PBSAV*, Fol. I. Letter from Richard Newnham to Jack Cope, August 30, 1963.

35 *Ibid.*

36 Penguin Archive, PBSV, Fol. 2. Letter from Jack Cope to Anthony Richardson, July 6, 1965.

37 Penguin Archive, PBSV, Fol. 1. Letter from Anthony Richardson to Jack Cope, July 15, 1965.

of applying to the government for an exemption for Penguin.[38] After mentioning this possibility in November 1965, the archive contains a gap until 1966 and the notion of an exemption or Cope's ban is never alluded to again. Since the book ended up being published, it is unclear whether Penguin received an exemption or whether Cope's name was cleared. The original document for "The List of Banned Persons" in 1966 does not contain Cope's name.[39] Thus, while acknowledging the gap in the Penguin archive, it is possible to deduce from the absence of Cope's name on the "The List of Banned Persons" in 1966 that Cope's ban was lifted.

After this censorship scare, from 1965–68, the archives reveal that Penguin became preoccupied with neutering the political nature of the book. Penguin, like many British publishers, knew that it was not its anti-apartheid stance which would get their works banned "but its particular execution" of politically sensitive material which might be cause for refusal by publishing houses (Ehmeir 1995, 112). It is to the way in which the anthology's political message was palatably executed through its "voluntarily censorship" and disguise that I will now turn.

"'Voluntary Censorship', or at Least Disguise"

The threat of a ban on the book resulted in a series of modifications to the text of both a concessionary and subversive nature. After receiving news of the ban and Penguin's letter about the possibility of exercising some sort of disguise, in 1966, Cope sent a draft version of an introduction for the book to Penguin. The platitudes and generic descriptions used to describe South African poetry, which, in Richardson's words, "read like a commercial",[40] indicate that the

38 Penguin Archive, PBSV, Fol. 1. Letter from Jack Cope to Anthony Richardson, November 6, 1965.

39 "List of Banned Persons 1966." *The Literature Police*. Peter McDonald, 2009. Accessed March 4, 2015. http://www.theliteraturepolice.com/documents/.

40 Penguin Archive, *PBSAV*, Fol. I. Letter from Anthony Richardson to Jack Cope, August 12, 1966.

introduction packaged itself as non-political. The introduction did not touch on the significance of the inclusion of translations of poetry from seSotho, isiXhosa, isiZulu, and Khoe and San languages into English. It merely stated that "in the African languages the transition from the spoken to the written form of poetry is still an active process, beset by difficulties".[41] Rather than highlighting the radical inclusion of the verse of Vilakazi, Cope makes no mention of the way in which his work broke down racial boundaries by bringing the struggle against segregation to the fore (Le Roux 2015, 57). Cope also reductively asserts, in a particularly exoticising passage, that the languages of the Indigenous African groups "reaffirm in the accents of stone-age man the poetry of magic or the magic of poetry".[42] In contrast, with four full pages devoted to it, in a seven-and-a-half page introduction, great attention is given to valorizing Afrikaans poetry and its history. Cope even goes so far as to state that "any new Afrikaans poet of merit finds almost immediate acclaim in university and other educated circles" and that "Afrikaans is probably the most anthologized in all modern literature".[43] In reply, Anthony Richardson chastises Cope for writing a banal introduction that speaks in platitudes about the significance of including English translations of poetry in Indigenous African languages and for his obfuscation of the fact that the policy of the nationalist government in relation to school textbooks is probably what helps the sales of Afrikaans poetry and is "no guarantee of quality".[44] Richardson instructs Cope to "write in more depth about the particular qualities of South African poetry and the South African experience".[45]

In defence of his introduction, Cope reveals that he was deliberately excluding the significance of including English

41 Penguin Archive, *PSAV*, Fol. I. 'Introduction' Manuscript from 1966, p. 3.

42 Penguin Archive, *PSAV*, Fol. I. 'Introduction' Manuscript from 1966, p. 4.

43 *Ibid.*, p. 4.

44 Penguin Archive, *PBSAV*, Fol. I. Letter from Anthony Richardson to Jack Cope, August 12, 1966.

45 Penguin Archive, *PBSAV*, Fol. I. Letter from Anthony Richardson to Jack Cope, November 4, 1966.

translations of poetry in Indigenous African languages in order to avoid inflaming political sensitivities. Referring to the draconian policies of the Cronjé report, Cope asserts that there is no way for him to deal with the "bloody awful picture" of the elision of African poets in South African publishing "in the urbane terms of an anthology forward". [46] Cope suggests that "the undoubted interrelation of political pressure and poetry" is problematic.[47] He enumerates all of the things excluded from the introduction, including: "the evil influence of Afrikaner nationalism" and "the dread of the politically more mature English population at what Afrikaners are doing". [48] Moreover, when it comes to the question of addressing the significance of including translations of poetry from seSotho, isiXhosa, isiZulu, and Khoe and San languages into English, Cope continues to condemn censorship, stating:

> African literature has been virtually 'taken over' by the Nationalists who publish nearly all books by African writers in the Bantu languages, mostly for schoolbooks and therefore censored into nonentity. One result is that we just don't see any new African poets with an individual voice, we don't know where they are if they exist. It's a bloody awful picture, you must admit, and how can one start to tackle it in the urbane terms of an anthology forward? So you may think we are guilty of cowardly evasion. No doubt. At the same time, it may be better to let the poetry speak for itself. And to hope that something of our peculiar horror comes through to the outside world.[49]

By characterizing his introduction as one that is evasive, Cope suggests that he is doing something more than simply practising

---

46 Penguin Archive, *PBSAV*, Fol. 2. Letter from Jack Cope to Anthony Richardson, November 12, 1966.

47 *Ibid.*

48 *Ibid.*

49 *Ibid.*

voluntarily censorship. Rather than executing a type of censorship aimed at exclusion, Cope reveals that this form of censorship is aimed at maximizing the content of the collection or its expressive possibilities. By submerging the political nature of the book beneath platitudes, Cope intends for the "poetry to speak for itself" so that the "peculiar horror" of apartheid comes through to the outside world. In this way, it is possible to conceive of this kind of voluntary censorship as one of disguise. By dissociating the intention of the paratext (the introduction) from the text, Cope was aiming to hide the political intention of the work.

This design appears to be a pattern in Cope's other editorial work. A disjunction between Cope's editorial policies and his editorial practice also existed in his work for *Contrast* magazine. In the first edition of *Contrast* magazine, Cope asserted that:

> In a policy-ridden country, here in the first place is a magazine with no policy. Its aims may be difficult just because they are so simple—to keep out of the rough and tumble of parties and groups and yet to cross all borders and to hold a balance even between conflicting opinions. (Cope quoted in Ehmeir 1995, 125)

This explicit statement in the editorial of the first issue, which suggested a "retreat from the political disturbances", is at odds with Cope's inclusion of Nadine Gordimer's 1960 story "A Chip of Glass Ruby" which foregrounded a resistance against the South African regime (Ehmeir 1995, 126). Considering Cope's history of withdrawing from politics, it is worth questioning whether this exercise of "voluntary censorship", subversively figured in the correspondence between Cope and Penguin as a form of political disguise rather than exclusion, actually represents, in Cope's words, a "cowardly evasion".

In spite of the ambiguity about whether or not Cope's deliberately banal introduction suggested that he was engaging with politics or retreating from politics, it is important not to overemphasize Cope's agency in shaping the introduction subversively. Cope's introduction was also diluted by concessionary modifications made to the text ordered by James Walton, Managing Director of Longmans Southern Africa. Walton's concern with getting the book published in South Africa resulted in the neutering of a passage in the introduction that alluded to the "suffering, exile and death" faced by "radical" poets owing to the repressive political climate in South Africa. [50] In this contentious paragraph, Cope attributes the suicide of Ingrid Jonker to the situation in South Africa. Walton cautions that "it is quite unnecessary and it implies that the suffering, exile and death of the poets mentioned are the direct result of South African Government legislation" and expresses his concern that "a paragraph of this nature will do untold harm in the selling of the book in South Africa even if it is passed by the Censor". [51] At the behest of Penguin and Longmans, Cope removed the mention to Jonker and diluted the passage from an explicit reference to "suffering" to a reference to "dissociation" and the mention of forced "exile" to one that is both "voluntary or perforce" (Cope and Krige 1968, 22). Walton remained opposed to any mention of coerced exile and demanded that the offending paragraph be removed.[52] However, Cope and Nick Stangos, an editor at Penguin, remained united on the need not to revise the passage any further, believing that "no unjustified inference should be made from what, after all, is an inherent characteristic of South African verse". In their view, "omitting this paragraph would be like refusing to acknowledge a salient aspect of South African poetry".[53] Despite the editors' small victory regarding the inclusion of this passage, a more politically explicit blurb for the book, stating that the poetry represented here

50 Penguin Archive, *PSAV*, Fol. I. 'Introduction' Manuscript from 1966, p. 7.

51 Penguin Archive, *PBSAV*, Fol. 1. Letter from James Walton to R.H. Clarke, June 20, 1968.

52 Penguin Archive, *PBSAV*, Fol. 2. Letter from James Walton to R.H. Clarke, 8 August, 1968.

53 Penguin Archive, *PBSAV*, Fol. 2. Letter from Nick Stangos to R.H. Clarke, August 20, 1968.

"crosses all barriers of race, belief, prejudice and custom, contributing to a common achievement in a new republic of the spirit", was cut from the final text.[54] It is likely that this statement of racial equality was expurgated as it challenged the idea of white superiority. Not only was the paratextual material altered but additional cuts were also made to the collection. Although Stangos stated that poems such as Currey's "Ultimate Exile", Vogt's "How Many Lives" and Griffiths's "The Last Three Bushmen" needed to be cut for "price reasons", the highly political nature of all of them seems more likely to have been the main reason for their expurgation.

This deduction appears to be confirmed by correspondence between Longmans and Penguin which reveals concerns about the political nature of the book and raises the possibility of producing a politically expurgated edition of the book for the South African market.[55] Discussing the possibility of gaining educational prescription, an editor from Longmans questions "if there were some poems not accepted, would it not be possible to omit those poems from the South African edition?"[56] Ultimately, Penguin decided that producing a more politically expurgated version of the book as a separate South African edition, as well as an unexpurgated version for international sales, would be too costly.[57] In the end, Cope's deliberately banal introduction, with the inclusion of the new diluted passage, was approved by Penguin and included in the final manuscript of the book published in 1968. Despite these concessions, rather significantly, the inclusion of Adam Small in the Afrikaans section and the inclusion of poems which criticised apartheid remained in the final text submitted to the censors.

54 Penguin Archive, *PBSAV*, Fol. 2. Blurb presented in Letter from Jack Cope to Nick Stangos, March 3, 1968.

55 Penguin Archive, *PBSAV*, Fol. 2. Letter from Nick Stangos to Jack Cope, June 22, 1966.

56 Penguin Archive, *PBSAV*, Fol. 1. Letter from L.M. Stegmann to D.M. Rogers, September 18, 1968.

57 Penguin Archive, *PBSAV*, Fol. 1. Letter from R.H. Clarke to D. Pevsner, October 1, 1968.

The censors' willingness to allow the political poems in the book to go through reveals that the image of the censor is not as close to the literary "hangman" analogy drawn by Cope. Although Cope's subversive modifications to the text point to a type of self-censorship aimed at enabling inclusivity rather than exclusion, Cope's concessionary modifications to the text demonstrate that the conceptualization of publishers and editors simply as creators rather than oppressors of their own work is not tenable. The liberal adjudication of the text in the censors' report demonstrates that the study of censorship in this case does not fit the simple binary of a battle between creation and oppression.

The Politics of the Censors' Verdict

Despite Longmans' concern that the book remained too political, the censors' report shows that the book was found to be "not undesirable". Longmans submitted the text to the Board on December 30, 1968. The text was reviewed and passed by the censors on February 21, 1969, the first year of the Kruger Board of assessors. The inconsistencies and idiosyncrasies that defined the Dekker Board of assessors can also be seen in the Kruger Board who assessed the book of poetry.[58] The text for the report is written in Afrikaans and includes comments from Merwe Scholtz and C.J.D. Harvey. Scholtz was an Afrikaans poet and literary academic whose expert advice on literature was sought during the Cronjé Commission. Harvey was a professor of English at the University of Stellenbosch and on the editorial board of *Standpunte* (McDonald 2009, 39). Scholtz and Harvey's comments in the censor's report reveal that the general intention of *The Penguin Book of South African Verse* was considered to be non-political. Describing the book, Scholtz asserts:

> An anthology of poems from South African poetry [*digkuns*, literally, poetic art] from all languages and racial groups. Some of the poems {insert: e.g. Vilakazi} take the racial

58 See McDonald (2009), 33–35 and 41–46.

> problem as a theme, but this is unavoidable [or inescapable]. The compilers appear not to have made the race problematic their starting point—it is a bona fide literary selection, even though one would not agree with [or endorse] all their choices.[59]

Scholtz's comment that the text "does not seem to take the race-problematic as its starting point" contradicts Penguin's original intention to make the issue of race the starting point in its construction of an inclusive and anti-apartheid book of verse. This final assessment seems to suggest that the "local sensitivities" that Penguin, Cope and Krige took into consideration, as well as Cope's attempt to disguise the book, ended up displacing the political intention of the text. However, such an easy conclusion, which confers all agency onto the publishers/editors, ignores the role of the censor.

As the report reveals, the censors did in fact register the political potency of the poems. Under the section in which the censors list objectionable features of the work, they cite pages "134,170,178" (Censor's Report BCS 5/69). These "objectionable passages" include three poems: "Sharpeville Inquiry" by Anne Welsh, "The Murder Trial" by Perseus Adams and "In Solitary Confinement, Sea Point Police Cells" by C.J Driver. Welsh's poem was explicitly political regarding the iniquity of racial segregation. As one passage of the poem states: "Hate is on exhibition/Inside that room;/And at the outside tap/A black servant rinses a teapot". It concludes: "And between the curled contempt of the 'public' benches/The line of suffering is growing/The bright sun sharpens it" (1968, 134.). This clear indictment of racial segregation should have made the passage objectionable under Section 5(2). Section 5(2) deemed a publication to be undesireable if it was prejudicial to the convictions of the Republic. A critique of racial segregation should have made this poem objectionable.

Despite the censors' detection of the book's political nature, the fact that it was allowed to be published shows a lack of

59 Censors' Report BCS 5/69. Original document translated by Peter D. McDonald.

correspondence between the legal parameters of Section 5 and the censors' literary assessment. This discrepancy suggests that the censors were transgressing the law. Unlike the British system of censorship, which took into account artistic merit or the literary quality of a work when deciding if content was obscene or not, South African law did not. However, as this document suggests, the censors saw themselves as guardians of the literary and contravened the letter of the law by "privileging questions of intentionality and readership" (McDonald 2009, 40). McDonald ascribes the censors' autonomy to the "vague formulations" of the Act which "gave the apartheid censors extraordinary discretionary powers" (2009, 35). This looseness was enabled by the contradiction between Section 6 and Section 5 (2). Part of Section 5 (2) stated that "a publication or object shall be deemed to be undesirable if it or any part of it" is "indecent", "obscene" or "harmful" to the amorphous and all-encompassing category of "public morals" and considered "blasphemous or is offensive to the religious convictions or feelings of any section of the inhabitants of the Republic" (Publications and Entertainments Act 1963, Section 5). However, Section 6 "contradicted the absolute criteria of Section 5 (2)" (McDonald 2009, 36) by stating that a publication could be banned if it "has the tendency to deprave or to corrupt the minds of persons who are *likely* to be exposed to the effect or influence thereof" (Section 6, my emphasis). Section 6 (a) introduced the notion of likely readership.

This "complication in the legislation's construction of the reading public" (McDonald 2009, 36) as the 'likely reader' is what enabled Scholtz and Harvey to pass *The Penguin Book of South African Verse*. This is evident in Harvey's comments on the text. He asserts that "banning the book would be absurd considering the likely readership" (quoted in Censor's Report BCS 5/69). Harvey's invocation of the notion of "likely readership" suggests that a sociological dimension governed the censors' conception of the literary. The censors do not explicitly mention who the likely reader is in their report. A text could be considered undesireable if it was "socially subversive" or "politically seditious" (McDonald 2009, 34). The censors' acknowledgement of the anti-apartheid poems in the text suggest that the likely readers, who would not, in their view, be incited to sedition or consider the poems offensive, would most likely be a politically neutral white South African readership. Despite being printed in paperback, it is also likely that the censors did not object to this text because poetry was seen as a medium that was unlikely to be bought widely. This point is echoed by Alvarez-Pereyre who asserts that, in matters of censorship in South Africa, "the poet is tolerated for so long as he influences only an extremely small part of the population" (1984, 265).

The fact that the censors passed this anthology because of their perception of it as a literary selection suggests that this was the main principle governing their decision-making. This point can be substantiated from an interview conducted in 2001, in which Scholtz admitted that, "if it was literature, then it was through" (McDonald 2009, 42).[60] This admission by Scholtz resonates with Darnton's assertion that "seen from the inside, and especially from the censor's point of view, censorship can appear to be coextensive with literature" (2014, 234). Thus, "to dismiss censorship as crude repression by ignorant bureaucrats is to get it wrong" (Darnton 2014, 231). In assessing the reasons that enabled the successful publication of *The Penguin Book of South African Verse,* the reality that it was a particular combination of factors which allowed it to be passed—including Penguin's dual scheme of disguise and expurgation combined with the censors' transgression of the law—suggests that the narrative of censorship, as a dichotomous story of creation and oppression, needs to be politicized.

The Politics of Censorship

An analysis of previously unexamined letters between Penguin and the editors regarding the making of *The Penguin Book of South African Verse* demonstrates that the story of censorship in South Africa cannot

60 H. van der Merwe Scholtz, personal interview with Peter McDonald, 22 Aug. 2001.

be reduced to simple binaries between heroic publishers/editors and oppressive censors. An interrogation of the cycle of transmission of *The Penguin Book of South African Verse* reveals the complex story of the way in which the text was able to be passed owing to the modifications made by Penguin. These modifications were shaped by conflicting local and global institutional pressures. Furthermore, the text was also published because it was read by two censors who were known for possessing a high-minded approach to the literary and who could tolerate anti-apartheid voices so long as they were not propaganda.

An analysis of the production of this multilingual book of poetry in South Africa contributes to an understanding of the tensions between the global and the national in the world literature field. Rather than providing a conventional account of how external, global institutional pressures shape national literatures, this case study adds complexity to the story of the intersection between world literature and national anthologies. Rather than assuming excessive agency on the part of British publishers in the commodification of national anthologies in South Africa, an analysis of the production of *The Penguin Book of South African Verse* reveals how the text was formed by competing national and global institutional pressures.

Furthermore, this study has complicated the conventional narrative and historiography regarding Penguin's uncompromising approach to anti-apartheid publishing by revealing the way in which its commercial concerns about gaining educational prescription in South Africa, rather than simply political concerns, caused Penguin to modify the text. With the spectre of the hangman's noose above their heads after the introduction of the Publications and Entertainments Act of 1963 and the gag-order placed on Cope in 1965, Penguin made concessionary and subversive modifications to the text to ensure its palatability to South African censors while maintaining its appeal to a global audience.

In this chapter's implicit acceptance of Penguin's use of the term "voluntary censorship" to describe its modifications to the text, it is important to distinguish between the types of censorship Penguin and its editors were doing in pre-publication control and the type of censorship censors carry out. The type of censorship that Cope was enforcing was geared towards inclusivity rather than exclusion. By altering the introduction, he hoped to enable a fuller expression of the work which would allow the voices of politically seditious poets to be published. This is in stark contrast to the type of censorship the censors did that resulted in the suppression of texts, imprisonment, exile, loss of career and, in some cases, suicide. The brutality of state-sponsored censorship is indicated in the "inflammatory" passage Cope insisted on keeping in the introduction which mentioned the dissociation and exile which characterized the lives of South African poets living through a time of apartheid censorship. According to Darnton, if the concept of censorship is extended to everything it means nothing. It should not be trivialized" (2014, 235). He elaborates that, although "power is exerted in many ways, I think it crucial to distinguish between the kind of power that is monopolized by the state" (2014, 235). This notion is echoed by J.M Coetzee (1996) in *Giving Offense: Essays on Censorship in South Africa* in which he asserts that social pressures should not be conflated with censorship. Indeed, the publishing house's "social intolerance" for politically incendiary passages that might harm their sales is "different in kind from official sanctions backed by the force of law" (Coetzee 1996, 19).

While this chapter has attempted to complicate the study of censorship, it should not result in an inversion. By revealing the way in which Penguin "censored" its own work through modification, and by revealing the way in which the censors' privileging of the literary over the political enabled censorship to be "seen as coextensive with literature" (Darnton 2014, 234), it is important not to reduce these inferences to a simple inversion in which the publisher/editor becomes complicit in apartheid censorship and the censor an agent of subversion. An investigation into the making of *The Penguin Book of South African Verse* simply shows that the story of censorship must take into account certain "strains of humanity" (Darnton 2014, 15) and "complexities of experience" that are often elided (Darnton 2014, 243). Indeed, to shift from the hero/oppressor paradigm to an equally monochromatic model, in which publishers are depicted as equivalent repressors to the censor, is equally as naïve.

Acknowledgements

I would like to thank Penguin Books for permission to quote from the Penguin Archive, held at the University of Bristol, and the staff at Special Collections, University of Bristol Library, particularly Hannah Lowery, for their guidance and expertise.

Bibliography

Archival Material

University of Bristol Special Library Collections, Penguin Archive: Penguin Books Ltd editorial files, Penguin African Library Series, The Penguin Book of South African Verse, DM1107/D109, Fol. 1.

University of Bristol Special Library Collections, Penguin Archive: Penguin Books Ltd editorial files, Penguin African Library Series, The Penguin Book of South African Verse, DM1107/D109, Fol. 2.

University of Bristol Special Library Collections, Penguin Archive: Penguin Books Ltd editorial files, Penguin African Library Series, Modern Poetry Series file, DM1107/D109, Fol. 1.

The Censor's Report (BPS 5/69) trans. by Peter McDonald.

"List of Banned Persons 1966." *The Literature Police*. Peter D. McDonald, web site, 2009. https://theliteraturepolice.files.wordpress.com/2018/07/list-of-banned-persons-1966.pdf

"The Publications and Entertainments Act 1963." *The Literature Police*. Peter D. McDonald, web site, 2009. https://theliteraturepolice.files.wordpress.com/2018/07/publications-and-entertainments-act-1963.pdf

Works Cited

Abrahams, Lionel, and Nadine Gordimer, eds. 1967. *South African Writing Today*. London: Penguin.

Alvarez-Pereyre, Jacques. 1984. *The Poetry of Commitment in South Africa (African Writers Series)*. Translated by C. Wake. London: Heinemann.

Coetzee, J. M. 1996. *Giving Offense: Essays on Censorship*. Chicago: University of Chicago Press.

Cope, Jack, and Uys Krige, eds. 1968. *The Penguin Book of South African Verse.* Harmondsworth: Penguin.

Currey, James. 2008. *Africa Writes Back: The African Writers Series and Launch of African Literature*. Athens: Ohio University Press.

Davis, Caroline. 2013. *Creating Postcolonial Literature: African Writers and British Publishers.* Basingstoke: Palgrave Macmillan.

Davis, Caroline, Archie Dick & Elizabeth le Roux. 2018. "Introduction: Print Culture in Southern Africa." *Journal of Southern African Studies,* 44 (3):377-381.

Decker, Michelle. 2016. "Entangled Poetics: Apartheid South African Poetry: Between Politics and Form." *Research in African Literatures* 47 (4): 71–90.

Darnton, Robert. 2014. *Censors at Work: How States Shaped Literature.* New York: W.W. Norton.

Dubow, Saul. 2014. *Apartheid 1948-1994.* Oxford: Oxford University Press.

Ehmeir, W. 1995. "Publishing South African Literature in English in the 1960s." *Research in African Literatures* 26 (1): 110–31.

Gordimer, Nadine. "Apartheid and Censorship." *Index on Censorship* 23, no. 3 (March 1994): 151–52. doi: 10.1080/03064229408535 714.

Helgesson, Stefan. 2014. "Postcolonialism and World Literature: Rethinking the Boundaries." *Interventions* 16 (4): 483–500.

Helgesson, Stefan, and Pieter Vermeulen. 2016. "Introduction: World Literature in the Making." In *Institutions of World Literature: Writing, Translation, Markets,* edited by Stefan Helgesson and Pieter Vermeulen, ix–23. London: Routledge.

Le Roux, E.H. 2015. *A Social History of the University Presses in Apartheid South Africa: Between Complicity and Resistance.* Boston: Brill.

McCleery, Alistair. 2018. "Minding Their Own Business: Penguin in Southern Africa." *Journal of Southern African Studies* 44 (3): 507–19.

McDonald, Peter D. 2009. *The Literature Police: Apartheid Censorship and its Cultural Consequences.* Oxford: Oxford University Press.

—. 2017. "Semper Aliquid Novi: Reclaiming the Future of Book History from an African Perspective." *Book History* 19: 384–98.

Moore, Nicole. 2012. *The Censor's Library.* St Lucia, Qld.: University of Queensland Press.

Ruiters, Michele. 2009. "Collaboration, Assimilation and Contestation:

Emerging Constructions of Coloured Identity in Post-apartheid South Africa." In *Burdened by Race: Coloured Identities in South Africa*, edited by Mohamed Adhikari, 104-134. Cape Town: UCT Press.

Sanders, Mark. 2006. "Undesirable Publications: J.M Coetzee on Censorship and Aprtheid." *Law and Literature* 18 (1): 101–14.

Van der Vlies, Andrew. 2007. *South African Textual Cultures: White, Black, and Read All Over.* Manchester: Manchester University Press.

—. 2012. *Print, Text and Book Cultures in South Africa.* Johannesburg: Wits University Press.

Wittenberg, Hermann. 2008. "The Taint of the Censor: J.M Coetzee and the Making of *In the Heart of the Country.*" *English in Africa* 35 (2): 133–50.

Penguin's People: The Information Research Department and British Publishing

Gareth Guangming Tan

In recent discussions of the Cold War, mentions of the United Kingdom's innocuously named Information Research Department (henceforth IRD) have cropped up with remarkable frequency, given the UK's perceived role as a relative bystander in what was to be, for all intents and purposes, a conflict between superpowers. What records remain of this now-defunct organization's inner workings have been steeped in the mystery and intrigue of the Cold War until relatively recently, but the slow yet steady process of declassification has created enticing new opportunities for researchers to examine them. This has coincided with recent work in Cold War historiography which has demonstrated that the assumption "that liberal democracies could not engage in propaganda" was more likely than not "part of the propaganda" itself (Risso 2007, 46). This conjunction of factors has made the present day a golden age for research into the history and methodologies of organizations like the IRD. Of particular utility have been opportunities to situate the organisation in broader efforts to preserve British imperial hegemony in an age of decolonization—an exercise which often went hand in hand with more explicitly acceptable anti-communist ideological compulsions. These exercises, taking place amidst the waning of Britain's material influence, inevitably found manifestation in its soft power outreach. That Britain's immensely influential publishing industry would find itself capable of playing a key role was therefore inevitable, given the sheer size of the postcolonial anglosphere.

This essay will, consequently, deploy material uncovered in declassified IRD documents at the National Archives, and corporate material from the Penguin Archives at the University of Bristol, in order to fill in gaps in contemporary conceptualizations of the IRD's methodologies. The objective here is to situate the IRD in a specific socio-economic context by examining attempts that were made to secure the cooperation of large British publishing houses such as Penguin, with a specific emphasis on the obstacles encountered during these undertakings. This will be accomplished through an overview of recent trends regarding research into covert propaganda organizations including the IRD, alongside a brief summary of the organization's early history and ideals. This will be followed by an examination of the relevance of authors, books and publishing more broadly to public debate and nation-building. Finally, I will examine documents from the IRD's archives pertaining to the organization's contact with larger publishers, and what these can be interpreted to mean in the broader context of the IRD's history and methodologies.

On Her Majesty's Intelligence Service: The IRD and the Cultural Cold War

The declassification of the IRD's documents has coincided with changing conceptualizations of the battlefields upon which the Cold War was waged. As Gordon Johnston (2010) notes, while much research into the Cold War continues to be "worked within the traditional categories of the 'economic', 'political', 'military' and 'diplomatic'", more recently "a significant amount of work has been undertaken on the 'cultural Cold War'" as well (292). Tony Shaw (2005) notes that this new emphasis on the Cold War's cultural dimensions arises in response to criticisms of Cold War historiography which assert that it "has been excessively concerned with high politics, diplomacy and military affairs, producing a top-down approach that has privileged the role of political elites during the conflict, over that played by the ordinary masses" (109). Greater emphasis on the cultural Cold War made possible by this approach enables examinations of the macro-conflict's manifestations "in national politics, in trade unions, among intellectuals, and in various forms of art and architecture, theatre, ballet and cinema, and music and literature" (Hopkins 2007, 925) facilitating the development of more holistic conceptualizations of the Cold War.

Research into the cultural Cold War has additionally cast new light on the efforts made by the two superpowers to influence mass opinion through propaganda and other means of narrative control. First, the concept of propaganda, as it will be used in this essay, requires definition. Propaganda (or psychological warfare) has traditionally manifested "in two distinct forms: overt and covert"—correspondingly coded white propaganda and black propaganda—with "white propaganda being that with an honestly identified point of origin and black being that for which the point of origin was either concealed or deliberately misattributed" (Cull 2013, 134). In the context of the Cold War, white propaganda often manifested itself as what was sometimes termed "Cultural Diplomacy"—a nation's attempts to emphasize the positive aspects of itself to its opponents. Black propaganda was, by contrast, the more aggressive work of slanderous, active disinformation, with its deployment typically being directly overseen by national espionage agencies. Grey propaganda, the primary output of the organizations to be explored in this chapter, was therefore a form of propaganda whose "precise origin was unclear, but [whose] true source had an ability to deny a role", though the boundaries between "white" cultural diplomacy and grey propaganda could become blurred (Cull 2013, 135).

The Soviet Communist Information Bureau (Cominform) would perhaps be the most immediately recognizable vector of this general class of activity, having become emblematic in the popular imagination of the mechanisms of propagandistic cultural control applied during the Cold War. However, more recent work, particularly that of Francis Stonor Saunders (1999), has cast a revelatory light on the USA's Congress for Cultural Freedom (CCF). Self-admittedly formulated in 1950 to counteract Cominform's "campaign to shape Western opinion", the CCF initially positioned itself as an independent advocacy group and engaged "in an extraordinary array of activities, including festivals, seminars and concerts, all designed to demonstrate to intellectuals the cultural advantages of political freedom" (Warner 2007, 44). The CCF was eventually discovered to have been covertly funded by the American Central Intelligence Agency (CIA) to "promote the ethos and politics of the so-called 'Free World'", especially in Europe, which was perceived as being particularly susceptible to Communist infiltration (Rodden 2013, 269). Nicholas Cull notes that despite the CCF's activities seeming to fall into the conceptual framework of white propaganda, "secrecy about its true source of funding placed this work beyond the pale of cultural diplomacy as a grey propaganda project" (2013, 136). Through influencing modes of cultural production and dissemination, the CCF—its subordinate organs consistently increasing in size and number—would grow to subtly control the nature and manifestations of Anglo-European cultural discourses, co-opting and manipulating the zeitgeist to better represent and serve US strategic interests.

Andrew Rubin (2012) has researched the CCF extensively, and notes that this influence extended into the realms of the literary as well, with the appearance of the CCF's literary publications, such as the famous *Encounter* magazine, marking "a significant stage in the history of literary and cultural production" (58). Rubin observes that with the use of these mechanisms, "the CCF help[ed] to consecrate writers through the sheer repetition and translation of their work", functioning to establish "both cultural capital and legitimacy" while simultaneously maintaining "a new kind of dominance over them by publishing their work on certain subjects and not on others" (58). The CCF was thus able to utilise its control over the dissemination of literary prestige to organize the disparate voices of the authors it managed into a unified chorus of US propaganda, simultaneously banking upon the credibility of said authors and curtailing any ideologically problematic tendencies and individuals as and when they arose. Martin Meyer (2001) elaborates upon the objectives of this approach:

> While the Soviets tried to convince the "bourgeois intellectuals", the Americans addressed the "non-Communist left" in Europe. Either group could be reached

> through books and a proven commitment to culture. Once convinced of either the capitalist route or the Communist way, these intellectuals would become mouthpieces, some people apparently thought, and help to pave the way toward Communism or capitalism. (165)

The CCF's operations in thereby manipulating literary production and control were targeted largely at the intelligentsia, in anticipation of their consequently serving as cultural vanguards for their fellow-citizens. While these methods would come to be regarded as hallmarks of the CCF's approach to cultural domination, they stand additionally as telling indicators of the approaches and objectives of similar organizations such as the IRD, with whom the CCF would actively collaborate over the course of the Cold War. Fundamentally speaking, the body of work that has been produced on the CCF has revealed its reach in both Europe and other parts of the world to be pervasive, consequently paving the way for further studies into the interconnectedness of similar organizations, and their effects on the over-arching dynamic of the Cold War.

It is in this context of heightened academic engagement with the organizations through which the cultural Cold War was waged that the significance of the IRD to more complete understandings of the period has become apparent. While research into the IRD has been conducted since IRD documents became earmarked for rapid declassification under the 1993 Waldegrave initiative, it is the body of work around the CCF that has formed the foundations of more recent inquiry into the IRD's mechanisms. Furthermore, as noted above, work into one has often been found to organically inform work into the other (Defty 2004, 2). Founded in 1948 and thus predating the CCF by two years, the IRD was "the first major Western initiative in anti-Communist propaganda" (Wilford 1998, 354). Unlike the CCF, it was a full department of the Foreign Office, and made few pretensions to being independent of governmental support, often operating out of British Embassies and High Commissions abroad. This is not to say, however, that the British government was transparent about the

IRD's activities; its founder the MP Christopher Mayhew was particularly concerned about its vulnerability to "the exigencies of British politics" (Wilford 1998, 357). Considerable secrecy, exemplified by the department's innocuous name, was consequently deemed "necessary to protect the new department from parliamentary scrutiny, as left-wing Labour MPs would have wrecked such a venture had they known about it" (Wilford 1998, 358).

Nevertheless, the IRD's relative visibility compared to the CCF was likely a reflection of the fact that, until the Second World War, US policymakers had "disdained the methods of the decadent old states of Europe who ran makeshift clandestine operations in foreign communities and in their own colonies" (Rodden 2013, 273). This initial cultural disjunction also meant that the dawn of the Cold War would see America's intelligence mechanisms developing from positions of methodological and infrastructural disadvantage relative to those of its European peers. The UK in particular was able to draw upon its experience with "the British Council and agencies developed for cultural propaganda in peacetime" such as the successive Ministries of Information (MOI) and the Foreign Office's Cultural Relations Department (CRD), to "forge ahead in information warfare during the late 1940s" (Aldrich 2003, 110). Richard Aldrich also notes that the IRD was therefore additionally notable for its fusion of aforementioned peacetime methodologies with wartime grey propaganda techniques, representing in many ways a "Whitehall battle to resurrect agencies developed for war"—namely the Special Operations Executive and Political Warfare Executive (110).

This melding of wartime and peacetime agencies had repercussions beyond just the methodologies which the IRD would see fit to deploy. It is important to consider that the immediate post-war period ushered in an Anglo-American dynamic which had not yet solidified into the "special relationship" of subsequent decades and the present day. Indeed, as Dianne Kirby (2000) notes, the IRD itself "had its intellectual roots in social democracy and [Christopher] Mayhew's early papers talked of creating a socialist 'third force' in Europe half way between Washington and Moscow" (402). Hugh

Wilford (1998) observes that the politicians who first conceived of the IRD had initially ascribed to it the task of "projecting Britain positively as a democratic socialist power capable of creating a Western European bloc independent not only of Soviet Russia but also of capitalist America" (354). As the Cold War developed, however, this proved to be an untenable dream for both Britain and the IRD. Almost from its inception the IRD engaged primarily in the negative anti-communist grey propaganda for which it is now best known. Wilford asserts that this was above all "due to its links with the British military and secret services, which wanted it to specialize in political warfare operations" to the detriment of white propaganda operations, which were once again given to the CRD and British Council (1998, 354). This apparent tension between the IRD's founding tenets and its eventual objectives reflected "the problematic relationship between [the] permanent officials and Labour ministers" in charge of British foreign policy, foreshadowing the doom of the "third force" idea, "as it succumbed to the concept of an Atlantic alliance" (Wilford 1998, 354). The IRD itself would also eventually fall in line as another mechanism in the said Atlantic alliance's anti-communist arsenal, though it consistently retained a certain jurisdictional authority vis-à-vis matters pertaining to the remnants of the British Empire, and later, the Commonwealth.

Books are Forever: Literature, Publishing and the IRD

Regardless of its ultimate fate, the IRD was, like the CCF after it, quick to recognize the importance of literature and books more generally in both ideologically bolstering areas vulnerable to communist influence and critiquing communism alike. The organization's collaborations with, and endorsements of George Orwell in particular are well documented, and an extensive academic corpus exists regarding his active participation in IRD propaganda operations. Tony Shaw (2003) notes that Orwell's attractiveness as an asset arose, paradoxically, from his formidable reputation as "a socialist paragon", whose consequent repudiation of communism "would ensure wider currency, stronger credibility and greater efficacy in the officials' ideological battle against the Soviet Union" (145). The IRD and later the CCF would continue to bank on Orwell's reputation long after his death, with the event fostering "his legendary status, and consequently boost[ing] the sales and authority of his works", with his absence also transforming his legacy into a "malleable, prized asset whose powerful rhetoric and vision would be 'clarified' and then spread as deeply and as widely as possible" (Shaw 2003, 147). Orwell was thus made into a symbol from which the IRD could continually draw legitimacy, with his works becoming immortalized across national and linguistic boundaries through the aforementioned cycles of repetition, translation and commemoration which Rubin observed were subsequently inherited by the CCF.

Emblematic of these cycles of commemoration was the extremely wide circulation of Orwell's *Animal Farm* during the Cold War. A readable novel that nevertheless retained its ability to pose a "challenge to the literary-minded", *Animal Farm* formulates a vigorous condemnation of Soviet Communism, consequently becoming a darling of the western Intelligence community, being consistently earmarked for translation or transliteration wherever there was perceived to be a looming communist threat (Shaw 2003, 146). This also tied into the fact that the novel was linguistically uncomplicated, being accessible even to children and thus, Shaw observes, easily translatable into different languages and artistic mediums (146). Fascinating insights into this process can be found in the extensive correspondence between the IRD and its various branch offices regarding its translation and adaptation, and discussions with Egyptian representatives regarding an Arabic translation of the text reveal the IRD's methods and approaches to this kind of enterprise. Initial proposals laid out in 1949 notably emphasized the need to liaise with Celia Kirwan, who served as the IRD's main link to Orwell himself, reflecting his continued personal involvement in these operations despite at this point being confined to a sanatorium for the

Figure 1: Draft illustrations commissioned for Arabic translation of *Animal Farm*

tuberculosis he would die from in 1950.[1] With regards to issues of cultural specificity, discussions with a Foreign Office contact in Cairo also eagerly emphasise the novel's translatability, further pointing to its special potency as a piece of propaganda, given that "both pigs and dogs", which feature as antagonists and stand-ins for prominent Communist figures in *Animal Farm's* narrative, "are unclean animals to Moslems [sic]".[2] Figure 1 demonstrates that this aspect of the novel's cultural relevance was emphasised in illustrations subsequently produced to accompany the text, all of which prominently feature pigs and dogs.[3]

1 Minutes of Discussion regarding Arabic Translation of *Animal Farm*, April 14, 1949, The National Archives (hereafter abbreviated as TNA), Kew Gardens, London, Foreign Office (hereafter FO) 1110/221

2 Letter from FO, Cairo to R. Murray of IRD, April 4, 1949, TNA, Kew Gardens, London, FO 1110/221

3 Draft illustrations commissioned for Arabic translation of *Animal Farm*, Date Unlisted (estimated 1950–51), TNA, Kew Gardens, London, FO 1110/221 & FO 1110/392 p.1

The IRD's respect for the influence books could have on ideological struggles, especially in the context of influencing the intelligentsia, was not restricted to the realms of literature. Indeed, in many ways, the IRD's specializations in the production of grey propaganda were even better suited to operations conducted outside literature's frequently allegorical realms. This is reflected in IRD records which indicate that the department was in contact with Sir Allen Lane of Penguin in 1949, who received internal memoranda from IRD researchers, sent in the hope of eventual publication by Penguin.[4] However, while Allen Lane subsequently notes that these memoranda seemed "admirably suited as a series of notes informing Press Attaches and others of the salient points of a subject", he nevertheless expressed scepticism regarding the prospect of their publication, noting that "unless there is something exceptional in the presentation of the material" such an endeavour would be difficult to justify and prove ultimately futile. [5] It should be noted at this juncture that Lane's objections to the project were predicated on his concerns regarding the form of the texts he was presented with, as opposed to the veracity of their content, which, in typical IRD fashion, was composed of grey propaganda and thus to a significant extent unverifiable. While records cataloguing the eventual conclusion of this conversation do not exist, Shaw observes that "Penguin later produced many editions of one such IRD paper, *The Theory and Practice of Communism,* written by Foreign Office Sovietologist Robert Carew Hunt", indicating that Lane was at the very least eventually provided with a document presentable enough to publish (2003, 148).

The IRD's interest in publishing such monographic works also extended to attempts to enable similar projects in non-aligned nations—an element of IRD policy which will be discussed later on.

4 Minute regarding meeting with Allen Lane, May 12, 1949, TNA, Kew Gardens, London, FO 1110/221 p.1 AND Minute to Watson & Murray from Leslie Sheridan, May 20, 1949, TNA, Kew Gardens, London, FO 1110/221

5 Letter from Allen Lane to Leslie Sheridan, May 25, 1949, TNA, Kew Gardens, London, FO 1110/221

Such attempts were undoubtedly influenced by perceptions regarding the vulnerability of these areas to Communist infiltration and influence. The IRD took particular interest in the protection of British ideological interests in its colonies, many of which began to actively agitate for independence in the 1950s. Examples of this interest, and of the kinds of action which the IRD was subsequently sanctioned to undertake, can be noted in the IRD's records regarding the situation on the ground in British Ghana on Africa's Gold Coast.

In a memorandum entitled "Ideological Defence in Immature Communities", intended for use by IRD personnel operating within or around West Africa, the IRD's objectives are stated as two-fold: the "defeat [of] the existing Communist attack" and the construction of "a positive/non-Communist ideology comprehensive enough to satisfy the aspirations and desires of the population and robust enough to prove a stronger attraction than Communism". [6] The memorandum asserts that these goals are doubly important because "there is well-established and vigorous nationalism, a suspicion of white men and especially the British—and the beginnings of a growth in literacy and of Higher Education", alongside a particular vulnerability to cheap Soviet literature due to "unsatisfied demand among the literate".[7] It concludes that the project of making local Nationalists in particular see that "however much they may wish to be free of Western domination, it is equally important for them to remain free of all domination", can be accomplished with ideological outreach manifested through contact in local universities, as well as through the targeted deployment of anti-communist materials.[8] A notable final suggestion also alludes to the possibility that the IRD could reach out to non-governmental organizations to acquire such material, with the specific mention of the Oxford University Press (OUP) as a source of

6 "Ideological Defence in Immature Communities—West Africa", Unknown Author, January 11, 1952, TNA, Kew Gardens, London, FO 1110/394. p.1

7 *Ibid.* pp. 1–2.

8 *Ibid*, pp. 3–5 and Letter from C.Y Carstairs, February 14, 1952, TNA, Kew Gardens, London, FO 1110/394.

"simple historical and economic studies".[9] There is thus a strong emphasis on the nature of books as vectors of national ideology through which the metropole can continue to affect the societal development of its colonies.

Moreover, it is a sentiment which was predictably echoed by members of the white British West African Intelligentsia, who actively collaborated with metropolitan agencies during this period. Correspondence in Penguin's archives at the University of Bristol indicates, for example, that academics at the University College of the Gold Coast in Ghana were in contact with Penguin over the course of the firm's development of its Penguin African Series. Published from 1953 to 1965 and edited by British-born academics David and Helen Kimble of the University College's Department of Extra-Mural Studies, the Penguin African Series represented the firm's first attempts to penetrate the West African anglophone market. It was clear, however, that for the Kimbles, this exercise was one that had much broader political repercussions as well. In the discussions recorded in Penguin's archives, Helen Kimble relates a sense of urgency regarding the publication of a monograph entitled *The Machinery of Self-Government,* in light of the issue of full self-governance that was shortly to go before the Ghanaian Legislative Assembly.[10] She also subsequently expresses concern at the lack of "facilities for Africans to purchase books", indicating her specific interest in informing the very local populations which the IRD's memorandum also notes as vulnerable to ideological misdirection.[11] The Kimbles' desire to involve this and other books in an ongoing national conversation thus speaks to their perceptions of the importance of these vectors of information in the context of developing a more informed society. They also speak to Penguin's participation in said events, in many

9 "Ideological Defence...", p. 7.

10 Letter from Helen Kimble to A.S.B Glover, 31 March, 1953, Penguin Archives (hereafter PA), Arts and Social Sciences Library (hereafter ASSL), Bristol, DM1107/WA4

11 *Ibid*, p. 2

ways positioning its involvement as an ancillary exercise in private sector nation-building.

Nevertheless, as Valerie Holman (2005) notes, "however potent their symbolism, books are first and foremost material objects whose very existence depends on the availability of raw materials, manpower, and machinery" (197). Consequently, their qualities as agents of national ideology were handicapped by their simultaneous existence as economic objects with a different, but no less important, significance to Britain's economic stability, especially in the context of the nation's recovering post-war economy. Amy Flanders (2010) notes in her seminal work on the post-war British book export drive that British publishing had dominated the international anglophone market prior to 1940, with "a general acknowledgement that Britain was a net exporter of books and that its products were valued around the world" (883). Indeed, books were such a directly profitable export that when the Publisher's Association, an organization composed of the nation's largest publishing houses, conducted a survey in 1937, it found that a full "33 1/3 per cent" of all books produced in Britain were exported (Flanders 2010, 880). Banking on this new evidence that "books really were essential export commodities" and that booming domestic circulation was vital to healthy exports, publishers were even able to lobby for exemption from the Purchase Tax (now the Value Added Tax), demonstrating the importance of books to the British economy at the time (Flanders 2010, 880).

The economic boon which the success of British publishing represented was furthermore perceived as having an additional dimension, because the proliferation of British books had the additional benefit of "persuading [foreign readers] to buy other British goods" as well (Flanders 2010, 875). However, the Second World War forced publishers to face "severe restrictions in the supply of materials—of paper, famously, due to the quota system, but also of binding cloth, boards for book covers and even glue", with subsequent restrictions on paper in particular not being lifted until 1949 (Flanders 2010, 878). These restrictions were applied to governmental institutions as well, with correspondence within the

IRD also noting potential issues regarding paper supplies as late as October 1950.[12] Flanders also notes that such shortages were compounded at the end of the war by the fact that "many firms had been damaged during the Blitz and hundreds of thousands of books had been destroyed". This, when combined with rising costs and disrupted distribution networks, "cut the supply of books to a mere trickle of the pre-war flood" (2010, 878). Finally, the problems faced by Britain's publishers were compounded by fierce competition from US publishers, who faced fewer supply issues during the war, and then began to intrude on markets which had previously been locked down by British firms (889–90).

What ensued in the immediate aftermath of the war, as the UK economy struggled towards recovery, was an immense nationwide export drive, with the book trade in particular spearheading the charge (Flanders 2010, 899). The efforts made to facilitate this recovery suggested that the project had assumed a certain nationalistic dimension as well, with private individuals such as "leading authors, publishers and booksellers donat[ing] their expertise, their vacation plans, their books and their profits to improve the prospects of book exports" alongside the efforts of larger governmental and private organizations (Flanders 2010, 905). Examples of this engagement can be found in the Penguin archives, which contain records of Sir Allen Lane's expeditions to many foreign countries, including journeys to Soviet Russia and Communist China in 1957, where his attempts to set up an exhibition for Penguin and other British firms received a cold reception, and he became thoroughly convinced of both nations' impenetrability to British exports. Flanders's work on this export drive demonstrates that reclaiming Britain's place as the world's top book exporter was a priority for both the government and private individuals, in light of the importance of the publishing industry to Britain's economic recovery.

---

12 "Project for Arabic Version of 'Animal Farm' by George Orwell" by R Parkes, October 25, 1950, TNA, Kew Gardens, London, FO 1110/221. p.1

From Penguin with Love: The IRD and Collaborations with Publishers

The relative strength of British publishers, stemming from sizeable private and public investments which had been made to vouchsafe their agency during this period of economic recovery, complicated the IRD's attempts to court their cooperation. Given the IRD's aforementioned respect for the potential influence of monographs and literary works alike, it is unsurprising that the institution attempted to reach out to publishers on several occasions. This was especially so when the IRD sought to penetrate foreign markets in which publishers had already established presences. A memorandum addressed to Christopher Mayhew himself notes the absolute "necessity for publishing firms being interested in IRD subjects", further indicating that several firms had already been contacted, including the OUP and the now-defunct Odhams Press. [13] This memorandum, obviously composed during the heyday of the "third force" concept, pointedly emphasized the possibility of projecting "'social democracy' as a successful rival to Communism in Burma".[14] Ultimately, however, few further references to any direct collaboration between the IRD and either the OUP or Odhams exist, though as mentioned earlier, the IRD subsequently continued to seek out independently published material from the OUP

Archives about the IRD are, additionally, replete with correspondence between the organization and various publishers regarding the acquisition of publication rights. While the quantity of these exhanges certainly attests to the existence of active lines of communication linking elements of the IRD and publishers, their often-fragmentary nature as they currently exist within the National Archives, combined with an inherent bureaucratic impenetrability, makes it difficult to determine the degree to which the IRD interacted directly with publishers. On the one hand, much of this

13 Memorandum to Christopher Mayhew regarding publishers, April 10, 1949, TNA, Kew Gardens, London, FO 1110/221. p.1

14 *Ibid.*

correspondence seems to have been composed by representatives of publishing firms who had received at least some contextual information regarding the situations in which the books would be deployed, with some correspondents openly expressing their personal support.[15] On the other hand, many requests were filed through the Foreign Office, occurring separately from prior exchanges with the IRD representatives who had initially requested the rights in the first place.[16] As such, a precise idea of how transparent the lines of communication actually were is difficult to establish.

A far more striking demonstration of the IRD's interactions with Britain's larger publishing houses exists in its discussions regarding interactions with Penguin. A memorandum dated September 7, 1951 records a meeting between C. Y. Carstairs of the IRD and Allen Lane, who had recently returned from a trip to West Africa with the idea that developed into the Penguin African Series mentioned above.[17] Carstairs indicates, first, an awareness on Lane's part regarding "the activities of Rosary Gardens" being conducted "under the counter" in Ghana – "Rosary Gardens" being in this case an oblique reference to the Soviet Information Agency.[18] Carstairs additionally notes that Lane had requested input regarding titles and content for his new enterprise.[19] These indications might suggest that Lane was functioning as an informant for the IRD. However, in a previous, more formal meeting, Leslie Sheridan of the IRD signalled that Lane was given "the usual cover story", indicating a contrasting need for misdirection.[20] Lane's distance from the IRD's operations is further reinforced when situated in the context of other IRD members'

---

15 Letter to D.R.M Ackland from George Allen & Unwin Ltd, April 5, 1951, TNA, Kew Gardens, London, FO 1110/849

16 Letter from M.R. Barraclough to IRD, March 13, 1951, TNA, Kew Gardens, London, FO 1110/849.

17 Memorandum regarding meeting between Allen Lane and C.Y. Carstairs, September 7, 1951, TNA, Kew Gardens, London, FO 1110/394.

18 *Ibid.*

19 *Ibid.*

20 Memorandum regarding meeting between Allen Lane and Leslie Sheridan, May 12, 1949, TNA, Kew Gardens, London, FO 1110/221.

responses to Carstairs's memorandum. Particularly telling is the reaction of one L. MacLaren, recorded in a meeting with Sheridan and a certain J. Snodgrass regarding actions to be taken regarding Allen Lane and Penguin. MacLaren described Penguin as an organization that was "in many ways of the greatest potential use, but full of all the most tiresome jokers", describing Lane himself as a "hard-headed citizen" possessed of an unpleasant "zeal to sell his wares". [21] MacLaren's vitriol apparently derived from his conviction that Lane was highly unlikely to "accept [Commonwealth Office] tutelage", suggesting prior attempts to convince Lane to cooperate which could only, given MacLaren's tone, have ended in failure.[22]

However, the response of Carstairs's office to suggestions later proposed by the aforementioned IRD functionaries is particularly telling. All attendees of the meeting in question had expressed serious concerns regarding Penguin's having in 1952 published a book entitled *I Choose Peace*, by the notoriously leftist Labour Party MP Konni Zillacus, who was suspected of sympathizing with the Soviet Union. [23] This developed into a consensus which suggested to Carstairs that any advice issued to Lane regarding titles and the like should be understood as being strictly conditional on Penguin's future avoidance of authors like Zillacus, with Sheridan and company assuming that it was Lane who had contacted Carstairs for information and advice. As the following excerpt from the response drafted by Carstairs's office indicates, however, these assumptions were incorrect:

> (1) Mr. Lane did not seek an interview with us; Mr. Carstairs sought an interview with him. We knew he had been in Africa and we wanted to find out what he had been up to.

---

21 Minutes of meeting involving T. Snodgrass, L. MacLaren and L. Sheridan, September 21, 1951, TNA, Kew Gardens, London, FO 1110/394. p.2

22 *Ibid.*

23 *Ibid.*

(2) We don't think the time has yet come to work out themes for Penguin Books. The project still has to get through Mr. Lane's directors. But this will obviously be worth pursuing if the project does materialise, and as Mr. Carstairs has a longstanding acquaintance with Mr. Lane it should not be difficult to sell him both ideas and authors.

(3) Penguins need no help from us in Africa and we are therefore in no position to make conditions. We shall obviously do all we can to keep in close touch.[24]

The unnamed author of this response swiftly and decisively disabuses Sheridan and company of their misplaced notions, and very pointedly notes that Penguin did not require the IRD's expertise at all, furthermore attributing Carstairs's influence upon Allen Lane to personal acquaintance alone. This is a singular testament to both the independence of Penguin and the embarrassing impotence of the IRD in matters regarding Britain's large publishers. It is also a reminder of the pervasive influence of old boy networks at the highest echelons of Britain's private and public sectors alike, demonstrating that if the IRD did eventually have any influence on the Penguin African Series, it was probably not brought about by coercion or a desire to collaborate with the state, but by the influence of "longstanding acquaintances".

One aspect of the IRD's inability to influence Penguin seems to have come about as a consequence of Penguin's predilection for creative control and its prioritization of political neutrality. Referring again to the meeting between the IRD members mentioned above, J. Snodgrass, who broaches the subject of Penguin's publishing of Zillacus, asserts that the act was undertaken "in an effort to be objective".[25] Editorial documents in Penguin's archive relating to

---

24 Letter to J.H. Peck, October 6, 1951, TNA, Kew Gardens, London, FO1110/394

25 Minutes of meeting involving T. Snodgrass, L. MacLaren and L. Sheridan,. p.1

Zillacus's book indicate that this may well have been the case as copy-editors were heavily opposed to its being published, noting that it read "like a speech made by some counsel for the defence of the Soviet Union", and recommending the excision of several chapters' worth of content.[26] That the text eventually made it to publication despite these radical opinions could be interpreted as a partisan move, given the controversy Penguin's editors no doubt knew they would cause. However, examining this gesture alongside Penguin's contrasting decision, discussed above, to publish in roughly the same time-frame (from 1949–50), IRD material written by R.C. Hunt, might instead point to an editorial desire to acquire credibility as a non-partisan publisher which could consequently derive legitimacy from across the political spectrum. Regardless of the motivations which led to these decisions, however, they make it quite clear that the IRD's desire for cooperation with Penguin was in no way mutual.

This state of affairs was also influenced by the fact that, even at this point, only a few years after its initial implementation, the IRD was already consistently being upstaged by its American rivals. The years leading up to the establishment of the CCF saw the Americans swiftly outgrow any stigmas regarding covert propaganda, leading to the exponential expansion of its operational capacities in this regard. The Americans' main weapon was the funding they were able to deploy, operating as they were from a position of much greater financial security than their British counterparts. Wilford quantifies this disparity, noting that by January 1950 "the US Government was pouring hundreds of millions of dollars into psychological warfare, as compared with the £100,000 available to IRD in 1949" (1998, 368). Apart from this, the US government also excelled at creating synergistic partnerships between publishers, intellectuals and the public organizations which formulated its anti-communist strategies. A series of communiques resulting from a particularly damning report by one G.F.N. Reddaway regarding the IRD's capabilities with regards to book circulation, which states that the IRD "are lagging far behind

26 Report on Zillacus Typescript, March 24, 1949, PA, ASSL, Bristol, DM1107/5157 p.1-2

the Americans", is telling.[27] An attached memorandum outlines America's faculties in this regard, and takes special care to emphasize the importance of Franklin Publications, a state-funded institution of considerable means, which "is said to form the spearhead of the American cultural effort in the Continent of Asia in the field of Book-distribution".[28] In the course of its undertakings, Franklin Publications is noted to work "in association with universities, foundations, government agencies, research institutes, and various cultural groups", with its board of directors being "composed partly of publishers and partly of representatives of the public interest".[29] The memorandum pointedly ends with Davy noting that "to compete with this obviously powerful consortium of the American Government, American Education and American Publishing houses the British publisher and book distributor has to work alone and unaided by the British Government".[30] Dated to 1958, this memorandum and the report which prompted its creation ultimately demonstrate the full scope of America's ascendance and Britain's contrasting decline as operators in this particular theatre of international espionage. In them is outlined the story of an internally cohesive American book-printing and distribution mechanism with staggering international coverage that had been growing from strength to strength, set against a barely extant British effort bereft of governmental support and languishing from a lack of funding and attention.

Conclusion

The IRD began its life as the carrier of an ideal and ended its existence in 1977 as a shadowy bogeyman, emblematic of pervasive governmental control. These perceptions have often made it difficult to conceive of the IRD as a real organization, staffed by real people

---

27 Report by G.F.N. Reddaway to Mr. Hepsen, June 16, 1958, TNA, Kew Gardens, London, FO1110/1060

28 "Book Distribution in Asia", A.E.G. Davy, June 24, 1958, TNA, Kew Gardens, London, FO1110/1060 p.1

29 *Ibid.* pp.1-2

30 *Ibid.* p.3

who faced real problems in bringing its objectives to fruition. This essay has thus expanded upon the context in which the IRD operated and attempted to situate it in the specific socio-economic circumstances of post-war Britain, in order to achieve a more holistic understanding of its scope as an organization. As such, documents produced by the IRD have been assembled and assessed in the context of existing critical analysis to create an outline of the IRD's capabilities and limitations. Taken as a whole, the image of the IRD produced by this assessment is of an organization of considerable means and experience which was nevertheless handicapped by being tied to a nation recovering from war, whose priorities lay in the acceleration of economic growth as opposed to the defence of ideology. The IRD was an organization formulated to present Britain's best side to potential allies, but most of its existence was spent disseminating misinformation about its foes. It keenly understood the importance of books to nation-building and ideological defence, but lacked the means to influence national publishers. Finally, it was an organization intended to vouchsafe Britain's independence and to enable it to assert itself on a global stage, but ended up as just another tool in the arsenal of an Atlantic alliance.

Bibliography

Archival Material

Special thanks to The National Archives at Kew Gardens and The University of Bristol's Arts and Social Sciences Library. Additional thanks to Ms. Joanna Price (Managing Director, Penguin General Books) for permission to access Penguin's archives and to Ms. Hannah Lowery and Mr. Michael Richardson of the University of Bristol's Special Collections for their hospitality during my visit.

The National Archives. Papers of the Foreign Office. Kew Gardens, London.

- Supply of publications and articles to posts; suggestions for book publishing; Russian language version of *Animal Farm*, FO 1110/221
- *Animal Farm*: production of strip cartoon; possibility of producing a successor, FO 1110/392
- Africa: future plans of Penguin Books Ltd; proposals for anticommunist information work in Africa, FO 1110/394
- Books: foreign rights for Bellman Books, FO 1110/849
- Asia: provision and distribution of commercial books, FO 1110/1060

The Penguin Archive. Arts & Social Sciences Library. University of Bristol, Bristol.

- Penguin Archive: Penguin Books Ltd editorial files on Konni Zillacus' *I Dream of Peace*, DM 1107/5157
- Editorial Files on Penguin West Africa, DM 1107/WA

Works Cited

Aldrich, Richard. 2003. "Putting Culture into the Cold War: The Cultural Relations Department (CRD) and British Covert Information Warfare." *Intelligence and National Security* 18 (2): 109–33. doi:10.1080/02684520412331306770.

Cull, Nicholas J. 2013. "Roof for a House Divided: How U.S. Propaganda Evolved into Public Diplomacy." In *The Oxford Handbook of Propaganda Studies*, edited by Russ Castronovo and Jonathan Auerbach, 131–44. Oxford: Oxford University Press. doi:10.1093/oxfordhb/9780199764419.001.0001.

Defty, Andrew. 2004. *Britain, America and Anti-Communist Propaganda, 1945–53.* Abingdon: Routledge.

Flanders, Amy. 2010. "'Our Ambassadors': British Books, American Competition and the Great Book Export Drive, 1940–60." *English Historical Review* 125 (515): 875–911. doi:10.1093/ehr/ceq163.

Holman, Valerie. 2005. "Carefully Concealed Connections: The Ministry of Information and British Publishing, 1939–1946." *Book History* 8: 197–226. doi:10.1353/bh.2005.0007.

Hopkins, Michael F. 2007. "Continuing Debate and New Approaches in Cold War History." *The Historical Journal* 50 (4): 913–34.

Johnston, Gordon. 2010. "Revisiting the Cultural Cold War." *Social History* 35 (3): 290–307. http://dx.doi.org/10.1080/03071022.2010.486581.

Kirby, Dianne. 2000. "Divinely Sanctioned: The Anglo-American Cold War Alliance and the Defence of Western Civilization and Christianity, 1945–48." *Journal of Contemporary History* 35 (3): 385–412.

Meyer, Martin. 2001. "American Literature in Cold War Germany." *Libraries & Culture* 36 (1): 162–71. doi:10.1353/lac.2001.0015.

Risso, Linda. 2007. "'Enlightening Public Opinion': A Study of NATO's Information Policies between 1949 and 1959 based on Recently Declassified Documents." *Cold War History* 7 (1): 45–74. http://dx.doi.org/10.1080/14682740701197672.

Rodden, John. 2013. "Of G-Men and Eggheads: The FBI and the New York Intellectuals." *American Communist History* 12 (3): 267–81. http://dx.doi.org/10.1080/14743892.2013.835560.

Rubin, Andrew. 2012. *Archives of Authority: Empire, Culture and the Cold War.* Princeton, NJ: Princeton University Press.

Shaw, Tony. 2003. "'Some Writers Are More Equal Than Others': George Orwell, the State and Cold War Privilege." *Cold War History* 4 (1): 143–70. doi:10.1080/14682740312331391774.

—. 2005. "Introduction: Britain and the Cultural Cold War." *Contemporary British History* 19 (2): 109–15. http://dx.doi.org/10.1080/13619460500080140.

Warner, Michael. 2007. *Origins of the Congress for Cultural Freedom 1949–50.* Central Intelligence Agency. April 14. https://www.cia.gov/library/center-for-the-study-of-intelligence/csi-publications/csistudies/studies/95unclass/Warner.html.

Wilford, Hugh. 1998. "The Information Research Department: Britain's Secret Cold War Weapon Revealed." *Review of International Studies* 24 (3): 353–69. http://journals.cambridge.org/abstract_S0260210598003532.

—. 2003. "Calling the Tune? the CIA, the British Left and the Cold War, 1945–1960." *Intelligence and National Security* 18 (2): 41–50. http://dx.doi.org/10.1080/02684520412331306730.

Section 2: Recognition through Prizes

V. S. Naipaul's Booker Prize for *In a Free State*

Carmen Thong

In book history research, Pierre Bourdieu's theories on the dynamics of power in the field of cultural production have been widely cited, and his models tried and tested for their exceptions and fallibilities. James English (2002) highlights what to him is the Bourdieusian model's main limitation in "Winning the Culture Game":

> Unlike the true disciples, I would concede that Bourdieu's economic model of cultural practice has failed to yield a very convincing theory of the subject, that he ultimately offers us an individual subject no less reduced in its agency to acquisitiveness and competition, and not much better articulated along axes of race, gender, or sexuality, than the Economic Man of neoclassical economics. (111)

Following English's critique, this chapter aims to identify the kinds of agency available to writers that are insufficiently accounted for by "Bourdieu's economic model of cultural practice", which will be analysed specifically within a case study of how institutional forces shaped the form of V.S. Naipaul's (1971) Booker Prize-winning text, *In a Free State.* In this chapter, I will first show how Bourdieu's model is useful in analysing how the perception or recognition of *In a Free State* as a novel has been instituted. However, like English, I suggest that this model still requires "certain modifications" to account for the agency of writers like Naipaul, whose relationship with institutions is one of "affiliation, patronage, emulation and competition" as well as "colonial antagonism" (Peter Kalliney quoted in Low 2011, 105–06). I conclude by charting how Naipaul's agency can be woven into the Bourdieusian field, and expanding the applicability of his model of cultural production to the subject.

The case study in this chapter centralizes around the debate about *In A Free State* (henceforth *IAFS*)'s form and its classification as a novel in 1971 by the Booker Prize. This debate commanded institutional stakes because, in order to qualify for the prize, *IAFS* had to be judged as a novel. It is easy to see why such a debate existed among the judges and prize committee. *IAFS* can be described as walking the fine line between a novel and a book of short stories. The book is framed by two short fragments from a travel journal. Within the frame, there are two short stories and one longer narrative with the same title as the book. All five segments contain different locations and characters, but share common themes like freedom and displacement. Its categorization as a novel could continue to be a matter of debate. Does the compactness of the 140 or so pages of the central narrative disqualify it as a novel? Would any other book, if composed of relatively unrelated and short pieces of text, be seen as a novel? Nevertheless, this chapter is less concerned with discussing the correct identification of the genre of *IAFS* than in examining how it came to be perceived as a novel within a model of cultural production. In other words, this chapter will focus on the "instituting" of form as a process whereby various sociological and economic forces come together to recognise *IAFS* as a novel. To this end, the chapter will study the documents found in the 1971 Booker Prize Archive at Oxford Brookes University, press cuttings in the same archive, and various editions of the book in subsequent years.

My use of Bourdieu's model of cultural production is focused on his theories of "field", which is "described as a separate social universe having its own laws of functioning", and "habitus", defined by Gail Low (2011) as "a set of predispositions to action or reaction or a set of generative structures that engender a course of action or response" (135). An anology would be that the field is like an ecosystem and the habitus is like the different layers and forces that make up the ecosystem and that interact within it. In this case study, the "field" is taken to be 1960s and 1970s London as a publishing metropole, and "habitus" to be the various institutions within that field (i.e. publishers, the Booker Prize, and the press). Any existing cultural item or subject would then find itself situated within such a "field" and occupying one or more "habituses" within said field. Bourdieu defines the act of actively situating oneself in the field as "position-taking", and one's positioning is always in dynamic and shifting relations with the position-takings of other entities in the field in order to compete and win literal or symbolic capital. Thus, these interactions create a structure of conflict, according to Bourdieu:

> [it is] not the product of a coherence-seeking intention of an objective consensus (even if it presupposes unconscious agreement on common principles) but the product and prize of a permanent conflict; or, to put it another way, that the generative, unifying principle of this 'system' is the struggle, with all the contradictions it engenders. (1993, 34)

The following study follows *IAFS*'s and Naipaul's position-takings in relation to habituses within the structure of conflict (for literal and symbolic capital) that comprises the field of 1960s and 1970s London as a publishing metropole. The study shows how the written form (the actual structure of the text) of *In a Free State*, and the gradual instituting of its perceived form (normalized recognition of *IAFS* as a novel), are characterised by "permanent conflict" between habituses and "the contradictions it engenders". The study also proceeds to track how a subject's agency cannot be reduced to that of the "Economic Man" who merely competes for power and capital, but can nonetheless be understood within an expanded Bourdieusian model.

In the first section of this chapter, I break down the "imbroglio" between the judges and Booker committee over the eligibility of *IAFS* for the Booker Prize. This deconstruction unfolds the structure of conflict that led to the "instituting" of *IAFS* as a novel. In the following section, I study Naipaul's own moves within this structure in order to question the extent of institutional reach and the rule of economic acquisition as overriding forces in the cultural production of *IAFS*. I map Naipaul's positionings in the "field" through his persistence in maintaining his chosen written form, which influenced the structure of the field itself. I show that a subject can become a disruptive player within the Bourdieusian field, and that such agency is capable of reshaping the structure within which the subject is situated. J. Dillon Brown (2013) points out that "the field is not an inert, impersonal force, but a flexible social space continually constituted via an accumulation of individual actions" (17). Brown suggests here that just as the Bourdieusian field determines the positions available within it to individuals, the disruption caused by individual agency can also very well shift the field's formation. Naipaul's show of authorial agency, not characterised by the logic of economic exchange, complicates Bourdieu's economic model of cultural production. While I identify the workings of a Bourdieusian model within the Booker Prize institution of 1971, I also show its limitations through the unfolding of Naipaul's authorial agency.

In the third section, I nuance my analysis of Naipaul's disruptive agency by noting his shifts in position in the Bourdieusian field as he gains more symbolic currency. With the later published editions of *IAFS*, Naipaul becomes less and less resistant to the perceived form of *IAFS* just as he becomes more and more embraced by the consecrating institutions of his time. This third section shows that subject agency can disrupt a field and yet continue to be responsive to the conflict for literal and symbolic capital that characterizes the Bourdieusian model. In charting the three movements of this field and Naipaul's position in it through the instituting of *IAFS*'s form, I extend Bourdieu's economic model of cultural production to also account for individual acts of agency.

As proposed by Flair Donglai Shi in the introduction of this volume, my study of the "creation" of *IAFS*'s perceived form via the Booker as a consecrating institution aligns with the collection's "sociological approach". Alongside my fellow authors in this section of the book, I aim to dissect the social processes through which literature, or world literature, is presented whilst also revealing how they are disruptive acts of institution in their own right.

Booker Prize Imbroglio: *In a Free State's* Perceived Form

In the Booker Prize Archive at Oxford Brookes University, a file entitled "Documents concerning the Booker Prize imbroglio, 1971" exists as a subset of the administrative papers of Booker plc in 1971. It was formerly owned by one of the judges of the prize that year (hereafter referred to as A). The documents chart the dissension between the judges and the permanent committee about the eligibility of Naipaul's *In a Free State* as a novel. It mostly occurred during and after the selection of the winner from the shortlist. The imbroglio began with the intervention of Tom Maschler, who was on the permanent committee of the Booker Prize. After *In a Free State*'s questionable eligibility (according to the newly drafted rules of 1971) was brought to his attention, he spoke about this to the chairman of the judges, John Gross. When this matter was eventually raised with the other judges, they invoked an existing rule that states that the judges' decision is final. There was an all-round general agreement that IAFS was eligible. Later, however, A rescinded his vote for its eligibility in a letter that he circulated to the other judges: Gross, Antonia Fraser, Philip Toynbee and Saul Bellow. This elicited a series of letters between the judges, Maschler, and John Murphy (who was also on the permanent committee). The issue was resolved when Gross sent out a document asking for each judge's YES/NO vote on the book's eligibility. The imbroglio between Gross and Fraser for YES and A and Bellow for NO was ended when Toynbee also voted YES, resulting in a narrow majority vote in favour of the book's eligibility.

On the basis of this imbroglio, I will analyse the various factors that led to the consecration of *In a Free State* as a novel. First, the influence of the commercial or "larger" field over the "restricted" literary field. Second, the interpretations and permutations of the rules. Third, the judging committee as a habitus; and fourth, the role of the press. Looking at these factors, I argue that the instituting of In *a Free State* as a novel is an impressive case of "misrecognition", which Bourdieu and Passeron describe as: "the process whereby power relations are perceived not for what they objectively are but in a form which renders them legitimate in the eyes of the beholder" (quoted in

Norris 2006, 141). This misrecognition is a result of the structure of conflict that makes up the Bourdieusian field.

The first, and probably the most important, factor for the instituting of *In a Free State* as a novel was the effect of the "larger" field in an institution that is usually expected to play within the rules of the "restricted" field. The "larger" field here includes the largest possible audience and is mostly governed by profit, while the "restricted" field relies on symbolic recognition from those within that field, usually associated with "high literature" valued for its own sake (Bourdieu 1993, 115). In the case of *IAFS*, its misrecognition as a novel was partly due to the commercial truth that novels sell better than other genres. The influence of the "larger" field was blatantly acknowledged by Maschler: "But in one small way we could protect the Prize and that was by eliminating [collections of short] stories. Stories sell less than novels. That's a fact" ("Letter from Maschler to A, September 22, 1971"). This fact had driven the Prize committee to reject, in the previous year, a collection of short stories —*A Time to Keep* by George Mackay Brown—and to subsequently use the word "novel" rather than "fiction" as an eligibility criterion in the rules. The Booker Prize narrowed itself to one form of fiction because it was set up not as a purely "restricted" and aesthetic project, but as one that sought to increase the commercial value of fiction written in English. Sharon Norris (2006) notes that:

> As far back as 1968 there were indications of a predisposition towards conflation [of the literary and commercial] in the Booker Prize, when the first press release stated that the sponsor hoped the award would "help to narrow the all too frequent gap between artistic and commercial success". (154)

The conflated accumulation of symbolic and monetary capital from both "larger" and "restricted" fields was necessary to elevate London's status as a literary hub, which "appeared embarrassingly slight next to those of New York and Paris" (Kalliney 2013, 253). To do so, it was necessary to award a literary prize to a form that was already commercially viable. Limiting eligibility to the novel ensured that the works awarded the Booker Prize had a higher chance of selling well, thus pleasing the publishers and ultimately adding to the success of the Prize itself. This meant that the Prize's permanent committee was motivated commercially to ensure that Naipaul's *In a Free State* was at least perceived to be a novel, even after they failed to stop the judges from deeming it eligible. The conscious instituting of the book as a novel to protect the commercial interests of the then fledgling Prize is clearly evidenced by Murphy's letter to Gross (22 September 1971). Murphy wrote that the most important thing is:

> making sure to all and sundry that the judges do indeed believe that the Naipaul book is a full-length novel—[. . .] I think with these bits of paper [votes of YES/NO by individual judges about the eligibility of the book] that everybody concerned with the Booker Prize, including the judges, is thoroughly protected.

In order to make up for not questioning the book's eligibility until it was too late, the Prize committee officially insisted that it was a "full-length novel". This is a clear example of Bourdieu's concept of "misrecognition": the power relations enacted upon the book allowed it to be perceived as a novel, and the Prize was consequently perceived as an institution that was able to consecrate and cultivate definitions of form, even playing a role in the creation of a commercial canon of literary fiction.

Aside from the Prize's permanent committee, the publisher of Naipaul's book, Andre Deutsch, also had clear commercial interests in submitting *In a Free State* to the Prize as a "full-length novel". He signed a form upon submission stating that *IAFS* is a novel, and therefore adheres to the Prize's rules. Despite even Naipaul's own refusal to call *IAFS* a novel, Deutsch was ready to declare it as such in order to compete for the Booker. This act of declaring *In a Free State* as a "full-length novel" made it so, in the eyes of one judge, Antonia

Fraser: "George Mackay Brown's book was offered as short stories. Nobody ever pretended that the Naipaul was being offered as such" ("Letter from Fraser to Gross, 1 October 1971"). Though A took this to mean that Andre Deutsch "monkeyed with" the rules ("Letter from A to Maschler, September 30, 1971"), this institutional and bureaucratic act of naming the book as a novel tautologically made the claim legitimate for Fraser. It plays a similar role to the YES/NO votes in showing how institutions colluded by exchanging symbolic currencies of legitimacy, wherein the act of institutional consecration establishes *IAFS* as a novel regardless of its formal written characteristics.

Nevertheless, one might wonder if Andre Deutsch merely made a mistake, considering the aforementioned rule change from "fiction" to "novel" in 1970 in order to disqualify George MacKay's short stories. He might simply have not caught up with the changes in definition. However, the history of Andre Deutsch's publishing relationship with Naipaul suggests otherwise. Naipaul's first book, the collection of short stories *Miguel Street*, had been rejected by Deutsch. Instead, Deutsch asked if Naipaul had a novel; luckily, he was writing one at the time (*The Mystic Masseur*). It was only after the publication of *The Mystic Masseur* that *Miguel Street* was given the green light. The demand for a straightforward novel is mirrored in the case of *In a Free State*. Patrick French (2008), in his biography of Naipaul, *The World Is What It Is*, writes in regards to *In a Free State* (here referring to the central narrative in the middle of the book) that "Diana Athill [. . .] suggested it be published alone, without the accompanying stories and material" (288). Naipaul refused, but Andre Deutsch decided to market the whole five segments as an entire novel anyway, despite having to use convoluted qualifications, which I will explore later. This publication history shows furthermore that the Prize in 1971 as a supposedly "restricted" literary field was in fact deeply interconnected with the "larger" commercial field. This specific construction of the intersecting forces of consecration (the Prize) and the purveyors of commercial success (publishers) is a part of the overall "field" that is the London literary hub.

The second factor that led to the consecration of *In a Free State* as a novel is the interpretation and permutation of the rules. The struggles and contradictions around the rules of the Booker show the prominence of the Bourdieusian field, with all its contingencies, in the instituting of form. Most of all, the rules in this case constituted a sub-field where struggles for authority played out.

As mentioned earlier, the rule regarding eligible form had been changed from "works of fiction" in 1970 ("Rules of the Competition") to "full-length novels" in 1971 ("Details and Rules"). *In a Free State* was so adamantly proclaimed as a novel because the word "novel" was the key to the symbolic capital of winning the literal capital of a £5,000 prize (one of the most lucrative prizes at the time, which gave the Booker more press attention, and therefore more symbolic capital). It is likely that Andre Deutsch and the judges would have been happy to call it by another name had it been published just a year earlier. This illustrates the contingencies of the field within which *In a Free State* was instituted. Another contingency was the rule that "the decision of the judges as to whether a book is eligible shall be binding" ("Details and Rules"). This was established for the sake of practicality as opposed to technicality, as the judges themselves acknowledged their lack of discussion in terms of *IAFS*'s written form. This contingency meant that the particular combination of judges, since it varied year on year, created completely different sets of standards by which books were measured. Hence, Naipaul's book might have been disqualified in another year. These contingencies prove that the field lacked "coherence-seeking intention" (Bourdieu 1993, 34). Furthermore, some of the judges' constant wielding of this rule in their opposition to Maschler shows that the rules are a site of "permanent conflict" (Bourdieu 1993, 34). Rather than discussing the arguments for or against the book as a novel, the focus of the discussion was on conflicts of power, like the conflict between Maschler (representing the permanent committee) and the judging committee. This pattern was repeated in A's letter, where the focus was more on defending against allegations or wrangling over who said what, than on the book itself:

> Neither [Gross] nor yourself has commented on the arguments against eligibility I set out in my letter—and what absolutely amazes me is that none of us (I am equally guilty, of course) ever raised these arguments at the time. ("Letter from A to Fraser, 2 October 1971")

Just as the discussion about eligibility in the letters turned into a struggle between different sets of interests within the judging panel, the rules of the Prize became a site of conflict too. Hence, the instituting of form in this case was swayed by transient conditions within the Bourdieusian field.

The effects of this struggle continued in the next year. The permanent committee responded to the judges' decision by changing the rules again, thereby reinstating its own authority: "Any full length novel [. . .]. Such a book must be a unified and substantial work. Neither a book of short stories nor a novella is eligible" ("Rules for 1972"). As both Maschler and Murphy of the permanent committee made clear that they were not convinced by the book's eligibility as a novel, the rule change was a clear response to the imbroglio of 1971. The word "unified" comments on the fact that the thematic unity of the various parts of In *a Free State* was contentiously held as the reason that it should be qualified as a novel.[1] The word "substantial" also seems to be a comment on the rather slim 141 pages of the book's "central novel". The permanent committee's reclamation of authority through this pointed rule change was a result of the rules as a site of conflict in 1971; but it also created long term effects as submitted books of subsequent years up until the time of writing were judged according to the words "unified" and "substantial". A spoke of his concern about this in a letter to Gross (28 September 1971):

> In addition, whatever the outcome of this year's competition, I imagine the rules and procedures will be changed next year to see that this situation never occurs again. I[t] seems rather ironic that all we shall have done is to provoke further

1 For more on thematic unity as qualification, see Appendix.

limitations; and perhaps condemn future borderline cases that could have been argued for more convincingly.

This condemnation of future cases echoed up till 2019, as the 2019 rules for eligibility contain the line: "1. e) Every submitted novel must be a unified and substantial work" (The Man Booker Prize, 2019). Interestingly, the 2019 rules mark the first change in definition of eligible submissions in nearly 50 years, from "novel" to "work" or "long-form fiction" (The Man Booker Prize, 2019). However, the criteria of being "unified and substantial' still remains from the committee's consideration of *IAFS* (as above).

The third factor that led to the consecration of In *a Free State* as a novel is the formation of habituses within the judges and committee members. Bourdieu's theory of "field" and "habitus" is particularly pertinent when it comes to the judges and the committee, as they clearly exemplify separate "habituses". Within each "habitus" exist sub-habituses, which have differing interests and predilections in the structure of conflict. This specific set of positionings contributed to the instituting of *In a Free State* as a novel.

The first such sub-habitus within the judging committee was that of "The School", which Bourdieu describes as one that "reproduces the social status quo, and ipso facto, the conditions of its own existence. It is also, together with the home environment, one of two key sites for the transmission of the aesthetic habitus" (quoted in Norris 2006, 144). This habitus can be identified among the judges in that four out of five of them studied at Oxford, with the one exception being Saul Bellow. Though it might be argued that the committee shared more common ground on the basis of literary credentials than on that of having studied at Oxford, those groups were so interlinked, as has been noted by critics like Graham Huggan (2001, 218–19), that it can be impossible to separate one from the other. Nonetheless, what can be ascertained is the presence of the "aesthetic habitus" shared by the judging committee; built by similar backgrounds in "home environment" and "school", i.e. similar class and cultural backgrounds.

However, the very existence of the imbroglio complicates the idea of this shared aesthetic habitus. A, who opposed the eligibility of *IAFS*, also graduated from Oxford. What needs to be pointed out then is the existence of sub-habituses within this larger aesthetic habitus; divided by either social groups or commercial interests. A was an author published by Jonathan Cape, which was headed by Maschler. As Maschler was the one who appointed A to the jury, and A, in his turn, called in Doris Lessing's shortlisted novel (Lessing was also under Jonathan Cape), A was tied down into a position of commercial interest. Whether he chose to or not, he inhabited a sub-habitus with Maschler and Lessing. A, Maschler and Lessing's sub-habitus is in contention with the other sub-habitus, which is comprised of Fraser, Naipaul and Gross. Fraser shared the same agent as Naipaul, and according to A's letter to Gross (28 September 1971), Fraser and Gross "declared [themselves] both close friends of [Naipaul]". This formed yet another sub-habitus—one that was perhaps influential in determining the eligibility of In *a Free State.* Maschler wrote in a letter to A (September 22, 1971):

> No[r] am I influenced by the fact that John Gross told me that Vidia Naipaul considers it to be a novel. Indeed, it seems to me quite unethical, or at lea[s]t, foolish, that the chairman of the judges should discuss the eligibility of one of the books with its author! That I consider a breach of confidence, and I'm surprised that John Gross should have committed it.

Fraser had also, as accused by A, supposedly tried to persuade Naipaul, alongside Andre Deutsch, to "drop the suspect material from the book" ("Letter from A to Gross, September 28, 1971"). Fraser later denied this by saying that she was not on such terms with Naipaul, and had not met him during the writing of the book ("Letter from Fraser to Gross, October 1, 1971"). Patrick French's (2008) record of this period in his biography of Naipaul provides an alternative perspective. French mentions that "from 1963 until the early 1970s, Lady Antonia gave Vidia significant hospitality and friendship. Her house in Campden Hill Square provided him with a remote idea of security and familiarity" (249). French also records Fraser as saying, about Naipaul, "After all, we had all been at Oxford together [and] the Sixties wasn't a time of social gaps. [. . .] The house was full of colonial people" (248). If nothing else, these sources confirm, at least, the existence of another sub-habitus made up by Gross and Fraser within the judging committee. French adds that:

> Through Antonia, Francis [Wyndham] and Anthony Powell (his wife, Violet, was Antonia's aunt), Vidia gained access to a new group of privately educated, well-connected British people who were willing to accept him as a curiosity, particularly once he gained the imprimatur of literary success. (247)

These sub-habituses created conflicts of interest within the judging process, despite the judges' best efforts to be impartial and objective. Their positions within these sub-habituses made it so that meetings inevitably turned into fields of conflict, where it was impossible to shed one's interests to create an environment in which literary merit became the primary concern. A, clearly frustrated, described it as such in a letter to Maschler (September 30, 1971):

> We had already, the previous week, started horse-trading: if you'll be nice to my A, I'll be nice to your B, that kind of thing—and the reverse. If I had "stopped" Naipaul, I knew I'd have at least two votes adamantly against my two [p2] horses—Richler and Lessing. [. . .] [I believe the] jury to be a disastrously dishonest method [. . .] It's not that A or B is corrupt; just that everyone starts playing poker—bluffing, misleading, combining, trading . . . all in a nice English way, of course.

These conflicting sub-habituses meant that a judgement on the book was no longer just a judgement on the book, but also a judgement on the trader of that "horse". This can be seen in the letters of the imbroglio, as the judges neglected to discuss the formal qualities of IAFS but instead traded allegations. The instituting of Naipaul's book as novel, as shown here, was largely made possible by the conflicts of habitus within the judging committee.

The final factor that allowed In *a Free State* to be perceived as a novel was the relative silence and passivity of the press regarding the imbroglio. This left the symbolic capital of the Prize intact and thus allowed for the continued misrecognition of Naipaul's book as a novel. The first reason for the press's silence on the issue was the Booker Prize's first ever scandal, which distracted from the imbroglio: "Muggeridge Quits in "Porn" Row" (Roberts 1971). Malcolm Muggeridge had initially been on the 1971 judging panel, but he resigned as he could not in good conscience award the Prize to any of the works he read, which he described as "pornographic". He was later replaced by Toynbee. The utility of this scandal was not lost on the organisers. An administrative letter at the time (July 29, 1971) states: "Personally, I feel that when we get near the time for the choice to be announced, we remind people unofficially of the exit of Muggeridge and sow seeds of speculation as to whether the Booker Prize has gone permissive". This strategy was in keeping with the Booker's idea to create a shortlist so that the Prize could become a topic of speculation. This scandal allowed the Prize to get widespread press coverage even before the announcement of the shortlist, and when controlled, created publicity without tarnishing the Prize's maximum potential for symbolic capital. James English in *The Economy of Prestige* describes this classic mechanism of leveraging on negative publicity as a 'system of exchange [. . .] which seems to secure cultural esteem by maximizing the flow of disesteeming discourse through and around it' (2005, 188). This safer form of scandal created a distraction from the judges' dispute on eligibility upon the announcement of the winner.

However, the word did get out. A few articles in the press hinted at the judges' dispute, but the focus was on the judges rather than on the eligibility of Naipaul's book. The article with the most obvious treatment of the issue hardly made much of a fuss, and still focused more on the judges than the book:

> Perhaps the most promising sign of the possibility of increasing general interest in this prize is at last the smell of scandal seeping out from the locked doors of the judging committee—why was the announcement postponed and is this connected with the vociferous complaint of some publishers that *In a Free State* is not, in fact, a novel at all but a series of short stories? (Hollis 1971)

The probable reason for the minimal impact of this judges' scandal is suggested in the same news article: "Does Naipaul's mopping up of so many prizes mean, in effect, that he is the best novelist around?" Naipaul was considered an established name, and as such, it was less likely that the press would doubt the merit, and the eligibility, of his work—especially when his publisher, the judges, and presumably Naipaul himself, all asserted that the book qualified as a novel. Most of the press articles skirted around the eligibility issue by emphasising Naipaul as a "novelist". Quite a few of them included the obligatory fact that Naipaul was an Oxford man, a fact which holds enough social capital to put weight behind I*n a Free State's* asserted novel form. The strength of Naipaul's name was also aided by his own role as a reviewer for newspapers and magazines, as evidenced by Athill's (2000) suggestion below. This hints at Naipaul's position in a sub-habitus (that of novelist-reviewers) within the habitus of the press:

> there was never any doubt about the making of his name, which began at once with the reviews and was given substance by his own work as a reviewer, of which he got plenty as soon as he became known as a novelist. (205)

Naipaul's intersection, along with other novelists, of two habituses—the literary establishment and the press—maps the movements of power unique to the "field" that instituted the form of

In a Free State. The efficient handling of the imbroglio, the fanning of the Muggeridge scandal and the currency of the Naipaul name allowed the eligibility issue to sink into obscurity. The legitimacy of the Prize escaped unscathed.

Even though it can be clearly seen that the perceived form of the book, or its "misrecognition", was the contradictory product of a Bourdieusian field and its habituses, the fact remains that these instituting acts were required because Naipaul refused to write a straightforward novel, or to discard the supporting materials that complicate the book's classification. Naipaul ignored these commercial and consecrating institutions' demand for a novel, causing them to bend over backwards in their effort to adapt to this anomaly. Naipaul's established literary success and his connections within the habituses of these institutions meant that they were willing to adapt in the first place. However, his insistence on producing a book that required them to do so is a testimony to the existence of creative agency within the Bourdieusian field of cultural production that cannot simply be subsumed under the "Economic Man of neoclassical economics" (English 2002, 111). The writerly creation of *In a Free State* is an example of a "disruptive intervention" (McDonald 2016, 40) within habituses' "generative structures" (Low 2011, 135). The slight but definite destabilisation caused by the book was felt by several institutions within London's publishing field. Despite their best efforts, the book's aberrant written form (five pieces: one central novella wrapped with seemingly unrelated narratives; two journal fragments and two short stories) could not be completely replaced by its misrecognised perceived form, adding to the system's contradictions. This proves the need to modify and expand Bourdieu's economic model to acknowledge such creative agencies. As such, my next section focuses on the germination of this "aberrant written form", and analyses the institutions and movements that Naipaul seems to position himself against in his various habituses. While my first section reveals the maneouvres of monetary, social and symbolic currency within the 1971 "imbroglio", my second section expands the

Bourdieusian model in considering Naipaul's agency and resistance as a type of positioning.

Writerly Agency and Literary Movements: *In a Free State*'s Written Form

Aside from eluding the institutional forces of the publisher, the prize and the press in terms of *In a Free State's* written form, Naipaul also stood counter-current to two literary movements that were prevalent in his habituses in the years leading up to *IAFS*. I will be analyzing the institutional forces surrounding Naipaul as well as the two literary movements as intersecting habituses in the field of London as a publishing metropole. A case study of *IAFS*'s written form and its writing process reveals what seems to be intentional positionings on the part of Naipaul either in resistance or response to those habituses—thereby asserting his agency within the Bourdieusian field.

The two main literary currents interacting with Naipaul at the time were The Movement, which reasserted the influence of literary realism, and the cultural nationalism of the Caribbean Artists Movement (CAM), which was set up in 1966. Naipaul's choice of an experimental written form for *In a Free State*, specifically in 1971, was primarily an exertion of his creative agency in defiance of the pressures of these two literary movements within the conflicted London publishing field.

During the late 1950s and early 1960s in London, West Indian or Caribbean writing mostly comprised the modernisms of the Windrush generation. At the same time, an opposing force was in play: "composed of English writers such as Amis, Donald Davie, Philip Larkin, and John Wain, the Movement had cultural convictions—proudly philistine, aggressively nationalist, and anxiously concerned with the changing dynamics of class (not race) within Great Britain" (Brown 2013, 16). It was also concerned with "the reconstruction of the tradition, when writers of an earlier period of realism, the

Victorian and Edwardian ages, were recuperated and made visible" (Bradbury 2001, 358).

Naipaul was strongly associated with the Movement in his writing style at the time, especially with works like *A House for Mr. Biswas*. He was lauded for being one of the writers who were able to revive 19th-century realism. Consequently, Naipaul was seen by his fellow West Indian or Caribbean writers as someone who sought to eliminate his own cultural identity in his attempt to ape the British. A.J. Seymour described Naipaul's writing career as having developed within "the colonial cocoon" (quoted in Walmsley 1992, 271). This reaction is unsurprising, as Naipaul had repeatedly suggested that "properly West Indian literature is British", and as such, seemed "to have aimed at aligning West Indian writing as closely as possible to an ostensibly stable, unchanging tradition of realism then being noisily revived by Amis's generation in English literature itself" (Brown 2013, 173).

However, this conservative realism is clearly not the written form that Naipaul chose for *In a Free State*. After writing within that tradition for years, why did he deviate from it in 1971? Judith Levy (1995) posits that the book marks a turning point into Naipaul's "second phase", when he began to deal with the "dual disillusionment: with himself in the role of English novelist, and with fiction as a vehicle for the creation and expression of self" (xvi). Alongside Levy's explanation, I posit that Naipaul transitioned because, in 1971, the experimental form was no longer the immediate characteristic of the Caribbean or West Indian writers' habitus. The modernism of the Windrush generation lent itself as a genesis to CAM's preference for experimental writing. Kamau Brathwaite, a leading figure in CAM, lamented in his 1967 essay "Jazz and the West Indian Novel" that "British publishing firms continue to display a "waning of interest [in] <<new>>, <<experimental>>, <<too parochial>>, <<too specialised>>, <<for too narrow a market>>, <<unknown>> Caribbean writing" (quoted in Brown 2013, 177; punctuation as in original). Later on, CAM's focus on formal and aesthetic experimentation dissipated when Brathwaite left for Jamaica in 1968 and created a branch of CAM there, whilst other members of CAM took over in Britain, dividing the movement into two different streams: one focusing on Caribbean cultural nationalism and another on Black British race politics.

As the writings of a bifurcated CAM were increasingly tinged with specific political goals, Naipaul could venture into new and different forms in his writing without being immediately associated with CAM, or with "West Indian writers" as a group. Even *In a Free State*'s thematic focus on placelessness is arguably antithetical to CAM's shift of focus to situated aesthetics (Caribbean versus Black British). The dispersion of a specifically West Indian or Caribbean trend for experimental writing enabled Naipaul to deviate from traditional British realism, without being immediately associated with labels which would be commonly attributed to Naipaul, like "West Indian Writer", "Emergent Third-Worlder", and "Transplanted Indian" (Theroux 1972, 7). Naipaul's active and desired dissociation was acknowledged in Frank Kermode's speech at the 1971 Booker Prize awards ceremony: "PARTICULARLY DELIGHTED WINNER A TRINIDADIAN ALTHOUGH REALLY A CITIZEN OF THE WORLD" ("Speech notes"). This amorphous phrase indicates the kind of stateless authorial image that Naipaul aimed for. It is possible that he worked so hard to assimilate into British literary circles in the first phase because he wanted to differentiate himself from the categories of Caribbean or West Indian, but as *In a Free State* and his subsequent writings show (works like *The Enigma of Arrival, 1987* and *A Way in the World, 1994* continue to trouble critics' efforts to classify them), he later also distanced himself from the British habitus through his deviant use of form, exactly when it is possible to do so without striding into the habitus of CAM.

I suggest that Naipaul's use of a deviant form in *In a Free State* was a part of his larger continued efforts to differentiate himself, in the London literary field, from the habituses of West Indian or Caribbean writers, and to a lesser extent, the British literary habitus. As Heather Dubrow (1982) states in *Genre*: "literary forms may perform a type of social function in that they establish their author's relationship to other writers: [. . .] demarcating a small circle of writers from the larger literary culture with which they uneasily coexist" (115). Naipaul's shifts in literary form were one way to establish his authorial identity in relation to other writers and movements around him. Naipaul constantly sought to demarcate his own creative agency, especially through form, despite his own conflicted sense of artistic isolation. He said as much in his interview with Linda Bradford in the *Telegraph* Sunday Magazine in 1979:

> You know, my work doesn't really exist. When people talk about trends, I'm never there. There is some element of discussion about [the] others of one's contemporaries—Updike, Bellow, Lessing, Amis—but my work will not be around. They won't give me a Nobel Prize. There'll be nothing in it for Them; I don't represent anything. One doesn't speak for anyone. This is not a complaint, you know. One is just stating a fact. (Naipaul quoted in Jussawalla 1997, 51)

Although his artistic choices could, to some extent, be explained as reactionary to the field of cultural production, his consistent strategy of deviant forms asserts himself as a proactive force within the field. Admittedly, these conflicts do show that the "unifying principle" of the field of position-taking is indeed that of the "struggle, with all the contradictions it engenders" (Bourdieu 1993, 34), especially for postcolonial writers within the metropole. Still, Naipaul's disruptive formal intervention shows that the Bourdieusian model has, as James English suggested, "failed to yield a very convincing theory of the subject" (2002, 111), as it still needs to account for the creative agency of writers like Naipaul—an agency based on assertion of subjecthood rather than the acquisition of literal or symbolic capital.

His strategy of resistance against the main currents of the field can be coherently fitted into the "structure of conflict", but does not seem to be motivated from an economic standpoint (no clear advantage in gaining various currencies). Naipaul asserts his own position of power via resistance by wielding his written form as creative agency. As such, the Bourdieusian model can be modified in order to take into account positionings in the field where resistance is for resistance's sake, or for absolute subject isolation. However, my next section yet again complicates this added perspective in Bourdieu's model. As Naipaul's own standing grows, he begins to move from a position of resistance into a traditional position of power, habituating himself to the consecrating institutions of the field. My third section adds a third dimension; a reciprocity between subject agency and institutional power. The ground that he gradually concedes in the presentation of *IAFS*'s written form shows the interrelations between positions of resistance and power, and perhaps even resistance as a possible strategy to obtain currencies of power.

Aftermath: *In a Free State's* Formal Evolution

While true at the time of the Booker imbroglio, Naipaul's creative agency through deviant form in the case of *In a Free State* is later deradicalised. As his name and symbolic capital grew, Naipaul became more and more willing to allow institutional forces to shape not just the perceived form of his book, but the written form as well. In this section, I will examine the evolution of *In a Free State*'s published and marketed form as new editions were rolled out. I will also look at these editions' paratexts as "as a zone not just of transition, but of transaction" (Genette and Maclean 1991, 262), where the publisher enters into a contract with the reader as to the perceived form of the book.

(Front cover of V.S.Naipaul's *In a Free State*, Andre Deutsch 1971 edition, taken from Man Booker Prize's Gallery.)

The Andre Deutsch edition of 1971 was published immediately after the announcement of the winner of the Booker Prize. This edition most accurately reflects the uneasy collaboration between Naipaul as writer and the publisher as institution. It is clear that Andre Deutsch tried to emphasise the book's status as a novel. They placed prominently, in a textbox at the top of the front inner flap, the £5,000 Booker win, followed by a blurb by Francis Wyndham: "I consider Naipaul the finest living novelist writing in English, and this his most important work". Wyndham repeated the press's strategy of calling Naipaul a novelist rather than calling the book a novel because Naipaul had made it clear that the book was a "sequence":

> To be sure that nobody at Andre Deutsch became confused over its form or its worth, Vidia drafted "a guide as to how the blurb can be written. [. . .] 'Sequence' is the key word: it is the word that I had in my mind during the writing. [. . .] This may be V.S. Naipaul's best book. It is certainly his most original and complete", [Vidia] suggested. (French 2008, 290)

The edition's description of the book was structured to move around the obstacle of the word "sequence" and to ensure that it was still perceived as a novel, one way or another. Whilst the paratext does say that "this is a sequence", it goes on to say that "at its heart is a novel", implying that even though the entirety of the book is difficult to classify as a novel, the most important part is a novel, and thus, the book is qualified as one, with or without its accompanying parts. By elevating the longest story of the book to the main element, namely the "central novel", the other four parts are cast as interesting yet disposable supporting material. On the back flap, this "central novel" is "given a deeper meaning by two long studies of other men. . . . The fiction is enclosed by two pieces of documentary, fragments from a journal" [my emphasis]. By casting the other stories as "studies" and "documentary", their pesky connotations as "fiction" was elided, which might suggest that the book is a collection of short stories. These convoluted paratextual manoeuvres indicate the contradictions of a field of struggle, but also the stubborn persistence of Naipaul's creative agency through the phrase "sequence" and his insistence on keeping the other material surrounding the "central novel".

(Front cover of V.S.Naipaul's *In a Free State*, Picador 2002 edition, taken from Abebooks.)

After Naipaul was awarded the Nobel Prize in 2001, Picador released new editions of his writing. Picador's 2002 edition of *In a Free State* has the line WINNER OF THE NOBEL PRIZE IN LITERATURE at the very top, above the emblazoned V.S. NAIPAUL, which shows the importance of his name. The words "A NOVEL" are printed in capital letters under the title, with the line "with two supporting narratives" underneath, italicised and in a tiny font.

Like the Deutsch edition, it uses the phrase "central novel" to elevate one story above the rest. This implied notion is reflected in Picador's choice to use "A NOVEL" rather than "THE NOVEL", which implies the central novel as one of many narratives rather than asserting the entirety of the text as "the novel". The paratext also emphasises the fact that "the theme is displacement", bringing back the notion of the thematically unified novel that was used to justify the book's eligibility during the Booker imbroglio. Picador's 2002 edition differs from the Deutsch edition in its abandonment of the word "sequence" and adoption of the phrase "with two supporting narratives". Moreover, the blurb is taken from Dennis Potter's comments in *The Times*: he calls it "a book". Despite moving away from "sequence", Picador still took pains in 2002 to account for its unconventional form, in contrast to the 2008 edition examined later. I would suggest that Picador's willingness to underplay the book's presentation as "the novel" in the whole is due first to the establishment of Naipaul's name as a Nobel Prize winner, and second to the fact that there was a larger awareness of the genre of literary fiction. Due to the consecration of the Nobel and the safety of an institutionalised genre that allowed for free experimentation with form, both Naipaul and Picador were assured of the book's ability to sell, despite its unconventional descriptors.

(Front cover of V.S.Naipaul's *In a Free State*, Picador 2008 edition, taken from Kobo store.)

The book's evolution into further formal conformity reached its apex in this 2008 edition, paralleling Naipaul's trajectory into the apex of his career. Here, the central piece that is also called "In a Free State" is published on its own. At this point, Naipaul had written most of his oeuvre, his last work being *Magic Seeds* written four years earlier. With a Booker and Nobel win, and a knighthood to his name, there was very little that could be done to shake his authorial status. As such, his sense of authorial power did not need to be compensated by the resistance of deviant form. From that perspective, or from the perspective of symbolic or literary capital, Naipaul ran no risk whatsoever in releasing the Picador 2008 for the "first time in a stand-alone edition". This edition is entitled "In a Free State: The Novel (Author's revised edition)". Note also the shift from "A NOVEL" to "The Novel". It contains a new preface by the author, in which Naipaul significantly states:

> But then, as the years passed and the world changed, and I felt myself less of an oddity as a writer, I grew to feel that the central novel was muffled and diminished by the surrounding material and I began to think that the novel should be published on its own.

Naipaul here abandons his concept of "sequence", and adopts the phrase "central novel", a move that he directly attributes to the fact that he feels "less of an oddity as a writer". In contrast to his conflicted statement in the 1979 Bradford interview, it is clear that the solidifying of his reputation has removed the need to continuously assert himself as an individual author.

In 1971, Naipaul refused to conform to the pressures of the Bourdieusian field in a tactical move to assert his own position within the field of position-takings, staying stubbornly neither West Indian nor Caribbean, nor wholly British. Later on, as can be seen in *In a Free State*'s formal evolution, his individual authorial image was safely established, becoming an institution in itself. This meant that he no longer needed to wield *In a Free State*'s deviant form as a way to assert his creative agency and autonomy. While I still acknowledge the need for an expansion of Bourdieu's model to account for creative agency, this closing section shows that *In a Free State*'s later formal permutations plays back into the very institutions where "all the powers of the field, and all the determinisms inherent in its structure and functioning, are concentrated" (Bourdieu 1993, 37). Once Naipaul achieved an entrenched position of power within this field, he relinquished his hold on his own creative agency.

Conclusion

Within this sociological approach to literature through the literary prize, I have striven to stretch Bourdieu's model of cultural practice beyond its economic basis to account for the movements of individual, creative agency. In my first section, I established the model's basic application through a case study of the 1971 Booker imbroglio over the form and eligibility of Naipaul's *In a Free State*. In that example, the instituting of *IAFS*'s perceived form can be explained through four factors: the commercial influence on the literary, the rules, the judging committee as a habitus, and the role of the press. These factors mapped the multiple "position-takings" that occurred among habituses within a structure of conflict, showing Bourdieu's model in practice. I added a second dimension to the model, however, by looking at Naipaul's authorial agency through his use of a deviant written form. This was spun out in the second section, where I suggested that despite the lack of a theory of subjecthood or agency in Bourdieu's model, it can still be productively modified to also map the positionings of creative agency within the overall field. While Naipaul's position-takings did not have a direct link to literal or symbolic currency, they were very much still plays that were generative and capable of changing the structure of the field.

Lastly, I complicated the independence of the second dimension by showing the reciprocity between agency and institutions of power. As Naipaul gained influence and standing, he slowly conceded his deviant written form and eventually conformed to the instituted presentation of *IAFS* as a novel. While the position of resistance was productive to him in 1971, he later shifted his position in the field as the field itself changed, especially as it changed to recognise his symbolic currency as an author. Perhaps his act of creative agency was, after all, an economic positioning that led him to the position of power that he held later in his career.

Bibliography

Archival Citations

(Oxford Brookes University Special Collections: Booker Prize Archive)

"Details and Rules of the Competition for the Prize to be Awarded in 1971." 1971. Booker Prize Archive 1971. Box 1, Folder BP/1/3/1/1. 35. Administrative papers of Booker Plc. Feb. 22, 2016.

"Documents Concerning the Booker Prize Imbroglio, 1971." 1971. Booker Prize Archive 1971. Box 1, Folder BP/1/3/1/1. 212. Administrative papers of Booker Plc. Feb. 18, 2016.

Hollis, Nigel. 1971. "Winners and Losers." *Literary*, Dec. 4 1971. Booker Prize Archive 1971. Box 3, Folder BP/1/3/2/2. 145. Book Trust press cuttings. Feb. 22, 2016.

"Letter 29 July 1971." 1971. Booker Prize Archive 1971. Box 1, Folder BP/1/3/1/1. 101. Administrative papers of Booker Plc. Feb. 18, 2016.

"Letter from Maschler to A, 22 Sep 1971." 1971. Booker Prize Archive 1971. Box 1, Folder BP/1/3/1/1. 220. Administrative papers of Booker Plc. Feb. 9, 2016.

"Letter from Murphy to Gross, 22 Sep 1971." 1971. Booker Prize Archive 1971. Box 1, Folder BP/1/3/1/1. 163. Administrative papers of Booker Plc. Feb. 9, 2016.

"Letter from A to Gross, 28 Sep 1971." 1971. Booker Prize Archive 1971. Box 1, Folder BP/1/3/1/1. 223, 225. Administrative papers of Booker Plc. Feb. 9, 2016.

"Letter from Maschler to A, 28 Sep 1971." 1971. Booker Prize Archive 1971. Box 1, Folder BP/1/3/1/1. 219. Administrative papers of Booker Plc. Feb. 9, 2016.

"Letter from A to Maschler, 30 Sep 1971." 1971. Booker Prize Archive 1971. Box 1, Folder BP/1/3/1/1. 228, 229. Administrative papers of Booker Plc. Feb. 9, 2016.

"Letter from Fraser to Gross, 1 Oct 1971." 1971. Booker Prize Archive 1971. Box 1, Folder BP/1/3/1/1. 236. Administrative papers of Booker Plc. Feb. 9, 2016.

"Letter from A to Fraser, 2 Oct 1971." 1971. Booker Prize Archive 1971. Box 1, Folder BP/1/3/1/1. 239. Administrative papers of Booker Plc. Feb. 18, 2016.

Naipaul, V.S.. 1971. "Life on Approval [Interview with Alex Hamilton]." *The Guardian,* Oct. 4: 8. Booker Prize Archive 1971. Box 3, Folder BP/1/3/2/2. 51. Book Trust press cuttings. Feb. 18, 2016.

Roberts, John. 1971. "Muggeridge Quits in 'Porn' Row." *The* Sun, July 30. Booker Prize Archive 1971. Box 3, Folder BP/1/3/2/2. 30. Book Trust press cuttings. Feb. 22, 2016.

"Rules of the Competition for the Prize to be Awarded for 1969 in 1970." 1970. Booker Prize Archive 1970. Box 1, Folder BP/1/2/1/3. 87. Papers of Marilyn Edwards. Feb. 22, 2016.

"Rules for 1972 Booker Prize for Fiction." 1972. Booker Prize Archive 1972. Box 1, Folder BP/1/4/1/1. 56. Papers of Booker plc. Feb. 18, 2016

"Speech Notes for the Award Ceremony". 1971. Booker Prize Archive 1971. Box 1, Folder BP/1/3/1/1. 186. Administrative papers of Booker Plc. Feb. 9, 2016.

Works cited

Athill, Diana. 2000. *Stet: A Memoir*. London: Granta.

Bourdieu, Pierre. 1993. *The Field of Cultural Production: Articles on Art and Literature.* Edited by Randal Johnson. Cambridge: Cambridge University Press.

Bradbury, Malcolm. 2001. *The Modern British Novel.* London: Penguin.

Brown, J. Dillon. 2013. *Migrant Modernism: Postwar London and the West Indian Novel.* Charlottesville, VA: University of Virginia Press.

Dubrow, Heather. 1982. *Genre.* London: Methuen.

English, James F. 2002. "Winning the Culture Game: Prizes, Awards, and the Rules of Art." *New Literary History* 33 (1): 109–35.

—. 2005. *The Economy of Prestige: Prizes, Awards, and the Circulation of Cultural Value*. Cambridge, MA: Harvard University Press.

French, Patrick. 2008. *The World Is What It Is: The Authorized Biography of V.S. Naipaul*. London: Picador.

Genette, Gérard, and Marie Maclean. 1991. "Introduction to the Paratext." *New Literary History* 22 (2): 261-272.

Huggan, Graham. 2001. *The Postcolonial Exotic: Marketing the Margins*. London: Routledge.

Jussawalla, Feroza F. 1997. *Conversations with V.S. Naipaul*. Jackson, MS: University of Mississippi Press.

Kalliney, Peter J. 2013. "Conclusion: Postcolonial Writing or Global Literature in English?" *In Commonwealth of Letters: British Literary Culture and the Emergence of Postcolonial Aesthetics*, 245–58. Oxford: Oxford University Press.

Levy, Judith. 1995. *V.S. Naipaul: Displacement and Autobiography*. New York: Garland.

Low, Gail. 2001-02. "Publishing Commonwealth: The Case of West Indian Writing, 1950-65." *EnterText* 2 (1): 71–93.

McDonald, Peter. 2016. "Instituting World Literature." *In Institutions of World Literature: Writing, Translation, Markets*, edited by Stefan Helgesson and Pieter Vermeulen, 39–52. New York: Routledge.

Naipaul, V. S. 1971. *In a Free State*. London: Andre Deutsch.

—. *In a Free State*. 2002. London: Picador.

—. *In a Free State*. 2008. London: Picador.

Norris, Sharon. 2006. "The Booker Prize: A Bourdieusian Perspective." *Journal for Cultural Research* 10 (2): 139–58.

The Man Booker Prize. 2018. "The 2018 Man Booker Prize for Fiction Rules & Entry Form." *The Booker Prize Foundation*. https://arts docbox.com/Books_and_Literature/81465951-Rules-entry-form-finestfiction-the-2018-man-booker-prize-for-fiction.html

The Man Booker Prize. 2019. "The 2019 Man Booker Prize for Fiction Rules & Entry Form." *The Booker Prize Foundation*. https://the manbookerprize.com/sites/manbosamjo/files/181210%20MB 2019%20Rules%20And%20Entry%20Form.pdf

Theroux, Paul. 1972. *V.S. Naipaul: An Introduction to His Work*. London: Andre Deutsch.

Walmsley, Anne. 1992. *The Caribbean Artists Movement: 1966–1972: A Literary and Cultural History*. London: New Beacon.

Appendix

"John Gross's Statement on Naipaul's Eligibility". Booker Prize Archive 1971. Box 1, Folder BP/1/3/1/1. 140. Administrative papers of Booker Plc. 9 Feb. 2016.

Dear John Gross,

As the Publishers' Association will already have told

140

In the opinion of the Judges V.S.Naipaul's In a Free State is eligible for the Booker Prize because it is a unified and coherent work rather than a collection of short stories. The successive episodes interlock and reinforce one another, while whatever the unorthodox technique may sacrifice in terms of conventional narrative consistency it more than makes up for by enabling the author to bring out the global dimensions of his theme without having to dilute his novelist's sense of concrete and individual detail.

Author's own image.

Resituating the Author: Arundhati Roy, the Booker Prize and the Rhetoric of Authenticity

Lubabah Chowdhury

In a 1997 letter to Booker Prize administrator Martyn Goff, novelist Ken Follett writes:

> I did think *The God of Small Things* was the best of a poor bunch [of shortlisted novels]. However, it is *very* derivative of Rushdie. There is even a pickle factory: I hope that was a conscious acknowledgement of debt. And one has read so many stories in which a woman's yielding to physical passion is linked with the death or injury of one of her children. This is such a tediously melodramatic theme. (Ken Follett to Martyn Goff, 29 October 1997)

Follett's orientation towards the Booker Prize and debut novelist Arundhati Roy's work typifies the attitudes of Booker Prize judges and the Booker's public relations firm Colman Getty. From A.S. Byatt claiming that the Booker Prize should have been awarded to an English novelist[1] to Carmen Callil lamenting the "execrable"[2] nature of the novel, Roy's win was yet another year in the Booker Prize's long history of literary scandals. These scandals, as James English (2005) writes in *The Economy of Prestige*, are part and parcel of prize culture and ultimately only further the legitimizing force and authority of the prize itself (25). But Follett's comments deserve special consideration because they both rebuke Goff for ostensibly failing to identify and reward the "outstanding book of the year" (Follett to Goff) and reveal

1 Channel 4, "Video of Channel 4's coverage of the award ceremony, 1997, presented by Melvyn Bragg and Muriel Gray."

2 *Ibid.*

the ways in which Third World women writers must prove their merit in order to be recognized by the global literary marketplace. Here, I purposely use the term Third World in order to refer to a political positioning as well as a geographic one (see Uma Narayan 1997, Chandra Mohanty 2003); I am equally deliberate in using Sarah Brouillette's (2007) term "global literary marketplace" because it defines the very terms and conditions of Roy's prize win and her subsequent fame. As Follett suggests, the Third World woman writer may only use images or tropes from her male predecessors if she is willing to acknowledge the debt she owes them; she must pay this debt while striking out on her own without being "derivative"; and it is best if she does not write about domestic life or romantic relationships at all, lest she resort to "melodrama".

These sorts of criticism, which characterized the rhetoric around Roy's 1997 Booker win, demonstrate the imperative to account for gendered and racialized particularities when discussing the circulation of world literature. As Flair Donglai Shi notes in his introduction to this volume, David Damrosch's definition of world literature as "all literary works that circulate beyond their culture of origin" does not account for *why* certain literary works are chosen by multi-national publication houses and prestigious prizes for promotion and recognition while others are not; furthermore, Damrosch's definition does not account for the particular sorts of pressures these modes of recognition place on Third World women writers. Using materials from the Booker Prize Archive at Oxford Brookes University, I examine how Roy's Booker Prize win relied upon her legibility as an "authentic" Third World woman authoress, whose observations of domestic life in Kerala reproduce her own life experiences in thinly veiled autobiographical form. I then outline how such demands for authenticity are part and parcel of the demands placed on the cultural worker in the creative economy. Drawing on Sarah Brouillette's (2014) *Literature and the Creative Economy*, I argue that the media's construction of Roy as an "authentic" Indian writer reveals the paradoxical expectations and pressures placed on writers in what the Warwick Research Collective calls "*capitalism as a world-system*" (cited in Shi's Introduction in this volume; my italics). I conclude by considering how Roy's orientation towards the Booker and her subsequent activism and non-fiction essays challenge the expectations placed upon her by the consecrating forces of the prize and the media.

Before returning to the rhetoric around Roy's novel and her person, it is important to note that most of the journalism and publicity materials I examine in this chapter fall neatly into the reading practices that Graham Huggan's (2001) *The Postcolonial Exotic* claims are rewarded by prize culture. Placing Roy in a genealogy of cosmopolitan Indian Anglophone writers such as Rushdie makes Roy's writing legible as an "Indo-chic" product. As Huggan notes, that term is not just a "appropriately catchy" "journalistic label" (67), but is also directly tied to India's emergence on the global market, an emergence due both to India's increased economic liberalization during the 1980s and 1990s and to the global North's continued exploitation of a formerly colonized nation-state:

> 'Indo-chic' and Roy's contribution to it, are not simply to be seen as naïve Western constructs; they are products of the globalization of Western-capitalist consumer culture, in which 'India' functions not just as a polyvalent cultural sign but as a highly mobile capital good. (67)

"Indo-chic" is only one of many ways in which literary critics in the global North—and those entities affiliated with the Booker Prize in particular—tend towards a voyeuristic expectation of insider knowledge of the postcolonial experience. A winning Third World writer, then, is rewarded for his or her ability to transport the reader to a little-known and exotic locale, to translate the experience of subjugation under colonizing forces and the personal, emotional and political turmoil therein for a western audience. In a word, the Third World writer is rewarded for an easily legible authenticity determined by institutionalizing bodies outside of his or her control.

The Booker plc's public relations firm Colman Getty best exemplifies these exoticizing attempts to "sell" India to a western audience: from the references in promotional materials to the twin protagonists' "diverse and exotic" family to the titillating details of Roy's £1 million advance, a sense of Roy and her novel's construction as a lucrative treasure from the Third World pervades both the Booker's publicity materials and the subsequent media coverage of the prize and the novel. The media's fascination with the substantial advance Roy received is not unusual; as John B. Thompson (2010) notes in *Merchants of Culture*, "authors carry their sales histories around with them like a noose around their neck" (199). What is striking about the conversations around Roy's lucrative novelistic debut, however, is how her financial success was often credited to the legitimising forces of experienced British publishers, particularly Roy's London-based agent David Godwin, rather than to her own merit. Godwin's October 1997 interview with *The Independent* rehashes the narrative of the marginalized Third World woman writer being permitted to speak by those who inhabit the cultural and economic core. Godwin's interview subtly effaces Roy's own literary efforts:

> And then the story of Arundhati Roy—this year's Booker winner—started. Her novel arrived one morning, sent to me via Patrick French, and when I read it I was overwhelmed. So I got on a plane to India, and Roy met me in Delhi, very wary of me. I spent a weekend with her, brought the book back here, and it's been a fairytale story. (*Independent*, "CV: David Godwin")

Godwin's formulation of his reaction to the book conspicuously places him as the active agent in the narrative, while configuring Roy—and in particular, her novel—as the passive recipient of his affective response and subsequent valuation and promotion of her novel. Claire Squires (2007) makes similar observations on this particular configuration in *Marketing Literature*:

"Godwin's account reads with the simplicity of a fable. [. . .] Godwin formulates the ensuing journey of the novel into the world as a 'fairytale,' in which he could well be cast as the fairy godfather" (138). Godwin's account casts him as a benevolent benefactor, eliding the other consecrating forces that led to Roy's recognition in the global literary marketplace.

To that end, Colman Getty's publicity material further serves as a useful example of the other accusation lobbed at Roy after her Booker win: namely, that her novel was too autobiographical, thereby undermining her merit as a fiction writer. The description Colman Getty gives of Roy's publisher Flamingo suggests that Roy would be in better company with memoirists and other feminized forms of writing than with literary giants such as Rushdie. While Colman Getty recognizes that Flamingo publishes "literary fiction", the publisher is also listed as publishing "memoirs [and] travel writing [. . .] in Britain and the Commonwealth". Huggan notes the endemic need to authenticate Third World woman writers by pigeonholing them as memoirists or as writers who deal first and foremost with their lived experiences: "Even when [postcolonial] writers—particularly women writers—have produced other literary forms, especially novels, 'their attempts to universalise their experience [have tended all too often to be] reduced to the particularities of a lived life' (Hawthorne 1989: 262)" (Huggan 2001, 155). Requiring such a claim to authentic life experience on the part of the Third World woman writer calls into question her ability to comment on anything besides the particulars of domestic life. Accordingly, while Malcolm Bradbury, the chair of the 1981 Booker judging panel, placed Salman Rushdie's novel in the western canonical tradition, comparing *Midnight's Children* to *Tristam Shandy* and *The Tin Drum* (see Appendix I), Colman Getty's 1997 press releases remark upon the restricted scope of Roy's novel, accrediting her work with a specificity of location that the Booker categorically did not attribute to *Midnight's Children*: "*The God of Small Things* is set in a pickle factory in Southern India". Furthermore, Bradbury insists that Rushdie's work is very much his own, assigning him an originality that is conspicuously absent in the discussions of Roy's novel: "But

[*Midnight's Children*'s] fertility is its own; it generates a remarkable metaphorical and symbolic code" (Bradbury 1981, 9).

These assertions differ from those made about *The God of Small Things*: while the judging panel's chairperson Gillian Beer clearly praised the novel, her praise is not only significantly more tepid but also focuses on the aesthetic rather than political success of the novel. Beer claimed that Roy's novel told "a tale fundamental as well as local", only furthering the project of constructing Roy as a storyteller concerned with the domestic, as opposed to Rushdie's mastery of Indian history and politics in *Midnight's Children*. Roy, unlike Rushdie, is not interested in the workings of the nation but in the workings of a "diverse and exotic" family; her characters, unlike Rushdie's, are not metonymic forms of the postcolonial nation-state but are mere children trying to reclaim their youth and innocence. Rushdie and Roy are also credited with two very distinct relationships to history within their novels in a way that suggests a marketing scheme very much influenced by gendered norms. Bradbury asserts in his speech that Rushdie "does not use form to evade the historical world, but to penetrate it in the largest way" (1981, 9). Rushdie's novel is constructed as not only dealing with history but actively engaging with it and perhaps even changing the reader's perception through his literary and political insight. On the other hand, Beer's comment that Roy "funnels the history of South India through the eyes of seven-year-old twins" ("Arundhati Roy wins") reduces *The God of Small Things*'s interaction with history to an instrumentalization of fact, wherein historical events inform the narrative when it pleases the author. It is difficult to fail to notice the gendered language here. While Rushdie "penetrates" history, Roy can only "funnel" it to meet her own ends; while he is constructed as a legitimate commentator on matters regarding India because of his active literary engagement with the question of history, any political or social critique her novel could have posited is elided by the story about children that serves as the narrative backbone of the novel. In the Booker's marketing of Roy's novel, the Indian pickle, an easily recognized consumer good, and the familiar if dysfunctional domestic narrative serve to ground a prospective western reader in the well-known and well-trod path of the woman writer whose strength lies in her ability to explore familial ties, albeit in a slightly unfamiliar setting. Both Roy and Rushdie are caught up in this particular legitimating institution, but the gendered implications of the distinctly different discourses surrounding them bestow institutional favor on Rushdie while offering a highly qualified form of the same institutional favor to Roy.

Furthermore, Roy's physical beauty served the media and other consecrating forces as a marker of her aesthetic capabilities while subtly undermining and discrediting the political valences of her writing. Indeed, most layouts for articles regarding Roy's Booker win barely leave room for written content, thanks to the large photographs of Roy that dominate nearly every newspaper and magazine spread: *The Independent on Sunday, The Times Literary Supplement* and the *The Eastern Eye* all supplement their articles with disproportionately large photographs of Roy. As Elleke Boehmer (2005) remarks in *Stories of Women*, "the elements that were repeatedly accentuated in the critical promotion of Roy in the west [. . . included] her intensely feminine, ineffably photogenic, elfin beauty" (161). In many instances, press commentary on her beauty exoticised and infantilised Roy. In the same *Independent on Sunday* article, Peter Popham comments on the very youth and beauty meant to catch readers' eye at the newsstand: "In her white cotton tank-top and slacks, wearing no discernable make up, [Roy] looks more like a beautiful teenage runaway than a 37-year-old literary phenomenon" ("Under fire", *Independent on Sunday*). The connotations of exoticism, inexperience and immaturity underpinning Popham's description of Roy's physical appearance are echoed in much of the criticism directed at *Small Things*. David Robson's scathing critique of Roy's debut and its lack of literary merit relies on the same depiction of the author as a naïve and too-young newcomer to both fame and the literary market: "The novel is vitiated by the faults of inexperience—precious metaphors, twee sermonising, tricksy narrative—and does not merit the amount of huge hype which Arundhati Roy has generated" ("Poor list", *The Weekly Telegraph*). These two reviews—

both published in prominent national newspapers and therefore both heavily implicated in the field of cultural production—demonstrate the conflation of Roy's general youthful looks with her apparently "immature" prose. Casting Roy as a teenager and characterizing her writing as "twee" juvenilia reaclls Boehmer's depiction of the link often drawn between a woman writer's personal aesthetic and her prose style: "Noteworthy, though not always typical, is also the singling out of a slight, feminine body shape as somehow corresponding to stylistic whimsicality, or specifically, Indian stylistic whimsicality" (2005, 162). According to the media, Roy's linguistic inventiveness is a result of not only her feminine subject matter but also of her inherent femininity. It is worth mentioning that these various literary critics and journalists chastise Roy for the very style that the same circle of cultural legitimators praise in "Indian writing" in general. The same imaginative—and by extension, linguistic—fertility that Malcolm Bradbury ascribes in his speech to *Midnight's Children* becomes childish experimentation when applied to Roy. The political thrust of Rushdie's formal decisions that Bradbury identifies in his speech devolve into mere aesthetics that echo the aesthetic beauty of Roy's person.

These observations, however, can only aid in the articulation of the problem with the sexist discourse surrounding Third World women writers. Huggan, English and other scholars of prize culture and postcolonial reception are invaluable in rehashing the sexist, Orientalizing discourse that shapes the field of cultural production and in holding responsible the consecrating forces primarily responsible for such discourses. But they offer precious few alternatives to such hegemonic readings of these writers and their *oeuvre*. There remain scant discussions and analyses of Roy's response and reaction to these claims and her own position-takings regarding her Booker win and her writing. Perhaps to even attempt such an analysis would be to underestimate the ways in which power works in the field of cultural production and operates upon the postcolonial woman writer herself. But I will attempt to do so nonetheless, not because I do not believe in the force of the consecrating powers of prize culture and the media, but because to begin and end the construction of the Third World woman writer with the institutions that attempt to define her is to disregard her agency and the legacy of a strain of postcolonial theory that insists that alterity is never definitively foreclosed (see Bhabha 1997). Indeed, Huggan himself admits that the author can be—and often is—a player in the field of cultural production, but he all too quickly moves on to discuss the institutions that he believes overshadow anything an author could possibly have to say about his or her work: "The writer himself/herself is only one of several 'agents of legitimation'—others might include booksellers, publishers, reviewers and, not least, individual readers and 'valuing communities' (Frow 1995)" (Huggan 2001, 5). Indeed, the author rarely, if even, reappears in Huggan's work, a fact that raises the question as to whether or not Huggan truly believes that the author is even an "agent of legitimation", let alone a subject upon whom power works while he or she tries to wield that same power. James English takes an even more fatalistic view of the role of the writer in speaking for himself or herself or contesting the discursive construction of his or her authorial self. Like Huggan, he rarely mentions authorial or countercultural resistance to mainstream consecrating forces such as the Booker, and then to lament the ways in which such dissent only shores up the cultural capital of the very institution it is meant to decry:

> For as we might anticipate, these unofficial and antibureaucratic counter-institutions [including dissenting authors] soon become part of the established institutional landscape, targets in their own right of the latest generation of contemptuous independents or outsiders. And while prizes, along with the societies or academies that sponsor them, do occasionally wither away, they generally perpetuate themselves long after the moment of resistance or opposition from which they arose has passed. (English 2005, 52)

To be clear, the impetus to set out the powerful consecrating force of the Booker Prize serves as an important counter to the rhetoric of colonial apologism into which the prize's promoters often slide. In his contribution to *Booker 30: A Celebration of 30 Years of the Booker Prize for Fiction* Sir Michael Caine writes that

> [Managing Director of the Booker Company Jock Campbell] was deeply conscious of the wrongs and hurts of slavery and the complex relationships of the African and East Indian populations in Guyana. Jock Campbell, who was an active supporter of independence movements, soon transformed Booker from a typical colonial business into a thriving enterprise esteemed by employees, shareholders and customers. (Booker plc. 1998, 6)

Caine's vague language regarding the Booker company's investment in Guyanese plantations and the establishment of the prize as a way to "apologise" for the company's involvement in British colonialism has come under fire from various scholars and critics of prize culture, including Huggan, who writes: "The Booker might be seen, in any case [...] as remaining bound to an Anglocentric discourse of benevolent paternalism" (2001, 111). However, the *overstatement* of the power wielded by such institutions leads to a disregard for the moments of resistance that winning authors themselves have often enacted.[3] By resituating Roy as an active participant in her authorial self-making, I want to resist the hegemonic narrative I have outlined

---

3 In perhaps the most notorious case of writerly resistance to the Booker Prize, John Berger repudiated the Booker's colonial legacy in his 1972 acceptance speech, saying: "The prize is given by Booker, who are a firm who have extensive trading interest in the Caribbean for 130 years. The extreme poverty [of the Caribbean] is the direct consequence of the exploitation of companies like Booker. [. . .] And so I intend, as a revolutionary writer, to share this prize with people in and from the Caribbean, people who are involved in a struggle to resist such exploitation and eventually to expropriate companies like Booker. I am actually going to give half the prize to the London-based Black Panther Movement" (Berger 1972).

thus far, wherein power can only act upon the writer and cannot possibly be wielded as a tool of resistance or dissent by them. Sarah Brouillette offers insight as to why and how scholars should resituate the author in reception studies discourse while still acknowledging the other powerful forces at play. In *Postcolonial Writers and the Global Literary Marketplace*, she writes:

> Attention to authorial self-construction need not be based in naively conceived readings that treat texts as though they have clearly intending, expressive authors in full control of their own meanings [. . .] the goal of this scholarship is patently not to revive a thoroughly discredited biographical criticism in an effort to exhume a text's intending intelligence. Instead the author in the text is resolutely, purposefully *figural*, based in a set of significations that mediate between the writer in the world and the world of the work, so much so that interpretation often identifies aspects of an author's posturing that the writer in question would most likely discredit. (2007, 44–45)

Like Brouillette, my interest does not lie in resurrecting the author in the interest of a pseudo-biographical or pseudo-psychological literary analysis. Rather, a critical discussion of the author's orientation towards his or her own text and his or her role in the production and reception of a text is necessary to a thorough understanding of the production and reception of the text as a whole. Especially in the postcolonial context, constructing the author as a figure who is purely at the whims of various consecrating forces, or as Pierre Bourdieu claims, "a hierarchically organized series of fields" (1994, 6) reinscribes her into the very structures of power her writing is often resisting. Brouillette later contends that "when Barthes promotes the proliferation of interpretations brought about by 'the death of the author' he also effectively denies authors some ability to defend their works against certain readings they might find problematic, or even [. . .] against political factions' appropriation or denigration of their very identities as writers" (2007, 68–69). What happens when we resituate the author so that she can not only defend her own work, but also challenge our perceptions of the social and political work writing can do, and how do we do so? While Brouillette articulates the problem with suppressing any discussion of the author's role in the literary marketplace, she does not necessarily provide any clear framework for serious engagement with the question of authorial agency and self-representation. It is for this reason that I turn to Sara Ahmed's work on orientations as a method that allows me to talk about Roy's attitudes towards certain consecrating forces and her orientations towards her fame and her writing while still remaining attentive to the consecrating forces themselves.

To be clear, the writer *is* most certainly locked in "a hierarchically organized series of fields"; to claim that artistic license and the false sort of authorial agency that Brouillette (2014) critiques in *Literature and the Creative Economy* allows the writer to somehow cast these socio-political realities aside is simply false. Rather, attentiveness to orientations allows for a formulation of authorial position-takings wherein the author's attitude towards these consecrating forces can and does shape the reader's own attitudes. Ahmed's understanding of the political work a study of orientations can do allows for a reading of seemingly totalizing forces such as the Booker Prize as objects that are still imbricated in power but that the subject can orient himself or herself in relation to, as well as for for a reading of racialized and otherized bodies as objectified entities that others can orient themselves around. Thus, while I treat the media's objectification of Roy's person as a possible impediment to her authorial agency, I argue that her interviews and writing reorient the reader towards her text and her political activism and carve out a space for self-representation amidst the sexist and racialised rhetoric that defined various consecrating forces' attitudes towards Roy and her work.

To take up a dismissive attitude toward the Booker Prize could be read as artistically fashionable. As Brouillette argues, the creative economy framework purported by management theory that she critiques requires the writer to forego worldly accolades in favor of introspection and self-expression: "The creative realm is a space of pure introspection unbounded by necessity and expedience, and [. . .] though creative people may work within markets, serious [writers] will be motivated by internal directives to which profit is irrelevant" (2014, 5). According to this formulation of "producers of culture", for a Booker Prize winner to be anything but reticent about the prize would suggest that they have abandoned their writerly obligations under the constraints of the creative economy; self-expression and freedom of thought, the hallmarks of the cultural worker, preclude any serious engagement on the part of the winner with the socio-political implications of prize culture. And yet, various Booker Prize winners have taken to the spotlight to voice their opinions: from John Berger condemning the prize money for its colonial legacy to Salman Rushdie's infamous fit at losing the 1983 Booker to J. M. Coetzee, winning writers' attitudes towards the Booker challenge the notion that Brouillette critiques: orientations towards the Booker reveal a deep engagement with the prize's socio-political valences rather than a uniform disdain for worldly recognition for literary excellence. Roy's comments shortly after her Booker win suggest yet another orientation—one that differs from Berger's stance of rejection or Rushdie's expression of thwarted desire. David Lister's report of Roy's comments suggests that Roy's attitude towards the Booker Prize cannot be reduced to simple animosity: "Ms Roy [. . .] said: 'The Booker Prize is about my past not my future. I will only write another book if I have another book to write. I don't believe in professions" ("Roy wins the Booker", *The Independent*). Rather than turning her back on her prize winnings, Roy places it and the authorial legitimation it ostensibly provides her in her past such that the reader is left facing her and only her while the Booker Prize faces her back. This ordering of things reveals Roy's orientation towards the social capital that Berger rejects and Rushdie wishes for. Ahmed elaborates on the importance of such seemingly subtle orientations: "What is perceived depends on where we are located, which gives us a certain take on things [. . .] and in seeing it, in this way or that, it becomes an 'it,' which means I have already taken an orientation toward it" (2006, 27). Roy's orientation towards her Booker win—her back to it because she has placed it behind herself—is distinct from Berger's refusal of his prize, but her comment resists the accumulation of cultural capital such a prize would allow her. As previously noted, the prize, combined with Roy's substantial sales advance, caused the media to turn towards her with both admiration and sharp criticism. As A.S. Byatt noted during the roundtable interview that preceded the announcement of the winner in the 1997 Channel 4 screening of the Guildhall ceremony, such a prestigious win for a debut novel can place a different sort of pressure from the necessity of success: namely, the necessity of continued success (Channel 4, "Video"). But Roy resists such pressure by temporally distancing herself from it: the consecrating force that, in the eyes of the media and the prize judges, launched her foundling literary career, devolves into a mildly interesting anecdote that forms part of Roy's backstory, an anecdote that leaves very little impression upon the present or future.

There exists, of course, a cynical reading of Roy's comment that only reinforces the construction of the cultural worker that Brouillette decries. By eschewing any sort of "profession", Roy could be said to be drawing on the popular notion of the writer as a detached outsider who has divested themselves of any worldly—read: socio-political—concerns. The writer does not work but *creates,* thus placing herself outside the purview of the economic or the political. Furthermore, Roy's lack of interest in any "profession" could allow her to be classified as a representative of David Brook's "Bo-Bo" or bourgeois bohemian, her resistant engagement with the Booker Prize and her sales advance indicating a state of material comfort and "post-scarcity" (Brouillette 2014, 37) rather than any sort of principled political stance against the exploitation faced by workers under capitalism. But Ahmed's reading of gender and phenomenology opens up other possible interpretations of Roy's comments and her subsequent career as a political activist and writer: "By showing how phenomenology faces a certain direction, which depends on the relegation of other 'things' to the background, [Ahmed considers] how phenomenology may be gendered as a form of occupation" (Ahmed 2007, 27). Roy's relegation of the Booker Prize to the background of her career becomes necessary under the regime of sexist rhetoric that attached her Booker Prize win to her "feminine" writing, both in subject matter and in style, should she wish to be a political writer and activist.

While Rushdie's Booker win granted him the authority to comment upon India, Roy's win relegated her to the position of a "women's writer" who only had the authority to comment upon the domestic and the particular rather than the political and the global. Huggan argues that: "Rushdie has played an ambivalent role as a 'cosmopolitan celebrity,' combining the seemingly incompatible positions of the freewheeling oppositional intellectual and the slightly unwilling cultural spokesperson, dispensing wisdoms for the embattled mother country from the relative comfort of the diaspora" (2001, 70). That Rushdie should be given such authority while Roy is subtly but decisively stripped of it also has as much to do with geographic positionality as it does with gender. As a diasporic subject, Rushdie is closer to the western audience who would turn towards him for direction as to how to "read" India and the Orient writ large; or, as Ahmed attests,

> the reachability of the other, whether the Orient or other others, does not mean that they become 'like me/us.' Rather they are brought closer to home, but the action of 'bringing' is what sustains the difference: the subject, who is orientated toward the object, is the one who apparently does the work, whose agency is 'behind' the action. (2007, 117)

To ask Roy's western audience to orient themselves towards her, then, becomes difficult under the powerful apparatuses of patriarchy and ethnocentrism.

Roy's writing projects after *The God of Small Things* are attempts to reorient the reader toward her novel as much as they are political tracts. Roy's introduction to her book *Power Politics*, written four years after her Booker win, reorients the reader not only as to how to read *The God of Small Things*, but as to the phenomenological importance of the Booker Prize itself. The tongue-in-cheek title "The ladies have feelings so [. . .] shall we leave it to the experts?" already begins to reformulate the political work Roy believes her writing can do; the rhetorical question raises further questions about the role of affect in determining policy and political action and about our constant turning towards "experts" in the midst of political crisis. Her attitude towards writing again relegates her fame and her Booker win to the background and foregrounds her political concerns:

> To be a writer—a supposedly 'famous' writer—in a country where three hundred million people are illiterate is a dubious honor. To be a writer in a country that gave the world Mahatma Gandhi, that invented the concept of nonviolent resistance, and then, half a century later, followed that up with nuclear tests is a ferocious burden. (Roy 2001, 4)

Roy does not once mention once the anglophone Indian writers she is often associated with—Rushdie, Amitav Ghosh, or Amit Chaudhuri, amongst others—but invokes instead the socio-political realities that are recentred time and again in both her fiction and her non-fiction. The reader is reminded that India is not a fictive setting for fiction writers, but a geographic location where non-violent anticolonial resistance, the threat of nuclear development and the deleterious effects of globalization have taken and continue to take place. But Roy's most powerful evocation occurs when she troubles the term "writer-activist" that was often applied to her after her Booker win and when she showed no indication of writing another novel:

> I've been wondering why it should be that the person who wrote *The God of Small Things* is called a writer, and the person who wrote the political essays ["The End of

> Imagination", "The Greater Common Good", and "Power Politics"] is called an activist? True, *The God of Small Things* is a work of fiction, but it's no less political than any of my essays. (2001, 10–11)

Roy's questions echo and evoke Ahmed's questions about the gendered division of writerly and political work:

> Women have taken up spaces orientated toward writing. And yet, the woman writer remains just that: the woman writer, deviating from the somatic norm of 'the writer,' as such. So what happens when the woman philosopher [or writer] takes up her pen? What happens when the study is not reproduced as a masculine domain by the collective repetition of such moments of deviation? (2007, 61)

In order for Roy to write both fiction and nonfiction, she must be bifurcated into a "writer-activist", and the reader must reorient his- or herself towards Roy according to what he or she is reading. And yet, Roy is clear about her orientation when she is writing: "I take sides. I take a position. I have a point of view. What's worse, I make it clear that I think it's right and moral to take that position" (2001, 11). Roy does not claim to face two sides at once or to inhabit two sides at once, but rather, to be on one side and to write from that side. For her, there is no divide between the writer and the activist, nor is there a writer-activist, but rather, a writer who is politically active and actively political.

As Ahmed writes: "To commit may then also be a way of describing how it is that we become directed toward specific goals, aims, and aspirations through what we 'do' with our bodies" (2007, 17). While Roy's articulation of her commitments cannot completely undo the sexist discourse created by various consecrating forces such as the Booker Prize or the media, her writing and her actions have made her commitments clear and have laid to rest any hopes that she would, in Ahmed's words, be "pressed into line" (17), that she would follow the genealogical line left by Rushdie and other anglophone

Indian writers whose work has been consecrated by Western accolades and praise. Roy's refusal to fall into line behind other Indian writers begins soon after her Booker win and indicates her ongoing resistance to globalization and new imperialist forms:

> When I was in America I went on a couple of TV shows with Rushdie. And he said [. . .] 'The trouble with Arundhati is that she insists that India is an ordinary place'. Well, I ask, 'Why, the hell not?' It is my ordinary life. The difference between me and Rushdie begins there. ("The Goddess of Small Things", *The Times*)

The marker of difference she places upon herself separates her from Rushdie, but more importantly, it separates her from the project of making India legible to western audiences. Roy definitively orients herself towards India: India is her lived and literary experience, an experience that she writes about because she feels personally compelled to do so, not because she wishes to package and market it for a western audience. At every turn, Roy resists the very social pressures that Ahmed attests press us into line and draws and redraws her own line that we are left to follow.

Bibliography

Archive materials

Press releases

"Arundhati Roy wins the 1997 Booker prize for fiction." Box 1, folder 1. *Papers of Colman Getty, 10 Dec. 1996–20 Jan. 1998.* Booker Prize Archive, Oxford Brookes University Library, Oxford, United Kingdom.

"Bookies battle over 1997 Booker favourite." Box 1, folder 1. *Papers of Colman Getty, 10 Dec. 1996–20 Jan. 1998.* Booker Prize Archive, Oxford Brookes University Library, Oxford, United Kingdom.

"Specifications for advertisements for regional newspapers." Box 1, folder 1. *Papers of Booker plc, 5 Nov 1980–26 Feb 1982.* Booker Prize Archive, Oxford Brookes University Library, Oxford, United Kingdom.

Newspaper articles

"Booker could do better." 1997. *The Guardian*, Sept. 16. Box 4, folder 1. *Colman Getty press cuttings, 1 Nov 1996–26 Oct 1998.* Booker Prize Archive, Oxford Brookes University Library, Oxford, United Kingdom.

Chauhan, Kalpana. 1997. "Teaching the English Small Things about Writing." *Asian Age*, Oct. 18. Box 4, folder 1. *Colman Getty press cuttings, 1 Nov 1996–26 Oct 1998.* Booker Prize Archive, Oxford Brookes University Library, Oxford, United Kingdom.

Cowley, Jason. 1997. "The Goddess of Small Things." *The Times*, Oct. 18. Box 5, folder 1. *Colman Getty press cuttings, 1 Nov 1996–26 Oct 1998.* Booker Prize Archive, Oxford Brookes University Library, Oxford, United Kingdom.

"CV: David Godwin, Literary Agent." 1997. *The Independent,* Oct. 20. Box 5, folder 1. *Colman Getty press cuttings, 1 Nov 1996–26 Oct 1998.* Booker Prize Archive, Oxford Brookes University Library, Oxford, United Kingdom.

Lister, David.1997. "Roy wins the Booker." *The Independent,* Oct. 15. Box 5, folder 1. *Colman Getty press cuttings, 1 Nov 1996–26 Oct 1998.* Booker Prize Archive, Oxford Brookes University Library, Oxford, United Kingdom.

Lockerbie, Catherine. 1997. "Indian pips Scot for Booker Prize." *The Scotsman*, Oct. 15. Box 5, folder 1. *Colman Getty press cuttings, 1 Nov 1996–26 Oct 1998.* Booker Prize Archive, Oxford Brookes University Library, Oxford, United Kingdom.

"Missing the plot." 1997. *The Sunday Times,* Sept. 21. Box 4, folder 1. *Colman Getty press cuttings, 1 Nov 1996–26 Oct 1998.* Booker Prize Archive, Oxford Brookes University Library, Oxford, United Kingdom.

Popham, Peter. 1997. "Under fire, but India is in my blood." *The Independent on Sunday,* Sept. 21. Box 4, folder 1. *Colman Getty press cuttings, 1 Nov 1996–26 Oct 1998.* Booker Prize Archive, Oxford Brookes University Library, Oxford, United Kingdom.

Robson, David. 1997. "Poor list means readers will lose." *The Weekly Telegraph*, Sept. 1. 1997. Box 4, folder 1. *Colman Getty press cuttings, 1 Nov 1996–26 Oct 1998.* Booker Prize Archive, Oxford Brookes University Library, Oxford, United Kingdom.

"Tough at Top. 1997." *The Daily Telegraph,* Oct. 2. Box 4, folder 1. *Colman Getty press cuttings, 1 Nov 1996–26 Oct 1998.* Booker Prize Archive, Oxford Brookes University Library, Oxford, United Kingdom.

Wareing, William. 1998. "Currying favour on Booker list." *Gloucestershire Echo*, Sept. 30. Box 4, folder 1. *Colman Getty press cuttings, 1 Nov 1996–26 Oct 1998.* Booker Prize Archive, Oxford Brookes University Library, Oxford, United Kingdom.

Meeting Minutes

"Booker Prize UK Management Committee Minutes of Meeting 10 December 1996." Box 2, file 1. *Papers of Martyn Goff, 6 Nov. 1996–12 Nov. 1997.* Booker Prize Archive, Oxford Brookes University Library, Oxford, United Kingdom.

Transcripts

British Broadcasting Corporation. "Camera script for the Booker McConnell Prize." Box 1, folder 1. *Papers of Booker plc, 5 Nov 1980–26 Feb 1982*. Booker Prize Archive, Oxford Brookes University Library, Oxford, United Kingdom.

Speeches

Bradbury, Malcolm. 1981. "The Booker Prize speech (20 October, 1981)." Box 1, folder 1. *Papers of the Booker Trust, 20 Oct. 1981*. Booker Prize Archive, Oxford Brookes University Library, Oxford, United Kingdom.

Letters

Ken Follett. 1997. "Letter to Martyn Goff, 29 October 1997." Box 2, file 1. *Papers of Martyn Goff, 6 Nov. 1996–12 Nov. 1997.* Booker Prize Archive, Oxford Brookes University Library, Oxford, United Kingdom.

Audiovisual material

Channel 4. 1997. "Video of Channel 4's coverage of the award ceremony, 1997, presented by Melvyn Bragg and Muriel Gray." Box 7, file 1. *Booker plc and Colman Getty audio visual material, 1997.* Booker Prize Archive, Oxford Brookes University Library, Oxford, United Kingdom.

Secondary sources

Ahmed, Sara. *Queer Phenomenology: Orientations, Objects, Others.* Durham, NC: Duke University Press, 2006.

Boehmer, Elleke. 2005. *Stories of Women: Gender and Narrative in the Postcolonial Nation*. Manchester: Manchester University Press.

Booker plc. 1998. *Booker 30: A Celebration of 30 Years of the Booker Prize for Fiction.* London: Booker plc.

Bourdieu, Pierre, and Johnson, Randal. 1993. *The Field of Cultural Production: Essays on Art and Literature.* New York: Columbia University Press.

Brouillette, Sarah. 2007. *Postcolonial Writers in the Global Literary Marketplace*. Basingstoke: Palgrave Macmillan. Ebook Library. Web. February 20, 2016.

—. 2014. *Literature and the Creative Economy.* Stanford, CA: Stanford University Press.

English, James. 2005. *The Economy of Prestige: Prizes, Awards, and the Circulation of Cultural Value*. Cambridge, MA: Harvard University Press.

Huggan, Graham. 2001. *The Postcolonial Exotic: Marketing the Margins*. London: Routledge.

Narayan, Uma. 1997. *Dislocating Cultures: Identities, Traditions, and Third-World Feminism.* New York: Routledge.

Roy, Arundhati. 1998. *The End of Imagination*. Kottayam: D.C. Books.

—. 2001. *Power Politics.* Cambridge, MA: South End Press.

Squires, Claire. 2007. *Marketing Literature: The Making of Contemporary Writing in Britain*. Basingstoke: Palgrave Macmillan.

Thompson, John B. 2010. *Merchants of Culture: The Publishing Business in the Twenty-First Century*. Cambridge: Polity.

Appendix I

Transcript of Professor Malcolm Bradbury's Booker Prize Speech, October 20, 1981, page 9 of 12

~~*novel*~~ *work of abstract comic joy,* ~~*[ambition?]*~~ *and tragic pain, a work*

...The other is Salman Rushdie's Midnight's Children, a / ~~book~~ of extraordinary ambition and abundance. It is another / work where the historical world is powerful but capable of / being seen and grasped only through radical distortion of / supposed fact, though the intrusion of the satirical meta- / phorical imagination. This makes it a book of amazing / imaginative fertility as well of political courage, a tale of the largest intentions, dealing with the emergence into / Independence of India and Pakistan but taking this as psychic as well as political fact. You can find behind it an extra- / ordinary fictional lineage—Tristram Shandy, The Tin Drum / and Thoman Pynchon's V. all seem consciously present behind / it. But its fertility is its own, it generates a remarkable / metaphorical and symbolic code, satirically bitter and biting, / and like Thomas's work it does not use form to evade the / historical world, but to penetrate it in the largest way. //...

Key:
"/" indicates an original line break.
"//" indicates the end of the paragraph.
Italic lettering indicates a handwritten section.

The Caine Prize for "African Writing": A Continental Reading and Rewarding

Sana Goyal

> Then Edward spoke. The writing was certainly ambitious but the story itself begged the question "So what?" There was something terribly passé about it [witchcraft and Pentecostalism] when one considered all the other things happening in Zimbabwe under the horrible Mugabe.
> [...]
> Edward chewed at his pipe thoughtfully before he said that homosexual stories of this sort weren't reflective of Africa, really.
> "Which Africa?" Ujunwa blurted out.
> [...]
> "This may indeed be the year 2000, but how African is it for a person to tell her family that she is homosexual?" Edward asked.
> [...]
> That evening, the Tanzanian read an excerpt of his story about the killings in the Congo, from the point of view of a militiaman, a man full of prurient violence. Edward said it would be the lead story in the *Oratory,* that it was urgent and relevant, that it brought news. (Adichie 2009b 171–72; 173; 175–76)

Chimamanda Ngozi Adichie's short story titled "Jumping Monkey Hill", first published in *Granta* in 2006, and later collected in *The Thing Around Your Neck* (Adichie 2009b), tells the tale of a fictionalised African Writers' Workshop held at the eponymous, secluded resort, located on the edges of Cape Town, South Africa. "Ujunwa found it odd that the African Writers' Workshop was held here, at Jumping Monkey Hill", writes Adichie. "The name itself was incongruous, and the resort had the complacence of the well-fed about it, the kind of place where she imagined affluent foreign tourists would dart around taking pictures" (2009b, 154). Adichie attended the first-ever, and Ford Foundation-financed, 2003 Caine Prize African Writers' Workshop held at Monkey Valley Resort in Noordhoek, suburban Cape Town after her short story "You in America" was shortlisted the preceding year. Here, she produced the story "Lagos, Lagos", which was later revised and retitled as the title story of *The Thing Around Your Neck*. In another act of retitling, the Caine Prize for African Writing became the Lipton African Writers' Prize in "Jumping Monkey Hill". This veiling aside, it is worth noting as Nathan Suhr-Sytsma makes clear in his reading, that "Jumping Monkey Hill" is "a work of fiction about the meaning of fiction, not just a condensed *roman à clef*" (2018, 1102).

Writing in 2013, the-then Caine Prize for African Writing administrator Lizzy Attree declared that "the workshops themselves are something of which the Caine Prize is particularly proud", and defends their choices of location by saying this: "it is possible that the workshops could move from their previously rural, isolated locations to more urban venues, but the benefits of isolation for writing are not to be dismissed too quickly" (Attree 2013, 38). Championing them as catalysts for building continent-based literary networks and connections, Attree adds that "involving twelve writers each year, the workshops have facilitated contact between authors from different countries, creating a self-sustained community, as participants stay in contact, share, and critique one another's work" (39).[1] Since their inception in 2003, the Caine Prize writing workshops have travelled to almost a dozen African countries, and in 2018 took place in Gisenyi, Rwanda. Thus, the Caine Prize for African Writing "can be said to be

1 The Prize website reveals that participants include shortlisted authors and "other writers who have come to our attention through the selection process", who then contribute their respective short stories to the annual Caine Prize anthology, published together with that year's shortlisted stories, and that these workshopped stories are automatically entered for the following year's Prize.

helping to produce as well as evaluate contemporary African writing", Attree concludes (39). It is not so much the Prize's production of contemporary African writing, but its evaluations, that critics tend to take issue with, and this will be tackled in due course.

Meanwhile, to return to the textual location of "Jumping Monkey Hill", Adichie's writer-characters—chosen and curated by the British Council, and commercially catalysed by the Chamberlain Arts Foundation—are expected to produce a story for possible publication in the *Oratory*, and this under the mentorship of their workshop moderator Edward Campbell. In stark contradiction to his feedback on the participants' stories quoted above, Edward clarifies his position as not "an Oxford-trained Africanist, but as one who [is] keen on the real Africa and not the imposing of Western ideas on African venues" (Adichie 2009b, 174). As Adichie's protagonist, Ujunwa, coupled with her writer colleagues, experiences the pressures of "the patronage that sometimes frames this [creative-writing workshop] process of literary production and canonisation" ("'Which Africa?' Ujunwa blurted out"), these pressures leave the layers of the meta-fictional text, and leak into larger discussions of literary production, canonisation, distribution, and consumption of African literature (Kiguru 2016a, 206; Adichie 2009b, 173). For Doseline Kiguru, "Jumping Monkey Hill" comments on "the act of inclusion and exclusion at the point of production as well as consumption of literature", and also explores the "nature of the canon formation process" (2016a, 208) through its particular focus on the creative writing workshop. Similarly, Suhr-Sytsma suggests that Adichie "attempts to reclaim the criteria of literary judgment from London literary gatekeepers—and to suggest the masculinist bias of representations of Africa" (2018, 1100). Whereas Attree considers the creative-writing workshops as supporting mechanisms for African literary production, Kiguru and Suhr-Sytsma showcase how this contribution is skewed, and not as straightforward as we are often led to believe.

Indeed, Edward's evaluation of the workshop stories—an embodiment of western-funded forces—is emblematic of the power dynamics, privileged positionality, and point of view at play: for him, Mugabe is manifestly a metonym for Zimbabwe, and Congo is construed merely as a container of violence. Furthermore, his feedback foregoes the personal in favour of the political: the story of the Senegalese writer grieving at the death of her lesbian lover is as *un*-"African" as the Tanzanian's is urgently, and news-worthily, "African". The critic Eve Eisenberg (2013) makes the case that, at its core, "[this] is a conversation [. . .] not only about good and bad writers, but about good and bad representers of Africa" (14). Edward, and by extension western publishing elites, expect the Zimbabwean "to produce a text that clearly and mimetically represents atrocity", she adds, and moreover, "to represent the atrocities specifically associated with her national origins, an expectation emphasized by Adichie's choice of identifying all the writers (except for Ujunwa) solely by their nationalities [the Zimbabwean, the Tanzanian, the Ugandan, and so on]" (15). Edward's reductionist national representations are further linked to his keenness on "the real Africa", and to continental generalisations. Suhr-Sytsma argues that Adichie's choice "may index the tendency to identify African writers with countries of origin, a tendency that can verge on patronizing tokenism" (2018, 1102). Indeed, the manner in which the Prize frames its shortlisted and winning writers through a national lens dismisses, and does a disservice to their diasporic (and also intra-continental) connections and affiliations, real or textual.

Adichie's own stance, specifically on the Caine Prize for African Writing, is no secret, and is worth a short digression here. In a 2013 *Salon* interview with Aaron Bady, who asks her opinion on the overwhelming number of Nigerians shortlisted for that year's prize (four of five), she says:

> Elnathan was one of my boys in my workshop. But what's all this over-privileging of the Caine Prize, anyway? I don't want to talk about the Caine Prize, really. I suppose it's a good thing, but for me it's not the arbiter of the best fiction in Africa. It's never been. I know that Chinelo is on the short list,

> too. But I haven't even read the stories—I'm just not very interested. I don't go the Caine Prize to look for the best in African fiction. [. . .] I go to my mailbox. (Adichie 2013, n.p.)

Following this, some of the shortlisted authors such as Abubakar A. Ibrahim, immediately took to Twitter angrily, accusing her of arrogance, and calling her out on her comments. On a related note: it is significant that Adichie has never won the Caine Prize for African Writing; she was shortlisted for "You in America" in 2002, the year preceding her workshop participation. While she has won the [then] Orange Broadband Prize for Fiction, and the prestigious MacArthur Foundation grant, both of which have propelled her to international success, it is interesting that she has done so by circumventing the Caine Prize for African Writing, often considered a rite of passage for African writers. In other words, as Suhr-Systsma says, "she fashioned this career without winning the Caine Prize" (2018, 1101). Do we read Adichie's scathing critiques of the prize as rooted in personal resentment or as reflective of bigger, bolder questions? Eisenberg certainly leans towards the latter opinion, as does Suhr-Sytsma (2018), and finds Adichie's meta-fictional short story as reflective of the actual African literary landscape and of the questions raised in Adichie's own fiction (hence Eisenberg's title: "'Real Africa'/'Which Africa?'"). Similarly, the central question posed by Taiye Selasi's (2015) piece in *The Guardian* is this: "Why must writers from Africa always bear the burden of representing their continent?" She then proceeds to point out the "prioritisation of perceived cultural allegiance over creative output" (n.p.). The "most scathing critique of the African writer is not that she is insufficiently talented, but that she is insufficiently African", Selasi writes. (n.p.). And lo and behold, as Adichie's short meta-fiction stages, this holds as true for African writer-characters as for their real-life counterparts. What is evident from Edward's crude comments is that some types of stories—those suffused with cultural and continental stereotypes—are relevant to, and reflective of, Africa *really*, while others fall short of such "African-ness", and are therefore not fit to be funded, or foregrounded on the global literary stage. Inspired by Adichie's meta-fictional critique, what Suhr-Sytsma identifies as her "strategic fiction" (2018, 1109), the following section of this chapter points to the plethora of writers who seek to avoid storytelling that is seen as stereotypically and expectedly "African".

Stereotypes and Ways of Storytelling

Chimamanda Ngozi Adichie's 2009 viral TEDx talk, "The Danger of a Single Story", signals how deeply stereotypes are embedded into our ways of storytelling: "Show a people as one thing, as only one thing, over and over again, and that is what they become", she says (Adichie 2009a, 9:25). Stereotypes, for Adichie, are solidified through relentless repetition and under-representation: "The single story creates stereotypes, and the problem with stereotypes is not that they are untrue, but that they are incomplete. They make one story become the only story" (12:56). "Of course, Africa is a continent full of catastrophes", but to cash in on such catastrophes, as Edward does, is to be complicit in the creation of a selective, "single story" that conveniently falsifies, filters, and falls short of, the full picture (13:24). Therein lie the "danger" and shortcomings of certain kinds of storytelling.

Binyavanga Wainaina's groundbreaking *Granta* essay, "How to Write About Africa", uses his particular brand of powerful and thought-provoking satire to subvert the storehouse of sweeping stereotypes used by journalists and novelists when writing about the African continent at-large:

> In your text, treat Africa as if it were one country. [. . .] Don't get bogged down with precise descriptions. Africa is big: fifty-four countries, 900 million people who are too busy starving and dying and warring and emigrating to read your book [. . .] so keep your descriptions romantic and evocative and unparticular.
> [. . .]

> Africa is to be pitied, worshipped or dominated. Whichever angle you take, be sure to leave the strong impression that without your intervention and your important book, Africa is doomed.
> [. . .]
> Remember, any work you submit in which people look filthy and miserable will be referred to as the 'real Africa,' and you want that on your dust jacket. Do not feel queasy about this: you are trying to help them to get aid from the West. (Wainaina 2005, n.p.)

"Africa, Wainaina reminds the would-be scribe, is a homogenous space in crisis", writes Madhu Krishnan (2014, 1); if for Adichie stereotypes are "incomplete" half-truths, Wainaina has a tendency to exaggerate them—and extend each stereotype. Ikhide Ikheloa, a literary journalist and blogger who has routinely followed, documented, and critiqued the Caine Prize for African Writing, restored the implied "not" in *Wainaina*'s title when composing his own his blog-post about the 2011 shortlist, "How Not to Write About Africa" (2011, n.p.).

Taiye Selasi (2015) offers a variant, if equally valid, interpretation of Wainaina's title and text, saying that: "Wainaina is telling us not how to write about Africa, but how to invent it" (7). She ignores the invisible "Not" in the title; instead, she suggests that Wainaina is addressing the likes of the Oxford-trained Africanist Edward, who "invent" "this singular Africa": "[it] doesn't exist: it must be imagined and insisted upon", she adds (7). Commentators on Wainaina's essay agree that the actual targets of his satire are those readers of "Africa" with a perilous predilection for continental readings, renditions, and reductions.

While Adichie and Wainaina attempt to smash stereotypes around "Africa", with their misrepresentations and exaggerations, Namwali Serpell and Taiye Selasi wrestle with the label "African literature", and its expectations and commercialisations. In an interview for *Africa in Words*, Lilly Kroll asks the 2015 Caine Prize shortlisted Serpell (who went on to win the award) if she could borrow a question from the author's own Twitter timeline: "How can we change the conversation about 'African' writing?" And "is it still possible to generate interesting debate around the age-old question, 'What is African literature' or should we be talking about something else entirely?" (Serpell 2015, n.p.), Kroll asks. Serpell suggests a starting-point:

> Yes, there are other questions that would generate different and more vibrant conversations. "What is African literature?" is essentially unanswerable and tends to devolve into rigid binaries (this is African literature v. this isn't) or sweeping vaguenesses (everything is African literature; there is no such thing as African literature). I find questions about the relationship between, say, form and politics, or genre and ethics much more interesting. Perhaps tweaking the question slightly to "What does African literature *do*?" would be a start. (n.p.)

This "tweaking" can be juxtaposed with Taiye Selasi's (2013) lecture, "African Literature Doesn't Exist", where she suggests that readers and writers wipe the slate clean of stereotypes, and start from scratch. Reflecting on this lecture later, she said:

> Selasi: I find that, as a rhetorical strategy, once you've *emptied* something you've given yourself the space to refill it, to reflect on what *should* go inside. In saying "African Literature Doesn't Exist" I was simply trying to empty the container, to ask then: now that it's empty, what should we put inside? If we didn't know what African literature was, if it did not exist *a priori*, what would we put in that container? What do we want it to be? (Bady and Selasi 2015, 156)[2]

---

2 In "From That Stranded Place" (2015), an edited transcript of a conversation between Taiye Selasi and Aaron Bady at the University of

"Why do we call [. . .] an Achebe novel a Nigerian one, worse, an African one?" asks Selasi in her aforementioned lecture. "Where does that instinct come from?" (Selasi 2013, 2). For a continent that has long been contained and characterised by its cartographical boundaries, a monolithic block on the map of the world, the commercial category "African literature" "is an empty designation", says Selasi—and one dangerously heavy with premeditations, preconceived notions, and prescriptions (2013, 1). As a consequence, three questions resolutely remain at the core of this category, she finds: "Who is an African writer, what should she write, and for whom is she writing?" (Selasi 2015, n.p.).

Of course, there are no conclusive answers to these questions, but the questions themselves remain valid. Perhaps the most desirable and determined feature of Serpell's and Selasi's approaches is the aspirational quality of their formulations of African literature: "What does African literature *do*?" "What do we *want* it to be?" As it turns out, these rhetorical questions are not redundant: while Selasi's strategy can be situated in a contemporary discursive space, these seemingly timely debates can be traced back over half a century. It was in the aftermath of the first African Writers Conference, "A Conference of African Writers of English Expression" (June 1, 1962), that Chinua Achebe declared that those attempting to define "African literature" had been similarly defeated:

> There was [one] thing that we tried to do and failed—and that was to define 'African literature' satisfactorily. Was it literature produced in Africa or about Africa? Could African literature be on any subject, or must it have an African theme? Should it embrace the whole continent, or south of the Sahara, or just black Africa? (Quoted in Selasi 2013, 4)

Historically, "African literature" has resisted definition—geographically, thematically, linguistically, artistically—and

---

Texas Symposium for African Writers, December 2014, Selasi cites and clarifies her 2013 lecture, "African Literature Doesn't Exist".

necessarily so. But a continental reading (and writing) impulse remains intrinsic to the commercial aspects of literary production, as does the market's and academy's capacity to canonise texts and circulate them conveniently. Going forward, the challenge lies not just in allowing for a container that is more accommodating, less *containing*, but also in critiquing those who create the container as it currently exists: the likes of Edward Campbell, western publishing elites, and other such literary gatekeepers. Yvonne Adhiambo Owuor's (2015) TEDxEuston talk "Words for Worlds" provides a bridge into the future gestured at by Selasi:

> Word of the season: Ebola.
> The other day, one of my friends was laughing over the alacrity with which the world surrendered the Rising Africa narrative to Ebola Africa.
> [. . .]
> Yet, the Ebola pandemic—this really sorrowful crucible—offers *our Africa* a profound gift. It commands us to face the force of Africa's crisis of meaning. It demands that we ask again—
> What does Africa mean for Africa? Before we bother with what Africa means for the world. (n.p.; emphasis in original)

Owuor stages Chimamanda Adichie's "single story" of stereotypes—"Ebola Africa", and in the process jumps onto the Binyavanga Wainaina-bandwagon and subverts it—"the Ebola pandemic [. . .] offers a profound gift"; like Serpell and Selasi, she poses open-ended questions—"What does Africa mean for Africa?" and "Where do we go from here?" I wish to use this as a starting-point to interrogate the Caine Prize for African Writing—its history and hints of colonial legacy; its identity and inner workings; its powers of canonicity, the controversies and critiques; and finally, its future.

This chapter will pursue Kiguru's (2016b) idea that the positions of The Caine Prize for African Writing and [The Commonwealth Writers' Prize] in the global literary marketplace "has greatly contributed to the canonisation of contemporary African literature and in this way made a substantial contribution to sustaining and influencing particular cultural images, both locally and globally" (2016b, 162). Here, Suh-Sytsma is in agreement. The Caine Prize for African Writing has "made itself an inescapable part of the machinery for selecting and publicizing early career writers of anglophone African fiction"; gained increased importance "with the discontinuation of other major literary awards for African writers", including the NOMA and the Commonwealth Writers' Prize; and "exerts an outsized influence on discussions about an emerging canon of twenty-first century African literature", he writes (2018, 1094).

It will also deconstruct the name of the Caine Prize for *African Writing* (my emphasis). Aaron Bady has observed that although prizes such as the Booker and the Commonwealth Writers' Prize afford African writers international attention, what the Caine Prize for African Writing has in common with them is the usage of "the continental adjective, without any serious effort at a continental scope" (2011, n.p.). This chapter does quite the opposite; it deliberately refrains from using the shorthand, and dissects the identity of the prize through its nomenclature. Is the Caine Prize for African Writing reflective of 54 countries? A quick survey of its 20-year history reveals that a handful of countries have been privileged (Nigeria, South Africa, Kenya, Zimbabwe, Uganda)—in terms of entries, shortlists, winners—if only inadvertently. Due to this, social media critics have quipped that it should be renamed as the "Caine Prize for Nigerian Writing" or the "Caine Prize for Diasporic Writing". It also maps the structure, successes and shortcomings of the prize thus far, culminating in some suggestions that attempt to articulate the *after*, taking its cues from Owuor's 2015 question "Where do we go from here?" and Aaron Bady's question: "If 'African literature' is having a renaissance, does it need a prize for emerging writers? What happens to the Caine Prize after African literature has emerged?" (Bady 2016, para. 19). In this, the 20th year anniversary of the Caine Prize for African Writing, it questions how we can look back and reflect on what the Prize has achieved and accomplished for African writers and African writing thus far, whilst simultaneously holding it accountable and looking to the future.

The Inception and Inner Workings of The Caine Prize for African Writing

The Caine Prize for African Writing, sometimes dubbed "The African Booker", is "not an African prize, but British, funded mainly by British and some US and African charities" (Pucherová 2012, 13). Named after the late Sir Michael Caine (former Chairman of Booker plc., and Chairman of the Booker Prize management committee for a quarter of a century), it was founded "to encourage the growing recognition of the worth of African writing in English, its richness and diversity, by bringing it to a wider audience" (*caineprize.com*). But as "a British prize for African writing", adds Dobrota Pucherová, "the Caine is unavoidably imbricated in the troubled history of postcolonial literatures in English, of which the primary site of evaluation and legitimation has been the west" (2013, 13). In an interview with Nick Mulgrew, its Director Lizzy Attree defends the Caine Prize for African Writing against charges such as not being "completely of Africa in the sense that it's foreign-run". "Prizes are often 'external' bodies; [they] are additional, if you like, but their ability to champion particular authors and texts can feed back into local industry and inform consumers' decisions about which books to buy and read" (Attree 2015, n.p.).

To better understand the importance and implications of the Caine Prize for African Writing for the present-day postcolonial literary industry, it is imperative to first position it within its larger legacy, and London-based location. It can be argued that the Prize is politically and postcolonially problematic; if its home is Britain, and its financial ancestor the Booker,[3] how does this frame the personality of the prize? Furthermore, how can the post-imperial metropolis be positioned and perceived in what Sarah Brouillette (2007) terms the "global literary marketplace" as the host city, and hegemonic source

3 For the full list of current donors and sponsors see the prize website.

of "charity",[4] for the Caine Prize for African Writing, as well as other prizes (such as the Commonwealth Writers' Prize), when the Prize celebrates emerging writers from a continent, several of whose countries were previously part of the British Empire?

What Cynthia Ozick (2012) writes in *The New York Times* of the [then] Baileys Prize for Women's Fiction [formerly the Orange Prize] can be applied to the origins of the Caine Prize for African Writing: "The Orange Prize, then, was not born into an innocent republic of letters" (para. 7). Ozick is of course, referring to the dearth or complete non-existence of female authors on prize lists, but one can appropriate her idea of "innocence" to trace the birth—scandalous at best, questionable at worst—of the case in point, and, additionally, to question institutions which are propelled by and have a penchant for prizing literatures, books, and authors based on where they are born.

As the "African Booker", the Caine Prize for African Writing "has not only inherited the positive but also the negative capital of the Booker", writes Doseline Kiguru. It "not only benefit[s] from the symbolic capital of the Booker but from the financial support from both the Booker and the Commonwealth foundations, too" (2016b, 168). She adds that what most taints the Booker is its corporate connection to a long history of economic and colonial oppression in the Caribbean Islands. Richard Todd (1996), Graham Huggan (1997), James F. English (2005) and Sandra Ponzanesi (2014) have all addressed evils of the Booker's colonial and historical connections in some capacity. Huggan, for example, describes the Booker McConnell firm which was the main funding body for the [Booker] Prize as "a leading multinational agribusiness conglomerate [. . .] initially formed in 1834 to provide distributional services on the sugar-estates of Demerara (now Guyana). [It] achieved rapid prosperity under a harsh colonial regime" (2001, 106–07). It is no surprise, then, that the Caine Prize for African Writing's primary and most powerful point of critique comes, similarly, from within its own birthplace and being.

4 "The Caine Prize for African Writing is a registered charity whose aim is to bring African writing to a wider audience using our annual literary award." (*caineprize.com*)

Samantha Pinto (2013) notes that:

> African writers and postcolonial critics have received the prize both as a practical reward to be pursued in the face of minimal continental support for African writing, and a double-edged gift from the "bloody colonizers" [Wainaina 2011, 188] [. . .], one given in exchange for compromised readings of African struggle and trauma. (142)

In his famous Twitter "Caineversation", Wainaina, himself a Caine-recipient, tweets of this gift as: "certificate of England" (@BinyavangaW Oct 13, 2014). There is a sense in which Owuor's notion of a "profound gift" (quoted earlier) and Pinto's point of view on this "double-edged gift" break down the binary that, according to gift theorist Mark Osteen (2002), forms the backbone of interpretations of gift practices:

> In one camp are those adhering to what Aafke Komte dubs the "moral cement" approach. These theorists emphasize the unifying effects of gift giving, gifts' capacity to forge or solidify social bonds. In the other camp are those who stress the ways gifts can be used to acquire and exercise power; these writers emphasise inequality and social disintegration. (17)

When one considers the Caine Prize for African Writing as a (post) colonial gift, it is clear that the two approaches—of solidifying social bonds and social disintegration—are not diametrically opposed. What is disguised as Komte's "moral cement approach" is layered with acts of neocolonial power acquisition and asymmetry.

Funding aside, the Prize's rules of entrance and eligibility have also engendered critique; eligibility, after all, is based on exclusivity—and rules are characteristically exclusionary. Lizzy Attree clarifies the rules thus:

> The content of the stories is *de facto* African, as the prize is for African Writing and the authors are limited to those "born in Africa, a national of an African country, or whose parents are African, [and those] whose work has reflected an African sensibility". As I stated earlier, different writers have their own sense of what "Africanness" is and how to write about Africa, or indeed any other subject they choose. (2013, 39)

The Prize stipulates a set of rules, as all prizes do, but rarely have rules been called into question as routinely, and a prize been reprimanded as relentlessly, as the Caine Prize for African Writing. Of course, the Booker and the Nobel are surrounded with their own "scandals" (English 2008). Generally, readers and critics have doubted the "Africannness" of shortlisted authors and winners, and over the years, displayed serious displeasure at the nomination of diasporic writers. Having said this, ironically enough, there have been instances where African authors have not been eligible for African literary prizes. More problematically, winning stories have been contested on grounds of their being "too African" or "not African enough". I am interested in Attree's use of the phrase "*de facto* African", and of the word "limited" and will return to them below. Krishnan, too, notices this usage: "more damningly, the prize *restricts* itself to works published in English, or available (in published format) in English translation, a pragmatic decision with far-reaching and often troubling implications for the shaping of African writing on a world stage" (2014, 135; my emphasis). Bushra al-Fadil's 2017 winning short story "The Story of the Girl Whose Birds Flew Away", translated from the Arabic by Max Shmookler, was the first time a story in translation was awarded in the Prize's history. Pucherová, meanwhile, reads the acceptance of Internet publications as "reflecting the significance of electronic publishing for a continent with poor publishing infrastructure" (2012, 14). Writing in 2013, Attree announced that, "since February 2, 2012, this unnecessarily limiting category ["African sensibility"] was eliminated" (39), but this has done little to lend total transparency to the Prize's expectations and criteria for evaluation. Krishnan writes of this tension between the need for African literature to be somehow identifiably "African" and the simultaneous impossibility of just that:

> Like the continent itself, the idea of 'an African sensibility' both alludes to a sense of closure while simultaneously defying any single statement of being or unified interpretation. It is this quality of the impossible, the multiple and the evershifting which the ambiguous wording captures, existing under erasure to open up the possibility of becoming otherwise. (2014, 146)

This struggle over the guidelines is symptomatic of broader questions regarding the reading and understanding of the African literature and its identity, she finds—it is simultaneously too specific so as to be indefinable. Before tackling head-on the Prize's Pandora's box of controversies and critiques, the next section showcases its contributions.

The Importance and Implications of The Caine Prize for African Writing

> It's hard to tell the story of contemporary African literature without talking about the Caine Prize for African Writing. It's the biggest and most prominent prize for African Literature—or at least the best publicized—and in the 17 years of its existence, what it means to say "African Literature" has changed quite dramatically, a transformation the Caine Prize has in part reflected, and in part helped to produce. (Bady 2016, para. 1)

A quick overview of academics' standpoints on the Caine Prize for African Writing (Pucherová [2012]; Pinto [2013]; Krishnan [2014]; Kiguru [2016a and 2016b]; Edwin [2016]) reveals that their arguments, while critical, almost always conclude in a celebration of the validation and visibility the Prize affords. For example: Kiguru questions the authors' "political and economic dependency" on the west, but eventually promotes James F English's notion of "positive patronage", which "allows the growth of literature from the less known areas" (2016b, 168; 171). "It is important for African writers to be able to seize these opportunities provided by international literary award institutions and, despite the patronage, tell their stories", she adds, before concluding (albeit with certain caveats): "hopefully, after getting the required [western] legitimation, these writers can then move on to write about the continent without the shadow of the patronizing empire or of the international prize" (2016b, 171). Indeed, Caine winners such as Binyavanga Wainaina (for "Discovering Home" 2002) and Namwali Serpell (with "The Sack" 2015) have embraced this "positive patronage". Wainaina used his Prize winnings to found and fund *Kwani?*, a Kenyan literary journal, which published Yvonne Adhiambo Owuor, whose "Weight of Whispers" won her the Prize in 2003. While Wainaina concentrated his resources into an instrument for local, East African literary publication, Serpell divided hers. In what she referred to as her "long over-due act of mutiny" (quoted in Primorac 2015, n.p.), the first Zambian recipient of the Prize cut up her £10,000 pie, and shared a slice with each of her fellow shortlisted writers:

> Prizes are often competitions, but this particular prize brings the shortlisted writers together for a week before the ceremony. [. . .] Writing to me has never seemed like a competitive sport. The more I thought about it, I figured the reason the prize is structured this way is because of the money. [. . .] I thought instead of attacking the prize, which is a wonderful thing, I'll go for the source of its structure, which, for me, seemed to be the money. (Doran and Serpell, 2015, n.p.)

Wainaina and Serpell answered the call of English's "positive patronage" in exceptional ways, but the question remains: Why must western legitimation still be a prerequisite for global success?

Similarly, with other academics, the overarching trend has been one of critique, ranging on the spectrum between subtle and stark, but ultimately submitting to praise of the Prize. Krishnan captures this trend and tension:

> Set in a context of increasing stratification, both of the global production of knowledge and of economic power, the prize has been described as simultaneously necessary for the growing transnational profile of African literature and debilitating in its inadvertent fostering of a certain 'aesthetic of suffering', to use Helon Habila's phrase, in global African writing. (2014, 136)

My argument here is not simply that the Caine Prize for African Writing is unimportant, nor is it designed to underestimate the effects of its investment in contemporary African literature—far from it. It is, however, to pinpoint that because the criticisms are not fully strengthened or fleshed-out, there remain unanswered (and new) questions that plague the Prize each year. Twenty years into the Prize's existence, it has never entirely managed to evade these questions and criticisms—and in this landmark year, it seems necessary, now more than ever, to raise them at the very least.

The representatives of the Prize itself speak of its achievement in the areas of literary production, publication, and publicity; Lizzy Attree has defended it on numerous occasions through tweets, interviews, panel discussions, and articles:

> The prize and the anthology together act as a showcase, a snapshot produced every year of current writing in Africa, and this is a brilliant platform for writers to become better known and more widely read. [. . .] the Caine Prize [. . .] is still one of the only prizes that recognises short stories with such a large financial reward, and so it remains important for that reason. The prize can make a significant difference to a writer's career, offering time to write and the opportunity to travel and make links with agents and publishers in Europe

> and the US. So I don't see a huge number of drawbacks. (Attree 2015, n.p.)

The Prize's website adds that:

> In addition to administering the Prize, we work to connect readers with African writers through a series of public events, as well as helping emerging writers in Africa to enter the world of mainstream publishing through the annual Caine Prize writers' workshop which takes place in a different African country each year. (*caineprize.com*)

Perhaps the quality for which the Caine Prize for African Writing is most prized, and on which it most prides itself, is the launching of "emerging" writers' careers—and there seems to be a more-or-less general consensus regarding the validity of this claim. Pucherová notes that the Prize has "tended to award early career writers" and "kick-started the careers of its winners by providing them with global visibility leading to publishing contracts" (2012, 14); Kiguru alerts that the award has "acted as a bridge for the transition from short stories to novels, from upcoming writers to global household names" (2016a, 204); and Attree herself has referred to it as "both a reward for excellence in literature as well as a development tool" (2015, n.p.). Aaron Bady's thought-provoking essay "Is the Caine Prize for Emergent African Writing, or the Best African Writing?" makes similar statements:

> The prize marks the transition from relative obscurity [. . .] into relative success: they each, shortly, became a writer with a *book*. [. . .] The list of winners tells the same, uniform story of How to Become an African Writer: write some stories, win the Caine Prize, then publish a novel.
>
> [. . .]
>
> In "emerging markets", writers lack the connections and material conditions to succeed, so the Caine Prize gives them a boost at a key moment in their development, allowing

> them to establish themselves and their careers to take off. [. . .] Established African novelists do not, as a rule, win the Caine Prize; it is a prize designed for and aimed at writers in a stage of *emergence*. (2016, paras. 3–6; emphasis in original)

For Pucherová the encouraging of young writers is a characteristic of the Caine Prize for African Writing, and for Kiguru, it can mark a substantial step in the journey of a writer's life. Bady, however, is critical of conferring this status on the Prize—indeed, on a single prize. Does the Prize succumb to a sort of stereotype—"How to Become an African Writer"—staging Adichie's "single story", and functioning similarly to the tendency Wainaina satirizes in "How to Write about Africa"? As Bady asks, "if 'African literature' is having a renaissance, does it need a prize for emerging writers? What happens to the Caine Prize after African literature has emerged?" These questions will resurface in the next section, but for the moment, they are here to signal that the accomplishments of the Prize are not beyond question.

Earlier, amidst the chaos of controversies in 2011, Aaron Bady took to his blog *Zunguzungu* to declare that: "a decade in, [The Caine Prize for African Writing] has become one of the more important institutions by which new African writing gets an international audience, an especially important function ever since Heinemann discontinued the African Writers Series" (2011, n.p.). If one thinks purely in terms of the Prize's contributions to the field of publishing, the idea of the Caine Prize for African Writing as descending from or replacing the "African Writers Series" becomes a better origin story than that of the Booker legacy. Indeed, the 2017 workshop, hosted in Tanzania, heralded new co-publishers across eight countries in the Horn and East Africa including Huza Press, *Kwani?*, FEMRITE, Jacana, and others, alongside the original UK publisher. The Prize has also supported local presses, and had symbiotic relationships with local institutions, where it has provided the bandwidth for publishing; in turn, published stories have been submitted to and shortlisted by the Prize. Shortlisted writers and winners have also featured heavily across some of the most celebrated short story anthologies to come out of the continent in recent times, such as *Africa39* and *The Granta Book of the African Short Story* (2011).

In her *Financial Times* review of *The Granta Book of the African Short Story*, curated, with a critical introduction, by Helon Habila, Petina Gappah (2011) gives credit where it is due:

> The anthology testifies to the depth of talent on the continent and in its diaspora; it also testifies to the strength and influence of the London-based Caine Prize for African Writing. As Habila observes, almost half of the writers here (including Habila himself) have come to prominence either by winning or being shortlisted for the award. [. . .] It is no coincidence that the Caine writers are among the best known from Africa. This raises the perennial question of the nature of African literary production that has preoccupied the continent's critics and thinkers since the first African writers were published in the west. (para. 5)

Once again, disguised in the Prize's successes are its various shortcomings. Even when the conversation about publishing is charted on the coordinates of the continent, the linkages with the "global literary marketplace" are evident, and it is increasingly clear that these Africa-based institutions and initiatives cannot be read entirely in isolation, innocent of western funding and forces. Consequently, we arrive at the literary traffic on the pan-African plane via a transit located in the geography of the "Global North". Therefore, as with the Booker legacy, it is true that the Caine Prize for African Writing is open to criticism in other areas too—and the following section reviews some of the controversies circling it, and the views of its critics.

The Controversies and Critiques surrounding The Caine Prize for African Writing

> The Caine Prize aims to be Africa's leading literary award but, of course, no one institution can act as the gatekeeper of African literature. (Attree 2015)

Before relaying some specific reasons that the Caine Prize for African Writing has been targeted for criticism, this section unravels the umbrella critique of the Prize: that, it has, in some respects, inadvertently become an institutional gatekeeper for African literature. Any British prize that "aims to be Africa's leading literary award" will, if it achieves its aim, inevitably do so at the cost of local, Africa-based institutions. To this end, four perspectives will be discussed—those of a former Caine Prize for African Writing judge, a non-winner, a recipient of the Prize, and a literary blogger.

It is instructive to begin with some thoughts from Ellah Allfrey, a former deputy editor of *Granta*, who has been Deputy Chair of the Council of the Caine Prize for African Writing, and who wrote in *The Guardian* of "The Winning Qualities of the Caine Prize", shortly after the shortlist was announced:

> How can one prize possibly claim to assess the literary output of a continent of over 991 million people and its diaspora? Is there any such thing as an "African writer"? Does the very existence of the prize encourage a continued inclination to ghettoisation of these writers and their work? Surely we've come far enough that Africans no longer need (if they ever have) the special consideration this categorisation implies? (Allfrey 2010, para. 3)

She concludes that one answer to these questions of definition and identity is that it permits the judges "the freedom to dismiss that unifying criterion [the African origins of the writers]" (para. 7), to take it as a given. While this gestures towards a judging process that is based purely on literary merit, it is also an opinion held from the narrow perspective of judging, and fails to account for questions of authority, power asymmetry, and continental category that continue to orbit the Prize. Petina Gappah (2017) picks up these pieces in her role as a kind of "a literary agony aunt". Obi from Ibadan writes in to say: "Dear Tete Petina, Once again I'm not on the Caine Prize shortlist". Gappah recalls her "own Caine adventure" (one of failure to win), and offers hope:

> It also helped enormously that a very kind friend said to me: "You know, you don't need the Caine Prize". This was an entirely new idea for me: that I could be a published writer without ever having been 'Caine-anointed.' At that time [2008], the Caine was so dominant in conversations about who got published that it seemed like a revolutionary, even sacrilegious idea, that really, we might all want to win the Caine, but no one truly *needed* it. (Gappah 2017, para. 6; original emphasis)

Here, though the format is playfully deceptive, Gappah has managed to make a big, bold statement. Though the Prize has come to be worshipped across continental and global African literary circles, she de-mystifies the aura and attraction surrounding it. Although appealing—achingly desirable even—it is not a requirement or a rite of passage for publication: one does not *need* to be "Caine-annointed". I want to reiterate here that Chimamanda Ngozi Adichie, and others such as Aminatta Forna and Taiye Selasi, have never won the Prize. And what are the consequences of idealising the Prize, placing it on a pedestal? The 2002 recipient of the Caine Prize for African Writing, Binyavanga Wainaina, reveals this through another unusual format: his famous Caine Prize Twitter rant—

> dear Caine Prize, DO NOT EVER, claim a central space in our literature. U r good, but we are not best employee certificate program. [sic]

> Dear Caine Prize, u made nothing, produced nothing, distributed nothing. U give a Prize of cash money and publicity. That is it. [sic]
> (quoted on http://bookslive.co.za/blog/2014/10/13/binyavanga-wainainas-twitter-outburst-dear-caine-prize-u-made-nothing-produced-nothing-distributed-nothing/)

This outburst can be traced back a few weeks, to a 2014 This is Africa interview with Chiagozie Nwonwu:

> I give the Caine Prize its due credit, but it just isn't our institution. [. . .] What is happening is you people are allowing the Caine Prize to receive funding and build itself as a brand and make money and people's career there in London while the vast majority of these [homegrown] institutions are vastly underfunded and vastly *ungrown,* and they are the ones who create the ground that is building these new writers [. . .] We need to focus on how we can grow our own ecosystem. (Wainaina and Nwonwu 2014, para. 14; original emphasis)

Wainaina's is a clarion call to bring the conversation back to the continent, and its institutions of publishing and prizing. He commends the work of Cassava Republic, of the Farafina Workshop, of magazines such as *Saraba* and *Jalada*. The year 2018 saw the Jalada Mobile Literary and Arts Festival, a cross between a traditional festival and a literary bus tour, which was awarded the nAnA (new Art new Audiences) grant by the British Council, and conceptualized in collaboration with Africa Writes (Royal African Society, UK), Jalada Africa Trust (Kenya), Huza Press (Rwanda), and a host of cultural institutions on the continent. With its foreign funding, and east African grounding (mapping five countries in the region), the first-ever travelling literary festival on the continent embodies intra- and inter-continental literary traffic. Also worth mentioning are The Huza Press Prize for Fiction (established by Louise Umutoni, founder of Rwanda's first publishing house, Huza Press), The Writivism Short Story Prize (also an annual literary festival, and administered by the Uganda-based Center for African Cultural Excellence (CACE)), the Short Story Day Africa Prize (whose sponsors include The Miles Morland Foundation and The Goethe-Institut, and several South African writers), and the shiny new NOMMO awards (announced by the African Speculative Fiction Society). Some of these institutions have foreign financial support, but Wainaina's larger concern, in my opinion, is to de-centralise the discussion of literary prizes and African literature, especially when one in particular prospers at the expense of others.

Although the Caine Prize for African Writing is not to blame for this imbalance in our priorities towards local prizes, the cultural status that the Prize has acquired allows it to enjoy this privileged position in the hierarchy of prizes. This is what blogger Ikhide Ikheloa would refer to as the "unintended consequences" of the Caine Prize. In an earlier piece, he writes: "The creation of a Prize for 'African writing' may have created the unintended effect of breeding writers willing to stereotype Africa for glory" (Ikheloa 2012). This leads one to perhaps the most controversial claim made about the Prize—one it encounters each year, and has been unable to entirely shrug off. The Nigerian novelist Helon Habila (himself a winner in 2001) reviews the 2013 novel, *We Need New Names* (an extension of the winning short story from the 2011 Caine Prize for African Writing "Hitting Budapest") for *The Guardian*, and accuses its author NoViolet Bulawayo of "performing Africa" in a "CNN, western-media-coverage-of-Africa, poverty-porn sense" (Habila 2013, para. 1). He further writes of her "palpable anxiety to cover every 'African' topic; almost as if the writer had a checklist made from the morning's news on Africa" (para 4.). His piece poses the question: is the new writing a fair representation of the existential realities of Africa, or just a "Caine-prize aesthetic that has emerged in a vacuum created by the judges and the publishers and the agents over the years, and which has begun to perpetuate itself" (para. 2)?

Habila's notion of a "Caine-prize aesthetic" encapsulates Pucherová's argument that "the prize participates in a system of postcolonial knowledge industry that both values and marginalizes postcolonial texts" (2012, 13). Ikhide too writes that "aided by some needy "African" writers, Africa is being portrayed as an issues-laden continent that is best viewed on a fly-infested canvas" (2012). Graham Huggan shifts the focus from the institution to the individual: "third-world writers are not only subject to but also actively manipulate exoticist codes of cultural representation in their work for their own ends, while choosing complicity with exoticist aesthetics and self-commodification" (2001, 32). Pucherová agrees: "The postcolonial author has emerged as a profoundly complicit and compromised figure whose authority rests, however uncomfortably, in the nature of his connection to the specificity of a given political location [and who] consciously deploy[s] aesthetics of postcolonial migrancy attractive to their Anglo-American readers" (2012, 3–4; 19). While Habila's attack on Bulawayo can be read as yet another case of male literary gatekeeping, the concern about the "Caine-prize aesthetic" has cropped up in constructive debate in recent years. And if Timothy Brennan's (1997) "geographical banners" of affiliation and aesthetic—banners that accompany the tendency to manipulate and market postcolonial writers in the west, are a "kind of literary passport that identifies the artist as being from a region of underdevelopment and pain" (38), such debates are useful in interrogating the identity of the Caine Prize for "African Writing". "The African literary text", in such circuits of consumption, commercialisation, and celebration, "is always received as more than just a text", writes Krishnan (2014, 2), and is read through Brennan's "banners" (and sometimes baggage) of geography and genealogy.

Conclusions, and Cues for the Future

> When people talk about the good things that the Caine Prize does for African writing, they tend to tell the story the way I've told it, as the story of individual writers, individual achievements. [. . .]If we go beyond the individual level, the Caine Prize is a more problematic entity. (Bady 2016, para. 9)

I believe that if one hopes to understand the personality and power of the Caine Prize for "African Writing", and also its identity crisis of being at once productive and problematic, one must look beyond its small successes. The Prize has hitherto functioned in extremes—doing too much or too little: for example, rewarding too many Nigerians and shortlisting the same authors twice over, or recognizing too few stories in translation, and too few North Africans. The identities of the Caine Prize for African Writing and of "African literature" and "African writer" have been inextricably interlinked—they are, somehow symbiotic, and feed into one another. And on the global scale, the Caine Prize for African Writing has become a synecdoche of African literary prizes in the same manner as "New Nigerian Writing" has become a synecdoche of contemporary African literature. The Caine Prize for African Writing has become the *Things Fall Apart* of literary prizes regarding the continent: a reduction, a point of fixed origin, a single prizing story, whose reputation leads to lazy assumptions.

As Ikhide Ikheloa has repeatedly suggested, "they [the Prize] should review the short-lists and winners since its inception, and put structures in place that ensure a more rounded set of offerings each year" (Ikheloa 2012); he also suggests that "it would be interesting to do a study of the places of abode of all the shortlisted writers since inception", especially in light of diasporic writers being accused of not being "African enough" of deserving the Prize (Ikheloa 2016). Shem Owino Otieno's unpublished masters dissertation, "The Caine Prize and the African Republic of Letters" (2017), takes Ikheloa's suggestion and does considerable statistical analysis (including of archived submissions and shortlist data). As part of my larger project, "Awarding Africa", I too am analysing similar data, searching for answers along gender, national, and linguistic lines, as well as combing through the digitised blog archives for press releases, judges' comments, notes on workshop experiences and prize ceremonies—to offer a full(er) picture of the Prize since it was born 20 years ago. Lizzy Attree's suggestion is also worth attending to: "It is the novels that Caine Prize winners go on to write (if they choose to) and the critical writing they produce about each other's work to which readers should look when attempting to discover how to appreciate writing about and from Africa" (2013, 45). My research also focuses on the winning writers' post-Caine Prize for African Writing trajectories—from these first prizes to their first books, and beyond.

The Caine Prize for African Writing, albeit inadvertently, asks of its authors and texts, "Where do [you] come from?", thus allotting "African literature" a geography-based banner and, in Adichie's words, one "single story". If, however, following Trinh Minh-ha (2011), we juxtapose "Where do we come from?" with the question "Where do we go?" we mediate between multiple worlds, and see writers, texts, and characters challenging citizenships and circumventing continental borders (13). Suhr-Systsma (2018) offers a fresh perspective, and a productive way of re-thinking and re-mapping, one that my project also aligns itself with:

> The literary geography of the Caine Prize is best represented, then, not as a unidirectional flow—whether of white British judgment of African writers or of African fiction being exported to the Global North—but as circuits of exchange among the UK, the United States, and various locations on the African continent where English is an official language (1109).

The conversation then oscillates between fixity and fluidity, is grounded and gives way to multiple geographies. The conversation, then, is one of connections beyond continental cartographies; one that is neither deliberately diasporic nor ethnically essentialist; and one of places and stories lost and found.

Bibliography

Adichie, Chimamanda N. 2009a. "The Danger of a Single Story." *Youtube*, uploaded by TED, www.youtube.com/watch?v=D9Ihs241zeg

—. 2009b. "Jumping Monkey Hill." In *The Thing Around Your Neck*, 153–85. London: Fourth Estate.

—. 2013. "Race Doesn't Occur to Me [Interview with Aaron Bady]." *Salon*, May 13. https://www.salon.com/2013/07/14/chimamanda_ngozi_adichie_race_doesnt_occur_to_me_partner/

Allfrey, Ellah. 2010. "The Winning Qualities of the Caine Prize." *The Guardian Books Blog*, April 27. https://www.theguardian.com/books/booksblog/2010/apr/26/winning-qualities-caine-prize

Attree, Lizzy. 2013. "The Caine Prize and Contemporary African Writing." *Research in African Literatures* 44 (2): 36–47.

—. 2015. "Caine Prize Gets the Sack [Interview with Nick Mulgrew." *Mail & Guardian*, July 10. https://mg.co.za/article/2015-07-10-caine-prize-gets-the-sack

Bady, Aaron. 2016. "Is the Caine Prize for Emergent African Writing, or the Best African Writing?" *Lithub*. http://lithub.com/is-the-caine-prize-for-emergent-african-writing-or-the-best-african-writing/

Bady, Aaron, and Taiye Selasi. 2015. "From That Stranded Place." *New African Fiction*: Special Issue of *Transition* 117 (1): 148–65.

Brennan, Timothy. 1997. *At Home in the World: Cosmopolitanism Now*. Cambridge, MA: Harvard University Press.

Brouillette, Sarah. 2007. *Postcolonial Writers in the Global Literary Marketplace*. New York: Palgrave Macmillan.

Doran, D'Arcy, and Serpell, Namwali. 2015. "Namwali Serpell is the Zambian Author Defying Convention and Starting a Mutiny." *Huck*. http://www.huckmagazine.com/art-and-culture/mutiny-lolita-afronauts-glimpse-namwali-serpells-world/

Edwin, Shirin. 2016. "(Un)solving Global Challenges: African Short Stories, Literary Awards and the Question of Audience." *Journal of African Cultural Studies* 28 (3): 359–71.

Eisenberg, Eve. 2013. "'Real Africa'/ 'Which Africa?': The Critique of Mimetic Realism in Chimamanda Ngozi Adichie's Short Fiction." 2013. In *Writing Africa Today, Vol 31: Writing Africa in the Short Story*, edited by Ernest Emenyonu, 8–24. Martlesham, Suffolk: Boydell & Brewer.

English, James F. 2008. *The Economy of Prestige: Prizes, Awards, and the Circulation of Cultural Value*. 2008. Cambridge, MA: Harvard University Press.

Gappah, Pettina. 2011. "The Granta Book of the African Short Story." *The Financial Times*, September 24. https://www.ft.com/content/e548b738-df98-11e0-845a-00144feabdc0

Gappah, Petina. 2017. "Dear Tete Petina: I Am Not on the Caine Prize Shortlist." *Brittlepaper*. http://brittlepaper.com/2017/05/dear-tete-petina-caine-prize-shortlist-petina-gappah/

Habila, Helon. 2013. "*We Need New Names* by NoViolet Bulawayo: Review." *The Guardian*, June 20. https://www.theguardian.com/books/2013/jun/20/need-new-names-bulawayo-review

Huggan, Graham. 2001. *The Postcolonial Exotic: Marketing the Margins*. London: Routledge.

Ikheloa, Ikhide R. 2012. "The Caine Prize and Unintended Consequences." Pa Ikhide Blog, March 11. https://xokigbo.com/2012/03/11/the-caine-prize-and-unintended-consequences/

—. 2016. "The 2016 Caine Prize: The Burdens of Identity and Fading Memories." Pa Ikhide Blog, June 3. https://xokigbo.com/2016/06/03/the-2016-caine-prize-the-burdens-of-identity-and-fading-memories/Kiguru,

Kiguru, Doseline. 2016a. "Literary Prizes, Writers' Organisations and Canon Formation in Africa." *African Studies* 75 (2): 202–14.

—. 2016b. "Prizing African Literature: Creating a Literary Taste." *Social Dynamics* 42 (1): 161–74.

Krishnan, Madhu. 2014. *Contemporary African Literature in English: Global Locations, Postcolonial Identifications*. Houndmills and New York: Palgrave Macmillan.

Kushkush, Isma'il. 2014. "One Foot in Each of Two Worlds, and a Pen at Home in Both." *The New York Times*, March 21. https://www.nytimes.com/2014/03/22/world/africa/one-foot-in-each-of-two-worlds-and-a-pen-at-home-in-both.html

Minh-ha, Trinh. 2011. *Elsewhere within Here: Immigration, Refugeeism, and the Boundary Event.* New York: Routledge.

Osteen, Mark. 2002. *The Question of the Gift: Essays across Disciplines.* London: Routledge.

Owuor, Yvonne. "Words for Worlds." 2015. *Youtube*, uploaded by TED. https://www.youtube.com/watch?v=T9Oe6U2zoAc

Ozick, Cynthia. 2012. "Prize or Prejudice." *The New York Times*, June 6.https://www.nytimes.com/2012/06/07/opinion/prize-or-prejudice.html

Pinto, Samantha. 2013. "The Caine Prize and the Impossibility of 'New' African Writing." *Journal of Commonwealth and Postcolonial Studies* 1 (1): 140–49.

Primorac, Ranka. 2015. " Acts of Mutiny: the Caine Prize and 'African Literature'." *Africa in Words* Blog, August 14. https://africainwords.com/2015/08/14/acts-of-mutiny-the-caine-prize-and-african-literature/

Pucherová, Dobrota. 2012. "'A Continent Learns to Tell its Story at Last': Notes on the Caine Prize." *Journal of Postcolonial Writing* 48 (1): 13–25.

Selasi, Taiye. 2013. "African Literature Doesn't Exist." Haus der Berliner Festspiele, 13th International Literature Festival Berlin, Berlin, Germany. Opening Speech. http://literaturfestival.com/medien/texte/eroeffnungsreden/Openingspeach2013_English.pdf

Serpell, Namwali. 2015. "Q&A: Namwali Serpell [with Lilly Kroll]." *Africa in Words* Blog, Sept. 4. https://africainwords.com/2015/09/04/qa-namwali-serpell/

Todd, Richard. 1996. *Consuming Fictions: The Booker Prize and Fiction in Britain Today.* London: Bloomsbury.

Suhr-Sytsma, Nathan. 2018. "The Geography of Prestige: Prizes, Nigerian Writers, and World Literature." *ELH* 85 (4): 1093-1122.

Wainaina, Binyavanga. 2005. "How to Write about Africa." In *Granta*

92: The View from Africa, edited by Ian Jack, 91–96. London: Granta Publications.

Wainaina, Binyavanga, and Chiagozie Nwonwu. 2014. "We Must Stop Giving Legitimacy to the Caine Prize." *This Is Africa*, Sept. 9. https://thisisafrica.me/lifestyle/must-stop-giving-legitimacy-caine-prize-binyavanga/

The Failure of the Man Asian Literary Prize and the Politics of Recognition

Flair Donglai Shi

In his article "Winning the Culture Game", James English (2002) states that "there is no form of cultural capital so ubiquitous, so powerful, so widely talked about, and yet so little explored by scholars as the cultural prize" (109). However, since the 1990s, there has actually been a proliferation of scholarship on this topic, most of which, such as Richard Todd's (1996) *Consuming Fictions: The Booker Prize and Fiction in Britain Today* and Graham Huggan's (2001) *The Postcolonial Exotic: Marketing the Margins*, has focused on the Booker Prize. The Nobel Prize in Literature and other more regionally focused prizes have also been thoroughly investigated from different perspectives.[1] Most of these studies, like English's own prize-winning monograph *The Economy of Prestige* (2005), have utilised Pierre Bourdieu's theorisation of different "forms of capital" to expose how prizes act as "the very means" of the production of value by facilitating the "circulations and interconversions of capital" (English 2014, 138; English 2005, 10). In these studies, the focus is on successful prizes that have had, and continue to have, significant influence on the field of literary culture either in global or regional contexts. Yet as James English has noted, the proliferation of cultural prizes and awards since the 1960s necessarily means that only a small number of prominent prizes like the Nobel and the Booker survive and dominate

1 For example, Rebecca Braun (2011) has studied the celebritisation effect of the Nobel Prize in Europe and Julia Lovell (2006) has investigated the complex entanglements between international recognition and national politics in the context of China's "Nobel Complex". Studies that focus on regional prizes, such as Sarah Bowskill's (2012) exploration of Spain's "The Premio Cervantes Prize", have also provided significant revisions of Bourdieu's and English's theories.

the economy of prestige, while others decline, becoming "defunct" and forgotten (English 2005, 123).

This chapter focuses on one of these defunct literary prizes, the Man Asian Literary Prize (2007–2012) (henceforth MALP), as a case of failure, in which the partial agency of the prize did not effectively intervene in or bring the desired changes to existing power structures in what Pascale Casanova (2004) calls "the international literary space" (25). The main body of this chapter is divided into two parts. Part 1 presents a comprehensive picture of the establishment, development and decline of the prize and makes observations about the shifting directions of recognition during its six years of operation. In this descriptive account, I bring together and examine a variety of textual and paratextual resources, including the two archival documents related to the prize's launch (See Appendices 1 and 2), the publicised longlists and shortlists in the prize's history, relevant media reports, as well as official publicity outlets such as the prize's YouTube channel and Facebook page. [2] Bourdieu's and English's theories about different forms of capital and their interconversions are also applied to this examination to emphasise the fact that in a case of failure like the MALP, the partial nature of "the agency of the cultural prize" is demonstrated through the prize's role not as the agent and source, but as the recipient and beneficiary, of recognition and cultural capital (English 2005, 320).

Part 2, with a more analytical focus, situates the prize and its failure in the debate on world literature as a cultural habitus and offers three possible explanations for the prize's failure, including the

---

2 More information, including the original announcements of each year's longlists and shortlists, used to be available on the prize's official website (www.manasianliteraryprize.org) during the six years of its operation. However, the site remained inaccessible for most of 2016 and 2017, and a brief check in the autumn of 2019 shows that it is displaying materials about Canadian women writers that are completely unrelated to the MALP. However, the Wikipedia page of the (Man) Asian Literary Prize (https://en.wikipedia.org/wiki/Asian_Literary_Prize) keeps a record of the lists and its accuracy can be verified through the different news coverages on the prize each year (last accessed on September 15 2019).

inadequacy of journalistic capital, the lack of cooperation with Asian countries, and the conservative elements in the operation of the prize that contradict its stated ambitions. Through these possible explanations, I caution against over-confidence in and over-reliance on prizes as the creator of value and argue that since they necessarily act as the mediator through which different players in the cultural habitus can exchange different forms of capital, their survival and prestige very much depend on the stakes they can build for these players. Ultimately, the failure of prizes, especially those like the MALP that aim to intervene in or challenge existing power structures, indicates that without decentring or diversifying the source of recognition in the existing paradigm, it is difficult for a new paradigm to be effectively established from within the power structures of a cultural habitus.

Part 1: From a Prize that Asian Writers Need to a Prize that Needs its Asian Writers

It was no coincidence that the old Hong Kong International Literary Festival changed its name to "the Man Hong Kong International Literary Festival" when it was chosen as the event at which the MALP would be launched in 2006.[3] The archival document on this launch, titled "Background to the Man Asian Literary Prize", lists Man Group plc and The Hong Kong International Literary Festival Ltd. as the two "founding parties" of the prize.[4] However, the connection between the two parties actually predated the prize's establishment. One of the founding members of the festival, Nury Vittachi, wrote in his blog that when Man Group plc became one of the sponsors of the festival in

3 Archival document (Press Release), "Major New Literary Prize Established in Asia." 2006. Box 1, Folder 1, Coll. BP/4/1, Booker Prize Archive, Oxford Brookes University Library. See Appendix 1, page 1.

4 Archival document, "Background to the Man Asian Literary Prize." 2006. Box 1, Folder 1, Coll. BP/4/1, Booker Prize Archive, Oxford Brookes University Library. See Appendix 2, page 3. Any citations of these two archival documents in the main text henceforth refer to the appendices given in the reference at the end of the sentence.

2002, his team was already planning to "launch and [sic] Asian Booker prize" with the knowledge that Man Group plc was recently enlisted by the Booker Foundation to become its title sponsor (Vittachi n.d., Chapter 1).

From a Bourdieusian perspective, this triangular relation between a literary festival, an investment company and a literary prize can be viewed as constructed by the flows of different forms of capital in the Asian literary field. In "The Forms of Capital", Bourdieu (1986) has defined capital as "accumulated labour [. . .] which, when appropriated on a private, i.e., exclusive, basis by agents or groups of agents, enables them to appropriate social energy in the form of reified or living labour" (46). He further proposes three different kinds of capital that can be converted into one another under certain conditions: "economic capital", "cultural capital" and "social capital". In the case of the MALP, Man Group plc provided economic capital, the only form of capital that is "immediately and directly convertible into money", to the festival and the prize through its sponsorship, which included prize money, administration fees and publicity costs (47). In turn, the Hong Kong International Literary Festival, as "the leading English-language festival in Asia", and the MALP, as the "major new literary prize established in Asia", provided cultural capital for the investment company (Appendix 1, page 2 and 1). As Bourdieu points out, "the most powerful principle of the symbolic efficacy of cultural capital [. . .] lies in the logic of its transmission" (1986, 49). The transmission in this case is obvious as it was institutionalised through the insertion of "Man" in the official titles of both the festival and the prize.

However, two factors further complicate the transmission of capital in this triangular relation. First, Man Group plc is also a source of cultural capital, which had been accumulating since 2002, when the Booker Prize changed its official name to "the Man Booker Prize" upon receiving sponsorship from the investment company. In the document "Background to the Man Asian Literary Prize", Man Group plc is described as one of its founding parties in three paragraphs, with the longest one solely focusing on introducing The Man Booker Prize for

Fiction. Indeed, rather than introducing Man Group plc in terms of its organisational nature—a business entity—the first paragraph states: "Man Group plc is the sponsor of the Man Booker Prize (the leading English-language literary award) and the new Man Booker International Prize" (Appendix 2 page 3). In this process, Man Group plc, by foregrounding its role as the sponsor for the existing Booker Prizes, transmutes economic as well as cultural capital to the newly established MALP.

Secondly, the social capital Vittachi and his team had gathered through the Hong Kong International Literary Festival is also important in the establishment of this triangular relation. For Bourdieu, social capital is "made up of social obligations" and embedded in "a durable network of more or less institutionalised relationships of mutual acquaintance and recognition" (1986, 47 and 51). According to Brian Moeran (2010), cultural events such as book fairs and literary festivals offer important opportunities for different participants in the field to have "short-term, face-to-face interaction in a structured environment" where "economic, social and symbolic values" can be defined and reasserted (138). As Vittachi's blog confirms, his job at the Hong Kong International Literary Festival enabled him to establish contacts with prize-winning writers such as Amitav Ghosh, Charles Foran and Pankaj Mishra, whose experiences with the economy of prestige in the anglophone world led him to believe that "prizes define authors" (Vittachi n.d., Chapter 4). However, the most crucial opportunity for Vittachi to expand his social capital from the Asian literary field to the field of global business connections was his meeting with the Regional Managing Director of Man Investments (Asia Pacific), Matt Dillon, introduced to him by the Australian writer Rosemary Sayer. In 2006, Vittachi gained an opportunity, through Mr. Dillon, to present his idea about a new literary prize for Asia at the headquarters of the company in London. As this was a time when Man Group plc was "expanding in Asia", the sponsorship was probably also seen by the company as a marketing opportunity where the cultural capital of the new prize could be converted into symbolic or even economic capital for the company in the long run (ibid).

With the support of these different forms of capital from the founding parties, the MALP was launched with two clear target groups and an ambitious focus on "newness". Firstly, as the prize "should be explicitly Asian", the target group of candidates (and winners) was restricted to writers who were citizens or residents of one of the selected 34 Asian countries (Appendix 2 page 2). As Martin Lewis and Kären Wigen (1997) have pointed out, the English word "Asia" is a "meta-geographical framework" by which "the myth of West and East" and "the myth of geographical concordance" can be evoked (xiii). In the case of the MALP, the 34 countries encompass the near East (e.g. Turkey) as well as Southeast Asia (e.g. Indonesia), reinforcing the old Victorian definition of the continent as separate from Europe. Notably, the Arabic-speaking countries in the Middle East had not been included in this big picture of "Asia", possibly due to the fact that a separate Arabic Booker (The International Prize for Arabic Fiction, 2008–present) was already under preparation, and this somewhat arbitrary selection indicates that the MALP's use of this "meta-geographical framework" also takes into consideration linguistic and institutional realities and is strategic in essence. Second, the target audience and market for the selected Asian authors comprise the "English-speaking peoples", especially those in "North America, Europe and Australia" whose dominant publishing industries were expanding in the emerging Asian markets through projects such as "Penguin India" and "Picador Asia" (Appendix 2 page 2).

This specific target audience has a direct influence on what is perceived as "new" by the prize organisers. One of the key criteria for submissions to the MALP at the time of its establishment was that the work had to be unpublished in English, so that the prize could fulfil its purpose to "support and facilitate new publication and translation rather than to merely reward existing publication activity" (ibid). This statement exemplifies what I mean by the prize's "interventionist" ambitions and it implies that some of the Asian countries with vibrant publishing industries in local languages would be prioritised over those with established circles of anglophone writers such as India. Indeed, many of the writers mentioned as examples of this target group in the background document, such as Su Tong, Yu Hua and Hotomi Kanehara, had been critically acclaimed in their home countries. Most of the six winning titles from 2007 to 2012 had been domestic bestsellers and won numerous important national literary prizes before receiving the MALP. For example, the inaugural winner—Jiang Rong's *Wolf Totem*—had been the bestselling novel in China for two consecutive years from 2004 to 2005, with more than 14 million copies (including pirated editions) sold (Henningsen 2010, 120). Similarly, the 2008 winner *Illustrado*, by the Filipino writer Miguel Syjuco, was awarded the Grand Prize at the Palanca Awards in Manila earlier in the same year. Many other authors in the MALP's longlists and shortlists had been nationally recognised in similar ways. From an Asian perspective, the majority of the nominated writers would not be considered new at all.

Moreover, the dominance of India and the anglophone writers from the Asian diasporas based in the west is specifically mentioned as one aspect of the literary status quo that the prize aims to address, constituting an interventionist agenda to further diversify the range of literary representations in the global literary marketplace. The background document states that while Indian and other "emigrant Asian writers [. . .] have long had significant publishing opportunities and have, as a result, long contributed to the corpus of world literature in English, Asian writers are only just now becoming increasingly important on the world literary scene" (Appendix 2 page 1).

However, it is this focus on newness that indicates the prize's awareness about the various structural imbalances in the sphere of world literature and defines its interventionist nature, which is manifested in three ways.

First, the rhetoric of "rising Asia" features prominently in the publicity around the MALP. When announcing the 2011 longlist, one of the judges, Vikas Swarup, made the remark that "everybody talks about the 21st century belonging to Asia; and now we are seeing Asia also is taking its place in 21st century literature".[5] This belief was echoed by the Chair of the Board of Directors of the prize, David Parker, who, in an online article entitled "Celebrating Asian Literature", emphasised the "growing cultural confidence throughout the region [Asia]" that the prize could help nurture (n.d.). Notably, both Franco Moretti and Pascale Casanova assign modern literature from Asia to the periphery of world literature and argue that Asian countries need to catch up with the "literary present" in the west according to "a law of literary evolution" (Moretti 2000, 60). However, as Asia accumulates more political and economic power in the age of globalisation, the organisers of the prize, such as Peter Gordon, Director of the Hong Kong International Literary Festival, expressed their strong belief that the region would be "an important source for new writing" (Appendix 1 page 1). Essentially, the rhetoric of "rising Asia", as employed by the prize organisers, demonstrates their awareness of the potential changes a prize focusing on promoting Asian writers in the anglophone literary space could make, and their constant evocation or performance of this rhetoric signalled their ambition to facilitate these changes in a proactive manner.

Second, not only were the prize organisers aware of the power imbalance between the west and Asia in the global literary system, they were also aware of the power imbalance in Asia's representation in the anglophone sphere. The aforementioned statement in the background document concerning Indian and other diasporic Asian writers indicates a desire to move from postcolonial writing to a more internationally-oriented world literature. As Sarah Brouillette (2007) has noted, postcolonial writers, usually consisting of migrant writers writing about their birth countries and their colonial histories within western empires, have significantly contributed to the multicultural discourse in the west, where they have come to dominate the representation of the geo-cultural Other through various kinds of intercultural "self-consciousness" (190). By

5 A video recording of the speech can be found on the official Youtube page of the MALP https://www.youtube.com/watch?v=Z31xLDZxBvc (last accessed on September 15 2019).

focusing on "new Asian voices" from "writers originating and writing from the region", the MALP was aiming to challenge the dominance of postcolonial Asian literature in the representation of Asia to the west (Appendix 2 page 2). This intervention is obvious in the fact that in the first few years of the prize's operation, the longlists contained a considerable number of South and Southeast Asian writers who write and publish in indigenous languages and address local realities (and thus were almost unheard of in the west), such as Laxmi Narayan Mishra, Lakambini Sitoy, N. S. Madhavan and others.

Third, the shift from diasporic Asian writers to nationally based and acclaimed writers from Asia presents a departure from the existing paradigm of the international economy of literary prestige. This paradigm, as James English argues, is built upon the "tendency of prizes, festivals, and related forms of competitive cultural events to facilitate exchange of symbolic capital between the indigenous and the metropolitan market places". English observes that following the acceleration of globalization from the 1970s onwards, the flow of symbolic and cultural capital between the global and the local has largely been achieved by "circumventing" the national (English 2005, 271). Addressing the relevance of this paradigm in the field of world literature, Casanova also posits a dichotomy between the international literary space, which she regards as the "autonomous pole", and the national literary space, the "politico-literary pole" (2004, 105). As I have discussed elsewhere, this antagonist dichotomy and the circumvention of the national are particularly strong in the politics of recognition, or "the dialectic struggle", between post-Mao Chinese literature and world literature (Shi 2016, 20). Andrew Jones (1994) has also pointed out that the international economy of prestige is characterised by the "problem" of "Western cultural hegemony vis-à-vis the so-called 'third world'" (176). As a result, "Chinese literature must rely on 'non-literary' factors" in order to gain the west's recognition, which explains the popularity of "banned in China" books with strong political themes in the "world literary economy" (Wang 2012, 580). However, the MALP sought to challenge this paradigm by proactively recognising the importance of the national. All of the

Chinese works longlisted for the prize, except for Yan Lianke's *Dream of Ding Village*, had been successful with their home readerships. In the last year of its operation, the prize even included in the longlist Tie Ning, the president of the China Writers Association and a member of the 18th Central Committee of the Communist Party of China, signalling its approval and promotion of nationally endorsed writers.

However, the prize's interventionist ambitions were never fully realised. The aim of discovering new writers who have not had their works published in English translations was only achieved in 2007 and 2008, and these two attempts failed to establish the winners' long-term presences in the anglophone literary market.[6] The 2007 winner *Wolf Totem* and the 2008 winner *Illustrado* were both bestsellers in their home countries, and *Wolf Totem* still holds the record as the most expensive Chinese book bought by any English-language publisher (10,000 US dollars paid by Penguin) (Henningsen 2010, 120). Yet despite their moderate successes in the anglophone market, the authors of these two works never again had any of their books translated into English (as of 2019).

The decline of the prize, in terms of the inability to realise its initial interventionist ambitions, can be observed in the significant rule changes in 2010 and its strategies of capital accumulation used thereafter. In 2010, two changes were made to the prize. First, the economic capital channelled into the prize was significantly increased as the prize value for the winning author was raised from 10,000 to 30,000 US dollars, and for the translator from 3,000 to 5,000 US dollars. Vittachi explains that this is the result of the "trust" built between the prize team and Man Group plc, but it can also be interpreted as a necessary strategy deployed by both founding parties to boost the inadequate cultural capital of the prize through greater investment in its economic capital (Vittachi, n.d., Chapter 6). Second, in that same year the organisers of the MALP gave up on the idea of only selecting works unavailable in English and changed the submission criterion to "works written in or translated into English

6 The 2009 winner, Su Tong, cannot be considered "new", as his previous works had been widely acclaimed both in China and abroad.

that have already been published" (Lau 2011, n.p.). This rule change significantly narrowed the scope of selection to the few established Asian writers who already had a substantial body of works written in or translated into English. More importantly, this change created an overlap between the target group of this prize and that of more prominent prizes such as the Man Booker International, the Commonwealth Writers' Prize and even the Nobel Prize in Literature. Such an overlap meant that the prize would gradually lose its distinct function in the literary field because, as James English states, the key to a new prize's success is for it to fulfil a certain "lack in its more esteemed predecessors" (2005, 63).

Indeed, after 2010, the "newness" of the longlisted and shortlisted names diminished, and the inclusion of internationally renowned Asian writers became the main source of the prize's "journalistic capital" (English 2002, 123). Nobel laureates Kenzaburo Oe and Orhan Pamuk were nominated in 2010 and 2012 respectively; other familiar names such as Amitav Ghosh, Anuradha Roy (both already Booker nominees), and Haruki Murakami also entered the longlists. Moreover, a significant event occurred in 2012, the final year of the prize's operation, when the Indian poet Jeet Thayil and the Malaysian novelist Tan Twan Eng were competing again for the prize with the same works (*Narcopolis* and *The Garden of Evening Mists* respectively), only months after they had lost the Man Booker Prize to Hilary Mantel. The inclusion of these prominent names did boost the "journalistic capital" of the MALP in terms of its increased "visibility and celebrity" in mainstream English-language media (ibid). However, as the thematisation of these prominent names in headlines such as "Nobel laureate leads Man Asian prize contenders", "Pamuk leads Man Asian Literary Prize shortlist" and "Murakami and Ghosh to compete for Man Asian Prize" reveals, the symbolic capital of the prize itself was easily overwhelmed by that of these writers. In this process, the prize's positionality in the flows of recognition shifted from active to passive, pushing it towards the receiving end of recognition and cultural capital. In other words, while this inclusion of big names might be regarded as a publicity strategy to boost the cultural and symbolic capital of the prize, the transference failed because it created instead a functionality overlap that resulted in the loss of the prize's unique desirability for writers. For example, when Tan Twan Eng won in 2012, the MALP was seen as an inferior "regional" and "particular" prize, given to him as a compensation for his failure to win the Man Booker Prize, or as the official website of the Man Booker Prize, in an article entitled "Second Chance for Jeet Thayil and Tan Twan Eng", euphemistically put it—"a chance at overcoming the disappointment of missing out on the Man Booker by winning its Subcontinental cousin".[7]

In October 2012 it was announced that the prize was "looking for a new sponsor" as Man Group plc decided to "dump" it (CNN 2012). Subsequently, the prize changed its title to "Asian Literary Prize" while waiting to be picked up by a new sponsor. As hinted by Sharon Norris (2006), even though the foundational power of economic capital is very important for new prizes, if the prize has successfully consolidated its own "symbolic profits" after a period of time, it may still possess the power to attract new sources of economic capital (142). This is certainly the case for the Booker Prize when it attracted Man as its new sponsor after its original funding from the company Booker-McConnell ended in 2002. When the announcement about Man's withdrawal from the MALP was made, most of the stakeholders in the field seemed quite confident that this would be the case for the Asian prize too. For example, Tan Twan Eng, upon receiving what would be the last MALP in 2012, said: "I am sure this particular prize will evolve and become an even greater force in the years to come".[8] However, without new sources of funding, the ambitious and

7 Even though the MALP's official website is not functioning anymore, this article can still be found on the main website of the Man Booker Prize (https://themanbookerprize.com/news/2013/01/11/weekly-roundup-second-chance-jeet-thayil-and-tan-twan-eng-new-novel-thomas-keneally) (accessed September 24, 2019).

8 This remark is from Tan's Facebook post on the 16th of March 2013, and it was reposted by the official Facebook account of the MALP two days later.

confident prize was virtually abandoned in 2013 and has remained defunct ever since.[9]

Part 2: The Failure of Intervention and the Partial Agency of Literary Prizes

The story of the MALP, as manifested in its initial interventionist ambitions, its gradual decline and eventual failure, provides a case for us to revisit English's optimism for "the agency of the cultural prize", especially its ability to intervene in and challenge existing power structures in "our globalised economy of prestige" (English 2005, 320).

In English's works, as well as those of Sharon Norris, Graham Huggan and Julia Lovell, the focus is mainly on highly successful cultural prizes and the celebrities they have created. In these cases, the economic, cultural, social and various other forms of capital invested in the prizes have been thoroughly absorbed, and as a result, these prizes would accumulate enough symbolic capital in and for themselves and secure their influence and power in the cultural habitus they were created to enter. For Bourdieu, the habitus is simultaneously a "structuring structure" and a "structured structure", where social differences and mechanisms of categorisation and distinction are not only practiced but also "internalised" by the players in the field. In such a definition, the habitus consists of dispositions shaped by past events and structures, and those that shape current practices and structures; its (re)production is "without any deliberate pursuit of coherence [. . .] without any conscious concentration" (Bourdieu 2010, 166). Take, for example, the Nobel Prize in Literature: when it was established in 1901, it relied on the economic capital provided by Alfred Nobel and the cultural and social

9 This defunct status can be confirmed by its altered website (where the original information concerning the MALP remains inaccessible as of late 2019), its inactive Facebook and YouTube accounts and its invisibility in the media since 2013. My personal correspondence with the Hong Kong International Literary Festival team in early March 2016 also confirms that none of the founding parties of the prize are still administering it.

capital of the Swedish Academy, but after its own symbolic capital had been secured through the interconversions of capital it built for these players as well as the prominent writers it recognised, its status as the "legitimating" arbitrator of excellence and the creator of literary value became assumed and naturalised in the habitus of world literary culture (English 2005, 58).

However, much less attention has been paid to the difficulties of consolidating symbolic power and securing a powerful position in any given cultural habitus, especially in cases where the support of economic and cultural capital seems to be more than sufficient. In the case of the MALP, three possible explanations can be found for its failure, which are illustrative of these difficulties as well as the partial nature of "the agency of the cultural prize".

First, the prize lacked the Bourdieusian "strategy of condescension" that is key to the accumulation of journalistic capital. In English's terms, "journalistic capital" is not only "visibility and celebrity" but also "scandal", or what he calls "negative affirmation" of the value of prizes (English 2005, 244). English claims that "Every new prize is always already scandalous. The question is whether it will attract attention for this latent scandalousness to become manifest in the public sphere" (192). In Bourdieusian terms, the journalistic potential for such scandalousness is located in the "suspension of belief and disbelief" where participants in the field, especially the recipients and judges of the prizes, need to balance between "indifference" and "enthusiasm" for the capital carried by the prizes, in order to generate enough media attention while maintaining their legitimate images in the politics of respectability (Bourdieu 1991, 67–68). This kind of "scandalous currency" and "strategy of condescension" can be found in the operations of almost all of the successful prizes mentioned (English 2005, 187–88). To understand the effects of these strategies, one only needs to recall the sharp contrast of anger and indifference of the two main contenders at the announcement dinner of the 1983 Booker Prize, where Salman Rushdie reportedly pounded his fists on the table when he lost to J.M. Coetzee, who did not even attend the event (*The Gurardian* 2008); or we can recall the international debates around democracy and censorship caused by the awarding of the Nobel Prize in Literature in 2000 to Gao Xingjian, a Chinese exile in France, whose idea of "Cold Literature" was supposed to overcome the politics surrounding literature (Lovell 2006, 164).

In contrast, in the case of the MALP, scandals had been rare and possibilities to create controversies were actually carefully avoided by the organisers. For example, when the rule change took place in 2010 and many established Asian writers were featured in the longlists for the 2011 award, a number of media reporters at the press meeting in Hong Kong asked questions about the fairness of such inclusions. In response, the chair judge, Monica Ali, provided the anodyne answer: "Literary merit is our sole criteria of judgement"—followed by no more questions. The same happened with the 2012 chair judge Maya Jaggi, who was also asked about the infighting among the judges and the arguments they had. But David Parker, in her stead, just said: "In the history of the Man Asian Literary Prize, I think the decisions have tended to be very unanimous".[10] Therefore, it can be said that in such efforts to hold on to their legitimate power of judgment, the prize organisers and judges failed to acquire enough journalistic capital for the MALP in the form of "negative affirmation", which resulted in the loss of the symbolic power it had accumulated in the habitus of world literature.

Second, the prize, founded by a London-based multinational investment company and an English-language literary festival in Hong Kong, lacked cooperation with national stakeholders in Asia itself. In fact, the prize's stated mission, namely to promote the translation, publication and distribution of Asian literature in the anglophone world without circumventing the national, was in line with the Asian countries' increasing interest in international soft power. As Bowskill's (2012) analysis of the Premio Cervantes Prize shows, such

---

10 Video recordings of these press meetings are available at https://www.youtube.com/watch?v=XumFbujISCc and https://www.youtube.com/watch?v=52AL7Oywd5U respectively (last accessed on March 29, 2016).

a new paradigm of international recognition, which seeks to facilitate the interconversions of cultural capital between the national and the international cultural habituses, demands the active participation of the nation states involved. She argues that rather than "the neo-colonial relationships which are said to characterise privately-run English-language awards such as the Booker", the relationship the Premio Cervantes creates between Spain and Latin America is more equal because the nation state, represented by the Spanish King's participation in the award ceremonies, has vested interests for the political capital the award carries to boost Spain's international image as a post-Franco democracy (308). The MALP also possessed this potential resource of political capital for the nation states in Asia, especially for a country like China, which is rich in economic capital but lacks the political credentials and soft power in an international sphere of culture dominated by western liberal values. By focusing on nationally endorsed writers like Tie Ning, rather than the "banned in China" books, the prize could have presented itself as an important vehicle through which to change the stereotypes about post-Mao Chinese literature created by the dominance of exiled dissident writers in the west. This kind of move can of course be risky, as the prize may be viewed as, by contrast to Bowskill's example, complicit with oppressive regimes in Asia, for whose economic capital the MALP's cultural integrity would be sacrificed; but this kind of risk might just as well generate the "scandalous currency" the prize needed in order to secure its significance in the habitus of world literature. None of these possible scenarios of collaboration happened with the MALP, as no national stakeholders were officially drawn into the field.

Third, as interventionist as the initial ambitions of the MALP were, its actual operation contained many conservative elements that contradicted its seemingly revolutionary focus on "newness". Although it sought to establish a new paradigm of international recognition by discovering "new voices" from Asia, the works in the longlists (those from China in particular) still seem to be confined to the "technologies of recognition" that Shu-mei Shih has outlined

(Appendix 2 page 2). In her essay "Global Literature and the Technologies of Recognition", Shih lists four "technologies of recognition" employed by "the West" to reaffirm its power as "the agent of recognition" vis-à-vis "the rest" as "the object of recognition", including "the systematic", "the allegorical", "global multiculturalism" and "the exceptional particular" (Shih 2004, 17). The first technology is especially relevant to the Chinese winners and longlistees of the MALP. In Shih's formulation, "the systematic" refers to the west's tendency to categorise modern non-western literature into structures such as nations and politics, so that it becomes "decipherable" and "manageable" (23). The example she gives is the proliferation of Cultural Revolution memoirs written by Chinese exiles in the west (which usually are not accessible in mainland China), which tend to shape western understanding of communist or even post-communist China in a very narrow-minded Cold War mentality. Indeed, the Cultural Revolution narratives still occupy a prominent position in the body of translated post-Mao Chinese literature in the west, and the MALP did not challenge as much as become complicit with this "systematic". Upon closer examination, three of the prize's six winners are Chinese, and yet all three titles are narratives about the Cultural Revolution, translated by the same person (Howard Goldblatt). Even when the prize nominated Tie Ning in 2012, it was *The Bathing Women*, a novel known for its humanistic portrayal of the Cultural Revolution in her large oeuvre, that had been featured in the longlist. Therefore, the extent to which the prize was really interventionist and "new" must be questioned.[11]

---

11 To be fair, it should be noted that not all of the Chinese books longlisted by the MALP are related to the Cultural Revolution. For example, Sheng Keyi's *Northern Girls*, longlisted in 2012, is a contemporary story of female migrant workers in South China, the frontiers of the country's economic reform and development. It was also the first book of Sheng Keyi's (a relatively unfamiliar name in the anglophone world then) that had just been translated in English. However, this does not change the fact that the MALP favoured narratives of the Cultural Revolution over works like Sheng's.

Moreover, even though the background document shows that the organisers of the MALP were aware of the dominance of diasporic Asian writers and intellectuals in shaping the understanding and representation of Asia in the west and sought to change it, the prize's governing structure of evaluation actually reinforced this dominance. To be more specific, while the implementation of the entry rules had been consistently strict and the longlistees were mostly Asia-based writers, the dominance of diasporic Asians based in the west continued in the form of judging panels (as gatekeepers). Notably, out of the 16 judges hired by the prize, nine were diasporic Asians based in developed anglophone countries such as America, Britain and Australia, while only the three Indian judges (Vikas Swarup, Vikram Chandra and Pankaj Mishra) were more or less based in Asia itself.[12] Hence, it could be said that the intervention made by the prize was, at best, a conservative one, directed from within the existing power structures in the global literary system.

The three explanations offered here are not exhaustive, but they do demonstrate the importance of maintaining a balance between accumulated capital and idealistic ambitions for the survival and success of new and interventionist prizes like the MALP. On the one hand, the prize organisers seemed to be over-confident in the successful transference and consolidation of the initial economic and cultural capital offered by Man Group plc and the Hong Kong International Literary Festival; without the active accumulation of "scandalous currency" and vested interests from Asian countries, it was assumed that the prize would create value and become a consistent agent of recognition, while the "complex mixtures" of flows of recognition and mutual dependencies in the field were more or less

12 The nine diasporic judges are: Adrienne Clarkson (Chinese Canadian), Gish Jen (Chinese American), Monica Ali (Bangladeshi British), Homi Bhabha (Indian American), Hsu-Ming Teo (Chinese Australian), Chang-rae Lee (Korean American), Maya Jaggi (Indian British), Monique Truong (Vietnamese-American), and Razia Iqbal (Pakistani Ugandan British). Notably, Vikram Chandra moved to the US in the 1980s and also holds American citizenship, but he often travels back to India and stays there for extensive periods of time.

ignored (English 2002, 137). On the other hand, such over-confidence was detrimental to the prize's self-reflexivity in terms of the structural constraints it still had in the face of persisting inequalities in the habitus of world literature. Namely, the hierarchies in the "cultural world-economy" (Casanova 2004, 110) are practised and reinforced instead of challenged, let alone toppled. Despite its short existence, the operation of the MALP has revealed that with the gatekeeping mediation of the Asian diasporic intellectual class in the west, the west is still expected to act as the recognising centre and the rest as the recognised periphery.

Therefore, as much as I agree with English's emphasis on prizes as the "creator", rather than the mere "vehicle" or "token", of cultural value (English 2002, 138), this case study of the MALP and its failure cautions us against such optimistic views and calls for more attention to the *partial*, and thus *limited*, nature of the agency of cultural prizes. This agency is often noted in contexts of success, where the flows of recognition can generate cultural capital for previously undiscovered cultural practices and products, and in this process the "symbolic efficacy" of the prize can be smoothly accumulated to strengthen the cultural habitus around it (English 2002, 133). However, the *partial* nature of this agency tends to manifest in contexts of failure, where the inadequacy in symbolic capital constantly demands prizes to receive recognition and other forms of capital from within certain pre-existing power structures, the cultural habitus of which usually centres around other cultural events and practices. As the case of the MALP shows, without drawing in a broader range of relevant stakeholders or building sufficient vested interests for existing stakeholders, the "symbolic efficacy" of a prize, as well as its mission to facilitate "pursuits of esteem" (ibid), is likely to be significantly compromised.

Epilogue: Han Kang's *The Vegetarian* and the Man Booker

Although the MALP became a defunct literary prize in 2013 and there have not been any signs of its resurrection, its interventionist ambition is not entirely lost to the main establishment of the Booker enterprise. In 2016, the Man Booker International Prize (MBIP) was awarded to the South Korean novelist Han Kang and her translator Deborah Smith for their book *The Vegetarian*, which was the author's first book to be translated into English as well as the first Asian work recognised by the MBIP. Moreover, it was also the first award given after the prize implemented an important reform in its selection criteria in the same year. Before 2016, the MBIP was given to an author whose literary output is largely available in English, including both works written in English and those translated into English, but after 2016, it has been awarded to recognise a single work translated into English in the previous year, and the prize money of £50,000 is shared equally between author and translator. In contrast to the 2010 rule change of the MALP, the MBIP's reconfiguration in 2016 is a successful endeavour that has mitigated the overlap between the Man Booker Prize and itself and carved out a niche, which has to a certain degree filled the void left behind by the MALP's failure.

Upon closer examination, it was indeed not surprising that the first post-reform MBIP was given to an Asian work. The MBIP was an international prize created in 2009 to complement the Man Booker Prize, which only covered anglophone countries in the Commonwealth prior to its own criteria update in 2014 to accept any English-language work published in the UK. However, the MBIP quickly became dominated by anglophone writers any case due to its wide coverage, and 4 out of 6 winners prior to 2016 are established authors who write in English, including Chinua Achebe, Alice Munro, Philip Roth and Lydia Davis. In this background, to showcase the result of its reconfiguration, it was highly likely that the MBIP would be given to a translated work that is not European (since both of the only two translated authors awarded the prize prior to the criteria reform, Ismail Kadare and László Krasznahorkai, write in European languages) and has not been covered by the prominent Arabic Booker. In this process, the functionalist agency of the MALP has at least been partially transferred to the MBIP, and the former's stated mission to promote new Asian writings to some extent fell upon the latter as well. Therefore, it can be said that Han Kang's award was implicitly facilitated by the very failure of the MALP. In a way, the MALP continues to emanate a kind of "posthumous" influence in the form of the reformed MBIP, even though "Asian" as a categorical distinction seems to be lost in the cultural habitus that is the Booker.

However, as the cultural habitus keeps shifting and restructuring, this loss is neither certain nor permanent. On 27 January 2019, the Booker Foundation announced the news that its partnership with the Man group would end in 2020 and the name of the prizes would revert to simply "the Booker" from mid-2019 .[13] One month later, it was widely reported in the newspapers that the British-American billionaire Michael Moritz had agreed to be the new sponsor of the Booker enterprise till at least 2025, with the possibility of extending the support to 2030. This seems to indicate that Asian stakeholders and potential sponsors may have to wait for another decade for new connections and opportunities to emerge, but when that happens, we may anticipate the many interesting ways in which the reversal of the MALP loss will play out. Alternatively, considering the rapid economic and cultural development in Asia, it is also very possible that by then, another cultural habitus of Asian literature—let us call it "X"—would have appeared outside the dominant structures of recognition handled by the west, and rather than Asian writers and readers restlessly chasing the "Asian Booker", we may look forward to an era when western stakeholders label their literature as the "western X" for prestige. As my analysis of the failure of the MALP has demonstrated, such reshuffling of rules can be an onerous task, but these initial attempts have at least given us some good reasons to remain optimistic.

---

13 The full statement is available at https://themanbookerprize.com/news/statement-booker-prize-foundation (last accessed on January 29, 2019).

Bibliography

Archival Material

Booker Prize Archive. Coll. BP/4/1. Oxford Brookes University Library.

Works Cited

Anon. 2013. "Second Chance for Jeet Thayil and Tan Twan Eng." *Themanbookerprize.com*. The Man Booker Prize, Jan. 11. Accessed January 25, 2019.

Bourdieu, Pierre. [1984] 2010. *Distinction: A Social Critique of the Judgement of Taste*. Translated by Richard Nice. London: Routledge.

—. 1986. "The Forms of Capital." In *Handbook of Theory and Research for the Sociology of Education*. Edited by J. G. Richardson, 46–58. New York: Greenwood.

—. 1991. *Language and Symbolic Power*. Translated by Gino Raymond and Matthew Adamson. Cambridge, MA: Harvard University Press.

Bowskill, Sarah. 2012. "Politics and Literary Prizes: A Case Study of Spanish America and the Premio Cervantes." *Hispanic Review* 80 (2): 289–311.

Braun, Rebecca. 2011. "Fetishizing Intellectual Achievement: The Nobel Prize and European Literary Celebrity." *Celebrity Studies* 2 (3): 320–34.

Brouillette, Sarah. 2007. *Postcolonial Writers in the Global Literary Marketplace*. London: Palgrave Macmillan.

Casanova, Pascale. 2004. *The World Republic of Letters*. Translated by M. B. Debevoise. Cambridge, MA: Harvard University Press.

CNN. 2012. "Man Asian Literary Prize Dumped by Man." *Edition.cnn.com*. CNN, Oct. 19. Accessed January 19, 2019.

English, James. F. 2002. "Winning the Culture Game: Prizes, Awards, and the Rules of Art." *New Literary History* 33 (1): 109–35.

—. 2005. *The Economy of Prestige: Prizes, Awards, and the Circulation of Cultural Value*. Cambridge, MA: Harvard University Press.

—. 2014. "The Economics of Cultural Awards." In *Handbook of the Economics of Art and Culture Volume 2*. Edited by Victor A. Ginsburgh and David Throsby, 119–43. Oxford: North-Holland.

Henningsen, Lena. 2010. *Copyright Matters: Imitation, Creativity and Authenticity in Contemporary Chinese Literature.* Berlin: Bwv Berliner-Wissenschaft.

Huggan, Graham. 2001. *The Postcolonial Exotic: Marketing the Margins.* London: Routledge.

Jones, Andrew F. 1994. "Chinese Literature in the 'World' Literary Economy." *Modern Chinese Literature* 8 (1): 171–90.

Lau, Doretta. 2011. "The Man Asian Literary Prize Switcheroo." *Blogs.wsj.com. Wall Street Journal*, Feb 15. Accessed January 24, 2019.

Lewis Martin W. and Kären Wigen. 1997. *The Myth of Continents: A Critique of Metageography.* Los Angles, CA: University of Carlifornia Press.

Lovell, Julia. 2006. *The Politics of Cultural Capital: China's Quest for a Nobel Prize in Literature.* Honolulu: University of Hawai'i Press.

Moeran, Brian. 2010. "The Book Fair as a Tournament of Values." *The Journal of the Royal Anthropological Institute* 16 (1): 138–54.

Moretti, Franco. 2000. "Conjectures on World Literature." *New Left Review* 1 (1): 54–68.

Norris, Sharon. 2006. "The Booker Prize: A Bourdieusian Perspective." *Journal of Cultural Research* 10 (2): 139–58.

Parker, David. n.d. "Celebrating Asian Literature." *Theculturetrip.com.* Accessed January 22, 2019.

Shi, Flair Donglai. 2016. "Post-Mao Chinese Literature as World Literature: Struggling with the Systematic and the Allegorical." *Comparative Literature & World Literature* 1 (1): 20–34.

Shih, Shu-mei. 2004. "Global Literature and the Technologies of Recognition." *PMLA* 119 (1): 16–30.

The Guardian. 2008. "Tears, Tiffs and Triumphs: 40 Years of Booker Prize Judges Dish the Dirt." *Theguardian.com*. The Guardian, Sep. 6. Accessed January 24, 2019.

Todd, Richard. 1996. *Consuming Fictions: The Booker Prize and Fiction in Britain Today*. London: Bloomsbury.

Vittachi, Nury. n.d. "A Brief History of the Man Asian Literary Prize." *https://mrjam.typepad.com/manasianliteraryprize/*. Accessed September 15, 2019.

Wang, Kan. 2012. "North America, English Translation, and Contemporary Chinese Literature." *Frontiers of Literary Studies in China* 6 (4): 570–81.

Appendices

(Documents from the Man Booker Archive at Oxford Brookes University)

Appendix 1

THE **MAN** HONG KONG INTERNATIONAL
Literary Festival 2006

Major New Literary Prize Established in Asia

Man Asian Literary Prize Will Recognise New Works By Regional Authors

HONG KONG – A major new literary prize was launched today to recognise the work of Asian writers and to bring them to the attention of the world literary community. The prize is a joint project of Man Group plc and the Hong Kong Literary Festival Ltd, which together announced the prize's creation.

Called the Man Asian Literary Prize, the award will seek entries from Asian writers for works that are yet to be published in English. Entries will be submitted in English, and the prize is intended to provide a broader platform for the cream of new Asian literature to be brought to the attention of English-reading audiences around the world.

The Hong Kong International Literary Festival, sponsored by Man Investments, is the region's most recognised festival highlighting the achievements of authors throughout greater Asia. Man Group plc (the parent company of Man Investments) is a leading London-based global provider of alternative investment products and solutions as well as one of the world's largest futures brokers.

Matt Dillon, Regional Managing Director of Man Investments, Asia Pacific announced its establishment at the conclusion of the 2006 Man Hong Kong International Literary Festival. The first annual prize will be awarded in Autumn 2007.

"Through this new prize we aim to foster the publication of new Asian voices in English and to help make those voices more widely heard", Mr Dillon said. "One of the most important tasks facing our world in recent times has been for the English-speaking peoples to have a better understanding of Asian society and culture. We very much hope this prize will encourage that activity".

Peter Gordon, Director of the Hong Kong International Literary Festival, said Asian writers were becoming increasingly significant on the world literary scene.

"Asia is becoming an important source for new writing for major international publishers and this award will help facilitate publishing and translating of Asian literature into English", Mr Gordon said.

THE **MAN** HONG KONG INTERNATIONAL
Literary Festival 2006

"Since the purpose of this prize is to facilitate publication and translation rather than to merely reward existing publication activity, the Prize will focus on 'new' works, as yet unpublished in English", he said.

The Man Asian Literary Prize will be administered by a new and independent not-for-profit entity. It is anticipated that the judging panel will be drawn from international literary and academic communities.

The Man Asian Literary Prize has a unique combination of features. It is explicitly focused on Asia, as distinct from, for example, the Asia-Pacific/Pacific Rim. It is based in Asia and it will be for currently unpublished works with the explicit objective of encouraging the publication of more works by Asian writers.

Further details including application procedures, eligibility and prize money will be finalised over the coming months and will be announced in Autumn 2006.

Man Group plc is also the sponsor of the Man Booker Prize for Fiction and the Man Booker International Prize, two of the world's premier literary prizes.

- Ends -

NOTE TO EDITORS

Background Paper attached

The Man Hong Kong International Literary Festival Ltd

The Man Hong Kong International Literary Festival was conceived by a group of journalists, publishers, editors, authors and academics in 2000 and was held for the first time in 2001. The Festival aims to entertain, educate and inspire through the promotion of English literature with an Asian focus. It is the leading English-language festival in Asia, and the only world-class festival focusing on writing with Asian roots. The 2006 Festival includes a 10 day programme with over 60 events and more than 40 authors from around the world, celebrating the best in fiction, narrative non-fiction, poetry and writing for children.

THE **MAN** HONG KONG INTERNATIONAL
Literary Festival 2006

Man Group plc
Man Group plc is a leading global provider of alternative investment products and solutions as well as one of the world's largest futures brokers. The Group employs over 3,000 people in 15 countries with key centres in London, Pfäffikon (Switzerland), Chicago, New York, Paris, Singapore and Sydney. Man Group plc is listed on the London Stock Exchange (EMG.L) and is a constituent of the FTSE 100 Index. Man Investments, the asset management division of Man Group plc, is a global leader in the fast growing alternative investments industry. Man Financial, the brokerage division of Man Group plc, is one of the world's leading providers of brokerage services.

Man Investments has supported the Festival since 2002 and is proud once again to sponsor the Man Hong Kong International Literary Festival 2006.

www.mangroupplc.com

For further information:

Peter Gordon
Director, Hong Kong International Literary Festival (www.festival.org.hk)
Editor, Asian Review of Books (www.asianreviewofbooks.com)
Publisher, Chameleon Press (www.chameleonpress.com)
Director, Paddyfield.com (www.paddyfield.com)
Tel: +852 2522 4224
Email: pgordon@iagroup.com.hk

Robb Corrigan
Global Head of Communications
Man Investments
Huobstrasse 3
8808 Pfäffikon SZ
Switzerland
Direct tel: +41 (0) 55 417 62 72
Direct fax: +41 (0) 55 417 62 61
Mobile: +44 (0) 7775 822 720
rcorrigan@maninvestments.com
www.maninvestments.com
A member of the Man Group

Sue Gourlay
Golin Harris (Hong Kong)
Direct tel: +852 2501 7936
Mobile tel: +852 9522 0135
sue.gourlay@golinharris.com

Appendix 2

THE **MAN** HONG KONG INTERNATIONAL
Literary Festival 2006

Background to the Man Asian Literary Prize

Executive Summary
The first Man Asian Literary Prize will be awarded in the Autumn of 2007 for an "Asian novel unpublished in English" and each twelve months thereafter.

The objectives of creating the Asian Literary Award are:

- To bring exciting new Asian authors to the attention of the world literary community.
- To facilitate publishing and translating of Asian literature in and into English.
- To highlight Asia's developing role in world literature.

The Prize is a joint project of the Man Group and the Hong Kong International Literary Festival Limited.

Definitions

- "in English" covers both works originally in English and translations of works already published in other languages.
- "unpublished" means that the work's publication date (if scheduled) must be after the scheduled date for awarding the prize.
- "novel" implies a substantial work of fiction.

In any given case, eligibility is at the discretion of the Prize.

Background and discussion
While writers from some countries, notably India, and emigrant Asian writers in such countries as the U.S., Britain, Australia and France, have long had significant publishing opportunities and have, as a result, long contributed to the corpus of literature in English, Asian writers (as defined here) are only just now becoming increasingly important on the world literary scene: Asia, from Japan to China and Southeast Asia, is now becoming an exciting source of authors, and as such, has been recognised by major mainstream publishers.

THE **MAN** HONG KONG INTERNATIONAL
Literary Festival 2006

Such recent industry announcements as the establishment of Penguin India and Picador Asia are clear evidence of this trend, as is the critical acclaim now being awarded to young, contemporary authors from China and Southeast Asia: writers such as Su Tong, Yu Hua, Jiang Rong, Tash Aw, Hitomi Kanehara and Rani Manicka.

An Asian Literary Award which concentrates on Asian writing based in Asia matches current developments in world literature. It also matches developments in world publishing where, as noted above, Asia is becoming an increasingly sought after source of important new writing for the major international publishers.

This particular formulation of the Prize was selected for the following reasons:

- Asia is a wide and diverse region with a large number of languages. Judging works across multiple languages was deemed to be impossible from a practical perspective and therefore the Award is limited to works in English.

- However, since many if not most of Asia's authors will be writing in a language other than English, translations of original works are included.

- The Prize should be explicitly Asian, rooted in the region and awarded to writers originating and writing from the region, rather than authors of Asian background writing from other regions.

- In spite of increasing publication of Asian writing, the publishing industry in most of the region is still underdeveloped and years behind that of North America, Europe and Australia: much good writing is still not available in the local language; it takes even longer for it to become available in English.

  The Prize also supports the craft of translation, an important part of the process of bringing new works to the English-language market.

  Publication is a commercial rather than creative reality. Since the purpose is to support and facilitate new publication and translation rather than to merely reward existing publication activity, the Prize will focus on "new" works, as yet unpublished in English.

In order to assist in this process of facilitating the publication of new and exciting Asian literature, a significant sum will be allocated to purchase copies of the winning book for distribution by the Festival to regional libraries and educational institutions.

THE MAN HONG KONG INTERNATIONAL
Literary Festival 2006

While it is expected that winners will be picked up by international publishers, if the works are not already scheduled for publication, Hong Kong's Chameleon Press (www.chameleonpress.com) has agreed to publish winning works that do not already have an international English-language publisher.

Founding Parties

Man Group plc is the sponsor of the Man Booker Prize (the leading English-language literary award) and the new Man Booker International Prize(see http://www.themanbookerprize.com). Man Investments is also the title sponsor of the Man Hong Kong International Literary Festival.

The Man Booker Prize for Fiction represents the very best in contemporary fiction. One of the world's most prestigious awards, and one of incomparable influence, it continues to be the pinnacle of ambition for every fiction writer. Now in its thirty-seventh year, the prize aims to reward the best novel of the year written by a citizen of the Commonwealth or the Republic of Ireland. The Man Booker judges are selected from the country's finest critics, writers and academics to maintain the consistent excellence of the prize. The winner of the Man Booker Prize receives £50,000 and both the winner and the shortlisted authors are guaranteed a worldwide readership plus a dramatic increase in book sales.

Man Group plc is a leading global provider of alternative investment products and solutions as well as one of the world's largest futures brokers. The Group employs over 3,000 people in 15 countries, with key centres in London, Pfäffikon (Switzerland), Chicago, New York, Paris, Singapore and Sydney. Man Group plc is listed on the London Stock Exchange (EMG.L) and is a constituent of the FTSE 100 index.

The Hong Kong International Literary Festival Ltd. is the body that organizes and runs the annual Man Hong Kong International Literary Festival, now Asia's leading English-language literary event, as well as the simultaneous Shanghai Literary Festival. Close to 10,000 people are expected to attend the 2006 Festival, which will feature more than 60 authors in more than 70 events.

Questions and Answers:

Q: How will the Prize be administered?
A: The Prize will be administered by a new not-for-profit entity.

THE **MAN** HONG KONG INTERNATIONAL
Literary Festival 2006

Q: How much will the Prize be?
A: Financial details are still being finalised. However, the award amount will be substantial. When appropriate, an additional sum may be awarded to the translator. Finally, in order to facilitate publication, it is anticipated that the Prize will also allocate a sum to purchase significant copies of the resulting book for distribution to regional libraries and educational institutions.

Q: Who will judge the manuscripts?
A: It is anticipated that judges will be drawn from the international literary and academic communities.

Q: What will be application procedure?
A: Details of the application procedure, eligibility, etc. will be available at a further announcement in the early Autumn of 2006.

Contacts
Additional comment on the Asian Literary Award will be withheld until the next announcement in early Autumn 2006. Contacts for the Award are:

Peter Gordon
Director, Hong Kong International Literary Festival (www.festival.org.hk)
Editor, Asian Review of Books (www.asianreviewofbooks.com)
Publisher, Chameleon Press (www.chameleonpress.com)
Director, Paddyfield.com (www.paddyfield.com)
Tel: +852 2522 4224
Email: pgordon@iagroup.com.hk

Robb Corrigan
Global Head of Communications, Man Investments
Huobstrasse 3, 8808 Pfäffikon SZ
Switzerland
Direct tel: +41 (0) 55 417 62 72
Direct fax: +41 (0) 55 417 62 61
Mobile: +44 (0) 7775 822 720
Email: rcorrigan@maninvestments.com
www.maninvestments.com

Sue Gourlay
GolinHarris, Hong Kong
Direct tel: +852 2501 7936
Mobile: +852 9522 0135
Email: sue.gourlay@golinharris.com

7

Section 3:
Minor Locations

Minor Literature, Minor Prizes: The Case of Mauritius

Rashi Rohatgi

Mauritian literature is not only minor but ultraminor: it is linguistically deterritorialized, thoroughly political, collectively charged, and its literary sphere consists of a relatively small number of book-buying participants (Rohatgi 2017). This small cadre of writers and readers has, however, long used institutions to respond collectively to the peripheralisation ultraminor literatures often face. Since the earliest days of permanent settlement on the island, Afro-Mauritians fled slavery and formed refugee societies in which vernaculars developed. Such a society is depicted, for example, in Bernardin de St. Pierre's ([1789] 1825) *Paul et Virginie*, although this work is, it should be stressed, not realistic fiction. Even before the end of the French colonial period, the French spoken on Mauritius was distinct from that spoken in France. When the British replaced the French in 1810, the Act of Capitulation protected the use of French, rather than English, in civic life. When Indians were brought as indentured labourers, they passed their language on through community recitations of religious works, particularly the *Ramayana*. Since independence in 1968, Mauritius has formally considered itself a multilingual nation, and Indo-Mauritians, especially, have been entitled to heritage language classes in public schools. The Kreol Morisyen movement agitated for a truly vernacular public education, and since 2012 Kreol Morisyen has been a medium of public education in Mauritius (Rohatgi 2014). It is quite possible that within a generation, Mauritian literature will not be minor at all, will not be linguistically deterritorialised, but rather be written primarily in Kreol Morisyen.

What remains to be seen is the effect this will have on Mauritian literary world-making: will an ultra-small but not ultraminor literature trade in hard-won global momentum in favor of a previously unthinkable, more insular creativity (Cheah 2016)? That institutions have been an important part of Mauritian literary world-making suggests that reading Mauritian literature alongside the works of Huggan (2001), Brouillette (2007), and English (2005), which analyse the role of literary institutions in the creation and maintenance of literary prestige, may provide clues. With no inhabitants, and thus no language or literature, before colonization, Mauritian literature can be seen as the quintessence of "the literature of the modern capitalist world-system", ripe for a sociologically-oriented critical world literature studies (Warwick Research Collective 2015, 15).

This chapter looks at one particular literary institution, the literary prize, in one particular decade, the 2000s, when literature in Mauritius was at its most multilingual: writers working in French, English, Hindi (and other Indian languages), and Kreol Morisyen were all publishing. Mauritian literature exists in every Mauritian language, but, as scholars of critical world literature theory would expect, the amount of published literature in each language does not neatly represent Mauritian demographics. Indo-Mauritians, linguistically comprised of speakers both of North and South Indian languages, make up almost three-quarters of the population of 1.2 million, whilst Creole Mauritians approximately one-quarter, Sino-Mauritians and white Mauritians—speakers of Mandarin, Cantonese, English, and French—are significant minority communities as well (the official demographic categories are Hindus, Muslims, Chinese, and General Population) (Rohatgi 2014).

Rather than reflecting either heritage language use or vernacular language use (citizens are united in their use of Kreol Morisyen), the Mauritian publishing industry reflects the country's history of double-colonisation, with many writers and readers acclimatised to reading in the French and English they were taught at school. That its two large publishing houses, the state-owned Editions de l'Océan Indien and school materials provider Editions Le Printemps, are not the primary publishers of the best known Mauritian fiction also reflects this history, as well as conforms to the expectations of readers of Damrosch (2003), Moretti (2000, 2003), and the Warwick Research Collective (2015). As with marginalised writers elsewhere, Mauritian writers' access to readers is often more effectively gained through Paris or London, even as their work can be seen as peripheral within anglophone or francophone literary worlds. Since 1901, when Mahatma Gandhi's visit to the island brought new energy to the Hindi language movement, Mauritians have worked to diversify the literary scene, popularising self-published works at literary gatherings and setting up small presses such as Vizavi Editions (Sundarajan 2006, 69). In the first decade of the millennium, on which this chapter is focused, the Kreol Morisyen movement gained significant ground. The two prizes here deal with literature in French and English, in the first instance, and Kreol Morisyen, in the second instance, reflecting a more reactive and a more aggressive response, respectively, to the disadvantageous position Mauritian literature finds itself in vis-à-vis major literatures.

The prizes discussed here are the Prince Maurice Prize, sponsored by the Prince Maurice resort hotel, and the Ledikasyon pu Travayer prize, sponsored by the eponymous labour collective. Neither prize has been successful at bringing Mauritian literature into the global consciousness and neither prize still exists in the form in which it was initially conceived. It would be easy to write off the Prince Maurice Prize for its gauche association with a resort in a country with devastating income inequalities, but the Booker Prize—sponsored by a company made successful through colonial sugar plantation holdings—is still very much with us, and this chapter will look at this prize specifically in relation to the Booker. While James English (2005) and Sarah Brouillette (2007) discuss the success of the Booker Prize, Graham Huggan (2001) in *The Postcolonial Exotic* traces its creation and trajectory, particularly its sponsorship by a sugar company that has now succeeded in erasing its primary affiliation with a troublesome industry. It would be easy to write off the Ledikasyon pu Travayer prize, for different reasons—as thus far too insular—but for advocates of minor literatures, how else is such literature to be made newsworthy, other than through the bestowal of a prize? For that reason, perhaps, this prize has been repurposed since Kreol Morisyen's ascendence as an educational medium, and this chapter will look at the intimations these changes offer as to how institutions might best play a role in a post-minor Mauritian literature. To be clear, this is a study of minor prizes: not minor in the Deleuze and Guattari sense, but minor in the measure of their global significance. At the heart of this critical endeavour is the argument that world literary studies must take into account failures, as well as successes.

The reasons for creating a prize are many and are often persuasive: to bring new writers to the fore, to bring minor literatures to the fore. Yet as Huggan (2001), English (2005), and Brouillette (2007) make clear, prizes more often make existing power more explicit and its voice louder, rather than allowing previously-unheard voices to be heard. We cannot say, however, at the last calculation, that the relative powerlessness of their sponsors renders prizes from the periphery totally toothless. The world they attempt to bring into being exists, if only in memory. The memory of these prizes in the minds of their applicants and of the readers of the prize-winning books integrates the Mauritian literary sphere ever more deeply with the global, fostering existing connections and forging new ones.

This chapter will proceed through five sections. First, a short summary of analyses of the Booker Prize's history makes evident that a prize's success depends on its ability to seem newsworthy. The ability to generate a scandal worth noticing is the key to making a prize stand out in the world literary marketplace. Before the discussion of the two prizes, the second section provides further context about the attention Mauritius receives in the world literary marketplace. The subsequent discussion of the Prince Maurice Prize describes the unsuccessful attempts made by prize chair Tim Lott to create scandal by playing into marginalising perceptions of the country. Discussion of the Lediskasyon pu Travayer prize describes the unsuccessful attempts of activists, including Commonwealth Prize-winning Mauritian author Lindsey Collen, to circumvent such perceptions while still garnering media attention. Since the

Lediskasyon pu Travayer prize celebrates literature in Kreol Morisyen, and the prize has recently been updated, this section focuses on 2004 prize-winner Rishy Bukoree's career trajectory as a writer following his victory. It suggests how the institutional groundwork laid by this prize could help future Mauritian literary prizes become more effective in advancing the cause of those Mauritians who push back against the marginalisation of their ultraminor literature. The conclusion takes a broader view of the topic, contextualising it in terms of current discussions of world literature studies.

The Booker Prize Model

In *The Economy of Prestige,* James English (2005) traces the birth of the modern prize phenomenon, noting its exponential rise in the last 100 years. Although excellence in literary activity has been celebrated throughout history, he notes that even now, concerns persist about the commodification of artistry (3). After all, these prizes exist in a world characterised by real inequalities in terms of distribution and representation. That the Booker Prize has been successful is not entirely surprising, as its patron is a company that, before it was a prize sponsor, was already both prosperous and politically advantaged as a sugar distributor with roots in Demerara. Through a celebratory lens, the founding of the prize is sometimes seen as part of a larger change of heart on the part of its then head, Lord Campbell. His obituary in *The Independent* depicts his transformation:

> He graduated into a bit of a tearaway, loving fast cars and fancy-free ways. Then he was sent to British Guiana to see how the family fortune was made and he had the shock of his young life. He saw the poverty on which a life of plenty was based. Those were the days, before the Second World War, when a ton of sugar might sell for as little as a cricket ball. All Campbell's abilities were suddenly converted into a faith that change must be possible, that Bookers had to forge a new deal with its working communities in the West Indies

> and black Africa. Demerara was Jock Campbell's Damascus. (Parker 1995, 1)

Alongside his not-insignificant changes to the company's treatment of workers, he also diversified the company, and his book division became profitable by buying up the copyrights of famous authors such as Agatha Christie. In such a narrative, taking the money earned from the reading public and returning it, in prize form, to that public, forms a natural conclusion. Booker's focus on Commonwealth Literature reflects its prior economic involvement with the Commonwealth. Huggan concentrates on the administrative side of the story. He notes that though the first prize was awarded in 1969, since 1971 the prize itself has been administered by a series of trusts. Its first administrators brought with them publishing expertise and contacts (through their experience with Jonathan Cape), but more importantly, they brought an understanding of the importance of newspaper coverage, and later (since 1981) television exposure (Huggan 2001, 109).

The Booker Prize committee—including authors, publishers, agents, booksellers, librarians, PR people, and a Booker-sponsored chairperson—takes entries from publishers, but the winner is chosen by five judges who are less industry-centric than the committee. They include academics and book critics, but also, always, celebrities who represent public opinion. At a televised gala, they announce a winner who, thus far, has tended to "belong to a recognized postcolonial canon" (Huggan 2001, 119). While this is by no means always the case, even those whom the prize has catapulted to a new level of renown tend to be writing from within a recognized framework of literary success. Marlon James, for example, was teaching writing by the time he won the Booker; his previous publications had led him to be seen as successful enough to earn a living as an expert practitioner in the field. More significantly, the winners often share a certain ideological bent: "more than half of the prizewinning novels to date investigate aspects of, primarily colonial, history or present a counter-memory" (111). While celebration of these works and their authors is unquestionably positive, Huggan's point is that "the discursive link is provided here by exoticist objectification" (111), even if the winning novels themselves have exactly the opposite intention.

The Prize is not famous, though, for its link to sugar or its postcolonialism, but rather for its unabashed incorporation of spectacle. As James English makes clear, literary prizes only matter when someone is arguing against them:

> The astonishing degree of journalistic interest in how the participants in an award ceremony behave, how the losers take the news, how the winners express their gratitude, how the old grudges and rivalries manifest themselves, is more than idle curiosity about celebrities. At stake in the minute and always ready-to-be-scandalized attendance to matters of prize etiquette is the very belief in the Artist as a special category of person, and hence in Art as a special domain of existence. (2005, 196)

The scandals allow society to have its say, renewed each year with the changing zeitgeist, on what art is. In 1981, John Banville wrote to *The Guardian* criticizing the elitism of the committee's shortlist choices—before winning in 2005. The 2011 shortlist, conversely, was panned by critics responding to judge Dame Stella Rimington's stated preference for so-called readable books over more experimental, complex, or literary choices (although Julian Barnes's *The Sense of an Ending* would eventually win) (Self 2011, 1). The establishment of the Booker may reflect Lord Campbell's change of heart, but its success was dependent on others in his community sharing that change of heart. We may protest against the Booker and its criteria, but having our say means making visible and legitimate the system of prize-giving in the first place.

The Mauritian Context

Mauritius parallels Guyana in its history. Like Guyana, Mauritius experienced waves of colonial rule, with the British arriving after the sugar plantation economy had already been established. In Guyana, after a long period of interaction with the Dutch and the French, the British consolidated their rule over the sugar-producing region of Demerara in 1814; in Mauritius, the British took over from the French in 1810. In the 20th century, Mauritius achieved independence in 1968, two years after Guyanese independence, leaving the governments and citizens of both nations to figure out how to move forward. Both countries struggled to create harmony among their various ethnic communities—during the colonial period, slaves brought over from Africa were joined by indentured laborers from Asia—and have them work together to overturn the ravages of the plantation past. Sugar continues to be produced, but diversification was clearly necessary. Since 1968, sugar production as a proportion of the Mauritian GDP has dwindled to single digits, but, with sugar production still occurring on 85 percent of the arable land in Mauritius, there is little chance that its symbolic significance will diminish.

In Mauritius, tourism has arisen to fill the economic void. Creating 30 percent of the national GDP (alongside rapidly growing IT and financial services industries), it is both controversial and undeniably here to stay. Girish Prayag et al. describe its manifestation:

> Since the start of the tourism industry in the 1950s, Mauritius has focused on enclave tourism. This—the principal development model used by tourism planners—has been shown elsewhere in the world to promote few economic or cultural linkages at local and regional levels. (Prayag et. al. 2010, 699)

This beach holiday model, though it requires minor cultural adjustment from locals, is less able to bring about infrastructure improvements that benefit the local population.

Governmental and business groups, aware of the inequalities and environmental degradation fostered by the luxury tourism model, have sought to mitigate tourism's risks. Since 2006, hoteliers have been required by the Tourism Fund Act to contribute a fraction of their profits towards a fund that goes towards infrastructure development for the country outside its resorts. Most of the Corporate Social Responsibility incursions, though, have been at the behest of the hoteliers themselves (Prayag et. al. 2010, 702). Le Prince Maurice resort hotel has been of particular note in this regard and has been awarded Green Globe certification (709).

With tourism as a mainstay of the new economy, the colonial languages of French and English have persisted, not only because of residual ideas of prestige, but because of their function in allowing the Mauritian workforce to communicate easily with business partners and hotel guests from around the francophone and anglophone worlds. The vernacular, however, has always offered an alternative to European languages; Mooneram (2009) notes that "independence in Mauritius saw the emergence of a politically and linguistically aware group of creative writers who choose to write in a creole vernacular" (6). Kreol Morisyen is a vernacular formed on the island, heavily inflected by the French and to a lesser degree by the African, South Asian, and other languages brought to the island by its inhabitants. Although since 2012 it has become the medium of education, this victory came after a concerted effort by writers to create, simultaneously, a canon and an orthography.

Efforts to unite the country around its vernacular have been carried out by non-governmental organizations, the most recognized of which is Lediskasyon pu Travayer. Noting that the predominance of French and English in official spheres has excluded from civic participation those who do not speak those languages, Lediskasyon pu Travayer fights not only for equality amongst languages, but also for equality between ethnic groups—with the island's Creole community least likely to have access to French or English—and economic classes. Those writers using Kreol Morisyen—most famously Dev Virahsawmy and Lindsey Collen—are stridently and intentionally political and postcolonial. Without this vernacular movement, the country would be even more severely subject to the literary version of a brain drain, described by Weinberg (2016) as follows:

> The phenomenon I have referred to as *text drain* has at least two faces: on the one hand, the newly asymmetrical forms of orientation and circulation of ideas and thought traditions; on the other, decontextualization and the loss of specificity. Here rests one of the components of the crises of the humanities: a shrinking of public spaces for dialogue, discussion, and joint construction and sharing, as well as a loss of the sense of specificity in artistic and literary practices. (76–77; italics in original)

With the inability of the publishing industry to meet the nation's literary aspirations, as discussed in the introduction, writers working in languages with international markets have been incentivized to make their work more relatable to readerships in those markets, rather than enmeshed in local literary conversations to the point of estrangement from those markets.

Already, many of the most successful Mauritian writers work in Hindi, English, or, mostly, French. From Abhimanyu Unnuth to Ananda Devi, writers have represented Mauritian culture not only from within, but with an outward orientation (Rohatgi 2014). The very act of being published by a foreign publishing house frames the reception of a text, reiterating, rather than rending asunder, the idea of Mauritian writers as peripheral parts of the Indian diaspora, or the *Francophonie*, rather than being at the center of a national literary sphere.

When long-esteemed French writer Jean-Marie Gustave Le Clézio won the 2008 Nobel Prize in Literature, readers were introduced through his acceptance speech (2008) to a new facet of this author, as they were through his subsequent paraliterary activity: Le Clézio was recognized as not simply French, but Franco-Mauritian. His ancestors had been (white) French settlers in the once-French island nation, and in his call for more extensive translation and circulation of works from decolonised spaces, he carefully draws attention to the Mauritian authors Malcolm de Chazal and Abhimanyu Unnuth (Le Clézio 2008, 1). They are two of many referenced, from all over the world; Le Clézio's speech is not primarily about his heritage, but for many outside of Mauritius listening to or reading it, this may have been their first exposure to these names—or indeed, to the existence of a Mauritian literary scene. These references served as a signal, too, of where his prize-money was to go: a large portion of it went to the co-founding of the Foundation for Interculturality and Peace with Mauritian intellectual Isa Asgarally. Jacqueline Dutton (2017) concludes that:

> when the opportunity arose to redeem his sugar plantation family name, Le Clézio stepped up to the challenge, lending his time and resources to create the FIP, promoting the aims of intercultural understanding for peace in a highly multi-ethnic and multi-lingual island locale. (48)

Le Clézio's career began with a prize: in 1963, he was awarded the Prix Renaudot. This first prize win, at age 23, allowed him to spend the entirety of his adult life as writer, and it is as a writer that he speaks when, in his Nobel lecture, he asserts that intercultural understanding is "above all the responsibility of readers—of publishers, in other words", equating action with access (2008, 1).

For South African-Mauritian writer Lindsey Collen, the equation of publishers and readers was initially a more concrete one: in 1990, her publisher, the labour collective Ledikayson pu Travayer, sold potential readers pre-purchase coupons in order to fund a Collen book project, "centralizing readers as active decision makers in dissemination of published fiction, rather than as consumers restricted to choosing between predetermined outputs" (Cousins 2018, 95). When, later, she was awarded the Commonwealth Writers' Prize for *The Rape of Sita* (1994), she recognised that international success would mean using international publishers and conventional publication models. She found the shift worthwhile, in part because of the exposure this brought her intersectional political causes, one of which was the championing of Kreol Morisyen, the national vernacular. She felt comfortable writing subsequent novels (including

Boy [2005]), which brought her a second Commonwealth Writers' Prize, ininitially in Kreol Morisyen, secure in the understanding that readers of an English translation would be given access to her work, and that it could function simultaneously as local and world literature. Her triumphs in the 1994 and 2005 Commonwealth Prize for Africa pushed against text drain and helped start a Kreol Morisyen literary movement around which future writers could coalesce.

Between Collen's victory in 1994 and Le Clézio's in 2008, literary prize victories brought visibility to Mauritian literature—and because of the responses of these two prizewinners, they brought visibility not only to two authors' contributions to Mauritian literature, but to the entire multilingual corpus. The Prince Maurice Prize and the Lediskasyon pu Travayer prize continue in this tradition, using the ability of prizes to generate prestige in order to counterbalance marginalization. However, as discussion of these prizes will show, the literary prize has no independent ability to convert graft into prestige. Prizes in minor literatures face often-insurmountable hurdles when attempting to push such literatures into the mainstream; instead, prizes are more effective when they reflect the prestige of their organisers and pull individual writers out of still-marginalised sectors. The endurance of Mauritian efforts to harness the power of the literary prize, however, underlines the role that literary prizes can play in drawing local attention to ultraminor literary worlds, and thus enlarging and solidifying them.

Le Prince Maurice Prize

The hoteliers of Le Prince Maurice are no strangers to the winning of prizes. By all accounts a well-run luxury resort, the hotel has been recognized in recent years by Trip Advisor in its Hall of Fame. *Jetsetter* commends its "splendid isolation, on a private peninsula devoid of beach vendors"; incursions of local culture are not absent, but rather highly curated—its architect, for example, is a highly regarded Mauritian, Jean Marc Eynaud, who garnered recognition for the hotel in the 2016 World Luxury Hotel Awards. This success allows the hotel some room to curate its visitors, as well, by making demands of them beyond what a hotel normally asks of guests: breathtakingly expensive gala dinners on Christmas Eve and New Year's Eve are compulsory. This weeds out those who simply want to gawk at the luxury and natural beauty. "Tourism proper", writes Sarah Brouillette, "is in a post-tourist phase". That is, tourists and the industry themselves do not simply exoticize; instead, they engage in "strategic exoticism" that requires a specifically-imagined voyeur, one who is not only "in need of [. . .] instruction" about the target culture, but who also shares with the host, the hotelier, an orientation towards the mode of discovery (2007, 43). Writers, with a whiff of the garret about them and their ethnographic perspectives, are not Le Prince Maurice's normal clientele; they are seldom factored into their prize-winning formula of luxurious exclusivity.

Although named after the bachelor prince Maurice van Nassau, the hotel proclaims itself, in its website, to be "inspired by passion". Thus the decision to curate a more literary reputation through the hosting of a literary prize for books about love was on-brand, and, indeed, an inspired choice for an island most famously depicted (in its day) by Bernardin de Saint Pierre's tragic love story *Paul et Virginie* ([1789] 1825). By offering a prize—a stay in the hotel, including the prize-bestowing gala dinner—that was both the best the hotel had to offer and the very asset the hotel needed to publicize in order to stand out in a crowded luxury market, Le Prince Maurice was proceeding with its characteristic curatorial panache. In the first decade of the 2000s, Le Prince Maurice was following Booker's lead in recasting an erstwhile plantation economy in a softer light by using its residual power to bestow cultural capital. The construction of the prize displayed the hotel's characteristic thoughtfulness: in alternate years, the prize celebrated global literary fiction on love in English and French, which made good use of the skills of the three multilingual Mauritian judges, Kumari Issur, Carl de Souza and Alain Gordon-Gentil, all of whom have published novels in French, and whose presence on the panel gave the prize its link with the Mauritian literary sphere. Foreign judges were freshly chosen each year by (foreign) chairs: Daniel Picouly for the French and Tim Lott for the English.

The Prize, then, was a natural fit for an island whose self-imaginary is steeped in the romantic. James English notes, though, that "even though prizes [. . .] seem automatically appropriate (like bringing flowers to a dinner party), each prize entails a lot of administrative work and continued patronage" (2005, 112). Any literary prize itself cannot consume the entire budget of its bestowing organisation, as there are also operating costs the sponsor must keep in mind. Whether or not enough money has been put aside is hard to gauge, because so many costs are incurred in a shadow economy of networking, professional and personal favours, and other exchanges of social, rather than monetary capital. One might think it would be tempting for Le Prince Maurice to attempt to forego these elements and instead, as both sponsor and organizer, stick to financial transactions to keep the planning more clear, but the type of press coverage a prize needs to survive can very rarely be bought. As English (2005) and Brouillette (2007) impress upon us, media attention—and therefore prize success—requires scandal.

"Every new prize is already scandalous", argues English (2005, 192), and perhaps the organizers at Le Prince Maurice understood only too well what their scandal would be: the very juxtaposition of the starving-but-noble artist and the luxe-but-sinister resort would make for headlines. And some attention did follow. In 2006, for example, recurring chairman of the jury Tim Lott was able to attract attention from both *The Guardian* and *The Independent* after convening a prize panel including Jacqueline Wilson, a longlist including works by Zadie Smith, Julian Fellowes, Rachel Cusk, and Kamila Shamsie, and, most importantly for the papers, actress Tilda Swinton as patron. Lott did this by imbuing the prize's origin story with scandal. "[It is] one of the more unusual prizes on the literary calendar", remarked *Guardian* reporter Michelle Pauli (2006, 1), referring not only to the sponsor but also to the prize's categorical vagueness. As Lott tells her the story, the prize was originally supposed to be given to works of romantic fiction, but Lott wanted instead to recognise "writers of the heart":

> the Booker, for example, rewards technical ability, but neglects humour and love stories. [. . .] the variety of literary love stories is incredible and there will never be clear boundaries—the book could have a tender voice or be about family love as well as romantic love. (Pauli 2006, 1)

Lott sets up a binary construction, dividing serious literature, with its intentional technique and defined genre, against popular literature, which he seems to champion but not quite define. Its writers have heart, and this heart comes through in their writing, regardless of style or subject matter, and these writers, he suggests, should be prized more than they currently are.

The decision of the hoteliers to bring in Lott was a canny one, and his decision to reshape the remit to make the most of his connections was also well-administered. But to give his prize more of a chance against the Booker, Lott would have had to move the prize back to the industry centre; after all, the Booker is based in London rather than Demerara. Yet to have done so would have stripped the prize of the inherent tension that buoyed it up: the very novelty, admirable and yet strange, of moving away from the centre by not, in fact, moving at all; by remaining, as *Independent* reporter John Walsh (2006) puts it, a "bizarre multi-media extravaganza" at "this hedonists' retreat in the Indian Ocean" (1). For "there's no threat, to the bigger prizes, from smaller ones doing the same thing. [Smaller prizes] can appear so slight as to be more slight than honour" (English 2005, 65).

The coverage by *The Independent* engages seriously with the Mauritian context of the prize, writing not only about the British judges and British nominees, but also about the Mauritians they met. These were primarily students and staff from the University of Mauritius, but also the Prime Minister, who spoke at the prize's dinner. Though the presence of a head of state at a literary prize dinner would generally be seen as an honour, the bemused tone of the article suggests that the Mauritian Prime Minister was not afforded the same reverence typically afforded the Queen, for example. Instead the account of the Prime Minister and the other Mauritians present recalls Brouillette's reminder that

> traditional ethnography was premised on the notion that the indigenous peoples studied by the participant observer do not themselves 'travel.' They do so neither literally, in the sense that they do not leave the space in which their 'culture' takes shape, nor metaphorically, since they cannot transcend the epistemological apparatus that defines their distinction. (2007, 23)

The *Independent* article describes some Mauritians' discomfort with certain sexual connotations in the readings, culminating in what would have been in the UK a tailor-made scandal: two women walking out of the prize dinner during Ben Markovitz's reading describing an erection. Instead, the issue is flattened: "two local women walked out in protest. Whoops" (Walsh 2006, 1).

After the year of Swinton's participation, however, the media fervour was not sustained; perhaps, indeed, the scandal—that the worlds of money and art lay so close together, that former sugar plantations could now be cultural arbiters—was no longer scandalous. Perhaps, alternatively, the implications of its location—that sugar plantations could reform themselves into cultural arbiters without participants having to travel to London or Paris—remained too scandalous. Indeed, just being a prize underpinned by the plantation economy had never been scandalous enough, even for the Booker; English writes that

> the Booker was a precarious enough proposition that the whole venture was very close to folding within just a couple years of its launch. [. . . Publishers] were threatening to stop nominating books; people invited to serve as judges were routinely declining to do so; Maschler insisted on acting like

> the head of the management committee, to the point where the actual chair resigned; the Book Trust was abruptly brought in to assume administrative responsibility, even though it had never administered a prize; and the sponsor, though contracted for an initial seven years of funding, was already making noises as if preparing for an early exit. (2005, 202–03)

For the Booker Prize to be successful, scandals were required: scandals which kept everyone focused on "the dominant optic of art-versus-money" rather than on the administrative minutiae which, when examined at any length, revealed the whole business to be one in which art and money are firmly intertwined (153). For the hoteliers of Le Prince Maurice, skilled as they are at curation, it should have become clear as the years went by that the Booker formula could no more make a space for Mauritius in the literary world—and therefore for Le Prince Maurice in the literary world—than *Paul et Virginie* (de Saint Pierre [1789] 1825) itself had. Despite their efforts, Mauritius would always be gazed at, never gazed with. By 2011, the French-language prize had evolved into "an important cultural exchange", most important to the prizewinner, who would be given a grant to study in Paris (Young 2012, 1). In the years when it was to have been awarded to an English-language novel, the prize was scrapped due to lack of funds: without scandal to sustain media attention, it could not differentiate itself enough from prizes like the Booker, which could provide more money and confer greater cultural capital (Young 2012, 1).

That Le Prince Maurice's literary prize has not eclipsed the Booker has not worn down its organizers. More recently, another prize was given top billing in the hotel blog: the Festival Culinaire Bernard Loiseau. Unlike the literary prize, it is properly in memoriam, and its commemoration does not aim to invoke the island's character (Loiseau was known for resisting the Asian culinary trends in the French restaurant scene); instead, the inclusion of Mauritian cuisine appears a practical, rather than ideological choice. Most of all, while still "a celebration of passion and creativity", it is very clearly "more than a culinary competition" ("2017 Festival Festival Culinaire Bernard Loiseau" 2017, 1). It need not bring scandal, only celebrity. And we can only hope that its 2020 participants will be well-chosen enough to properly appreciate its last, most important event: the gala dinner.

Ledikasyon pu Travayer Prize

Whilst Le Prince Maurice prize brings in non-Mauritian writers, the Ledikasyon pu Travayer prize hopes to bring greater recognition to Mauritian writers. In the strictest reading, the prize is not necessarily intended to send Mauritian writers out of the country; the prize is not a grant to study abroad, nor does its administration include foreign involvement. Its focus is more specific than promotion of the nation's literature: it aims to promote the nation's *vernacular* literature, and to legitimize the use of Kreol Morisyen as a language in the fullest sense of the word. By mapping literature on to a local enterprise, the Ledikasyon pu Travayer prize shows writers that they are a part of the literary world regardless of geographical and cultural isolation—it bestows upon them a calling card. But it cannot, by itself, change the people on whom those writers would need to call in order to enjoy global and financial success.

The most successful Mauritian writers, in terms of global reputation and financial renumeration, are those who write in languages not specific to Mauritius: English, French, even Hindi. Their works are more likely to be published by presses with global reputations and deeper pockets, and their potential readerships are greater. For writers who use Kreol Morisyen, then, being translated would be a more obvious reward than winning a prize. As Lindqvist (2016) notes, "translation is [. . .] a form of consecration in its more general sense; it constitutes the principal means for access to the literary world for writers outside the centre" (75). However, were Ledikasyon pu Travayer to scrap its prize in favour of a policy through which it pledged to translate one work into English, French, and Hindi each year, the benefits would not accrue year upon year unless the translated works were certain to be reissued by a press with a larger global reach. Prizes, however, grow more important, however slightly, by the simple virtue of enduring another year: each prizewinner joins a community that can be represented by whichever work is most relevant at any given time. To win the Ledikasyon pu Travayer prize may mean more to its beneficiaries several years after the fact, if all goes well.

Like the Booker, the Ledikasyon pu Travayer prize is a general one—its focus is language and quality rather than subject matter. It joins a host of other national awards; English writes that

> within this McWorld of awards, we can see how the outcome of one prize competition immediately registers as a factor in other, geographically remote ones—the sort of "action at a distance" that, for Anthony Giddens, characterizes the era of globalization. (2005, 260)

Like the Booker, these prizes are both independent of other awards and in conversation with them—and, like the Booker, in postcolonial nations the conversation they are having is often about the legacy of colonialism. The message the Booker sends about colonialism and its aftermath is murkier than it intends; the message Ledikasyon pu Travayer sends by holding a vernacular prize for local authors is clearer. (And the prize is inclusive as well as just local: its guidelines make clear that writers from internationally marginalised regions of Mauritius, such as Rodrigues, are welcome to participate, as are writers working in different genres, including poetry, prose fiction, and translation.) If the Ledikasyon pu Travayer prize were eventually to build up as prestigious a reputation as the Booker, its message—like that of similar prizes around the world—would be significant. Yet without the background infrastructure of globally-known publishers, the likelihood of this is slim. Whereas Le Prince Maurice is also part of a sub-community of prizes rewarding books about love, the Ledikasyon pu Travayer prize is only part of a global community that is shaped by the same forces of globalization that have made the need for such a prize so glaringly obvious.

Rishy Bukoree, winner of the 2004 Ledikasyon pu Travayer prize for his poetry collection *Poezi enn Rebel*, has gone on to write several subsequent chapbooks: in 2004, he worked with the Parisian publisher Publibook to produce *Arteries*, and since then has shifted to 100 percent self-publishing for *Words*, *Vers-Stem*, and *Solfatare*. Bukoree was born in 1977, and had worked as a journalist, a teacher, and in communications by the time he won the prize. It did not lead him to become an activist-writer focused on nurturing a Kreol Morisyen literary scene. His post-award decisions were instead decidedly pragmatic: he continued to write in French and English as well as in Kreol Morisyen, and to combine his writing talent with his training in International Relations at a day job in communications for the Mauritian Ministry of Agricultural Industry and Fishery. Whilst the prize did not attract the attention of major publishing houses, it did serve as an entrée into the more official strata of the Mauritian literary community: shortly after the win, he embarked on an MA in Social Studies and Humanities at the University of Mauritius, writing about literature. However, he did not study the fledgling Kreol Morisyen literary sphere. Instead, he wrote about diaspora in post-independence francophone Mauritian literature. This led to a lecturership in contemporary history at his alma mater, the University of Mauritius—the centre, in a parallel but quite different way than Ledikasyon pu Travayer, of the nation's cultural life.

Even before entering the prize, Bukoree was aware of the ways in which global inequalities continue to shape global interaction in the postcolonial world, writing to *Newsweek* after the 9/11 attacks that

> because the 'world' looks through the eyes of western media and western leaders, it seems to belong to the happy few who can laugh and cry, talk and mourn, and do whatever they want with an arrogance that flouts wisdom and truth. ("International Mail Call" 2001, 1)

In an interview with Radio Maurice, he spoke about the effect of this neocolonial gaze on the way Mauritian literature is received, noting that while exoticizing has been a successful strategy for authors like Arthur Martial or Clément Charoux, works like Marcel Cabon's (1965) *Namasté*, which employ what Bukoree sees as an authentic gaze upon the Indo-Mauritian community ("le regard de Cabon est authentique", he writes) are often disproportionately ignored ("Marcel Cabon" 2004, 1). For Bukoree, this novel—a love story in the vein of *Paul et Virginie* (de Saint Pierre [1789] 1825), in which Cabon's protagonist, Ram, loses his wife to a tropical storm and goes mad—is one of the greatest ever written, rather than one of the greatest Mauritian novels ever written (2004, 1). Published, in 1965, just three years prior to independence, this is one of the relatively few francophone Mauritian novels set in a poor Indo-Mauritian village, and, in its descriptions of Ram's ecstatic relationship to the printed word, is truly a writer's novel. Rich in allusions to the Hindu epics, it portrays life that is often glossed over by western media as too complex to assimilate.

Bukoree's prizewinning poetry is similarly full of allusions. Sedley Richard Assonne, in the introduction to *Poezi enn Rebel*, notes that the collection includes references to everyone from Indian poet/lyricist Gulzar to seggae star Kaya (Bukoree 2004, 7). Bukoree's poem "Namaste" is a direct response to Cabon's novel. In the poem, the speaker, the eponymous rebel, transcends the limitations of time and reality, speaking with Cabon at a funeral procession at the sacred inland lake Ganga Talao, setting the pair of Cabon's characters, Ram and Oumaouti, alongside other oppositional pairs such as Kuru and Pandu and Mao and Maggie (Thatcher) (Bukoree 2004, 36). The final pairing presented in the poem is that of Mahé de labourdonnais and Mahatma Gandhi, who might serve as bookends to the Mauritian national imaginary, with the first coming from France and turning a disparate peoples into a coherent nation (albeit one within which there are huge inequalities) and the latter visiting at the turn of the century (in 1901) and drawing the Indo-Mauritian struggle clearly into the global and national struggles for self-determination.

In her writing on the Mauritian literary heritage, Anjali Prabhu (2012) has noted that Cabon, who is of Creole ethnicity, depicts the Indo-Mauritian labour struggle in French as a part of the Mauritian national story, thus countering the rhetoric of communalism with cultural pluralism. Prabhu suggests that Cabon paved the way for Indo-Mauritian writers' depiction of their own struggles (for example, Abhimanyu Unnuth and his *Lal Pasina*) to be seen as Mauritian, rather than simply diasporic Indian, literature (64–65). Certainly Cabon has paved the way for an Indo-Mauritian like Bukoree to write in his national, rather than ethnic, vernacular, and to center a local/national understanding in his writing on the global politics of Mao and Maggie. *Poezi enn Rebel* makes sense as a prizewinner not only because of its literary merit but because its victory is in line with the political aims of Ledikasyon pu Travayer: its engagement with Mauritian literature in all of its previously disparate streams concretizes poetry in Kreol Morisyen as unifying, important, and central to the future of Mauritian literature. It's hardly scandalous, and like its opposite, Le Prince Maurice prize, it has hardly made a splash.

In the context of other kinds of institutional literature advocacy in Mauritius, however, the prize seems less like a failed experiment and more like a call to action. In the same year that Ledikasyon pu Travayer bestowed their literary prize on Bukoree, they were awarded a prize from a much more internationally-recognised organisation: they won the UNESCO International Literacy Prize. This recognised their wide-ranging approach: in addition to writing literature in Kreol Morisyen, Ledikasyon pu Travayer gave those novels' primary imagined readership actual access to the texts by putting on adult literacy classes and by producing and publishing the types of books in Kreol Morisyen that would be necessary if and when the language became the medium of education: most importantly, a regularised orthography and dictionary. Set next to already-popular works by Dev Virahsawmy, plays and adaptations of Shakespeare and Hindu tales that announced loudly and clearly that Kreol Morisyen was not insular, these materials made possible the institutionalisation of Kreol Morisyen (Rohatgi 2014, 147). The orthography, it should be noted, was influenced by, rather than in opposition to, speakers of the creole language: text messaging and internet use created new sites for Kreol Morisyen writing, particularly by its young people, and the orthography followed developing traditions (Rajah-Carrim 2009, 505). On the website of Lalit, the organisation's affiliate political party, Lindsey Collen, Rada Kistnasamy, and Alain Ah-Vee (2011) passionately and comprehensively outline the measures taken to achieve the 2012 inclusion of Kreol Morisyen as a language of education. While too long to quote in ther entirety, the measures outlined in this document are particularly relevant here:

> *Lalit* distributed 10,000 to 12,000 leaflets on average 3 times a year over the years, with 1,500 words or a total of 36 x 3 x 1,500 = 162,000 words, for a total of 1,188,000 leaflets. These leaflets are well-nigh never thrown away, but are folded up by the recipients, who often share them with others in their transport to work, at work, and then at home and in the neighbourhood in the evening. 3 or 4 times more people read a *Lalit* leaflet than receive one. All this gives an idea of the massive scope of the *Lalit* production in Kreol—for a population only now reaching 1.3 million.
> [. . .]
> [. . . We] in LPT are not just some technical "adult literacy" do-gooders. [. . .] LPT, in order to promote the Kreol language, did not only teach literacy to thousands of adult pupils, and train hundreds of volunteer teachers, and write manuals and teachers' guides and texts. Nor did we just publish and print on a mind-boggling variety of subjects, in Kreol. Nor did we just hold seminars, forums, exhibitions, meetings, conferences in favour of Kreol. Nor did we just organize petitions. Nor did we just prepare Charters in favour of the Mother Tongue, adhered to by hundreds. (paras 10–18)

Although the Ledikasyon pu Travayer prize never launched the career of a writer as successful as Collen (or, indeed, Le Clézio), it brought an institution of world literature to Kreol Morisyen free of the market forces which both underpin world literature and should be pinned up and studied as part of critical world literary studies.

Ledikasyon pu Travayer has recently introduced another prize (Konkur Literar 2003, 1). This one is more limited and, within these limitations, seems certain to be more effective: the prize asked applicants to translate a canonical short story into Kreol Morisyen in order to create a world literature reader to be used in schools. Though the stories translated were from a variety of languages, including Tamil, Telagu, Japanese, and Chinese, the majority of works were from the western canon. This prize will bring the world to students of Kreol Morisyen, but those students will have to take on the work by which the neocolonial impact of such classroom readers can be dismantled.

Conclusion

Mauritius, since its inception as an independent nation in 1968, has enjoyed post-sugar success, diversifying its economy with resort hotels nestled between erstwhile plantations and perennially beautiful beaches. Its literature has always exhibited a tension between the island's role in a global imaginary as the Edenic escape portrayed in St. Pierre's 18th-century literary phenomenon *Paul et Virginie* ([1789] 1825) and its historical significance for local residents as a site of blood, sweat, tears, and the rise of solidarity portrayed in Abhimanyu Unnuth's (1977) *Lal Pasina.* The two prizes explored here exemplify both sides of the literary spectrum, with Le Prince Maurice appropriately offering a prize for global romantic literature and Ledikasyon pu Travayer highlighting works in the local vernacular.

The current chapter has traced the failure of either prize to gain the prominence, legitimacy, or commercial success of the Booker for their institution and for prizewinners such as Rishy Bukoree. While the Booker, operating at the centre, further legitimizes British centrality by bestowing inclusion upon writers from anglophone peripheries, Le Prince Maurice and Ledikasyon pu Travayer face institutional barriers in their quest to go against the grain of history and use the same method—the bestowal of a prize—towards the same ends. International newsworthiness requires departure from a pattern, so that the prizes, trying to escape the patterns imposed on them by the distorting lens of the world literary marketplace, could not be made "interesting" enough to survive. Their failures echo other failures of world literature in Mauritius, such as the inability of Le Clézio-celebrated Hindi writer Abhimanyu Unnuth to be read as anything but a national writer, but they also form part of a longstanding Mauritian push for the demarginalisation of minor literature by institutional means. Considered briefly, minor literatures' minor prizes seem unable to exhibit the agency Cheah describes (2016), but a closer look reveals ways in which these prizes speak to and around the barriers described in Huggan (2001), Brouillette (2007), and English (2005), as well as in conversation with the case studies gathered here. Prizes, even ephemeral ones, can play a role in the long-term creation of minor literary worlds, through which writer and readers can feel integrated as equals into a world of literature.

Bibliography

"2017 Festival Culinaire Bernard Loiseau." 2017. Constance Hotels. https://www.constancehotels.com/en/news/2017-festival-culinaire-bernard-loiseau/.

Ah-vee, Alain, Rada Kistnasamy, and Lindsey Collen. 2011. "Victory Begins to be Won for the Kreol Language in Mauritius." *Lalit*, December 31. https://www.lalitmauritius.org/en/newsarticle/1335/victory-begins-to-be-won-for-the-kreol-language-in-mauritius/

Brouillette, Sarah. 2007. *Postcolonial Writers in the Global Literary Marketplace.* London: Palgrave Macmillan.

Bukoree, Rishy. 2004. *Poezi enn Rebel.* Mauritius: Ledikasyon pu Travayer.

Cabon, Marcel. 1965. *Namaste.* Port-Louis: Eds. de l'Océan Indien.

Cheah, Pheng. 2016. *What Is a World? On Postcolonial Literature as World Literature.* Durham, NC: Duke University Press.

"Constance Prince Maurice." n.d. *Jetsetter.* Accessed August 14, 2018. https://www.jetsetter.com/hotels/africa/mauritius/view/constance-prince-maurice/

Cousins, Helen. 2018. "Lindsey Collen's Narrative Gift: A Challenge to the Commodification of African Literature." *Research in African Literature* 49 (2): 87-106.

Damrosch, David. 2003. *What is World Literature?* Princeton, NJ: Princeton University Press.

Dutton, Jacqueline. 2017. "Narrating Expiation in Mauritius and the Indian Ocean Aquapelago." *Shima Journal* 12 (1): 48–65.

English, James. 2005. *The Economy of Prestige: Prizes, Awards, and the Circulation of Cultural Value.* Cambridge, MA: Harvard University Press.

Huggan, Graham. 2001. *The Postcolonial Exotic: Marketing the Margins.* London: Routledge.

"International Mail Call." 2001. *Newsweek,* October 7. http://www.newsweek.com/international-mail-call-153927.

"Konkur Literer Dan Langaz Kreol Morisyen." 2003. *Lalit,* October 21. https://www.lalitmauritius.org/en/newsarticle/89/konkur-literer-dan-langaz-kreol-morisyen/

Le Clézio, Jean-Marie Gustave. 2008. "In the Forest of Paradoxes." *Nobel Prize Lecture.* December 7. https://www.nobelprize.org/prizes/literature/2008/clezio/25790-jean-marie-gustave-le-clezio-nobel-lecture-2008/

"Le Prince Maurice Prize for Romantic Literature." 2011. *Constance Hotels Experience.* June 16. https://constancehotels.wordpress.com/2011/06/16/le-prince-maurice-prize-for-romantic-literature/.

Lindqvist, Yvonne. 2016. "The Scandinavian Literary Translation Field from a Global Point of View." In *Institutions of World Literature,* edited by Stefan Helgesson and Pieter Vermeulen, 174–86. New York: Routledge.

"Marcel Cabon." 2004. Radio Maurice, October. http://www.radiomoris.com/forum/56941-post2.html

Moretti, Franco. 2000. "Conjectures on World Literature." *New Left Review* 1 (Jan–Feb): 54–68.

—. 2003. "More Conjectures." *New Left Review* 20 (Mar–Apr): 73–81.

Parker, Peter. 1995. "Obituaries: Lord Campbell of Eskan." *The Independent,* January 4. http://www.independent.co.uk/news/people/obituaries-lord-campbell-of-eskan-1566530.html

Pauli, Michelle. 2006. "'Love Story' Prize Unveils Longlist." *The Guardian,* January 18. https://www.theguardian.com/books/2006/jan/18/news.michellepauli

Prabhu, Anjali. 2012. *Hybridity: Limits, Transformations, Prospects.* Albany, NY: State University of New York Press.

Prayag, Girish, et al. 2010. "Hotel Development and Tourism Impacts in Mauritius: Hoteliers' Perspectives on Sustainable Tourism." *Development Southern Africa* 27 (5): 697–712.

Rajah-Carrim, Aaliya. 2009. "Use and Standardisation of Mauritian Creole in Electronically Mediated Communication." *Journal of Computer-Mediated Communication,* Volume 14 (3): 484–508.

"Recognition." Jean Marc Eynaud Architects. http://www.jmeynaud

architects.com/recognition/.

Rohatgi, Rashi. 2014. *Fighting Cane and Canon: Abhimanyu Unnuth and the Case of World Literature in Mauritius.* Newcastle upon Tyne: Cambridge Scholars Publishing.

—. 2017. "Rainbows and Rain: Foreigners in Ultraminor Genre Fiction." *Journal of World Literature* 2: 217–35.

de Saint Pierre, Jacques Henri Bernardin. [1789] 1825. *Paul et Virginie.* Translated by Helen Maria Williams. London: Jones and Co.

Self, John. 2011. "Booker Prize Populism May Well Backfire." *The Guardian*, October 17. https://www.theguardian.com/books/2011/oct/17/booker-prize-populism-backfire

Sundarajan, Saroja. 2006. *From Bondage to Deliverance: Indentured Labour in Mauritius and British Guiana.* New Delhi: Allied Publishers.

Unnuth, Abhimanyu. 1977. *Lāl Pasīna.* New Delhi: Rājkamal Prakāśan.

Walsh, John. 2006. "The Prince Maurice Award: The Luxury Literary Prize." *The Independent,* June 1. http://www.independent.co.uk/artsentertainment/books/features/the-prince-maurice-award-the-luxury-literary-prize-480638.html.

Warwick Research Collective. 2015. *Combined and Uneven Development: Towards a New Theory of World-Literature.* Liverpool: Liverpool University Press.

Weinberg, Liliana. 2016. "The Oblivion We Will Be: The Latin American Literary Field After Autonomy." In *Institutions of World Literature,* edited by Stefan Helgesson and Pieter Vermeulen, 67–78. New York: Routledge.

Young, Toby. 2012. "Oh for the Prince Maurice." *The Spectator,* August 25. https://www.spectator.co.uk/2012/08/toby-young-oh-for-the-prince-maurice/#.

Cypriot Literatures and the World: Language, Nationalism, and the *bildungsroman*, 1960–1974

Daniele Nunziata

After almost a century of British imperial rule, the modern history of Cyprus is marked by a violent decolonisation movement (1955–1959), its independence in 1960, and, following the eruption of intercommunal conflict, partition along ethnolinguistic lines by 1974. These junctures are emblematic of colonial and postcolonial histories across the Commonwealth. The so-called "emergency" experienced in the 1950s was a term comparably used in reference to political turmoil in Kenya and Malaya. Its partition repeated the fate of many post-colonies across Asia, from the Holy Land to the Indian subcontinent. Even its decades of civil unrest occurred in parallel with the neighbouring Yom Kippur War of 1973 and the Lebanese Civil War beginning in 1975.

In dividing the island into discrete linguistic spaces, the partition created a barrier between Cypriots according to sectarian and nationalist dogmas. The majority of Turkish-speaking Cypriots now live north of the Green Line (in the breakaway "Turkish Republic of Northern Cyprus", recognised only by Turkey), while the south is predominately home to Cypriots who speak Greek, as well as Cypriot Arabic and Armenian (in the territory under the *de facto* control of the Republic of Cyprus, recognised by every UN member except Turkey). It was only in April 2003 that seven openings were made in the border, allowing Cypriots to cross the physical and ideological line which has come to define the island.

Despite the similarities between Cyprus and other erstwhile British (and French) colonies, significant differences mark its peculiar status. Notably, the complex linguistic environment of Cyprus elides simple categories of "pre-colonial", "colonial", and "national" languages. While often referred to reductively as the site of a Greek-speaking side and a Turkish-speaking side, the languages of the island are more multifaceted and intersectional. There is the English official in the British Sovereign Base Areas of Akrotiri and Dhekelia, home to British military personnel, and the presence of Cypriot communities who speak Cypriot Arabic and Armenian, each afforded minority status in the south. The official languages of the Republic of Cyprus are Greek and Turkish, both in the forms standardised in Athens and Ankara, respectively. It is these standard forms which prevail in education, politics, and the media (Hadjioannou, Tsiplakou, and Kappler 2011). On the one hand, the everyday vernaculars of Cypriots, however, are Kypriaka ("Cypriot Greek") and Kıbrıs Türkçesi (or Kıbrıslıca, "Cypriot Turkish")—both denied standardisation or official status, and both derided as rural *dialects* by nationalists who privilege the cultural forms of Greece or Turkey. On the other hand, for (predominately left-wing) Cypriots who advocate total independence, not only from British imperialism, but other neo-colonial manifestations of socio-political hegemony, these vernaculars are bestowed with greater cultural value and the potential to be standardised or even consecrated as languages. Standard Greek and Standard Turkish can be viewed as nationalist—and, indeed, neo-colonialist—interventions which estrange Cypriots from indigenous vernaculars in ways comparable to the imposition of British English a century earlier. Of symbolic importance, the national anthem of the south is the same as that of Greece, and that of the north is the same as that of Turkey.

Most Cypriots are diglossic, speaking either Kypriaka and Greek, or Kıbrıslıca and Turkish, with equal fluency (Arvaniti 2006). Often, the two blend into each other, consciously or otherwise. The majority also speak English with a high degree of fluency. Cypriots from the smallest ethno-linguistic communities often speak three or four languages simultaneously, splicing words from one form into another, creating mixed languages through code-switching (Tsiplakou 2006). The Cypriot languages already exhibit significant degrees of lexical borrowing, with loan words from Arabic, Greek,

Turkish, and Western European languages (Romance and Germanic) interspersing into each other (Gulle 2011). As a consequence, the very notion of a "first or native language" becomes impossible to define for Cypriots who speak one (or two) language(s) privately—the vernaculars of the home—and another one or two publicly: the official languages of the island's political structures and the omnipresent English of academia.

Such linguistic complexity helps us understand some of the inadequacies of the term "the world" when used in the phrase "world literatures". Cypriots navigate multiple worlds simultaneously. There is the entire world of cultural production, in which English is an international auxiliary language and within which connections can be made with other Commonwealth and postcolonial spaces. In addition, however, there are the "Greek world" and the "Turkish world"—cultural spaces within which participation depends on the extent to which Cypriot writers make institutional affiliations between their works and the national locations of publication. Most Greek-speaking Cypriots publish in southern Cyprus, Greece, or the UK, while most Turkish-speaking Cypriots publish in northern Cyprus, Turkey, or the UK. Publishing in English in London allows for Cypriot texts by Greek-speakers and by Turkish-speakers to exist in conversation with each other in ways that publication in Greece or in Turkey might otherwise limit. The publishing industries of Greece and Turkey are associated with the cultural capital of each country's national or nationalist identities. In contrast, publication in English in London eschews these parochial nationalist ties in favour of a wider readership containing Cypriots of different backgrounds as well as non-Cypriot readers.

As a consequence of these issues, Eastern Mediterranean cultures and identities exist in *layers*. For Cypriots, these layers, from most local to most global, are: the side of Cyprus within which they live; the wider trans-border island; the spheres of influence of Greece and/or Turkey; the anglophone Commonwealth; and ultimately the entire multilingual world. They are not simply citizens of Cyprus and the world, but also of the medial "Greek world" and/or "Turkish world" in between.

While some Cypriots write in standardised Greek or Turkish as perceived local, native, or postcolonial tongues, many compose in English instead (Papadakis 2005, 173). While debates have long existed on the merits of writing in English, notably from the dialogue between Chinua Achebe and Ngũgĩ wa Thiong'o (Ngũgĩ 1986) onwards, Cyprus offers a complicated standpoint on this perennial linguistic issue. Cypriots often cannot compose long prose works in the non-standard Kypriaka, Kıbrıslıca, or Cypriot Arabic. As a consequence, both English *and* the standardised languages of Greece and Turkey are linguistic forms at a remove from the quotidian vernaculars which preceded both British imperial rule and the nationalist movements of the mid-20th century. As all three languages can be considered comparably foreign, albeit with different genetic relationships with the island's indigenous tongues, the choice of language for Cypriot writers is more complicated than deciding between so-called "local" or "foreign" materials. While Franco Moretti (2000) employs the idiom of distance to express his understanding of world literatures, for Cypriot writers, any standardised linguistic form involves an inevitable and irrevocable distance from the quotidian. As all three languages—English, Greek, and Turkish—are hegemonic in their institutional status, and as the oral vernaculars have yet to be fully transliterated, modern Cypriot writers are compelled to choose between these forms in order to employ the one most appropriate for their literary *and political* aspirations. Writing in English, for instance, allows writers to visibly eschew affiliation with nationalist movements by creating works that can be read in a language understood by most Cypriots. It is also one which expands their readership to the rest of the Commonwealth and to global marketplaces beyond Greek and Turkish literary spheres.

Developing Pan-Cypriot Literature: Taner Baybars and Costas Montis

This chapter will investigate these literary and linguistic tensions through a comparison of the Turkish-speaking Taner Baybars (1936–

2010) and the Greek-speaking Costas Montis (1914–2004), both poets and novelists, whose prose works, *Plucked in a Far-Off Land* (Baybars [1970] 2005) and *Closed Doors* (Montis [1964] 2004), were first published in the period between independence and partition. The majority of Montis's texts were composed in Standard Modern Greek and published in Greece, while Baybars's oeuvre, since 1963, has been predominately in English and first published in London (including translations of Cypriot contemporaries like Mehmet Yaşın). Each, to varying degrees, considers identifications with the hegemons of Greece and Turkey and both are—although perhaps Montis more so—interpellated into the wider, delineating categories of "Greek literature" and "Turkish literature" consecrated in Athens and Ankara, respectively. However, despite differences in linguistic form, parallels in both their early lives and their literary constructs suggest that, beyond the expected polarising of culture from this period up to and including partition (1955–74), these two writers share related narrative tactics as constituent parts of a pan-Cypriot, postcolonial literary movement.

The two texts are semi-fictional, first-person, prose *bildungsromane* concerning the experiences of adolescent narrators: for Montis, the brother of an anti-colonial EOKA (*Ethniki Organosis Kyprion Agoniston*) insurgent killed in combat; for Baybars, an aspiring poet in the years leading up to his emigration from Cyprus to the UK. They draw on the writers' own experiences in the colony yet are compounded with elements of fictionality. Notably, Montis names the brother after his own, Nikos, who also died prematurely but of leukaemia, not in war. Importantly, in the afterlives of the works, the new millennium witnessed an increase in their readerships as *Closed Doors* was first translated into English in 2004, and *Plucked in a Far-Off Land* was republished in English in the Republic of Cyprus the following year.

Like the Cypriot politicians Archbishop Makarios and Rauf Denktaş, both authors emigrated in their youth to read law abroad—Montis in Athens, Baybars in England—although neither was able to practise. Montis was disallowed upon his return to colonial Cyprus due to the non-British provenance of his degree; Baybars abandoned his studies and remained in Britain as a full-time writer and translator. Experiences of exile and overseas degrees in law (completed or otherwise) indicate the imbrication of the legal, political, pedagogical, and literary within their migrant worldviews although the different metropolitan centres in which they were based accounts for the emergence of their distinct linguistic affiliations. During a historic moment when forms of anti-colonial violence categorised variously as "liberation", "paramilitary", and "terrorist" competed with the sanctioned violence of the colonial administration, early Cypriot writing was consciously concerned with the legal parameters of how imperialism can be challenged and usurped. As Stephen Morton (2013) has demonstrated in his research on colonial "emergencies" of the mid-20th century, albeit without specific reference to Cypriot contexts, there exists an important "relationship between law, state violence and colonial sovereignty" which anti-colonial and postcolonial writers attempt to navigate (2). For Michel de Certeau (1984), whose theoretical opposition between *strategy* and *tactic* elucidates the dichotomy of the authorised and resistant, "[f]rom birth to mourning after death, law 'takes hold of' bodies in order to make them its 'text'" (139).

For anti-colonial writers, the colonised Cypriot body is one textualised and regulated by a series of literary and legal discourses awaiting reinscription. While fleeting comparisons have been made between colonial Cyprus and other "emergencies" in Kenya and Malaya, the former offers a unique set of legal factors in that most anti-colonial political movements were generated, not towards the creation of a new nation state, but a legalised re-administration of the island by Greece or Turkey instead. As will be shown, Baybars's narrative, not written in one of the two national languages rendered official in 1960, strays further from representations of, and allegiance to, nationalist violence than Montis's account of the youth fighters of EOKA, an organisation he was tangentially involved with. Nonetheless, the two engage, through similar generic forms, in the projects of *simultaneously* rewriting colonial discourse and reflecting on the contemporary rise of nationalisms in cultural and political fields. The two are set before independence (Montis's between 1955 and 1960; Baybars's between 1938 and the late 1940s), and yet they equally gesture to the politics of the post-independence era in which they were published.

This temporal doubleness indicates the dual politics of Cypriot narratives which mediate the sanctioned ideologies of colonialism and nationalism/s, concurrently. The full title of Montis's text, *Closed Doors: An Answer to* Bitter Lemons *by Lawrence Durrell*, signals a direct writing-back to the British writer's 1957 Orientalist narrative exploring Cyprus. Montis achieves this, in part, by pressing on the *closed doors* of internment camps established by the British Empire to confine anti-colonial protesters. It is, therefore, necessary to consider these writers' chosen linguistic and textual interventions into the narratives of nationalism which were, and still are, extant on the conflict-ridden island.

Crucially, while the two authors are from different ethnolinguistic communities and utilise different linguistic forms, the important stylistic, generic, and thematic similarities between their works reveal a shared grounding of their literature in a common socio-political context. Beyond the reductive notion that no "Cypriot" literature exists, either in this period or now, these two texts are evidence of the existence of a pan-Cypriot literary zeitgeist, dating back to the 1960s. The two are most powerfully read in tandem, not as works from diametrically-opposed literary traditions. The very possibility of this has only come to light because of the translation of Montis into English, and the publication of Baybars in southern Cyprus, following the symbolically-important opening of the border in 2003. Concerned with providing testimony for their experiences *as Cypriots*, Baybars and Montis move beyond a simple affiliation with the "Greek world" or "Turkish world" of politics and cultural production. The two, therefore, create works of world literature, not only through allusion to other colonial contexts or Baybars's use of the anglophone form, but through their desire to put pressure on colonial, national, and nationalist borders, both on the ground and within literature.

This consideration is informed by existing scholarship which challenges how "the world" in "world literature" has long been understood. Following Francesca Orsini (2018), there is a need "to counter the identification of world literature with English by highlighting the multilingualism and the many factors that contribute to regional and transnational literary fields" (1). This is particularly prescient in the Cypriot setting precisely because its "multilingual" environment has led Cypriot authors to fluctuate in their associations with the cultural and publishing industries of different regions, namely Britain, Greece, and Turkey. Beyond the simple framework of centre and periphery long employed in the study of postcolonial and world literatures, the movements of Cyprus's culture are multidirectional, poised between different existential and institutional sites. As Pheng Cheah (2016) has observed, there are significant limitations to "equat[ing] the world with circulatory movements that cut across national-territorial borders [which] reduce the world literature's normative force to the barest minimum" (3). This includes a reluctance to understand the multiple layers in which borders exist. For Cypriot writers, in addition to the borders between the island and the British metropole, are the borders of languages and politics which divide Cyprus between Greece and Turkey, as well as those segregating Greek-speaking Cypriots and Turkish-speaking Cypriots. Given the existence of these overlapping "worlds", we must reconsider paradigms which ignore these layered divisions, and illustrate how literature moves between different ideological spaces through multiple languages. This allows for new literary spaces to emerge, including a pan-Cypriot literature which rejects any simple affiliation with the "Greek world" or "Turkish world" which would sustain ideological borders between Greek-speaking and Turkish-speaking Cypriots.

In short, the case study of this chapter will be a comparison of these two authors to show the importance of reading Greek-speaking and Turkish-speaking writers in tandem. The two use comparable stylistic devices to respond to the same social context which is distinct from Greece and Turkey, neither of which was colonised by the British Empire in the way that Cyprus was. The chapter will show that the generic similarities between the Turkish-speaking Baybars and Greek-speaking Montis, composing in the same juncture, gesture to the existence of an understudied pan-Cypriot literary movement which puts pressure on the distinct cultural fields—or "worlds"—of Greece and Turkey. Despite differences in linguistic form, the two authors have more literary commonalities than differences, stressing their significant relationship as Cypriots. The chapter will be divided into two sections to illustrate these parallels. The first, "Language as Imperial Violence", will demonstrate how Baybars and Montis respond to the linguistic imperialism of Britain, with the latter viewing English as a mode "cutting" Cypriots apart, and the former understanding English as a language inextricably tied to British military violence. The second section, "Language and Nationalism", will show how both authors use their adolescent narrators to symbolise how nationalism is indoctrinated into Cypriot youth through pedagogy performed in either Standard Modern Greek or Standard Modern Turkish. The two respective narrators move away from the propaganda of their elders, and of venerated Greek and Turkish politicians, to gradually express new, mature identities as Cypriots. Both prose texts are heavily concerned with metatextual representations of the languages of English, Greek, and Turkish through which they explore how each is tied to its own political hegemony and geopolitical "worlds". Each author is forced to consider which "world" they associate with their works, be it the anglophone Commonwealth, of Greece, or of Turkey. These overlapping anxieties in Baybars's and Montis's texts and the similar ways they are expressed—chiefly through the young narrators of Cyprus-based *bildungsromane*—indicate a pan-Cypriot literary movement from this period which is unique to the island.

Language as Imperial Violence

Both *Closed Doors* and *Plucked in a Far-Off Land* are interested in exploring the relationship between words and violence. The two metatextually depict warfare as a discursive act in order to consider its inextricable relationship with the comparable discursivity of colonial and national identities. These ideological and existential categories are presented in parallel with the violence of modern Cyprus, vividly represented by both authors. Montis's text is, as one might expect, replete with allusions to Durrell's travelogue. It uses colonial textual representations of the island, both literary and administrative, to interrogate their culpability in inscribing "the game of divide and rule" (Montis 2004, 113) onto the lives of colonised Cypriots. Assigning blame to the British Empire for the growth in intercommunal violence, the narrator asks, "hadn't they done so in similar circumstances in India and other places in their empire?" (24). In an act of unwitting, and almost prophetic, foreshadowing, the reference to British colonial policy posits a relationship with comparable situations across the Empire, especially the lingering memory of the Indian subcontinent, to accurately predict Cyprus's own partition in 1974. As well as showcasing the island's political and historical links with contexts outside the Greek-speaking world of its Athens readership, it simultaneously frames social division as an import from outside the island, alluding to its complex spatial identity formation between categories of inside and outside. How Cyprus is read and written abroad is paramount to Montis's excavation of how it should be re-written in the uncertain post-independence juncture.

In *Bitter Lemons*, acts of literary production and violent destruction are frequently compared. After quoting the EOKA Oath, Durrell (1957) metaphorically describes how nights were "punctuated by [. . .] grenades" (195) within "the tragicomic landscape of the Near East" (186). Likewise, in opposition to "a series of attacks by Athens radio" (210), a British civil servant is shown arriving on the island "armed [. . .] with a copy of the *Iliad*" (206). Analogous to his own anti-colonial testimony, Montis similarly textualises the conflict by suggesting that Cypriot guerrillas "had to rise up and face their special end [. . .] to write their own story [. . .] on the rock" (14). Like the project of a realist writing-back to the fantasies of Orientalism, anti-colonial violence is depicted as a re-inscriptive process which alters the physical landscape of the island—from its foundational "[bed]rock"—and challenges the perceived illegitimacy of the imperial administration. Earlier in the text, violence is presented in both physical and imagined forms. When EOKA's first shipment of weaponry arrives on the island, it is conceived of as a source of public morale: "Arms? . . . What was this word that echoed (exploded really) upon our slumbering servitude?" (6). It is worth noting the tacit link being made between arms and pens as instruments similarly held in an individual's hands. Here, the anticipation of violence, spread by words, challenges the stability of empire in a manner more profound than artillery or conflict. The very "word [. . .] exploded" *before* any actual weapons were fired. Specifically, however, it is the oral dissemination of "this word", in juxtaposition with the written legislation of empire, which allows its anti-colonial sentiment to be realised.

Indeed, while describing the dissemination of EOKA pamphlets, the narrator reminds the reader that "[t]here was also a war against the English language—against English road signs. [. . .] The war was to completely eliminate their language from our lives" (Durrell 1957, 36). Demonstrating the epistemic dimensions of anti-colonial warfare, he is invested in a campaign to target the cultural imports of empire, beginning with an iconoclastic destruction of anglophone edifices, physical and symbolic, on the island. Supplemented by boycotts against British goods, demanding "'Nothing English' [. . .] in that [. . .] Cypriot voice", the narrator replaces British textiles with Cypriot "alajia" (88). The textualities of fabric and paper are implicitly analogised. Specifically, the reaction against material Englishness takes the form of a pre-colonial *and* pre-nationalist "Cypriot voice", mimetically represented by "alajia", a word of Turkish etymology (*alaca*) denoting a local, pan-Cypriot textile based on Syrian designs. This avowal is a rare departure in a work which often valorises Greek national emblems and parades.

Notably, the affricate consonant [dʒ] is markedly uncommon in Standard Modern Greek, and the Greek alphabet lacks a single letter to denote the sound. It is a loan-sound, within a loanword, from Turkish, which has been naturalised as an example of the island's intersectional *sprachbund*. The signified, the local material shared by all Cypriots regardless of ethnolinguistic or religious background, is denoted by a signifier which transcends (Greco-Turkish) linguistic dichotomies. It offers a moment of departure from the standard conventions of Athenian Greek, drawing on both Kypriaka and its diverse etymological origins, revealing the narrator's attempt to frame anti-colonialism as uniquely local (not pan-Hellenic) and intercommunal. Interestingly, it is a word that would need to be translated for readers in Greece, yet would be understood, when spoken aloud, by Turkish-speaking Cypriots. It therefore foreignizes the language and context for Greek readers. Yet, surrounded as it is by Standard Modern Greek in the original publication, and written in the Greek alphabet, it would be effectively invisible in a text largely unreadable by most Turkish-speaking Cypriots. The passage attempts to briefly gesture towards a Cypriot cultural alternative to British imperialism that cannot be contained simply by the Greek language and its alphabet as they currently exist in Athens. However, it inevitably fails to create a cultural form which effectively contends with the island's polyphonic, polyalphabetic environment and which can be consumed by all Cypriots, regardless of language affiliation.

Throughout the work, resistance to English is metatextually manifested through acts of counter-consumption. The narrator's father is depicted translating English newspapers to accommodate "new ways of seeing" (Durrell 1957, 8) for the local community. Radio transmissions from Britain, Cyprus, and Greece, in opposition to Durrell's fear of the device, is described as a beacon that their family "laid siege to" (25). Furthermore, the heteroglossic narrative interweaves English words to present the otherness of both their cultural signification and their Latin form in a hellenophone work. He states, in one chapter, "*curfews* (I use the English word because it is weighed down in such pain [. . .] [without] equivalent [. . .] in Greek.)"

(67), as part of his repudiations of "[e]xpressions from a foggy northern country, political spin with no relation to our lives" (29). Unlike Baybars's choice of linguistic form, Montis's work rejects the English language as politically, culturally, and geographically Other, viewing it as insidiously harbouring an essential violence which cannot be translated into another language. An act of resistance to colonialism, for Montis and his narrator, involves an active rereading and rewriting of its discourses which, seen as engaged in the "political spin" and violence of the empire, can only be countered by an expulsion of the English language itself from Cyprus and its literary endeavours. However, despite the reference to *alajia*, a pan-Cypriot vernacular does not exist to replace English, accounting for Baybars's reluctance to use of the English linguistic form to overcome the *divide and rule* it has performed. While Montis's work is invested in repealing British colonialism and the language it introduced, it does not fully address the linguistic divisions inherent within anti-colonial national identities.

Echoing this cynicism towards English, Baybars's narrative employs the motif of *cutting* to ambivalently represent the impact of the language on Cypriot culture/s. The final paragraph, referencing the narrator's composition of poetry in England, 1963, details the cutting involved in his circumcision—symbolic in his and specific other cultures of maturation—meditating on how, "childhood is over. The paradise is lost", creating "a certain dividing line in my life" (Baybars 2005, 222). As in Montis's text, youth is used to refer to both personal and social (anti-)development, and cutting to represent an abrupt end to "childhood" as the post-lapsarian loss of innocence in the face of conflict. If, as Vangelis Calotychos (2004) suggests, Durrell "portrays the pre-EOKA days [of Cyprus] as edenic" (180), then Baybars re-iterates this trope to stress the idealism of an era, if not nominally *pre*-colonial, then before the layers of imperialist and nationalist politics which are metonymic of his adolescence. The dating of the poem symbolises that colonialism not only *cuts* Baybars off from his native home but is complicit in the construction of lacerations across Cypriot communities, including the "dividing line" emerging between Greek-speaking and Turkish-speaking citizens in 1963–64. Indeed, there was very limited cooperation between these two Cypriot communities against British imperialism. This resulted in decolonisation being viewed through nationalistic lenses which saw the future of the island as linked to those of Greece or Turkey.

Similarly, he refers to his dual identity between nexuses of periphery and metropole—rural/urban, Cyprus/London, English/ Turkish—as the "duplicity" (Baybars 2005, 191) of lives "trans Mutated" and "translocated" (194). His "urge to return, to migrate"—to Cyprus as a denaturalised adult—"was not to be fulfilled" (191). Notably, these descriptions of unwitting "transmutat[ion]" appear in the same chapter in which the narrator first learns English. The language produces a "duplicity" in his cultural life: on the one hand, it is the medium through which he composes his (anti-colonial, anti-nationalist) works, and yet on the other, its elevation in the globalised island creates ruptures both between colonial and pre-colonial cultures, and Turkish-speaking and Greek-speaking Cypriots who learn English rather than the other pre-colonial vernaculars of the island. The narrator, for instance, describes his experience of "English words gradually *cutting* into my tongue" at school (192), as a form of symbolic violence *cutting* him off from Kıbrıslıca and/or Turkish, before depicting Hollywood movies as "American heavies [. . .] with the[ir] ugly charm [. . .] mov[ing] across the white screen like a pair of *scissors*" (215, *emphases mine*). Anglophone British and American (cultural) imperialisms are framed as discourses which perform irreparable divisions in the identities and cultures of the post/colonial world.

Although this attention to linguistic imperialism is a common trope of postcolonial literatures, Baybars's narrative extends this further to demonstrate its specific impact on the already linguistically-heterogeneous island. Learning English, idealised for its exotic appeal and global reach, is "a new wonderful experience, more so than learning Greek words because I had not seen a Greek textbook, had only heard and spoken the few odd words" (Baybars 2005, 195). Recounted in the same chapter as his description of English "cutting into my tongue" (192), these reflections, in proximity, suggest that the dominance of the language within colonial education, whereby English books replace "Greek textbook[s]", facilitates the social division of Cypriots. Unlike his father and uncles, who are frequently depicted as speakers of both Turkish and Greek, Baybars's generation, on the receiving end of colonial pedagogical reforms and burgeoning US commodity excess, are increasingly *cut off* from one another. Whether by migration or linguistic segregation, Cypriots experience a loss of the "paradise" of the symbolically pre-colonial at a time of greater pan-Cypriot unity. Ironically, however, it is only *through* English that a Cypriot narrative can disseminate across all linguistic communities due to the preponderance of English speakers on the island. As Jamaica Kincaid (1988) asserts in her semi-autobiographical counter-travelogue of Antigua, "the only language that I have in which to speak of this crime [of imperialism] is the language of the criminal who committed the crime" (31). The poem at the end of *Plucked in a Far-Off Land*, an anti-epigraph on circumcision, indicates that, while English has estranged the narrator from his first "tongue", it can also be appropriated to *begin* a new narrative from the remains at the end of his former life in Cyprus. Circumcision, when "Boy becomes a man" (Baybars 2005, 222) symbolises the completion of one stage of existence and the emergence of a new identity. Interestingly, detailing this Muslim cultural practice in English, while shifting from prose to poetry, illustrates how these identities constantly move between expected categories.

Language and Nationalism

Elaborating on the relationship between empire and postcolonial nationalisms, the two narratives consider the linguistic, literary, and political implications of the national/ist identities developing in the mid-20th century. *Plucked in a Far-Off Land*, like many of Baybars's works, offers a vigorous resistance to Greek and Turkish nationalisms, often with greater vehemence than his reactions against British rule. Conversely, *Closed Doors* puts forward a more ambivalent stance which gradually transforms, at the beginning of the text, from an appropriation of Greek symbols within an essentialist identity in opposition to British hegemony, to a greater consideration of a uniquely Cypriot—albeit, perhaps, specifically *Greek* Cypriot—historical consciousness by the end.

In 1998, Baybars discussed his sense of internal conflict living "under the nationalist oppression on a small island. Poets are always forced to accept prevailing ethics and social roles to become a part of the collective national struggle of a minority community" (quoted in Pattie 2012, 159). Related to both his migration away from the "small island" and his use of English as a non-"nationalist" literary language, Baybars's resulting oeuvre puts pressure on the restrictive discourses of nationalist identification through specific, self-reflexive commentaries on his relationship with Turkey—rather than critiques of Cypriots of other ethnolinguistic backgrounds. In his poem "Letter to Homeland", a fictional piece of correspondence from London to his father, the first-person speaker describes himself as one with an "alien past", alleging that "I've never had a home", before and after his departure from the island (Baybars 1963, 19). He is both homeless as a colonial immigrant, and devoid of historical continuity as the native of a space without a simple pre-colonial past. Comparably, "Summer Incident", one of the few third-person poems within the same anthology, *To Catch a Falling Man* (1963), represents a silent man found deserted on a beach. A crowd congregate asking, "Who was this mysterious man?/Why did he never speak? Why the colour/of the cresset was white instead of red?/So they whipped him [. . .] And his lips never told" (24). The use of the symbolic colours, "red" and "white", demonstrates how the man espouses an identity which struggles to fit into established and expected categories but which tacitly associates itself with the whiteness of the newly-designed Cypriot flag, in contrast with the redness of the Turkish alternative. His political subversion leads to physical violence as well as an epistemic silencing. Withholding and self-censorship —which may include the disavowal of a standard linguistic form, and in Baybars's case, the Turkish language—are marked as modes of resistance. Yet, in this poem, he lacks the agency to speak in the first-person mode.

In "Two Cases of Identity", which, as the title suggests, discusses a dual identification between Cyprus and Britain, the speaker infers that his identity has always been fragmented, ruptured, and unconventional, asking in one line, "Why am I outcast? I'm myself as always been. It hurts" (Baybars 1963, 58). He is doubly an "outcast" as an ethnic minority in 1960s London and as a counter-nationalist writer from post-independence Cyprus. Across these poems, the use of rhetorical questions suggests a set of ongoing interrogations of his cultural identity which, nonetheless, evade simple solutions. Overall, Baybars's oeuvre is one of the earliest to engage with and tacitly promote notions of a pan-Cypriot identity. It is, however, a movement in nascent development and without a fully-formed set of parameters.

Plucked in a Far-off Land, as well as demonstrating how the sectarian policies of the British empire culminated in "a certain diving line" between Cypriots by 1963 (Baybars 2005, 222), reveals the simultaneous complicity of nationalist cultural movements in this process—including those the narrator, as a child poet, once participated in. He is presented as a child encouraged to recite nationalist poetry in public. As the text progresses, however, he is shown to challenge these nationalist assumptions and affiliations. Crucially, the *bildungsroman* and *künstlerroman* elements of the text represent the narrator's progress from naïve childhood faith in nationalism to a mature, anti-nationalist worldview.

In one description of a Turkish National Day (on either April 23 or May 19), the narrator publicly recites Turkish poetry, verses from *National Poems for Turkish Children*, to mark the event at his cousin's behest. He recalls,

> father and mother [. . .] were both pleased and disturbed. [. . .] I remember how my feelings towards the Greek and Armenian neighbour children suddenly changed as I rehearsed the poems standing on the window sill. I ceased to be a Cypriot. The language was the only tie between me and Turkey whose history I was learning as a matter of course. A record of a conquering past. [. . .] similar stories

> were circulating among the Greeks but only on National Days would we feel that there was a ditch between the two communities. [. . .] Uncle Hasan often told me to hear [the Armenian neighbour, Hamparsum] carefully so I could appreciate the beauty of our pure language. He [Hasan] didn't much care for the Turkish Cypriot dialect. (2005, 116–17)

The liminal standpoint of the "window sill" from which he performs, and the imbrication of past and present in nationalist discourse, gesture to the inherent paradox of the nation state. In short, its "objective modernity" is in antithesis with its "subjective antiquity in the eyes of nationalists" who frame modern nations as the products of ancient history (Anderson 2006, 5). It is here complicated further by an investment in the nascent Turkish nation through reference to an Ottoman past, at odds with the contemporary, secular, and post-imperial Republic, and recounted here outside Turkey's territorial borders. As well as the "disjunctive temporality of the nation" (Bhabha 2004, 212), the account's emphasis on the relationship between historiographic education and public display exemplifies Homi Bhabha's theory of "the contest of narrative authority between the pedagogical and the performative" within the dissemi*nation* of national identities (212). It is through participation in nationalism and theories of "pure"—not heteroglossic—languages, histories, and identities, that social divisions occur between Cypriot linguistic groups. Indeed, the narrator stresses that it is "only" during such performances of nationality, such as this civic expression of literature and flags on a day specifically honouring Turkish history, that ruptures emerge between Cypriots. As a consequence, he "ceased to be a Cypriot", repudiating this intercommunal identification, viewing Greek- and Armenian-speakers through a xenophobic and elitist lens. Identity is here a conscious choice and, in the face of colonialist claims of Cypriot non-history, an interpellation into "a conquering past" of an *established* nation—in this family, Ottoman Turkey; in others,

Classical Greece, Phoenicia, or Greater Armenia—becomes the chosen tactic of existential resistance.

However, the account problematizes this simple identification with Turkey, not least because it is framed by his parents' ambivalent response, both "pleased and disturbed", as members of a polylingual generation raised before both Atatürk's birthing of the Turkish state and the Cyprus conflicts of the 1950s and 60s. His parents are not metonyms of the mythicized parent-land of Turkey. According to his uncle, the actual vernacular of the narrator, Kıbrıslıca, reductively considered an impure and inferior alternative, is at a remove from "pure" Turkish cultural forms and is denigrated and marginalised by Turkish nationalists like Hasan. The actual components of their everyday cultural lives are abandoned in nationalist discourses, in favour of imports from outside the island. If English is a foreign hegemonic language which *cuts* Cyprus, then the hegemonic cultures of the national parent-lands (Greece and Turkey) perform similar roles in dividing Cypriots from each other and from their indigenous so-called "dialect[s]". They estrange Turkish-speakers from their "Greek and Armenian neighbour[s]", and vice versa. Ironically, the revelation that Greek-speakers (or, Kypriaka-speakers) had similar stories but that only on National Days would these stories of difference emerge, illustrates how nationalist performances are ubiquitous across the island's linguistic groups. They are social phenomena which unify Cypriots through the parallelism they unwittingly reveal between the layers of Cypriot culture/s. Nationalism is not unique to one discrete group but a pan-Cypriot issue through which neo-colonial axioms of "pur[ity]" and difference compete. In short, the motifs, idioms, and methods employed by Turkish nationalists are shared and repeated by Greek nationalists under a nominally different guise.

The narrative goes on to destabilise these nationalist myths by celebrating the linguistic and religious heterogeneity of the island. As well as detailing Cyprus' historic cultural layers, it alludes to the participation of Cypriots in religious events hosted by other denominations, Christian or Islamic (Baybars 2005, 115).

Comparatively, Montis's narrator in *Closed Doors* describes Nicosia as an essentially-diverse space "with Greek, Turkish, and Frankish quarters" within its Venetian walls (2004, 74). Stressing that "[w]ithin a few steps of one another were churches, mosques, covered Venetian balconies, the square of Serai where the Turkish Pasha's palace had stood" (74), the narrative imagines a cosmopolitan city where distinct religious buildings coexist peacefully.

Indeed, in the final chapters of Montis's work, almost all references to Greece and Hellenism are suspended. The final, albeit brief, allusion appears within a depiction of the processions celebrating the advent of Cypriot independence. Through parallelism with the Greek national days extolled vividly in the first chapter (Montis 2004, 3–5), the narrator asserts that the budding Cypriot alternative, the first of its kind, "was a real parade, not like the ones on the 25th of March or the 28th of October" (115), Greek Independence Day and Greek National "Ohi" Day, respectively. The fulfilment of decolonisation performs a celebration of the Cypriot nation which usurps the erstwhile observation of dates honouring events of Greek history. In the re-writing of Cypriot public spaces, the narrator implores the reader to "[p]aint all of Nicosia in one embrace, clinging tightly and crying [. . .] And paint the city throwing its school cap into the air [. . .] Call out its name a thousand times. It knows its name again" (115). Here, the city as a discursive structure, without any reference to specific linguistic groups, is manifested as an embodiment of social unity. Decolonisation is viewed as the fulfilment of adolescent maturation. It is a graduation in which one's (nationalist) "school" education is completed, if not abandoned, in the search for a future identity. It is a common *bildungsroman* trope projected onto the island as a whole. This identity, one of a unified Nicosia, reclaims the "name" it had lost as a result of nationalist anti-colonial violence spilling into intercommunal conflict. It revives the pluralist past the narrator had previously lauded without reducing the past to a Greece- or Turkey-centred reading of its history.

This tacit correlation of anti-colonialism with anti-nationalism also appears in the representation of EOKA's first attacks.

Following them, a "diverse crowd suddenly fill[s] the street, half asleep, half dressed, wandering aimlessly" (Montis 2004, 15). Images of "half"-ness are metonymic of its heterogeneous "divers[ity]". For the narrator, "space had so shrunk that all of Nicosia seemed without sections or neighborhoods [. . .] You had the sense that the explosions had [. . .] banged on your door and asked you to come outside" (15-16). In one of the first allusions to "doors" in the text, the relationship between the violence against the closed doors of imperialism and the destruction of delineating urban structures suggests a theorising of anti-colonialism as actively participating in the deconstruction of physical and symbolic divisions between Cyprus's "diverse" linguistic groups. The violence brings Cypriots together into urban spaces – rather than simply Greek-speakers on Greek national days, for instance – and eradicates the demarcations of ethnolinguistic "neighborhoods". As Elias Canetti (1962) has argued persuasively, a crowd's "destruction of representational images is the destruction of a hierarchy which is no longer recognized" (19). Like iconoclastic, epistemic violence against the English language depicted throughout the narrative, this scene of a pan-Cypriot crowd demonstrates how counter-colonial movements are involved in a "destruction of [the ethnic] hierarchy" which the empire had inscribed onto the colony through its census, sectarian policies, and education reforms. Divide and rule is combated in these representations of Nicosia through tropes of unity wherein no character is marked as "Greek" or "Turk", identifiers conspicuous by their absence in these chapters. Counter to Canetti's theory of humans' intrinsic fear of being touched by strangers (1962, 15), it is a Nicosian population that enthusiastically "embrace[s]" one another and effectively challenges the strictures of colonial curfews and segregation.

Elsewhere, Montis's text decentres the discursive authority of Greek nationalism and its dissemination through text, implying that it, in conjunction with British imperialism, is responsible for the marginalisation of Cypriot identities. In response to the perceived heroism of anti-colonial guerrillas, the narrator repudiates his earlier celebration of moments from Greek history "books" by asserting that

> [i]t was the worst possible time to read heroic tales of other people, other places. [. . .] our struggle was so blind that it would admit of no comparisons or analogies [. . .] even with such beloved names as Thermopylae or Maniaki [anti-Ottoman resistance sites in Greece from the previous century]. (Montis 2004, 37)

This pedagogical discourse is disavowed in favour of creating a new historical record valorising (Greek-speaking) Cypriots as identifiable idols, expunging the cultural "analogies" made earlier with Greece, now re-written as a site of alterity and the source of textualities *belonging* to "other people, other places" foreign to the Cypriot present. He imagines a Cypriot self is born through the reimagining of Greece as "other". Doing so, the narrator creates a counter-discourse within which (Greek-speaking) Cypriots can stage a sense of immediate identification and belonging. Earlier, upon discovering that the anti-colonial movement was generated locally, he states that "however much we came to admire the Greeks from our readings in school. We wanted those who took up arms to be Cypriots. [. . .] How could we envision those arms in the hands of others?" (2004, 22). The account uses similar motifs of resisting Hellenocentric education to create a distinctly "Cypriot" political and historical consciousness which marks "Greeks" as a separate category of ontological "others". Even the image of "hands", in addition to holding ammunition, suggests that Montis's writing is a mode of self-expression which reclaims Cypriot agency from representations of the island composed by the "hands" of Greeks—writing here "in our own name" (22).

Therefore, as well as writing back to the Orientalism of Durrell, the text participates in a depiction of Cyprus independent from the travelogues of Greek writers like Nikos Kazantzakis and Giorgos Seferis. Notably, in 1959, the Greek writer Rodis Roufos first published a response to Durrell entitled "Sour Grapes", anthologised in *The Age of Bronze* (Roufos 1960). Half a decade later, Montis's work becomes the first published narrative to write the pre-independence era from an autonomous *Cypriot* perspective. This transition echoes Frantz Fanon's (1961) urtext of anti-colonialism, *The Wretched of the Earth*:

> The native intellectual accepted the cogency of [the west...] ready to defend the Greco-Latin pedestal. Now it so happens that during the struggle for liberation, at the moment that the native intellectual comes into touch again with his people, this artificial sentinel is turned into dust. All the [northern] Mediterranean values [. . .] become lifeless [. . .] dead words. (37–38)

Ultimately, in reaction to centralised Hellenism, the narrator challenges the mythos surrounding Eleftherios Venizelos (1864–1936), the Greek Prime Minister whose support for irredentism often saw him compared to the similarly nationalistic Mustafa Kemal Atatürk (1881–1938), the founder of the Republic of Turkey. While Venizelos initially appears as a literal and figurative icon in the narrator's family home, after his lack of support for Cyprus' anti-colonial movements, "[h]is portrait in the living room was knocked a bit off-centre. [. . .] After the first hangings we came to hate him. [. . .] The house deserted him. We never let him back in" (Montis 2004, 56). The domestic space of the Cypriot home is represented as one which rejects both the politician and the Venizelism he espoused, "de-centr[ing]" his authority in the colony. If anti-colonial violence opens "doors" between Cypriots, then in the same period, it leads to the closing off of forms of Greek nationalism blind to the sanctioned violence of the British Empire. Venizelos is depicted as "a stalwart friend of the English" (56), above and before his relationship with Cypriots. As the *bildungsroman*'s narrator grows, the Cypriot home becomes a symbolic site in the establishment of an independent identity and one which consciously rejects the selective expansionist politics of Venizelism—a hegemon seeking to interpellate the island into its nation with limited concern for the welfare of its citizens.

Comparatively, and in contrast with contemporary pro-Turkey sentiment, Baybars's opening chapter in *Plucked in a Far-Off Land* trivialises the death of Atatürk. Bluntly informing his parents of the event, the young narrator states, "Atatürk is dead. [. . .] Let's eat. [. . .] You mustn't be sad, you've got me. I'll be a great man when I grow up" (2005, 13). In a *bildungsroman* of diachronic textual progress, its focal character attempts to usurp the authority of the former Turkish leader with his own future career as a writer from, and of, *Cyprus*. The domestic space, and the narrative which surrounds it, does not mourn the loss of the iconic nationalist or herald the legacy of Kemalism. They both instead privilege the consumption of local products, in this case, Cypriot village food. Both narratives are inevitably complicated by their choice of languages. Baybars's English departs from local languages, while Montis's Standard Modern Greek creates a Cypriot history with a bias towards its Greek-speaking population. Neither are endemic Cypriot vernaculars. Nonetheless, these linguistic modes, rupturing extant historiographic models and integrating the heteroglossia of subversive counter-perspectives within shared images of nationalist parades, challenge the simplicity of nationalist epics which, structurally and thematically, espouse purity and conformity. Unlike other postcolonial epics of the nation, however, these nationalist discourses are ones generated from the outside (in Greece and Turkey) and ones which Baybars and Montis re-foreignize by mixing local and foreign textual materials.

Conclusions

Counter to the assumption that Cypriot writers, including those from the 1955 to 1974 generation, can be segregated simply into the categories of "Greek" and "Turkish" literary fields, parallels in the works of Taner Baybars and Costas Montis reveal how they respond to the same context through related narrative tactics—creating comparable *bildungsroman* forms to write-back to British imperialism while simultaneously complicating nationalist discourses which encourage political and cultural union with either Greece or Turkey. This, ultimately, suggests a participation in a uniquely Cypriot, or pan-

Cypriot, literary movement which is distinct from the literature produced by authors from Greece and Turkey. It is necessary, therefore, to compare Greek-speaking and Turkish-speaking Cypriot writers to understand how they engage with the same social and cultural context through similar stylistic means. As the close comparisons between Baybars and Montis demonstrate, the commonalities between Greek-speaking and Turkish-speaking Cypriot authors are more abundant than divisions based on their linguistic background would suggest. Both share the same concern towards British linguistic imperialism which has not impacted Greece and Turkey in the way it has Cyprus, a colony of the British Empire until 1960.

Both authors also address the pervasiveness of the two nationalist discourses on the island, Greek and Turkish, which are encouraged through pedagogy but which Baybars's and Montis's comparable adolescent narrators seek to problematise over time. Cypriots must contend with the overlapping "worlds" of Cyprus, Britain, Greece, and Turkey which render this postcolonial context unique. Few other post-colonies have a relationship with three competing metropoles in the way that Cyprus does. Related to Pheng Cheah's challenges to how the term "the world" is used within postcolonial theory, it showcases how "the world" in "world literature" can no longer refer simply to one amorphous literary space in which all writing enters. Cypriot authors are forced to manoeuvre through layers of linguistic, cultural, and national spaces which seek to claim their identities: the "worlds" of the anglophone British Empire and Commonwealth as well as those created by irredentist Greek and Turkish politicians like Venizelos and Atatürk. In lieu of these political spaces, Baybars and Montis try to create literary sites that allow Cypriots to speak as Cypriots, despite the difficulties caused by divisions in everyday spoken languages.

While noting the two authors' stylistic similarities, however, it is important to observe how the two authors differ in their choice of linguistic form. The pressures of the three hegemons of Britain, Greece, and Turkey influence how Cypriot writers understand the political impact of choosing to write in English, Greek, or Turkish. For Montis, whose text involves copious references to resisting English textualities, writing in Standard Modern Greek, a language associated with Greek nationalism, realises his foremost concern, to contest British imperialism. For Baybars, the importance he places on revising nationalism compels him to appropriate the colonialist, but non-nationalist, language. English allows him to express cultural networks between Cypriot readers. Baybars uses the international auxiliary language of English as a tool for communication between, and across, linguistic groups.

Baybars and Montis, therefore, manifest radical and iconoclastic revisions of nationalist discourses, disavowing the (Greek or Turkish) pan-national in favour of the exchange of culture across the island's linguistic sects and in opposition to nationalist ethnocentricity. Related to the theories of Cheah (2016) and Orsini (2018), these Cypriot writers demonstrate how they exist in the limens of multiple "worlds". It is from this position that they push against existing and expected forms of political and linguistic division to challenge affiliations with nationalist-regionalist hegemons in favour of Cypriot identities which draw on cultural intersections between Greek-speakers, Turkish-speakers, and the language of the British Empire. If these forms of revision, which involve literary representations of anti-imperialist and anti-nationalist unity, are at an early stage in the pre-1974 period, then they re-emerge more fully in post-1974 works such as the first English translation of *Closed Doors* and the first Republic of Cyprus edition of *Plucked in a Far-Off Land.*

Bibliography

Anderson, Benedict. 2006. *Imagined Communities: Reflections on the Origin and Spread of Nationalism*. London and New York: Verso.

Appadurai, Arjun. 1996. *Modernity at Large: Cultural Dimensions of Globalization*. Minneapolis, MN: University of Minnesota Press.

Arvaniti, Amalia. 2006. "Linguistic Practices in Cyprus and the Emergence of Cypriot Greek." *San Diego Linguistic Papers* 2: 1–24.

Baybars, Taner. 1963. *To Catch a Falling Man*. London: Scorpion Press.

—. 1978. *Narcissus in a Dry Pool*. London: Sidgwick & Jackson Limited.

—. 2005. *Plucked in a Far-Off Land: Images of Self-Biography*. Nicosia: Moufflon Publications.

Bhabha, Homi K. 2004. *The Location of Culture*. Oxford and New York: Routledge.

Calotychos, Vangelis. 2004. "'Lawrence Durrell, the Bitterest Lemon?': Cyps and Brits Loving Each Other to Death in Cyprus." In *Lawrence Durrell and the Greek World*, edited by Anna Lillios, 169–87. Selinsgrove, PA: Susquehanna University Press.

Canetti, Elias. 1962. *Crowds and Power*. Translated by Carol Stewart. London: Phoenix Press.

Cheah, Pheng. 2016. *What Is a World? On Postcolonial Literature as World Literature*. Durham, NC: Duke University Press.

de Certeau, Michel. 1984. *The Practice of Everyday Life*. Translated by Steven Rendall. Berkeley, CA: University of California Press.

Durrell, Lawrence. 1957. *Bitter Lemons of Cyprus*. London: Faber and Faber.

Fanon, Frantz. 1965. *The Wretched of the Earth*. Translated by Constance Farrington. London: MacGibbon and Gee.

Gulle, V. Ozan. 2011. "Structural Borrowings in Cypriot Turkish from Cypriot Greek." *Mediterranean Language Review* 18: 91–113.

Hadjioannou, Xenia, Stravoula Tsiplakou, and Matthias Kappler. 2011. "Language Policy and Language Planning in Cyprus." *Current Issues in Language Planning* 12: 503–69.

Kincaid, Jamaica. 1988. *A Small Place.* New York: Farrar, Straus and Giroux.

Montis, Costas. 2004. *Closed Doors: An Answer to* Bitter Lemons *by Lawrence Durrell.* Translated by David Roessel and Soterios G. Stavrou. Minneapolis, MN: Nostos.

Morton, Stephen. 2013. *States of Emergency: Colonialism, Literature and Law.* Liverpool: Liverpool University Press.

Ngũgĩ wa Thiong'o. 1986. *Decolonising the Mind: The Politics of Language in African Literature.* Nairobi: East African Educational Publishers.

Orsini, Francesca, et al. 2018. "Multilingual Locals and Significant Geographies. For a Ground-up and Located Approach to World Literature." *Modern Languages Open* 1 (article 19): 1–8.

Papadakis, Yiannis. 2005. *Echoes from the Dead Zone: Across the Cyprus Divide.* London and New York: I.B. Tauris.

Pattie, Susan. 2012. "Imagining Homelands: Poetics and Performance among Cypriot Armenians." In *Cyprus and the Politics of Memory: History, Community and Conflict,* edited by Rebecca Bryant and Yiannis Papadakis, 140–67. London and New York: I.B. Tauris.

Roufos, Rodis. 1960. *The Age of Bronze.* London: Heinemann.

Tsiplakou, Stavroula. 2006. "Code-Switching and Code-Mixing between Related Varieties: Establishing the Blueprint." *International Journal of Humanities* 6: 46–66.

"The Page Becomes a Tape Recorder": The Development of an Oral Literary Aesthetic through Caribbean Radio

Lucy Steeds

What can the tape recorder offer the writer that the page cannot? In examining the development of anglophone Caribbean literature, studies have predominantly focused on the role of print media, publishing houses, and written traditions in producing a modern literary culture. This chapter argues that radio played a central role in the early phases of modern anglophone Caribbean literature. It contends that it was the centrality of radio, and its very dynamics, that conditioned the aesthetics of literature at the time. Radio, the "little magic box of sound" as George Lamming (1990, 14) described it, was a formative influence in the shaping of modern anglophone Caribbean literature.

The Page and the Tape Recorder: The Origins of Anglophone Caribbean Literature

There is a critical consensus about the dearth of anglophone Caribbean literature in the early 20th century. In 1949, Jamaican poet Una Marson claimed that "in our island home the writers who have reached professional status can be counted on the fingers of one hand" (quoted in Donnell and Lawson Welsh 1996, 185). Fellow Jamaican poet John Figueroa (1966) echoed her sentiments nearly 20 years later, observing that "until recently there was no West Indian publishing house" (xiv). Philip Sherlock argued that the "first West Indian voices belong to the 1930s" and that "not until the 1940s did the West Indian novel emerge" (quoted in Figueroa 1966, vii). Institutions of literary culture, such as publishing houses, professional writers, and established readerships were decidedly absent in the early part of the 20th century. Anglophone Caribbean literature was conspicuous in its absence, until what Alison Donnell has called the "boom" of the 1950s (2005, 185). The post-war years of the mid-20th century witnessed a significant surge in the Caribbean literary movement, and this historical "cleavage" (14) should not be underestimated: "the 'emergence' of a dozen or so novelists in the British Caribbean [. . .] between 1948 and 1958, is in the nature of a phenomenon", wrote Lamming (1960, 29). Why did this happen? And what role did the apparently ephemeral medium of radio play in the solidification of a Caribbean literary tradition during this formative period?

The answer, I argue, can be understood through an examination of *Caribbean Voices*, a BBC radio programme that was produced between 1943 and 1958. In the programme's 15-year history, over 1,500 stories and poems were broadcast on the BBC's West Indian Service, featuring, in a region with few professional writers, a total of 372 contributors from across the Caribbean. The programme was instigated by Una Marson, and subsequently edited by Henry Swanzy from 1946 to 1954, and V. S. Naipaul from 1954 until its final broadcast in 1958. It was during this formative period in the late 1940s and 1950s that the radio became a central space for the promotion and development of Caribbean literature. The explicit aim of *Caribbean Voices* was to provide an outlet for Caribbean writers. In an environment where "there were few opportunities to publish" (Figueroa 1966, xiv) and "the literary world of the region [. . .] was restricted and uneven" (Nanton, 2000, 64), the radio offered writers exposure, encouragement, and remuneration. "The purpose of the programme", according to Swanzy, was "to attempt to build up some kind of contemporary tradition by the exchange of writings between the islands" (quoted in Nanton 2000, 66). At a time when forums for exchange and opportunities for publishing were limited, radio became a primary site in which literature was developed.

By examining the transcripts from *Caribbean Voices*, which include not just a record of what was read on air but also traces of the editorial process through marginalia and handwritten amendments to the typed script, we can glean a greater understanding of how this literary culture was produced on air. Transcripts from the Caribbean Service held at the BBC Written Archives provide a written record of an oral history, and often the very scribal nature of the documents reveals the tensions between written and spoken literature. By correlating sound recordings, held at the BBC Sound Archives at the British Library, with written transcripts and correspondence, researchers can use the scribal history that hides behind this oralised literature to investigate the details of its production. In addition to the transcripts themselves, broadcasting notes and production documents (held at both the BBC Written Archives and the Cadbury Research Centre at the University of Birmingham) reveal the technical processes of translating literature into radio content.

Radio Geographies: a Renegotiation of Space in the 20th Century

The dynamics of radio initially seem divorced from the conventional understanding of literature as a textual and bibliographic tradition, but I argue that it was in fact the very qualities of radio broadcasting that enabled Caribbean literature to develop so organically. Looking back at the origins of Caribbean literary traditions, Edward Kamau Brathwaite (1984) said that people had "come from a historical experience where they had to rely on their very *breath* rather than on paraphernalia like books and museums and machines. They had to depend on *immanence*, the power within themselves, rather than the technology outside themselves" (19; original emphasis). But what happens when this notion of "breath" and the technology of radio are combined? This chapter examines the ways in which the immanence of Caribbean tradition and the material paraphernalia of colonial literary culture interact to produce an independent literature within the framework of a colonial institution.

Radio is often thought of as a "spaceless" medium (Mildorf and Kinzel, 2016, 121). It is thus particularly important to note the geographies involved in the production of *Caribbean Voices*. How does a medium that transcends physical locality negotiate the dynamics of metropole and periphery? How can we perceive of Caribbean literature being "in motion" in this instance? Even though *Caribbean Voices* featured Caribbean literature and was broadcast exclusively to the Caribbean, its organising centre was London. Arthur Calder-Marshall (1955), who was often featured on the programme, noted that "London, rather than Kingston, Port of Spain, or Georgetown, is the cultural centre for West Indian writers" (452). Whilst an independent literature was striving to emerge, the centre of its formation was still the colonial capital, 4,500 miles away. There exists an interesting dynamic clearly pertinent to Shih's (2004, 17) "technologies of recognition", whereby the "agent of recognition" remains the colonial centre.

Writing for the programme was sourced locally in Jamaica by a literary agent, Gladys Lindo, who advertised for and actively solicited scripts from across the Caribbean. The "pick of the bunch" was then sent to Broadcasting House in London, where Swanzy would make the final selection, and the literature was read on air and beamed back to the Caribbean on shortwave radio (Gramaglia and McIntosh 2013, 49). The centralising and organising presence of London in a Caribbean space is a reminder of the colonial power of the radio as a technology.

The advent of radio in the 1920s signalled "a truly major reshaping of the spatial organisation of social relations at every level, from local to global" (Massey, 1994, 161), and it is important, in an age of television and the Internet, to remember that radio at its inception was the most technologically exciting and experimental medium of communication in the world. John Reith (1924), the first Director General of the BBC, stated that:

> wireless [. . .] ignores the puny and often artificial barriers which have estranged men from their fellows. It will soon take continents in its stride, outstripping the winds; the divisions of oceans, mountain ranges, and deserts will be passed unheeded. It will cast a girdle round the earth with bands that are all the stronger because invisible. (222)

There is at once the freeing imagery of overcoming barriers, and the binding imagery of an invisible girdle here. Considered in the context of empire, this invisible binding that Reith imagines has significant political potential. By abolishing the spatial divisions between the heart of the empire and its peripheries, "the microphone can achieve what the printed word and the philosophical formulation of doctrine have failed to bring about [. . .] a quiet and secure linkage with the *stoep* and fireside audience" (Reith, 1935, 4; original emphasis). The radio provided a sense of the dissolution of space, and it is this initial spacelessness of the acousmatic voice that necessitates particular attention to the actual geographies of broadcasting. The radio encourages what Adorno (2009) calls "the illusion of closeness", via an acousmatic voice whose "radio physiognomics" defy conventional understandings of voice and locality (77). The voice of the coloniser could seep into the colonial subject's everyday life without the intrusion of physical presence.

The geo-cultural displacement between the source, production, and audience of *Caribbean Voices* is crucial in understanding the colonial implications of the BBC's role in the development of Caribbean literature. This jarring geographical reality was not lost on Swanzy, who admitted "I realise how galling it must be to have persons of no great literary achievement criticising from three thousand miles away" (quoted in Butcher 1989, 79). Whilst radio did bring disparate people into contact with one another, taking "continents in its stride", the geographical dislocation between the microphone and the radio itself constituted a colonial distancing that secured a connection between geographically disparate people. It served to remind the Caribbean of an omnipresent yet intangible colonial presence. The BBC, Swanzy acknowledged, could easily be interpreted as "the imposition of alien standards to a regional culture which ought to develop itself" (quoted in Gramaglia and McIntosh, 2013, 49). These geographies of radio production are all the more potent because of their invisibility—the quality intrinsic to radio which Reith himself had lauded in 1929. Considering the intricacies and contradictions of the diffusion routes involved in *Caribbean*

Voices, what remains most striking is the Caribbean response to the programme's work. Caribbean writers involved in the programme, including some of the most prominent figures of modern Caribbean literature, have expressed their belief in its significance as promoting the development of an anglophone literary culture. Derek Walcott (2009) asserted that "it's a debt you feel you owe to people who opened a door for you, and without whom you probably would not have entered that house at all". Lamming (1960), too, has claimed that "at one time or another, in one way or another, all the West Indian novelists have benefitted from [Swanzy's] work" (67). Whilst this colonial dependence is itself a reflection of British hegemony and influence, it is important to note that Caribbean writers used this space to their own advantage. Philip Nanton (2000) declared that *Caribbean Voices* became "the most important focus for the development and promotion of the region's literary output" (61).

By examining Swanzy's private correspondence with these writers, which in itself is telling of the degree of investment he placed in them, the relationship between Caribbean writer and Irish broadcaster sheds an interesting light on the dynamic between metropole and periphery. In response to Swanzy's concern about his place in Caribbean literary culture, Brathwaite wrote to him in 1953 to say;

> You're always doing your good word with a certain sense of trepidation, considering yourself as an "outsider." But may I say that without this balanced self-consciousness on your part, West Indian writers, like myself, might [. . .] have lost all sense of successful proportion? I say that you're doing a good job well.[1] (MS42/1/9)

This vociferous support for the programme's format acknowledges Swanzy's imposed presence but, as Brathwaite

1 Brathwaite to Swanzy, 30 March 1953. Papers of Henry Valentine L. Swanzy. MS42/1/9. All future archival citations will be noted by MS number. Please refer to bibliography for more detail.

acknowledges, it shows an understanding that an absence of local publishing opportunities meant that, in Lamming's words, "it was London, or nothing" (1960, 67).

In fact, encouraging a local literature from a geographically remote and divorced locality could be beneficial to Caribbean writers seeking wider recognition for their work, as recognised by V.S. Naipaul, who asserted that Swanzy "took local writing seriously and lifted it above the local" (quoted in Nanton, 62). By so doing, the radio allowed this writing to be read and heard as a global literature rather than a peripheral specialism. Whilst *Caribbean Voices* was only broadcast in the Caribbean, the affirming stamp of the BBC gave writers and Caribbean writing an international mark of recognition. Figueroa, too, has noted this surprising effect of geographical disparity, showing that:

> there was an ironic twist in all of this—one that was hardly noticed, and possibly could not have been avoided at the time: the local was being given status by something that was happening abroad! The metropole was strengthening the periphery! (quoted in Butcher 1989, 79)

The seeming disadvantage of geographical dislocation could be subverted so that "peripheral" cultures were strengthened by the good word of the metropole—the global reputation of the BBC, in this case.

Brathwaite has claimed that *Caribbean Voices* was "the single most important literary catalyst for Caribbean creative and critical writing in English" (1984, 87), and Samuel Selvon (1990) has simply said that "it was the greatest thing that ever happened really" (71). This chapter will examine the role that radio played in the "boom" of anglophone Caribbean literature in the post-war era, by analysing the original scripts and production memos from *Caribbean Voices*, the correspondence between Swanzy, Lindo and the writers who appeared on the programme, and the original recordings of the programme from the BBC's sound archives. It can then be understood to what extent this literature was conditioned by the dynamics of radio, and how an oral aesthetic developed in Caribbean writing of the 1940s and 1950s. Finally, this chapter will consider the ways in which Caribbean writers used the medium of radio subversively, and the ways in which their writing challenged the hegemony of English literature and of the place of Eurocentric literary standards in the Caribbean.

"Local Colour"

One of the few criteria for submitting work to *Caribbean Voices* was that the literature should reflect "local colour". When returning rejected manuscripts to Lindo on August 13, 1946, Swanzy noted that they "all have something in common, and that is a complete absence of local colour" (MS42/1/2). Swanzy later claimed that he only wanted material that "legitimately came under the title 'Caribbean Voices'" (MS42/1/2) and not "general effusions that could be written anywhere in the world" (MS42/1/3). The stress was on local specificity. In attempting to build up an authentic Caribbean literary culture, Swanzy's greatest focus was on filtering work that displayed what he called a "West Indian sensibility" (20946/8, 743).[2] This determination to focus on the local, from a vantage point of over 4,000 miles away, complies with a troubling exaltation of "representative" literature. Swanzy's desire to include only "legitimate" Caribbean literature builds a problem that Walcott later elucidated in "The Schooner *Flight*" (1979): "either I'm nobody, or I'm a nation". To get their voices heard, Caribbean writers had to write in expression of their origins, as if their individuality was entirely represented through their national belonging. In an article in *Caribbean Quarterly* Swanzy (1949) declared that "all the better writers show signs of their origin, even when they are not specifically describing the West Indian scene" (24).

---

2 Swanzy, 31 August 1952. BBC Written Archives. Acc No 20946/8, 743. All future BBC Written Archives citations will be noted by Acc. No. and page number. Please refer to the bibliography for more detail.

What are these "signs of origin", though, and how did they manifest themselves?

The greatest barrier to developing an individual literary tradition was the hegemony of English literature. In a colonial and even postcolonial Caribbean society, the greatest struggle of creating an independent literary culture was the effort to detach "literature" from "English literature". A Caribbean literature could not become Caribbean until the domination of the English canon, and the Eurocentric standards of aesthetics and criticism that accompanied it, had been disavowed. The hegemony of English literature was deeply entrenched in the aesthetic values of Caribbean writers and readers: "we had nothing but the words, the music, the images, the plays of the conqueror; and these were merely discards from the work benches of the familiar alien", asserted Victor Stafford Reid (1996, quoted in Donnell, 177). Readers read literature that did not express their lived experience. There was nothing for readers that reflected the realities of their own lives, and so the production of any literature was stifled by what Swanzy called "the uninspired shibboleths of teachers who are not creators, [who] have in fact saddled past generations of West Indian children with English classics" (1949, 22). Selvon recounted that "in the hot tropical atmosphere I dreamed of green fields and rolling downs, of purling streams and daffodils" (quoted in Sindoni 2010, 225). Figueroa, too, lamented children "conned by rote" who "recited with powerful glee poems about daffodils without ever having seen a daffodil" (Butcher 1989, 73). The colonial exaltation of the very English Romantic movement was not just an aesthetic ideology, but a determining force in what could be considered "literature" at all. What was read influenced what was written, and the struggle to articulate a Caribbean poetics stemmed from the dominance of the English literary canon in the region. If literature meant "English literature", then how could a local literary culture develop in a colonised society?

In the Foreword to the anthologised collected verse of *Caribbean Voices* compiled by Figueroa, Philip Sherlock articulates this artistic subjugation, and its consequential muteness:

> I was brought up on Tennyson and later Browning and Wordsworth, Keats, and later Shelley. But something was missing. I knew that I lived in a region of bewitching beauty but I found no poets to open magic casements on my fields of bananas and orange trees in the way that Keats transformed, or Wordsworth illumined, the English countryside. [. . .] I belonged to a people without a literature. (Figueroa 1966, vii)

In the English interpretation of "literature", the Caribbean was defined by its lack. There were no voices, as there were no outlets for these voices. *Caribbean Voices* changed that.

To create the "individual voice" anew, poets first had to dismantle the old. Poets began to define themselves in opposition to the standard tropes of English canonicity, asserting an identity through their own lack. Daniel Williams identified Caribbean writers as "We Who Do Not Know the Snow", in direct reference to the hegemony of Romantic English literature. The idea echoes throughout the collection, with H.D. Carberry's claim in "Nature" that "We have neither summer nor winter / neither autumn nor spring", H.A. Vaughan's assertion that "In our land / Poppies do not spring" ("In our Land") and Frank Collymore's reaffirmation of "No winter in this equinoctial land" ("At Easter"). By defining themselves and their own experiences in direct opposition to the English canon, Caribbean writers made the first step towards translating a Caribbean experience into a poetic one.

This was not just an issue of subject matter, but also form. When Lamming's first novel, *In the Castle of My Skin* (1953), was reviewed by *The Times*, it was noted that "it was West Indian in content, but within the English tradition" (20946/13, 1032). Addressing this assessment on *Caribbean Voices*, Naipaul declared that it was equally applicable to most writing to come out of the Caribbean. The script for the programme reveals the strength of this feeling amongst Caribbean writers. Naipaul's section of the script reads

> The British tradition remains the basic tradition
> in the West Indies; and after
> reading the work of West Indian writers in bulk, one
> experiences a sort of
> embarrassment relief
> emotional ~~suffocation~~, and one longs for ~~air~~.[3]
> (20946/13, 1032)

In a continuation of his redacted metaphor, Naipaul asserted that a "welcome breath of air to the tears and torture of West Indian poetry" can be found in the work of Edward Kamau Brathwaite (20946/13, 1032). Brathwaite had poetry, prose and drama broadcast on *Caribbean Voices* between 1943 and 1958, and even when his subject was Europe (as in "Poems on Italy" and "Trafalgar"), the form was experimental. "The Rite of Spring", broadcast on May 11, 1958, is particularly notable for its experimentation, with readers warned in advance that "it is an experiment [. . .] it isn't the sort of thing everyone will enjoy. In fact, probably some people might not even want to call it poetry" (20946/22, 1336). The unpublished poem is a long song in free verse with a tempo that accelerates and slows from line to line, using onomatopoeic language to evoke the sounds of drums, cymbals and human voices:

> Drums
> Drums
> And the trumpets of rain
> Again,
> Feet
> (lines 13–17)

The poem is a rallying cry for a people to resist the powers of an oppressor, to refuse the "sacrifice" (line 9), and instead to use the

---

3 "Suffocation" has been crossed out and replaced with "embarrassment"; "air" with "relief".

music of the earth to assert their natural place on it. Against the oppressor, Brathwaite cries:

> Fall fall fall on your knees
> For tall one, he comes, the rising and wise one.
> O shout shout
> Let us
> shout
> Lift up your hands
> Lift lift lift up your hands and
> Shout
> (lines 57–64)

Whilst the poem is celebratory, it is also subversive. It concludes with the toppling of the hierarchical order. The very act of broadcasting this poem on the BBC was a subversion of the radio's nationalistic impetus, and a bold move both by Brathwaite in writing it and Swanzy in broadcasting it. Whether or not the BBC was in fact impartial, it stood for a very British reality, and one that was undeniably colonial. To use this service, designed to reinforce the heart of the empire by connecting it to its peripheral dominions, to challenge the hierarchy, was a deliberate inversion of its purpose.

In a 1976 lecture at the Caribbean Festival of the Arts, Brathwaite argued that it was form, far more than subject, that constrained Caribbean writers. The pentameter "carries with it a certain kind of experience, which is not the experience of a hurricane. The hurricane does not roar in pentameters" (1984, 10). The question Brathwaite asked of his fellow Caribbean writers was "how do you get a rhythm which approximates the *natural* experience, the *environmental* experience?" (10; original emphasis).

The beginnings of an answer lay in the spoken voice. Specifically, T.S. Eliot's voice. Brathwaite asserted that "what T.S. Eliot did for Caribbean poetry and Caribbean literature was to introduce the notion of the speaking voice, the conversational tone" (1984, 30). Caribbean writers could not instantaneously forget the literature they had been brought up to read, but they could use that literature and direct the influence it had over their own writing. As Brathwaite continues:

> for those who really made the breakthrough, it was Eliot's actual voice—or rather his recorded voice, property of the British Council—reading "Preludes", "The Love Song of J. Alfred Prufrock", *The Waste Land* and *Four Quartets*—not the texts—which turned us on. (31)

The crux was radio. It was Eliot's recorded voice, broadcast over the airwaves, which gave life to his poetry in the Caribbean, far more than the printed texts. Significantly, Eliot himself worked for the BBC's Empire Service, and here developed many of his ideas about modernism, technology, and the voice. In fact, the sleeve note of Brathwaite's copy of the *Four Quartets* noted "what a recording of a poem by its author can and should preserve, is the way that poem sounded to the author when he had finished it" (1984, 31). This is what the tape recorder can offer the writer, whereas the page cannot. The recorded voice emphasises rhythm, inflection, pace and orality. Eliot was aware of these qualities that were amplified by the radio as opposed to the page and, in turn, Caribbean writers adopted those aspects of Eliot's art which spoke, quite literally, to them.

Eliot's influence over what Victor Stafford Reid, rather ironically, called the cultural "wasteland" of the Caribbean points to the beginnings of the importance of orality in modern Caribbean literature (Reid in Donnell and Lawson Welsh 1996, 178). An emphasis on the speaking voice, foregrounded by radio, was the starting point for the development of a highly oralised literary aesthetic. Philip Sherlock's Foreword to the *Caribbean Voices* anthology looks back to Reid's cultural "wasteland" and asks: "there was beauty; my island, like Prospero's, was full of sweet sounds; but why were there no voices?" (Figueroa 1966, vii). Radio gave these voices an outlet. *Caribbean Voices*, via the modern technology of radio, gave writers a means of expressing their voices whilst detaching their art from the scribal and bibliographic traditions of European literature.

Orality: the Development of Identity through Sound

In his diary on 16 May 1946, Swanzy wrote that he didn't "feel greatly enthused" by the prospects of Caribbean literature, "but old Harold Stannard was enthusiastic about the possibilities of the region, full of oral life, combining the traditions and folk lore" (quoted in Gramaglia and McIntosh 2013, 49). This, it transpired, was where the future of Caribbean literature lay: in the "oral life" of the region which at once combined an oral literary heritage with an Eliot-esque modernism. It is important to note that "in the field of Caribbean cultural diglossia, English represents a textualised language in the sense of Walter Ong [. . .] it marks a special intensity in the relationship of language to writing" (Döring 2003, 8–9). A move away from the English canon is thus implicit in the use of oral literature, even though it involves literary hierarchies. As Ong (2002) has shown, western academies have ranked written literature over oral literature, and the European "scholarly focus on texts [has] had ideological consequences" (10). Oral literatures have traditionally been seen as less refined, and less worthy of study than written texts. To use this "inferior" form of literature was thus a subversive move by Caribbean writers, but it drew on a rich tradition of oral literature, song, and folk tale. By using the radio, these writers were declaring that these traditions were relevant, modern, and worthy of being incorporated into a national literature. A second effect of broadcasting poetry and prose over the airwaves was the sudden accessibility of literature. Where literature once required literacy, radio meant that literary appreciation became an act of listening, not just of reading. Where one of the alienating aspects of the English canon had been its strong scribal history, radio provided a more egalitarian, accessible form of literary consumption.

In an interview with Stephen Spender on *Caribbean Voices* in 1951, Swanzy asked "when did you personally get to hear Caribbean poetry?" (20946/7, 638). The question is interesting, for Swanzy does not ask Spender when he first read Caribbean poetry, or even when he first heard *of* it, but when he heard it. Orality became the distinguishing trait of independent literature in the Caribbean in the 1940s and 1950s. It embodied "local colour", and the speaking voice became the primary medium through which to express this independence. Radio provided a literary medium which foregrounded speech inflections, rhythm, dialect and music, features that are often lost on the printed page. Laurence Breiner (2000) has argued that

> it was a great piece of luck for the development of West Indian poetry that the cachet of metropolitan approval came first of all not in the form of publication by a British anthology or magazine [. . .] but in the form of a radio program. (7)

The radio encouraged linguistic experimentation in a way that print publications did not. Over the course of its existence, *Caribbean Voices* enabled writers to experiment formally with language, and to use this as an expression of their identity.

Caribbean identity could be expressed through radio because it connected modern writing to a long tradition of oral literature. Brathwaite, in *History of the Voice*, asserts that the first thing to note about Caribbean languages is that they are oral rather than scribal. This orality means that language "is based as much on sound as it is on song [. . .]. The noise that it makes is part of the meaning", and so when it is written down, "you lose the sound or the noise, and therefore you lose part of the meaning" (1984, 17). This statement points not just to the long tradition of oral literature in the Caribbean, but crucially to the insufficiency of textualised literary traditions and, implicitly, the western canon. As a means of expressing an oralised history, radio is a more faithful representation of traditional spoken literature in the Caribbean than the printed word. The radio thus became a modern medium in which to express this heritage, simultaneously honouring tradition and asserting a modern, technological identity for Caribbean literature.

The ability to express this spoken literary history was important because it connected Caribbean writers to a history of West African orality. Oscar Dathorne has shown that many spoken and oralised traditions in the Caribbean are connected to West African practices, including the spoken ritual of santería, brujería, voodoo, the queh-queh from Guyana, the Shango shouts of Trinidad, and the songs of Pocomania and Myal in Jamaica (cited in Sindoni 2010, 220). By expressing this heritage on the airwaves, Caribbean writers were able to assert a historical identity which had often been denied to them, as was a literary identity, after centuries of oppression. Sandra Pouchet Paquet (2005) has shown that Caribbean ancestry has been "effectively silenced if not erased" (126). Oral literature worked against this silencing, and the radio gave a wide-reaching, technologically-advanced platform for reclaiming this history. The Caribbean context might also be read in terms of Marianne Hirsch's (2008) theory of "postmemory": the second generation's experiences of trauma that preceded their births, transmitted in ways that make them memories in their own right. Oral literature can be read as a resistance to the trauma of colonisation, where recovering the eradicated past functions as a resistant act (103).

One of the strongest expressions of oral Caribbean literature on *Caribbean Voices* is folk literature. Folk traditions provided an alternative literary heritage to the European canon: "perhaps in the proud march of our folklore we may bring our peasant people to the fore more readily than [. . .] by the imitation of the British Council dummy", declared Doreen Goodwin (quoted in Simpson 2011, 83). Even in terms of genre, folk stories are politically charged, for, "folk poets are the spokesmen whose whole concern is to express the experience of the people rather than the experiences of the elite" (Brathwaite 1984, 26). Anancy folk stories which featured on *Caribbean Voices* are derived from the Anansi tales of the Ghanaian Ashanti traditions, and feature the fabular figure of Anancy, often depicted as a spider. The 1952 broadcast of Louise Bennett's "Anancy and Monkey" is particularly illuminating, as is its subsequent critique by Calder-Marshall on the air. The story includes acknowledgements of the historical tradition from which it originates, ending with a sense of temporal continuity: "From dat day to today Monkey dah laugh after Anancy an any time you see Monkey running up an down troo an laughing is Anancy him remember. Jack Mandora me no choose none" (20946/7, 668). The final line is a motif; the end of the Anancy story in Caribbean and Ashanti storytelling. Each of Bennett's Anancy stories ends with this phrase, signalling that "I take no responsibility for the story I have told". "Jack Mandora—Keeper of Heavens door. Me noh choose none—It is not of my choosing".[4] This final linking of her own story to the Anancy tradition imbues Bennet's authorial role with a sense of fate and determinism, and connects her story to her heritage and ancestry. These stories are part of her identity, and not just of her choosing. In tying "Anancy and Monkey" into the Anancy tradition, "from dat day to today", Bennett ends by surrendering the authorship of her own story, confirming its relative unimportance in oral literatures by contrast to written ones.

After "Anancy and Monkey" was read on air, it was followed by a critique by Arthur Calder-Marshall. He concluded that "Louise Bennett's story belongs to this simple un-alphabetic age, when nobody thought of books, far less of print" (20946/7, 668). He praised the story strongly, but his critique exposes the orientalist trope of "anachronistic space," as defined by Anne McClintock (1995, 9), in which cultures distant from the metropole are associated with distance in time. "'Anancy and Monkey' is straight out of the Garden of Eden", Calder-Marshall asserted, in a Christianised reading which negates the Ashanti origins of the story. What Bennett asserted, and what Calder-Marshall indicatively refused to recognise, was the presence of an African literary tradition in modern Caribbean literature, one that has been subjected to the value-system implicit in the hegemon of the European literary canon. Calder-Marshall also explicitly acknowledged the oral qualities of Bennett's story, but, rather than expound the oralised potential of the story, he patronised

4 Louise Bennett, 2005. "An Exclusive Interview With Miss Lou." *Jamaicans.com.* http://jamaicans.com/misslouinterview/Accessed June 12, 2016.

it by comparing it to the monolith of written European literature: "Bennett's story belongs to this simple un-alphabetic age" (20946/7, 668). To be un-alphabetic is to be backwards in time, in Calder-Marshall's logic.

Dialect, Acrolect and Nation Language: Orality on the Airwaves and on the Page

As the transcript to Bennett's "Anancy and Monkey" demonstrates, a crucial part of orality is dialect, a key part of identity. Derek Walcott, who was himself promoted on *Caribbean Voices* at the age of 18, said that "tonally the individual voice is a dialect. [. . . It] shapes its own accent, its own vocabulary and melody in defiance of an imperial concept of language, the language of Ozymandias, libraries and dictionaries" (quoted in Döring 2003, 4). Dialect is another means of rejecting the "paraphernalia" of "books and museums and machines", and radio becomes a productive medium in which to hone the literary understanding of dialect.

Swanzy understood dialect as being a central expression of Caribbean literature. In a broadcast on July 11, 1948, after hearing poems by Harry Milner and Michael Smith, he noted that "when we hear these poems, we wonder about dialect" (20946/3, 255). Neither Milner's nor Smith's poems used dialect, and Swanzy's reflections reveal a feeling that something was missing. He contrasted the poems with "[dialect's] brilliant exponent" Louise Bennett, by broadcasting "Bans a Killin" (20946/3, 255). The poem defends dialect in both its subject and language, by raising Jamaican dialect to a parity with English dialects. Addressing the Englishman who wants to "kill dialec" (line 4) in the name of high literature, Bennett asks "Yuh gwine kill all English dialec / Or jus Jamaica one?" (lines 7–8). Defending the legitimacy of Jamaican dialect as a literary language, Bennett compares it to the esteemed history of dialectical English verse:

Yuh wi haffi kill de Lancashire,
De Yorkshire, de Cockney,
De broad Scotch and de Irish brogue
Before yuh start kill me!
(lines 25–28)

There is violence in this poem, and defiance, as the reader has to examine their own assumptions of literature and dialect "Before yuh start kill me!". Bennett exposes the hypocrisy in literary evaluation, and goes back to the hallowed names of the English canon that for long dominated Caribbean literary education. If critics wanted to banish dialect,

Yuh wi haffi get de Oxford Book
A English Verse, an tear
Out Chaucer, Burns, Lady Grizelle
An plenty a Shakespeare!
(lines 29–32)

The evocative use of dialect, "vocabulary, idioms, syntax, and speech rhythms", constitutes what Susan Gingell (2009) calls Bennett's "see-hear aesthetics" (32). When transcribed, Bennett's verse has to convey the inflections of her speech and so an experimental, or unconventional, use of spelling, grammar and syntax is employed. The radio was a modern and complementary medium for these "see-hear aesthetics". Before *Caribbean Voices*, and before being published in print, Bennett spent many years performing her poetry in music halls and theatres, giving live performances of her work. The radio thus provides an aesthetic continuation of this performative style, but one which is technologically modern, with far greater reach. Crucial to the understanding of radio dissemination, however, is that even though it is wide-reaching, taking "continents in its stride", it sustains Adorno's (2009, 77) "illusion of closeness"—a sense of intimacy regardless of proximity. This is complemented by dialect poetry, which, as Dennis Cooley (1987) notes, creates intimacy through the recreation of a sense of familiarity: "in sound we gain nearness. We feel the rasp and buzz of the vernacular" (213). There is overt parallelism here with radio, which creates a sense of proximity over distance through the buzz of sound over the airwaves. *Caribbean Voices* created localised space through the "nearness" inherent in dialect and broadcasting.

The dynamic between dialect and acrolect was explored in a broadcast of October 20, 1957. The programme, produced by Guyanese novelist Edgar Mittelholzer, featured the short story "The Storyteller" by Trinidadian writer E.M. Thorne. Mittelholzer opened with a reassertion of the division between written and oral literatures, saying that "most of the stories we receive for *Caribbean Voices* are written in a style more suited to magazine publication than to radio broadcasting" (20946/21, 1264). Thorne's story was different, however. The prose used "the free and easy manner of the raconter [sic]" (20946/21, 1264), mimicking speech in a way that complemented radio format, where literature is heard rather than seen. This is a clear demonstration of how the *Caribbean Voices* selection process shaped the development of anglophone Caribbean literature: stories with a greater oral quality, in the "free and easy manner of the raconter", were favoured as they were best suited to radio performance. These were the best-received stories, and their writers the most successful in becoming re-commissioned, and thus furthering their literary reputations and careers, as well as redefining the qualities of Caribbean literature. Practically, the BBC encouraged this as well. In a letter to Swanzy on September 14, 1946, Lindo noted that "the Copyright Department is now paying more for pieces specially written for broadcasting" (MS42/1/2). Rather than assuming written literature could be adapted to radio performance, Lindo's letter shows that writing that was specifically crafted with an ear for the radio, and for oral performance, was actively encouraged.

Thorne's "The Storyteller" begins by evoking oral storytelling: "Come, child; you want to hear a story? Come: I will tell you a story" (MS42/1/2). Thorne also evokes a distinctly Caribbean listening experience. The "local colour" of the story is the implicit locality of the listening audience:

> open the window little bit and let the night come in, so that we could hear the wind racing through the mango and cedar. Just push it open a little wider and if you listen good you will hear the owl hoot-hooting in the cedar tree and you will hear the ripe sapodilla fall when the bat suck it up to the stem.

Thorne clearly emphasises listening as crucial in the appreciation of his literature. The story in question blends dialect with Standard English, so that the dialogue is in dialect, and the narrative in standard acrolectal English. There thus develops a linguistic distinction between the lived and the narrated experiences, where dialect denotes the real, first-hand experience of the protagonist. Nearly a month later, on November 17, 1957, Mittelholzer broadcast another of Thorne's stories, "The Failure of the Early Rose", which explicitly addressed dialect. Using Trinidadian patois, Thorne reflected on the internalised prejudice Trinidadians held toward their own dialect:

> "Il tombé", she said.
>
> I winced. Patois always made me wince. I had learnt respectable French at school and I had always insisted to my mother that patois sounded like the gobbling of turkeys.

Acrolectal French is "respectable", yet patois is animalistic. Thorne touches here on the view instilled in Trinidadians that dialect, or patois, was inferior to acrolectal French. Overcoming European standards of aesthetics did not simply mean challenging European literature and literary figures, but also addressing such assumptions about language and hierarchy. J.E. Clare McFarlane declared in 1956 that dialect "is a 'broken tongue' with which it is impossible to build an edifice of verse possessing the perfect symmetry of finished art" (quoted in Simpson 2011, 84). This was an opinion held by many in the Caribbean as well as in Europe, and so the challenge of asserting an individual national literature was immensely complicated by the inferiority felt by Caribbean writers and readers, promoted by colonial teaching that patois was "broken" and "imperfect". This "special complicated Caribbean 'colonial' attitude" was questioned by *Caribbean Voices*, however (Figueroa in Butcher 1989, 61). The programme emphasised that Caribbean voices, and Caribbean dialects, were literary and that imitation of English accents, and conformity to European literary values, were not necessary for the successful production of Caribbean literature.

The comparison of acrolect to dialect naturally positions dialect as inferior, which is why Brathwaite rejected the term in favour of what he later called nation language. "I use the term in contrast to *dialect*", he said, in his lecture "History of the Voice" (1984, 13). Nation language is "the *submerged* area of that dialect which is more closely allied to the African aspect of experience in the Caribbean" (1984, 13; original emphasis). One of the greatest paradoxes of postcolonial anglophone literature is the very use of the English language. Writers who wish to assert a post- or anti-colonial sentiment often do so in the language of the coloniser. As Ashcroft, Griffiths and Tiffin (2002) show, however, by abrogating this language, the colonised subject can dismantle the "illusory standard of normative or 'correct' usage" assumed by the colonising power (37). Nation language is a resistance to this power, acknowledging the loss of African languages and using dialect to dismantle the paradox of English language in the Caribbean. Nation language is a form of speech that is based on sound and expression, and, as Brathwaite shows, "it may be in English: but often it is an English which is like a howl, or a shout or a machine-gun or the wind or a wave. [. . .It] is English and African at the same time" (1984, 13). Dialect was seen in the mid-20th century as a "debased deviation" of English (Sindoni 2010, 217). By giving this creolised language a new name, one that emphasised nationhood and independence, Brathwaite reclaimed the identity which "dialect" expresses. Braithwaite claimed nation language so as to laud the qualities of Caribbean dialects without defining them as dialects.

Bennett made a similar point in a 1984 radio broadcast, outlining the hypocrisy of the English understanding of how language develops:

> Like my Auntie Roachy say she vex any time she hearing the people a come style fi we Jamaica language as "corruption of the English Language". You ever hear anything go so? Aunt Roachy she say she no know why mek dem no call the English language corruption of the Norman French and the Greek and the Latin where they say English is derived from. Oonu hear the word: English 'derive' but Jamaica "corrupt". No, massa, nothing no go so. We not corrupt and them derive. We derive, too. Jamaica derive![5]

Bennet's point is all the stronger for being made in nation language itself. Nation language is the "submerged" language which moved "from a purely African form to a form which was African but which was adapted to the new environment and adapted to the cultural imperative of the European languages" (Brathwaite, 1984, 7). It is a language of survival, which connects Caribbean expression to African origins. Brathwaite's analysis shows that, simply by using nation language, writers could be subversive, and radio was a particularly productive medium for cultivating this literary nationalism.

The "Authentic" Voice: Individuality and Representation in the Spoken Voice

One of Swanzy's strongest commitments to orality was his insistence that texts should be read on air by Caribbean voices, so that "it should be an all-West Indian programme if possible" (MS42/1/3). There is a distinct irony in Swanzy saying this, and his essentialisation of the Caribbean voice, as well as of "local colour", as noted earlier, verges

5 Bennett in "Caribbean Connections", bl.uk (BBC Continuing Education, 1984). Web. June 12. 2016.

on exoticism. The authority of "native vision" is vehemently dismissed by Gayatri Spivak (1994), who affirms the danger of equating regional belonging with critical responsibility. To "fetishise national origin" is to burden the colonial subject with representation (143). This is a clear problem in the Caribbean, where there is not one but many "Caribbean" voices from many individuals and nations. As Gramaglia asserts, the "burden" emerges from the fact that representatives are often taken as models, the views of a single mind transmuted into a gestalt statement on a whole way of life" (2013, 52). It is important to read the voice as an expression of the individual, rather than just the national or the geographically specific.

In spite of the essentialist colonial dynamics surrounding the production of the programme, the feedback for *Caribbean Voices* reveals that listeners were receptive to the prioritisation of the "authentic" voice. Telemaque said that "the reading [of his own poems] by the Jamaican [reader] was indeed beautiful, added to which was his understanding of the quality and theme of the poems" (MS42/1/3). To have a reader whose voice could reflect the orality with which the poem was written aided the communication of poetry from writer to audience. An interesting letter from Edwina Melville on October 20, 1953 noted that "only <u>once</u> have I listened in to Caribbean Voices and heard a story that I liked [. . .]. The lady who read it had a beautiful voice. [. . .] It made little chills run down my spine" (MS42/1/9). The first thing Melville notes about the story, and indeed, her reason for liking it, was the way it was read. Stories that were less well-read, she said,

> seemed to be [read by] West Indian fellows who had forgotten their own way of speaking and had "put on" what we Guianese call "the AXe-ford Occent". It was hateful and most embarrassing to hear one of your own boys trying to imitate the englishman [sic]. Why can't we be proud to be us? (MS42/1/9)

The voice is a clear representation of identity, and it thus became a tool for nationalist expression. Caribbean poetry was more highly appreciated if it was read by a Caribbean voice, highlighting the importance of nation language to literature.

The transcripts of *Caribbean Voices* give an illuminating insight into the written aspects of this reading process. Brathwaite's "The Rite of Spring", for example, was read by two people. Mittelholzer's introduction to the poem reads:

> are and John Stockbridge in alternate cantos
> Here ~~is~~ Gordon Woolford ~~to read for you..~~

The decision to have two readers was clearly a last-minute one, as the emendations and additions are written in pencil above the typed script. Two readers were possibly used due to the length of the poem (totalling 303 lines), but there are artistic reasons as well. The productive value of having multiple readers sit around one microphone to read poetry instilled a sense of poetic community. The Englishman Stockbridge sat alongside the two Guyanese writers Woolford and Mittelholzer in a collaborative rendering of Brathwaite's poem, suggesting that *Caribbean Voices* was cultivating a neo-Andersonian imagined community across the airwaves (Anderson, 2006). Radio can far outstrip the physical boundaries dictated by print and newspaper circulation, and the translation of an imagined community onto a spaceless dimension fostered a literary community that had both the authenticity of the local and the authority of the metropole.

As Benedict Anderson notes, "radio brought even illiterate populations within the purview of the mass media" (1994, 320). Community is also a crucial aspect of oral literature. As Brathwaite articulates, "reading is an isolated, individualistic expression. The oral tradition on the other hand demands [. . .] the griot by the audience to complete the community" (1989, 18). Radio could enable this community, central to oral literature, in a way that written expression and print media could not. By emphasising the importance of the reader's role in creating a modern literary culture, *Caribbean Voices* paid homage to the oral roots of Caribbean performance and tradition, as well as foregrounding the "authentic" voices of Caribbean readers and writers themselves.

The strong focus that *Caribbean Voices* placed on the reading of literature has clear parallels with oral tradition and performance. However, the individuality of the voice raised questions of how translatable this literature was into print. If the oral performance is so unique, is something lost when that literature is transcribed? For example, Bennett's poetry, it was agreed, was enhanced by being read not simply by a "Caribbean" voice, but by her own. Bennett's work was in fact first broadcast only when she made the journey to London: on June 4, 1950 Swanzy announced "we are making use, our first use in this programme of Louise Bennett's visit to London, by asking her to read some of her own inimitable dialect poems" (20946/6, 478). This idea of "inimitability" is a literary concept which is successfully conveyed by the radio, where the nuances of the individual voice are clearly replicated. Bennett's readings are frequently described as "performances", as Calder-Marshall affirmed on hearing "Anancy and Monkey": "Louise Bennett is an actress. She gave a performance. It is impossible to say where the story as such ended and her performance began" (20946/7, 668). It can easily be concluded, then, that Bennett's poetry is fundamentally dependent on its performance.

What is most interesting, however, is that Bennett's printed texts are also described in terms of performance. In a *Times Literary Supplement* review of *Jamaica Labrish* in 1966, the anonymous reviewer notes "in print these ballads are like a phonetic libretto for performance" (quoted in Morris 1982, 49). Bennett's texts are replete with the cornerstones of oral literature, including "memorable antithesis, aphorism, aural effectiveness of onomatopoeia, contrasting voices in dialogue, verbal surprise, puns and wordplay, inventions of pig-Latin or pseudo-French", but, Morris asserts, "none of these effects is unavailable to the silent reader willing to hear and visualise as silent reading often requires" (52). Thus, it should not be assumed that the highly oralised quality of Bennett's work makes it unsuitable for print, but rather we should reconsider what the text is, and can be.

Ong notes that "the electronic age is also an age of "secondary orality", the orality of telephones, radio, and television, which depends on writing and print for its existence" (2002, 3). Radio provides a bridge between oral literature and the printed word, where literature is at once textual and vocal. Having been developed on the radio, Caribbean literature could be transferred to print in a way that respected and responded to traditional oral forms, but incorporated the permanence of print. In a 1990 interview, Sam Selvon was asked by Professor John Thieme, about his use of "dialect" and whether he agreed that he had "invent[ed] a new language form" (Selvon 1990, 72). Selvon refuted the idea that he invented anything, and emphasised that dialect is a natural reflection of the way people speak: "what I've been trying to do is convert this oral impression into a visual one, so that the page becomes a tape recorder as it were" (72). This is evidence of the productive effect that radio had on Caribbean literature: in encouraging literature through an oral mode that still necessitated a written element, a literary style developed in which the page became a voiceprint. It began with the radio, with the "tape recorder", and was then considered in terms of text. Transcripts show the conversion of an "oral impression into a visual one", in which the strictures and structures of standard English are subsumed by the desire to accurately convey on the page what is created by the voice. Radio scripts require a recreation of the voice, far more than an adherence to the formalities of Standard English.

Conclusion

The voice is highly political. Metaphors of the voice abound in discourses of resistance, and the radio provides a very literal embodiment of the voice's political potential. This chapter has examined the ways in which the radio voice encouraged nationalism, and how the individual Caribbean voice served to dismantle the authority of the English language and English literature.

In the same years that Frantz Fanon was realising that "the radio set was no longer a part of the occupier's arsenal of cultural oppression", Caribbean writers, half a world away from Radio-Alger, undertook a similar "decision to embrace the new technique and thus tune [themselves] in" (Fanon, 1967, 84).

The literature on *Caribbean Voices* served an ideological purpose. Whether or not it was explicitly, or even intentionally, political, the effect was to empower the voiceless and to encourage faith in the literary potential of the region. Figueroa asserted that "one of the great contributions of *Caribbean Voices* was that it offered an outlet to all and sundry" (in Butcher 1989, 72). The inclusion of folklore, oral tradition and nation language raised the status of Caribbean literature, forming an individual tradition which reflected every strata of Caribbean society.

In his final address to the programme, and one week before its final transmission, Naipaul noted: "every West Indian writer is now using dialect. Two years ago this wasn't so" (20946/23, 1392). To have reached a point where, in less than ten years, every Caribbean writer was using dialect is, in Lamming's words quoted earlier, "in the nature of a phenomenon". By encouraging oral aesthetics and creating pride in local oral traditions, *Caribbean Voices* promoted a literary upheaval and a national language revolution.

Caribbean Voices did not simply provide a platform for anglophone Caribbean literature, but actively encouraged the development of an oralised literary aesthetics. Caribbean literature developed in a medium which foregrounded orality and individual identity, where the voice, in all its political and nationalist manifestations, was recognised for its literary potential. As Andrew Salkey concluded in one of the programme's final broadcasts: "Walcott and [Cecil] Herbert may differ in their accents, but the voice is the same" (20946/23, 1364). The spoken voice, as an expression of identity, could combine the oral heritage of the Caribbean with a modern medium that propelled Caribbean literature across the airwaves, beyond the local.

Bibliography

Archival Material

- "Papers of Henry Valentine L. Swanzy", Cadbury Research Library, University of Birmingham.
  - MS42/1/2.
  - MS42/1/3.
  - MS42/1/9.
- "Caribbean Voices", BBC Written Archives, Caversham Park.
  - 20946/3, 255.
  - 20946/6, 478.
  - 20946/7, 638.
  - 20946/7, 668.
  - 20946/8, 743.
  - 20946/9, 808.
  - 20946/13, 1032.
  - 20946/21, 1264.
  - 0946/22, 1336.
  - 20946/23, 1364.
  - 20946/23, 1392.

Works Cited

Adorno, Theodor. 2009. *Current of Music*. Hoboken, NJ: Wiley.

Anderson, Benedict. 1994. "Exodus." *Critical Inquiry* 20 (2): 314–27.

—. 2006. *Imagined Communities.* London: Verso.

Ashcroft, Bill, Gareth Griffiths, and Helen Tiffin., eds. 2002. *The Empire Writes Back*. 2nd ed. London: Routledge.

Bennett-Coverley, Louise. "An Exclusive Interview with Miss Lou." 2005. Jamaicans.com. http://jamaicans.com/misslouinterview/

Brathwaite, Edward Kamau. 1974. *Contradictory Omens*. Jamaica: Savacou.

—. 1984. *History of the Voice*. London: New Beacon.

Breiner, Lawrence A. 2008. *Black Yeats: Eric Roach and the Politics of Caribbean Poetry*. Leeds: Peepal Tree Press.

Butcher, Maggie, ed. 1989. *Tibisiri*. Kingston-upon-Thames: Dangaroo Press.

Calder-Marshall, Arthur. 1955. "Caribbean Voices." *Times Literary Supplement,* August 5: xvi–xvii.

"Caribbean Connections." 1984. BBC Continuing Education. "Caribbean Connections". The British Library. http://www.bl.uk/learning/histcitizen/21cc/lang/shared1/caribbean1/caribbean.html

"Caribbean Voices—Part One". 2009. BBC World Service, July 24. https://repeatingislands.com/2009/07/24/bbc%E2%80%99s-caribbean-voices/

Cooley, Dennis. 1987. *The Vernacular Muse*. Winnipeg: Turnstone.

Donnell, Alison, and Sarah Lawson Welsh, eds. 1996. *The Routledge Reader in Caribbean Literature.* London: Routledge.

Donnell, Alison, ed. 2005. *Twentieth-Century Caribbean Literature*. London: Routledge.

Döring, Tobias. 2003. *Caribbean-English Passages*. London: Routledge.

Fanon, Frantz. 1967. *A Dying Colonialism*. Translated by Haakon Chevalier. New York: Grove Press.

Figueroa, John, ed. 1966. *Caribbean Voices: An Anthology of West Indian Poetry*. London: Evans Brothers.

Finnegan, Ruth, 1992. *Oral Traditions and the Verbal Arts: A Guide to Research Practices*. London: Routledge.

Gingell, Susan. 2009. "Coming Home through Sound." *Journal of West Indian Literature* 17 (2): 32–48.

Gramaglia Letizia, andMalachi McIntosh. 2013. "Censorship, Selvon and *Caribbean Voices*." *Wasafiri* 28 (2): 48–54.

Hirsch, Marianne, "The Generation of Postmemory.", *Poetics Today* 29:1 (Spring 2008), 103-128.

Lamming, George. 1960. *The Pleasures of Exile*. London: Michael Joseph.

McClintock, Anne. 1995. *Imperial Leather*. London: Routledge.

Massey, Doreen. 1994. *Space, Place and Gender*. Minneapolis, MN: University of Minnesota Press.

Mildorf, Jarmila, and Till Kinzel, eds. 2016. *Audionarratology: Interfaces of Sound and Narrative*. Berlin: De Gruyter.

Morris, Mervyn. 1982. "Louise Bennett in Print." *Caribbean Quarterly* 28 (1/2): 44–56.

Nanton, Philip. 2000. "What Does Mr. Swanzy Want?" *Caribbean Quarterly* 46 (1): 61–72.

Ong, Walter. 2002. *Orality and Literacy*. London: Routledge.

Reith, John. 1924. *Broadcast over Britain*. London: Hodder and Stoughton.

—. 1935. *Report: Union of South Africa: Broadcasting Policy and Development*. London: BBC.

Selvon, Samuel. 1990. "Oldtalk: Two Interviews with Sam Selvon [with John Thieme and Alessandra Dotti]." *Caribana* 1: 71–84.

Simpson, Hyacinth M. 2011. "The BBC's *Caribbean Voices* and the Making of an Oral Aesthetic in the West Indian Short Story." *Journal of the Short Story in English* 57: 81–96.

Sindoni, Maria Grazia. 2010. "Creole in the Caribbean: How Oral Discourse Creates Cultural Identities." *Journal des Africanistes* 80 (1/2): 217–36.

Swanzy, Henry. 1949. "Caribbean Voices: Prolegomena to a West Indian Culture." *Caribbean Quarterly* 1 (2): 21–28.

Section 4:
Translations beyond the Anglophone

Making a World of Literary Relations: The Representation of Indian Literature in the Chinese Journal *Yiwen/Shijie wenxue*, 1953-1962

Yan Jia

David Damrosch's (2003) seminal book *What Is World Literature?* opened new avenues in the scholarship of world literature by shifting focus from canon to translation/circulation and from *one* world literature to *many* world literatures. "For any given observer", Damrosch reminds us, "even a genuinely global perspective remains a perspective *from somewhere*, and global patterns of the circulation of world literature take shape in their local manifestations" (27; emphasis in original). Challenging Pascale Casanova's ([1999] 2004) Eurocentric approach, Damrosch astutely points out that her claim for a "world republic of letters" with Paris acting as the definitive centre is not a satisfactory account of world literature but at best "a good account of the operation of world literature *within the modern French context*" (2003, 27; emphasis added).

This chapter, focusing on a prestigious literary journal that was Socialist China's first systematic project of world literature, follows and reflects on Damrosch's call for a located perspective.[1] However, I do not build my analysis upon the assumption that there are certain "global patterns of the circulation of world literature" as such and examine how the Chinese "manifestation" conforms to or deviates from these patterns. Instead, I take the journal itself as my starting point, to investigate the ways in which world literature was conceptualised and put into practice, and then reflect on how the

1 For a recent and more detailed articulation of the "locations" and "locatedness" of world literature, see Orsini and Zecchini (2019), who argue that location "is not simply a geographical, historical, or cultural context but a standpoint, a position, an orientation, a necessarily partial and particular view, however ample and multiversal it may be" (2).

Chinese experience can enrich our understanding of world literature in general. Such a "bottom-up" approach draws inspiration from several precursors, who work proudly and creatively with local stories and archives (non-western ones in particular) and attend to the complex social, historical, cultural, and linguistic conditions of specific sites. An excellent example in this respect is the notion of "significant geographies" proposed by Karima Laachir, Sara Marzagora and Francesca Orsini (2018) to rethink world literature from a "located" perspective, replacing the binary local and global with specific geographies that are significant to a location or an actor. I am also drawing on Karen Thornber's (2009 and 2014) studies of the East Asian "literary contact nebulae" that suggest a regional world literature by examining various types of contact between Chinese, Japanese and Korean literary spaces in the Japanese empire. These studies have proved that a located perspective—particularly one that makes visible and valorises non-western experiences—can produce a richer and more nuanced understanding of the complexity of world literature than the systemic approaches proposed by Casanova, Franco Moretti and the Warwick Collective.

What languishes in obscurity together with the local perspective in Casanova's configuration of "world republic of letters" is the political vector—that is, the political ambition of an author and the political function of a text. Mapping Pierre Bourdieu's (1993) analysis of the "literary field" onto an international scene, Casanova envisages an autonomous "world literary space" that is relatively free from political, national, diplomatic and other "extrinsic limitations" ([1999] 2004, 350). For her, there is a "structural internationalism" comprising "the most literary countries" where writers "stand united against literary nationalism, against the intrusion of politics into literary life" and that thereby the autonomy of the world of letters can be safeguarded (86). What is problematic about this statement is not only the political register through which Casanova claims an apolitical identity for the "international literary field", but also her notion of the separability of literary and political factors in a given writer's outlook and practice. A good counter-example is that of Jean-Paul Sartre.

Although regarded by Casanova as a key "gatekeeper" of the literariness of the world republic of letters, Sartre was in fact also an advocate for an "engaged literature" (*littérature engagée*) and an enthusiastic participant in various political and intellectual movements from the 1930s onwards (Bondy 1967). This chapter seeks to show that turning to local practices of world literature with due awareness of their political significance can serve as a productive method that helps lead us beyond Casanova's model.

In the following sections, I first present the Cold War period as an exciting lens through which the plurality, locatedness and political significance of world literature can be observed. Situating the journal *Yiwen/Shijie wenxue* in the Cold War context and tracing its change along the "worldly" and "literary" axes in relation to China's geopolitics, I then elaborate on the journal's anti-Eurocentric characteristics and increasing emphasis on projecting a China-led "literary international" by including a large number of Asian, African and Latin American literatures. Through the lens of the journal's representation of Indian literature as analysed in the last section, I argue that *Yiwen/Shijie wenxue*'s world literature project features a creative enterprise of building within its textual and material limits a "world of literary relations", a notion that draws on Karen Thornber's (2009) concept of "literary contact nebulae" and Shu-mei Shih's (2015) concept of "relational comparison". This enterprise involves various acts of direct or mediated "relationing"—foregrounding existing relations, creating imaginative relations, or concealing problematic relations—activated by a great deal of curatorial and editorial work. The purpose is not only to justify the inclusion of certain authors and texts, but also to project the newly-liberated China as occupying an important position in the "literary international" it imagined.

Cold War-Era World Literatures and *Yiwen/Shijie wenxue*

The Cold War is an important period and context for considering the political signigicance of the idea of world literature, because it was during this period that contrasting national/regional versions of world literature emerged in different parts of the world, each reflecting a way of perceiving the post-war world orders and literary modernity. On the one hand, there were self-centred models produced by the two superpowers that aimed at establishing their own cultural supremacy. A quintessential US-centric project, the anthology *Masterpieces of World Literature in Digest Form* compiled by Frank Magill, included in its first two volumes (1949, 1955) 1,007 western titles as opposed to three non-western ones (i.e. *The Thousand and One Nights, The Tale of Genji*, and *The Shakuntala*). Although the following two volumes (1960, 1969) set out to include more titles "from the vast reservoir of Oriental literature", the presence of such voices remained nominal: of 1,008 authors only 23 are non-western (Damrosch 2003, 124–27). By contrast, Nikolai Tikhonov, vice-Chairman of the Union of Soviet Writers, put forward the concept of "world progressive literature" at the Second Conference of Soviet Writers, held in 1954. Tikhonov conceived of world literature as the "solar system" with Soviet literature lying at the centre as the sun and progressive literatures from other parts of the world moving around it on five concentric orbits. These orbits, according to their positions relative to Soviet literature, are: (1) literatures of the people's democracies in East Europe (Poland, Hungary, Bulgaria, etc.); (2) literatures of the people's democracies in Asia (China, Mongolia, Vietnam, etc.); (3) progressive literatures of non-socialist Asian countries that are subject to Soviet influence (India, Turkey, Iran, etc.); (4) progressive literatures of capitalist countries (the United States, Italy, Denmark, etc.); and (5) Latin American literature (Liu 2010, 12–13).

At the same time, however, counter-hegemonic configurations of world literature emerged in Asia and Africa, where literary movements associated with processes of nationalist struggle and decolonisation had been underway since the early 20th century. These politically-charged literary movements together gave rise to what Michael Denning (2004) has called an "international of writers" or more specifically a "novelists' International" (51–52). As Denning notes, these literary movements converged after the 1955 Afro-Asian

Conference of Bandung, increasingly linking together different parts of this writers' international—in reality mainly through an array of Afro-Asian writers' congresses and publications (64). Both Hala Halim's (2012) study of the journal *Lotus: Afro-Asian Writing* (published in Cairo) and Duncan Yoon's (2015) of the anthology *Afro-Asian Poems* (published in Colombo), though focusing on two different subcurrents of the Afro-Asian literary movement, display how Asian and African writers sought cultural decolonisation and self-determination for the Global South by establishing a transcontinental literary community that rejected western intervention.

While attending to these supranational literary movements emerging during the Cold War, we should not forget how world literature was perceived from local viewpoints and accounted for in local languages. In surveying the reception of world literary texts in 1950s Southeast Asia, Tony Day (2010) shows that many Indonesian and Vietnamese writers, including Pramoedya Ananta Toer and Trần Dần, were similar in choosing socialist realism over western modernism as the primary source of inspiration, although both forms were available at their disposal. Day points out that while "almost none of the books Casanova considers central to the modernist canon, such as the novels of James Joyce or William Faulkner or the plays of Henrik Ibsen, were translated into Indonesian or Vietnamese in this period" (154), the works of leftist writers from China and the Soviet Union such as Ding Ling and Vladimir Mayakovsky were well received in Southeast Asia. In Day's view, the affinity of writers from this region with socialist realism was not so much because of their ideological affiliation to communism, but because they found the genre more capable of addressing Southeast Asian experiences and concerns that shared more similarities with those of China and the Soviet Union than with western countries (154). In all these non-western modes of imagining and moulding world literature that emerged during the Cold War, we see different constellations of Asian and African writers stand in solidarity and act to challenge, bypass, and even invert the western "centre" as posited by Casanova and Franco Moretti (2000;

2003; 2006) in the alleged "world republic of letters" or "world literary system".

In the context of early Cold War-period China, the state-sponsored literary monthly *Yiwen/Shijie wenxue*, the archival focus of this chapter, offers a conspicuously anti-Eurocentric configuration of world literature that reflected Maoist China's perception of and positioning in the world. Launched as *Yiwen* (Translated Literature) in July 1953 under the tutelage of the Chinese Writers' Association (CWA), the journal was renamed *Shijie wenxue* (World Literature) in January 1959.[2] It ceased publication when the Cultural Revolution broke out in 1966. Resumed in 1977, it continues to the present day. The fact that *Yiwen*'s founding editor-in-chief Mao Dun was a leading Chinese novelist and also the incumbent Minister of Culture and President of the CWA testifies to the journal's significant position in the PRC's cultural life.

Throughout the 1950s and 60s, *Yiwen/Shijie wenxue* was the only openly-published Chinese periodical devoted to introducing, translating, and assessing foreign literature.[3] Yet as Nicholai Volland (2017a) observes, "*Yiwen* was designed to be more than just a translation journal"; rather, "it was a complete guide to world literature, as well as a window onto this new world" (169). Like other non-western articulations of world literature that emerged during the Cold War, *Yiwen/Shijie wenxue* featured a clear anti-Euro-American-centric approach in its selection of texts. With 634 titles of literary works and critical articles published between 1953 and1966 from Asia, Africa and Latin America, along with 636 from the Soviet Union and socialist countries in Eastern Europe, and 588 from western

---

2 In the rest of this chapter, I will refer to the journal as *Yiwen/Shijie wenxue* in a general sense and as *Yiwen* and *Shijie wenxue* respectively for the period 1953–58 and 1959–63. See Cui (2009; 2012) for discussion of the journal's literary taste and ideological inclination.

3 It should be noted that *Yiwen/Shijie wenxue* was not the only medium through which Chinese readers could read translated foreign works in the 1950s and 1960s. For other mediums, such as private/underground reading and restricted publication for internal distribution, see Volland (2017b) and Iovene (2014, 72–76).

countries (Liu 2010, 17), *Yiwen/Shijie wenxue* offered a seemingly unbiased and egalitarian version of world literature that contrasted dramatically with Magill's American version that presented "the world" simply as the western world. Furthermore, the journal's vast geographical span, which covered 124 states/regions ranging from India to Italy, from Senegal to the Soviet Union, from Ukraine to the United States (Cui 2012, 4–6), eclipsed that of *Lotus*, whose range of selection seldom moved beyond the Afro-Asian ambit (Halim 2012, 578–83). Before specifying how India was positioned and represented in *Yiwen/Shijie wenxue*, I will first explain the changing politics underlying the creation of this exceptional "literary internationalism" that unfolded in the journal during the early years of the Cold War.

The "Worldly", the "Literary" and Literary Internationalism in *Yiwen/Shijie wenxue*

According to Damrosch, "a given work can enter into world literature and then fall out of it again if it shifts beyond a threshold point along either axis, the literary or the worldly" (2003, 6). The shifting nature of any given work makes the entire body of world literature liable to change. The same holds true if we put Damrosch's statement in a somewhat different way: a locally envisioned world literature like *Yiwen/Shijie wenxue* can include a foreign work and then exclude it if the work shifts beyond a threshold point along either its worldly or literary axis.

Already, in the foreword to *Yiwen*'s founding issue published in July 1953, editor-in-chief Mao Dun had laid down the worldly and literary foundations, on which the following issues developed and from which they deviated. He divided the literary world into three sections: The Soviet Union and people's democracies (i.e. the socialist bloc), capitalist countries (i.e. the capitalist bloc), and former or current colonies/semi-colonies (Mao 1953, 2). This taxonomy, different from the "us versus them" dichotomy that generally characterised the Cold War, was largely in line with Mao Zedong's "three-way division of the world" posited in 1947, which interposed between the socialist and capitalist blocs an "intermediate zone" stretching from numerous colonial and postcolonial countries in Asia, Africa and Europe and including China (Bhattacharjea 1995, 24). Mao's "intermediate zone" theory assumed that the American imperialists could not wage direct war with the Soviet Union unless they had first taken control of the intermediate zone. The theory emphasised, according to Jian Chen (2008), that "the real thrust of the American-Soviet confrontation lay in the competition over the intermediate zone", and that "since China occupied a crucial position in the intermediate zone, the development of the Chinese revolution would play a central role in defining the path or even determining the result of the global Cold War" (213). After the PRC declared its membership of the socialist bloc in 1949, Mao decided that China would continue to occupy a crucial place in the intermediate zone, which, together with the socialist bloc, formed a vast "international united front" against American imperialism.[4]

It was precisely to the three geographical sections that Mao Dun, the journal's editor-in-chief, further assigned particular literary tasks: what deserved to be introduced into the journal was "excellent socialist realist literature from the Soviet Union and people's democracies" as well as "revolutionary and progressive literature from various capitalist countries, [former] colonies and semi-colonies" (Mao 1953, 2). Clearly, geographical inclusiveness was accompanied by literary selectiveness. By singling out socialist realist works from the Soviet Union and other countries in the socialist bloc and putting works from the other two sections under the same rubric of "revolutionary and progressive", *Yiwen* set out a hierarchical scheme with a distinct Soviet centrality. Yet this scheme, as we shall see, was to be altered dramatically in 1959 due to deteriorating Sino-Soviet relations.

As an official Chinese journal brought out in an era of high Cold War politics, *Yiwen/Shijie wenxue*'s literary project was inevitably tied to political and ideological rhythms. The "threshold

---

4 For a thorough study of Mao's changing conceptualisation of the Cold War world, see Chen (2010).

point" of either its worldly or literary axis was subject to the PRC's mutable self-positioning in the "global geopolitical architecture" (Volland 2017a, 155). From 1953 to 1958, the PRC followed the "lean-to-one-side" (i.e. the Soviet side) policy and regarded the Soviet Union as a model in almost all aspects, including literature. During this period, *Yiwen* had a pronounced preference for contemporary literary works and theoretical chapters written by Soviet authors while welcoming, to a lesser extent, texts from other countries. Moreover, interpretative essays written by Soviet critics were customarily invoked to vouchsafe the legitimacy of non-Soviet authors or artists. Paola Iovene (2014), for example, shows how the February 1957 issue of *Yiwen* used the prominent Soviet writer Ilya Ehrenburg's essay "On Pablo Picasso" to justify the appearance of a painting by this "controversial artist" in the journal (63–65).

The dominance of Soviet literature within *Yiwen*'s literary space remained unchallenged between 1956 and 1958, despite the Chinese leaders' disagreement with Khrushchev's denunciation of Stalin in early 1956 (Iovene 2014, 58). Meanwhile, the Hundred Flowers Campaign launched between 1956 and 1957 briefly opened China's literary climate and hence allowed greater space in *Yiwen* for an aesthetics-based selection and evaluation of foreign texts. Not only were French modernist works like Charles Baudelaire's *Les Fleurs du Mal* introduced (Cui 2015), but an effort was also made to produce a canon of world classics, such as the works of Goethe, Stendhal, Tagore and Premchand, by launching a new column called "Wenxue yichan" (Literary Heritage), which lasted from late 1955 to mid-1957 (Cui 2012, 272–73).

Yet the most dramatic change took place in January 1959 when the journal was renamed *Shijie wenxue* (World Literature), a decision that was made against the backdrop of mounting Sino-Soviet tension. *Shijie wenxue* set out to decentralise the Soviet Union in its new map of world literature, mainly by shifting its geographical focus from the Soviet Union to the many countries in Asia, Africa and Latin America. What Robert Young ([2001] 2016) has termed "tricontinentalism" (427–28) had its manifestation in the textual space of a Chinese journal seven years before it materialised in actual form in Havana in 1966, when the first Conference of the Organisation of Solidarity of the Peoples of Africa, Asia and Latin America was held. The transition from Soviet-centred to tricontinental was completed when Soviet literature entirely dropped off the journal's map of world literature from July 1963 onwards (Cui 2012, 396).

This shift mirrored China's reorientation of foreign policy, which was characterised by its aspiration to gather global revolutionary strength and build a China-led united front to fight against both "American imperialism" (*meidi*) and "Soviet revisionism" (*suxiu*). For this reason, the journal's redefined objective not only evoked an expansion of the "worldly" but also a broadening of the "literary". The first issue of *Shijie wenxue* published in January 1959 carried an editors' note entitled "From *Yiwen* to *Shijie wenxue*", which stated: "From now on, our journal will primarily introduce works that reflect the real lives and revolutionary struggles of the people of all nations in the world *in modern times*" (The Editors 1959, 2; my emphasis). While previously-favoured modern and contemporary progressive fiction and poetry continued to appear, some less literary genres and texts such as political commentaries, features, sketches, speeches and reportages were also read *as* literature and assembled in the journal so as to "*quickly* reflect crucial events taking place in people's lives all around the world" (2; my emphasis). This generic diversification amplified the periodical's journalistic character, which during the period of *Yiwen* was primarily embodied in the special column "Shijie wenyi dongtai" (World Trends in Literature and Arts), not in the literary works selected. Moreover, the time-related terms emphasised in the quotes, such as "in modern times" and "quickly" suggest a sense of urgency, indicating an intensified need to bring world literature to the "here and now" of the Chinese revolution. In this situation, classic works produced before the 20th century, which had already had a secondary place in *Yiwen*, were further sidelined in *Shijie wenxue* due to their political irrelevance and uselessness.

As this overview has shown, *Yiwen/Shijie wenxue*'s ostensibly egalitarian representation of literatures from the socialist bloc, capitalist bloc and the Third World from 1953 to 1966 was but a result of accumulated selective moves. The official background and intrinsic political orientation of the journal mean that it could not simply be an exhibition of literary works collected from the world, though aesthetic merit was indeed given varying degrees of attention at different times.

On top of this "selective inclusiveness" both geographical and generic, this chapter aims at exploring a more implicit yet no less important strategy that was frequently used by the journal editors to include non-western/non-Soviet literatures and enhance the journal's political agenda of literary internationalism. In order to elaborate this strategy, I propose the notion of "world of literary relations", which denotes a space comprising both actual and imagined "textual contact", "writerly contact" and "readerly contact"—terms that Karen Thornber (2009) usefully adopts to define the East Asian "literary contact nebulae" in the Japanese Empire (2).[5] I prefer this new concept to Thornber's "literary contact nebulae" for two main reasons. First, as a journal emerging from post-liberation China (i.e. the People's Republic of China [PRC], founded in 1949), *Yiwen/Shijie wenxue*'s interactions with foreign literatures, in most cases, did not take place in the midst of conflicting power relations such as those that Thornber unequivocally situates in the "literary contact nebulae". Second, in Thornber's discussion, the concept of "literary contact nebulae" operates more in a descriptive way that helps present literary encounters as they *actually* happened in history. Drawing on yet moving beyond Thornber's perspective, I propose the term "world of literary relations" to designate not only a body of actual exchanges between and within different literary

---

5 According to Thornber's definition, "'readerly contact' refers to reading creative texts (texts with aesthetic ambitions, imaginative writing) from cultures/nations in asymmetrical power relationships with one's own; 'writerly contact' to interactions among creative writers from conflicting societies; and 'textual contact' to transculturating creative texts in this environment (appropriating genres, styles, and themes, as well transculturating individual literary works via the related and at times concomitant strategies of interpreting, adapting, translating, and intertextualizing)" (2009, 2).

traditions in the world, but also a space in which different literary texts and agents are *brought into contact* with each other to form a world, that is, an active project of world-making or of what Shu-mei Shih (2015) has called "relationing". Inspired by world history studies, Shih champions the method of "relational comparison", which she defines as "the bringing of certain entities into relation" or an active act of "Relation", that can work "directly upon objects, terms, languages, texts, peoples and societies". "Doing comparative studies as relational studies", Shih argues, "means setting into motion relationalities between entities brought together for comparison and bringing into relation terms that have been traditionally pushed apart by certain interests" (436).

As we shall see in the case study of modern Indian literature, the journal *Yiwen/Shijie wenxue* functioned as more than a collection of foreign texts in Chinese translation. It involved painstaking curatorial and editorial work of "relationing" made by editors, translators and other literary agents in order to project, establish and maximise within the journal's physical and creative boundaries non-textual forms of literary contact—writerly contact in particular. The representation of these contacts helped create the sense that the newly-founded PRC occupyed a pivotal position within an emerging "literary international" where progressive texts, writers and movements from different parts of the world came into relation, creating a sense of anti-hegemonic solidarity.

As I will show in the following case study, examining a journal of world literature as a constructed world of literary relations requires a two-level method. The first level entails reading a given literary text in relation to its surrounding "paratexts" (Genette, 1997)—e.g. the author's biography, translator's postscript, editor's note, illustration, and report on literary trends—in the same issue, for it is often from the paratexts that we understand why certain texts are selected, how they are interpreted, and how the authors' literary and political identities are (re)framed. The second level entails reading across and comparing different issues so as to find traces of continuity such as patterns, cross-references and intertextuality, while not ignoring evidence of rupture. Unlike book-form anthologies of world literature that usually have a static set of texts, periodicals like the monthly one under discussion offer a corpus that is in constant flux yet still follows certain discernible logics. Only by attending to how editors take advantage of the periodical's material characteristics, such as regular frequency, topicality, layout flexibility and copious space for editorial apparatus, to foreground existing relations, create imaginative relations, or cover problematic relations, can we better understand the politics behind their making of world literature.

The Arts of Relationing: *Yiwen/Shijie Wenxue*'s Representation of Indian Literature

I have chosen Indian literature as my case study not only because it is most closely related to my academic training and research interests, but also because Indian literature had considerable presence in *Yiwen/Shijie wenxue* in the 1950s and early 1960s, with 85 titles published (more than the number for British literature) and thus can serve as a valid lens through which the journal's representation of literatures from the Global South can be observed.[6]

Mulk Raj Anand (1905–2004), one of the finest modern Indian authors writing in English, qualifies as a valid point of entry, for he was the only Indian author who made it into the journal from the very beginning. *Yiwen*'s founding issue (July 1953) published translations of two English short stories by Anand: "The Cobbler and the Machine" (1944) and "A Kashmir Idyll" (1944), translated by Yan Shaoduan and Hai Guan respectively. The former story depicts the wretched life of an old Dalit cobbler, who desires a sewing-machine but eventually works himself to death simply to pay off the debt on the machine, while the latter ridicules the corrupt feudal aristocracy in Kashmir. Both stories reflect on the structural economic oppression

---

6 According to Cui Feng's (2012) survey, the ten most translated national literatures in *Yiwen/Shijie wenxue* from 1953 to 1966 were those from: Russia/the Soviet Union (525), Japan (173), France (166), USA (149), Vietnam (112), GDR (93), India (85), UK (83), Albania (72) and Cuba (65).

in colonial India from a Marxist perspective and sympathise with the lower-caste villagers who are powerlessly deprived of the means of production in an increasingly capitalised society. In this sense, the two stories by Anand served as quintessential examples of what Mao Dun called in his foreword to the same issue "revolutionary and progressive literature from [former] colonies" (Mao 1953, 2); hence their inclusion in *Yiwen*'s founding issue.

Attached to the two stories is a postscript written by Hai Guan, translator of "A Kashmir Idyll". Interestingly, the postscript, though named after the two stories, is not so much about the texts as about the author. It offers an overview of Anand's literary career, his representative works and a detailed account of his political activism, indicating that the journal valued both the artistic and the socio-political merits of the author. Included in the postscript is a particular reference to Anand's role as one of the founding members of the Indian Progressive Writers' Association (PWA), a nationwide organisation of literary radicalism founded in the mid 1930s by a group of leftist or Marxist writers. Closely associated with the Communist Party of India (CPI), the movement suffered a setback in the years immediately following Independence in 1947 due to political turbulence caused by the CPI's turn to armed revolutionary uprising, which provoked Congress repression.[7]

A sharp-eyed reader would at once link this reference about the PWA to a news report in the "World Trends in Literature and Arts" column of the same issue, which deals with the sixth PWA conference held in Delhi in March 1953. Yet this report, written by Yan Shaoduan, translator of "The Cobbler and the Machine", is more than an introduction to this particular conference. It traces the historical trajectory of the progressive movement of India as an "anti-imperialist united front" from the mid-1930s to Partition in 1947, when the united front crumbled due to communalism and political sectarianism. The report also contains a full translation of the conference's manifesto, which "set out new directions for the future

7 For a fine study of the progressive literary movement, see Ahmed (2009).

development of India's progressive literary movement" (July 1953 *Yiwen*, 241). By holding together the past and the future, the report captures the PWA at a critical juncture, when Indian writers reunited after years of disconnection to breathe new life into the movement.

I read the juxtaposition of Anand's short stories with the translator's postscript and the report on the PWA conference in the founding issue of *Yiwen* as a strategic arrangement on the part of the editors. They took advantage of different editorial devices such as the postscript and the news report column to create a narrative within the journal aimed at providing the reader with a multi-layered example of the kind of "progressive literature" that Mao Dun had generally designated, by holding together and "relationing" the textual, individual and organisational dimensions. In so doing, they stretched the term's meaning from a set of writings to a group of writers in action and a reviving literary force.

It should be noted that behind this explicit act of relation-building was the editors/translators' implicit silencing of broken relations. Presented simultaneously as the author of the two stories and founder of the PWA, Anand apparently acted in this case as an intermediary who linked the textual and socio-political ends of the progressive literature of India. However, the editors and translators of *Yiwen* might have purposefully concealed a fracture in this linkage, because when Anand entred China's literary scene in the early 1950s he was no longer institutionally associated with the PWA. The ultra-left turn of the Communist Party of India between 1948 and 1951 radicalised almost all organisations associated with it, including the PWA.[8] Falling victim to the growing dogmatism initiated by the Communist-dominated Bombay group of the PWA, Anand was edged out of the Association in 1949 mainly because "he did not portray in his poor all the virtues the party line demanded" (Cowasjee 1977, 31). Nonetheless, *Yiwen*'s editors silenced Anand's actual estrangement from the PWA—a fact that they would have very likely known through frequent contact on occasions of cultural diplomacy or through their

8 For more information about the CPI's changing policies from the 1920s to the late 1950s, see Sen Gupta (1972, Chapter 1).

exchanges of correspondence, and consequently they projected him as a representative of the ongoing progressive movement in India.

Anand's appearance in the founding issue of the state-backed journal *Yiwen* was, I argue, a consequence not only of the historical role he played in initiating the PWA but also of his active presence in India's cultural diplomacy with China in the early 1950s. Two different yet overlapping platforms can be identified: the India-China Friendship Association (ICFA) and the All-India Peace Council (AIPC). While the ICFA was an Indian civil society organisation dedicated to fostering bilateral cultural exchanges with the PRC, the AIPC was the Indian chapter of the World Peace Council (WPC), headquarter of the multinational World Peace Movement initiated and directed predominantly by the Soviet Union. Anand's engagement in both organisations after his divorce from the PWA was largely an attempt to seek an alternative path for his abiding leftist activism, a path that turned from the domestic to the international.[9]

The establishment of formal mechanisms of China-India cultural diplomacy in the 1950s enabled organised, frequent and direct writerly contacts between Anand, among other Indian authors, and the leading figures of China's literary circles. The dynamics of these writerly contacts were only occasionally seen in previous decades, except for Rabindranath Tagore's phenomenal yet controversial visit to China in 1924 (Das, 1995; Tan, 1998). As a member of the 1951 Indian goodwill mission, Anand was one of the first Indian writers to visit the PRC and have face-to-face conversations with authorities from China's socialist literature such as Ding Ling and Zhou Yang (Sundarlal 1952, 154–59). Playing a key role in both the ICFA and the AIPC, Anand was also responsible for receiving visiting Chinese cultural delegations in Delhi or Bombay,

9 In the 1950s, Anand served as vice-president of the AIPC and represented India on the World Peace Council, along with certain other Indian intellectuals. He was also one of the founding members of the ICFA Bombay branch in 1951. For more details on Anand's engagement with leftist cultural movements, see Overstreet and Windmiller (1959, 411–32).

organising seminars for visiting Chinese writers, and sharing with them knowledge of Indian literature and society. Moreover, the many international conferences of the world peace movement offered additional locations (usually in European cities like Warsaw, Berlin, Vienna and Stockholm) where Anand could meet with leading Chinese cultural bureaucrats such as Guo Moruo and Mao Dun, who represented the PRC on the WPC Bureau. In short, frequent and growing contacts with China's cultural and literary figures, facilitated by both bilateral and multilateral channels of cultural diplomacy, had greatly increased Anand's presence and stature in the Chinese literary sphere by the time his stories appeared in *Yiwen* in mid-1953.

That Anand's connections with China-related cultural diplomacy were detailed in the postscript to his two short stories published in *Yiwen*'s founding issue attests to their significance in the eyes of the journal editors. For them, these direct connections were effective channels through which Anand could undergo a decisive process of image building. The process conferred on him various favorable traits that facilitated a positive reception in the PRC: he was presented as an accomplished novelist, a spokesman of contemporary Indian literature, a sympathiser with global leftist movements, a pacifist, and a friend of China. It is particularly noteworthy that the translation of Anand's literary works received an unprecedented impetus in China after the WPC awarded the prestigious "International Peace Prize" to him in 1952. In this case, it was an honor for his multinational cultural-political activism rather than a prominent international literary prize that acted as the predominant agency of recognition and enabled his works to have an "*effective* life as world literature" (Damrosch 2003, 4; emphasis in original).

In fact, *Yiwen*'s editors were enthusiastic about making traces of their relations to foreign authors perceptible to their readers. They usually gave a clear indication of the source of a text whenever it came directly from the author. This helped to strengthen the idea of an ever-expanding, transnational network of connected writers and travelling texts, with Beijing serving as a "literary hub". For instance, surveying the notes and postscripts of *Yiwen*'s issues published in 1956, we know that Balwant Gargi and Amrita Pritam, two Punjabi writers, directly mailed their works to *Yiwen*'s editorial department, and Mulk Raj Anand even contributed a novella that he wrote specially at the editors' invitation. Published in the 1956 June issue and entitled "The Road" (*Lu*), this special contribution bears the same name as the first part of Anand's autobiographical novel *Seven Summers: A Memoir* (1951). Both works tell anecdotes about a boy, Krishna, in a nostalgic style, and mirror the author's own childhood reminiscences. But the short piece Anand contributed to *Yiwen* is not a truncated version of the novel but rather a new piece of writing derived from the same setting with new characters and events.

Highlighting the editorial board's special connections with writers abroad was so important to *Yiwen*'s project of world literature that during the second half of 1956 attempts were made to formalise them through a column devoted to publishing letters from foreign writers. Published letters came from two North American Communist poets (Joe Wallace from Canada and Walter Lowenfels from the United States) and two leftist Asian novelists (Seiji Shimota from Japan and Anand from India), all of whom had previously published work in the journal. All the letters are celebratory in tone and most of them are emotionally dense. For example, "exhilarated" after learning that his poems had been published in *Yiwen*, Wallace wrote: "There is hardly any honor I have earned throughout the sixty-five years of my life that can compare with this one" (August 1956 *Yiwen*, 184). By publishing such remarks, *Yiwen*'s editors showcased the journal's international status and influence, especially among proletarian writers. Moreover, they helped construct an elevated image of the journal as an attractive site that writers from both east and west aspired to enter, thus projecting China as a rising hub in the socialist literary world.

Compared to the other letters, Anand's was less effusive but no less typical in terms of championing the world of literary relations that *Yiwen* was seeking to build. His letter dated May 31, 1956 and published in *Yiwen*'s 1956 November issue, reads as follows:

> I went to the countryside for a while to recuperate after having had a slight pleurisy, and just returned to Bombay this week. I read your letter dated 11th May, which made me very gratified.
> I have finished a revised draft of the novel *The Old Woman and the Cow*, and am currently writing up my second autobiographical novel, *Morning Face*. When this work is done, I am about to publish a collection of short stories entitled *The Power of Darkness and Other Stories*. By that time, I will have to deal with the heavy workload of the Asian Writers' Conference Secretariat.
> Whenever I go to Delhi, I will send the manuscript of *The Old Woman and the Cow* alongside some short stories to China. [. . .] But, more importantly, there should be more translations of modern Chinese works into different Indian languages. (187; my translation)

At first glance, this is simply a short message about the author's recent activities and work plans. But the letter tells us more if we read it together with the earlier and later issues, as a loyal reader of the journal would read in the 1950s. First of all, though published in such an official periodical as *Yiwen*, the letter strikes a rather informal tone. The use of second person singular form "you" (*ni*) points to a specific correspondent on the editorial board and the act of sharing personal information like health conditions, travel itinerary and details about his writing progress suggests Anand's closeness to his Chinese correspondent. We do not know exactly who this letter was addressed to. It could have been either the journal's chief editor Mao Dun or the deputy chief editor Xiao Qian, both of whom had been acquainted with Anand for years by the time he wrote the letter. That this was a letter written in reply to a previous one sent from China indicates an array of exchanges of correspondence, through which friendship could be maintained and familiarity enhanced. By making such a personal letter visible on the journal's pages, the editors transferred that familiarity to the reading public. Instead of letting the writer speak to his Chinese readers only through the characters in his works, they made him speak in a more tangible form—as himself.

Second, Anand's promise to send the manuscript of his latest novel to *Yiwen*'s editorial department as soon as possible indicates that China was indeed a literary platform that he valued. We do not know whether or not Anand eventually sent the manuscript (the Chinese translation did not materialise for unknown reasons), but we do know that the noted writer Xie Bingxin (also known as Bing Xin) did translate Anand's *Indian Fairy Tales* (1946) at the author's request when they met in India in 1953. Part of the collection was published in the December 1954 issue of *Yiwen*. In fact, by the time this letter was published Anand had become the living Indian author most translated into Chinese: nine of his works had appeared in *Yiwen* and three novels and two anthologies in book form.[10] This not only shows the dynamics of India-China textual contact in the 1950s but also suggests a positive correlation between writerly contact and textual contact. That is, the more personal presence a foreign writer had in the Chinese literary field, the more likely it was that his or her works would be translated. Therefore, translation was not solely dependent on the host culture but was determined by the host and guest cultures *together*.

Third, if we take further notice of Anand's reference to the Asian Writers' Conference, the letter functioned as an advertisement for this upcoming international literary event, the first meeting of Asian intellectuals since the last Buddhist Conference in the 6th century CE. under Harsha, as Anand framed it (1993, 183). One month after the letter was published in *Yiwen*, a Chinese writers' delegation led by the journal's editor-in-chief Mao Dun met Anand in Delhi. The letter was further echoed in a report in the "World Trends of

10 These translations include, on *Yiwen*, two short stories, "The Cobbler and the Machine" and "A Kashmir Idyll" (July 1953), six stories selected from *Indian Fairy Tales* (Dec. 1954), and a special contributed novella entitled "The Road" (June 1956); and, in book form, *Untouchable* (1954), *Selected Stories of Mulk Raj Anand* (1955), *Coolie* (1955), *Two Leaves and A Bud* (1955), and *Indian Fairy Tales* (1955).

Literature and Arts" column of the February 1957 issue, which summarised and praised the Delhi conference. Recognising Anand's important role in the conference as general secretary, the reporter calls attention to the announcement Anand read out at the closing ceremony. Highlighted in the announcement was a call for advancing Inter-Asian cultural cooperation that had been interrupted for centuries by western imperialists. Similar ideas were articulated in the speeches given by several delegation leaders such as Mao Dun and Faiz Ahmed Faiz, who collectively appealed to Asian writers to unite for the cause of freedom and peace (February 1957 *Yiwen*, 193). In this respect, Anand's writerly, textual and readerly relations with the Chinese journal *Yiwen* had indeed given this imagined Pan-Asian literary community a practical form.

While embracing Mulk Raj Anand and other contemporary Indian authors who had been keeping in contact with China's literary field in one way or another, the editors of *Yiwen/Shijie wenxue* showed no less interest in bringing to view canonised Indian writers like Rabindranath Tagore (1861–1941), who had died before the journal was launched. From 1953 to 1962, *Yiwen/Shijie wenxue* published ten pieces by Tagore, including seven short stories, two letters and only one poem (the narrative poem "Dūī Bīghā Jomi"). None of these was selected from the poetry anthologies that had been previously hailed in the west, such as *Gitanjali*, *Stray Birds*, *The Crescent Moon* and *The Gardener*. By consciously circumventing the works of Tagore that had been widely acclaimed in Europe and silencing the 1913 Nobel Prize completely in the contextual notes attached to the works selected, the *Yiwen/Shijie wenxue* editors invalidated the west's authority to determine a non-western writer's international recognition.

Before the 1950s, Chinese readers knew Tagore primarily as a poet. This impression owed much to the Nobel Prize judges, who granted the award to Tagore for "his profoundly sensitive, fresh and beautiful verse" (quoted in Levinovitz and Ringertz 2001, 154). However, Tagore's poetic output in general did not fit well with *Yiwen*'s preference for modern writers adopting realism and social subjects. In order to make Tagore more relevant to Socialist China's world literature, *Yiwen*'s editors and translators foregrounded his connections with the Soviet Union, the ideological and literary model of China during most of the 1950s. Here, the act of relationing is not direct (as in the case of Anand) but rather mediated.

Tagore made his debut in *Yiwen* with an abridged translation of *Rāśiyār chiṭhi* (Letters from Russia), a collection of letters the author wrote while paying his first and only visit to the Soviet Union in 1930 (November 1955 *Yiwen*). In *Yiwen*'s decision to publish this particular work in the heyday of the Sino-Soviet alliance, one can discern a process of mutual endorsement. On the one hand, the editors intended to reinforce the centrality of the Soviet Union on the journal's map of world literature by borrowing symbolic capital from Tagore, an important writer who had been widely recognised not only in China but globally. This is testified to by the fact that when Tagore's letters appeared in the journal, they were grouped together with a set of Russia-related writings penned by several world-renowned western intellectuals, such as Romain Rolland and Henri Barbusse, in a special column celebrating the 38th anniversary of the October Revolution. Highlighting the nationality of each writer, the column carved out within the non-Socialist world a widespread pro-Soviet discourse that spanned both east and west. On the other hand, as texts centred on the Russian revolution and its effect, *Rāśiyār chiṭhi* itself legitimised Tagore's entry into *Yiwen*'s literary world, especially at the height of Sino-Soviet brotherhood.

However, a closer comparison between the abridged Chinese translation and the complete English translation of the letters (Tagore 1960) reveals *Yiwen*'s silencing of Tagore's problematic relations with Russia while foregrounding the favourable ones, a strategy we have seen earlier in the case of Anand and the PWA. According to the complete English translation, Tagore's impression of the Soviet Union was a mixture of fascination and apprehension. While convinced by the "marvellous progress" the Russian government had achieved in terms of feeding and educating millions of common people (209), the author cautioned against some of the means by which these achievements had been carried out, such as "violence" and "dictatorship" used to "suppress the individual in the name of collectivity" (110, 114, 92). As one can anticipate, the Chinese translator Jin Kemu selected the positive appraisals while pruning out all the unfavorable comments. Moreover, his selection gravitated to those paragraphs that denounced western colonisers or compared them unfavorably with the Soviet Union, which resulted in an English translation published in *The Modern Review* in 1934 being banned by the British Raj (Tagore 2011, 748).

Before the Sino-Soviet alliance explicitly broke in 1959, highlighting the relations between or "relationing" a non-leftist writer/text from a non-Socialist background with the Soviet Union was a method of progressivisation frequently used in *Yiwen*. Selecting pieces that were thematically related to the Soviet Union/Russia, such as *Rāśiyār chiṭhi*, was one such strategy. A more frequent strategy, as Volland (2017a, 162–63) has shown, was to attach an interpretative essay about this particular writer/text written by a leading Soviet writer or critic as an endorsement. Yet occasionally we see *Yiwen*'s editors implement the strategy in a more nuanced way. As the following example shows, they bestowed upon Tagore a progressive "afterlife" not by overtly publishing a Soviet critical article that assessed the author against socialist realist yardsticks, but instead by covertly putting him into a historically unachieved interaction with Ilya Ehrenburg, one of the most eminent Soviet writers of the 1950s, within the latter's travel work, *Impressions of India*.

Originally published in the June 1956 issue of *Inostrannaja Literatura* (Foreign Literature), a Soviet journal that *Yiwen* consulted regularly, *Impressions of India* was serialised in *Yiwen*'s March and April issues in 1957. A veteran novelist, journalist and world traveler, Ehrenburg offers in this work a panoramic account of his recent travel experience in the subcontinent as well as insightful discussions about Indian history, religion, society, arts and literature in comparison with Russian, Western European, Chinese and other civilisations. Towards the end of the essay, Ehrenburg used Tagore as an example to illustrate the complexity and contradiction embedded in Indian culture. He rightly noted Tagore's dual character: "an extremely sensitive lyric poet" and at the same time "a tireless social activist" (April 1957 *Yiwen*, 151). The latter character led to a discussion of Tagore's 1930 visit to the Soviet Union. Disagreeing with Tagore's self-assessment made in 1921 that "I am a poet [. . .] I am not a fighter by nature" (Tagore 2011, 112), Ehrenburg saw his entire life as "a history of fighting—fighting against British rule, violence, deception, ignorance and hunger" (April 1957 *Yiwen*, 152). Quoting an impassioned speech Tagore had made after returning from the Soviet Union, in which he encouraged his countrymen to draw on the experience of the Russian revolution and participate in the Indian independence struggle, Ehrenburg concluded: "Only a *fighter-poet* can make such remarks" (153, emphasis added). The hyphenation is of special interest here for it offers a rewriting of Tagore's life trajectory by linking an identity that he admitted with one that he denied or, in Ehrenburg's interpretation, could not have realised at the time. In this rewriting, the Soviet trip was presented as a catalyst that helped Tagore develop his rebellious quality to an unprecedented extent. Also noteworthy is Ehrenburg's account of Tagore's death in August 1941, news of which he heard from P.C. Mahalanobis, Tagore's affectionate companion and an Indian statistician closely associated with Sino-Indian scientific exchanges in the 1950s (Ghosh 2016). Revealing the fact that the last words spoken by Tagore concerned the Soviet Union's situation in the face of German invasion, Ehrenburg not only recalled the humanitarian, internationalist and anti-imperialist spirit of Tagore, which had been stressed repeatedly in *Yiwen*, but also added to the relations between him and the Soviet Union a personally emotional touch.[11]

---

11 This echoes Yan Shaodan's (1958, 6) recounting of the veteran Hindi writer Premchand's life story. In the preface to his translation of the novel *Godān* (The Gift of a Cow, 1936), Yan included an episode in which Premchand grieved over the Russian writer Gorky's death before his own departure that occurred a few weeks later.

Conclusion: *Yiwen/Shijie wenxue* and the Making of World Literature

As a literary program formulated in the shadow of the Cold War, *Yiwen/Shijie wenxue*'s imagination and making of world literature was bound up with geopolitical considerations, and one such consideration was to build a China-based literary international. Focusing primarily on Indian literature, I have tried to understand the politics behind the journal's creation of world literature. Such a located perspective enables a nuanced inquiry into the invisible space between literary texts and agents. As I have shown, what the journal editors and translators attempted to build was not just an ever-increasing body of foreign literary works in Chinese translation, but also a world of ever-multiplying literary relations, with China occupying a crucial position.

Highlighting the constructive process of the "world of literary relations", this chapter has presented *Yiwen/Shijie wenxue*'s literary internationalism not only as different sets of literary texts that were geographically, ideologically, thematically or aesthetically interconnected, but also as groups of literary agents such as writers who related to each other because of their similar outlooks, experiences or tastes. Here, writerly contact is understood not only in Thornber's sense as "interactions among creative writers" (2009, 2) who actually met and befriended each other (Mulk Raj Anand's exchanges with Chinese writers and editors). It also incorporates connections between those writers who had not met, yet were imaginatively brought into indirect dialogue by Chinese literary agents (Rabindranath Tagore and Ilya Ehrenburg). The building of a world of literary relations also carried temporal significance, for it always involved establishing links between different foreign texts/writers with China's literary present. In the case of Anand, it means maximising the visibility of his dynamic ongoing interactions and friendships with Chinese writers, editors, translators and readers. In the case of a deceased writer like Tagore, it entailed bringing his literary aesthetics and political outlook closer to the Soviet Union, a reincarnation of the "literary future" that China had once followed. If "solidarity", a term that is sometimes used interchangeably with "community" and "unity", is central to forming internationalism, it is precisely from these interconnections between texts and relationalities between literary agents, both real and constructed, that the sense of solidarity emerges and becomes visible to the reader.

Acknowledgements

I would like to thank Francesca Orsini and Adrian Plau for their valuable comments on an earlier draft of this chapter. I also thank Neelam Srivastava for putting together the panel "Provincializing World Literature: Multilingualism, Resistance and Literary Internationals" at the 2017 ACLA conference, where my preliminary findings and arguments were presented. My gratitude also goes to the China Scholarship Council, whose funding has made this research project possible.

Bibliography

Ahmed, Talat. 2009. *Literature and Politics in the Age of Nationalism: The Progressive Writers' Movement in South Asia, 1932–56.* London, New York and New Delhi: Routledge.

Anand, Mulk Raj. 1993. "Mulk Raj Anand Remembers." *Indian Literature* 36 (2): 176–86.

Bhattacharjea, Mira Sinha. 1995. "Mao: China, the World and India." *China Report* 31(1): 15–35.

Bondy, Francois. 1967. "Jean-Paul Sartre and Politics." *Journal of Contemporary History* 2 (2): 25–48.

Bourdieu, Pierre. 1993. *The Field of Cultural Production: Essays on Art and Literature.* Translated by Randal Johnson. New York: Columbia University Press.

Casanova, Pascale. [1999] 2004. *The World Republic of Letters.* Translated by M. B. Debevoise. Cambridge, MA: Harvard University Press.

Chen, Jian. 2008. "Bridging Revolution and Decolonization: The "Bandung Discourse' in China's Early Cold War Experience." *The Chinese Historical Review* 15 (2): 207–41.

—. 2010. *Mao's China and the Cold War.* Chapel Hill, NC & London: The University of North Carolina Press.

Cowasjee, Saros. 1977. *So Many Freedoms: A Study of the Major Fiction of Mulk Raj Anand.* Delhi and New York: Oxford University Press.

Cui, Feng. 2009. "Wei Yiwen suyuan: cong Mao Dun de Yiwen Fakanci shuoqi" (A Study of Mao Dun's "An Opening Statement from Editors" for Yiwen). *Zhongguo bijiao wenxue* 77 (4): 80–88.

—. 2012. *Zhengzhi, wenxue yu fanyi: yi "shijie wenxue" wei li, 1953–1966 (Politics, Literature and Translation in the People's Republic of China: A Case Study of "World Literature", 1953–1966).* Unpublished doctoral dissertation. Singapore: Nanyang Technological University.

—. 2015. "Bieyang zhanfang de 'E zhi hua': 'Shuangbai' shiqi Yiwen de xiandaipai wenxue yijie" (The Translation of Western Modernist

Literature in *Yiwen* during the 'Double Hundred Campaign': The Case of *Les Fleurs du Mal*). *Dongfang fanyi* 2015 (2): 46–54.

Damrosch, David. 2003. *What Is World Literature?* Princeton, NJ: Princeton University Press.

Das, Sisir Kumar. 1995. *A History of Indian Literature 1911–1956: Struggle for Freedom: Triumph and Tragedy*. New Delhi: Sahitya Akademi.

Day, Tony. 2010. "Still Stuck in the Mud: Imagining World Literature During the Cold War in Indonesia and Vietnam." In *Cultures at War: The Cold War and Cultural Expression in Southeast Asia*, edited by Tony Day and Maya H.T. Liem, 131–69. Ithaca, NY: Southeast Asia Program, Cornell University.

Denning, Michael. 2004. *Culture in the Age of Three Worlds*. London: Verso.

Genette, Gérard. 1997. *Paratexts: Thresholds of Interpretation*. Cambridge: Cambridge University Press.

Ghosh, Arunabh. 2016. "Accepting Difference, Seeking Common Ground: Sino-Indian Statistical Exchanges 1951–1959." *BJHS: Themes* (1): 61–82.

Halim, Hala. 2012. "*Lotus*, the Afro-Asian Nexus, and Global South Comparatism." *Comparative Studies of South Asia, Africa and the Middle East* 32 (3): 563–83.

Iovene, Paola. 2014. *Tales of Futures Past: Anticipation and the Ends of Literature in Contemporary China*. Stanford, CA: Stanford University Press.

Laachir, Karima, Sara Marzagora, and Francesca Orsini. 2018. "Significant Geographies in Lieu of World Literature." *Journal of World Literature* 4: 290–310.

Levinovitz, Agneta Wallin, and Nils Ringertz, eds. 2001. *The Nobel Prize: The First 100 Years*. London and Singapore: Imperial College Press and World Scientific Publishing.

Liu, Hongtao. 2010. "Shijie wenxue guannian zai ershi shiji wushi zhi liushi niandai zhongguo de liangci shijian" (Two Practices of the Concept of World Literature in China in the 1950s and 1960s). *Zhongguo bijiao wenxue* 80 (3): 10–18.

Mao, Dun. 1953. "Fakanci" (Foreword). *Yiwen* 7: 1–2.

Magill, Frank, ed. 1949, 1955, 1960, 1969. *Masterpieces of World Literature in Digest Form*. 4 vols. Pasadena: Salem.

Moretti, Franco. 2000. "Conjectures on World Literature." *New Left Review* 1: 54–68.

—. 2003. "More Conjectures." *New Left Review* 23: 73–81.

—. 2006. "Evolution, World-system, Weltliteratur." In *Studying Transcultural Literary History*, edited by Gunilla Lindberg-Wada, 113–21. Berlin: de Gruyter.

Orsini, Francesca. 2015. "The Multilingual Local in World Literature." *Comparative Literature* 6 (4): 345–74.

Orsini, Francesca, and Laetitia Zecchini. 2019. "The Locations of (World) Literature: Perspectives from Africa and South Asia." Special Issue of *Journal of World Literature* 4: 1–12.

Overstreet, Gene D., and Marshall Windmiller. 1959. *Communism in India*. Berkeley and Los Angeles, CA: University of California Press.

Sen Gupta, Bhabani. 1972. *Communism in Indian Politics*. New York: Columbia University Press.

Sundarlal, Pandit. 1952. *China Today*. Allahabad: Hindustani Culture Society.

Tagore, Rabindranath. 1960. *Letters from Russia.* Translated by Sasadhar Sinha. Calcutta: Visva-Bharati.

—. 2011. *The Essential Tagore*, edited by Fakrul Alam and Radha Chakravarty. Cambridge, MA: The Belknap Press of Harvard University Press.

Tan, Chung. 1998. "Tagore's Inspiration in Chinese New Poetry." In *Across the Himalayan Gap: An Indian Quest for Understanding China*, edited by Tan Chung, 335–56. New Delhi: Gyan Publishing House.

The Editors. 1959. "From *Yiwen* to *Shijie wenxue*." *Shijie wenxue* 1: 2–4.

Thornber, Karen Laura. 2009. *Empire of Texts in Motion: Chinese, Korean, and Taiwanese Transculturations of Japanese Literature*. Cambridge, MA: Harvard University Press.

—. 2014. "Rethinking the World in World Literature: East Asia and

Literary Contact Nebulae." In *World Literature in Theory*, edited by David Damrosch, 460–79. Hoboken, NJ: John Wiley & Sons.

Volland, Nicolai. 2017a. *Socialist Cosmopolitanism: The Chinese Literary Universe, 1945–1965*. New York: Columbia University Press.

—. 2017b. "Clandestine Cosmopolitanism: Foreign Literature in the People's Republic of China, 1957–1977." *The Journal of Asian Studies* 76 (1): 185–210.

Yoon, Duncan. 2015. "'Our Forces Have Redoubled': World Literature, Postcolonialism, and the Afro-Asian Writers' Bureau." *The Cambridge Journal of Postcolonial Literary Inquiry* 2 (2): 233–52.

Young, Robert J.C. [2001] 2016. *Postcolonialism: An Historical Introduction*. Oxford: Blackwell.

The Curious Case of Exotic Translations in the South-East Balkans

Galina Rousseva-Sokolova

If the concept of World Literature, notoriously coined by Goethe, appears to us today as more of a problem than an object of study (Moretti 2000, 55), we can nevertheless easily empathize with the enthusiasm of the great German poet, reflected in his dialogues with Eckermann (commented on by Damrosh 2003, 1–4). In the context of his time Goethe envisions *Weltliteratur* as the dawn of a new era in the cultural history of mankind, a way out of the constricted self-centred enclosures of national literary traditions, an escape from the worn-out comforts of home into an open space of free intellectual exchange with endless opportunities for enrichment, cross-fertilization and inspiration.

Yet, his fervour is tempered by what Damrosh calls "provincial anxiety" (2003, 10): the fear that German literature may not meet the standards set by the English and the French, that in this emerging borderless arena comparisons will inevitably yield hierarchies in which German letters (and his own voice in them) will come out as a lesser competitor, resulting in self-consciousness and frustration. If, as Moretti puts it, the field of World Literature is one, it is nevertheless unequal, with a small central core surrounded by vast overlapping peripheries (2000, 55–56). Goethe assumed that the intrinsic aesthetic and humanistic quality of the respective national literatures would inevitably determine, in time, their position in the pantheon of World Literature. We have learned since then not only to be circumspect about presumably universal markers of beauty, but also to connect the dissemination of texts beyond the territory of their origins to a multitude of extra-literary factors, involving power dynamics, socio-economic circumstances, as well as the specificity of book markets, circulation and production.

This chapter aims to delineate some general features, trends and characteristics of translations from "Eastern" languages (Chinese, Korean, Sanskrit, Hindi, Japanese and a few others) that first appeared on the Bulgarian book market, on the institutions involved, on the political and economic circumstances, on the vision behind the editorial choices, and, to some extent at least, on their contemporary reception.[1] It will try to explain the tremendous impact of the political changes which swept Eastern Europe in 1989 in the field of book production and marketing as well as the shifts in readers' tastes, expectations and behaviours up to the present day.

The research has been conducted mostly through interviews with publishing house executives, editors and owners, sometimes the same interviewee combining all three functions. The relatively small sample of interviewees was selected for their long-term engagement in the publishing business throughout part or most of the period in focus here, which starts from the mid-1970s. Their testimonies have been crucial for making sense of the human narrative behind the facts and figures. A second source of information has been the database of the Bulgarian National Library, where the librarians kindly introduced me to the advanced functionalities of their website's search machine. The book by Valentin Karamanchev (2016), a long-time head of the National Publication Agency during the communist period, reads like a memoir and has been used to corroborate some of the information acquired through interviews. Finally, some relevant statistical information on the current characteristics of the Bulgarian book market was retrieved from the website of the National Statistical Institute.

Bulgaria, a small country on the Balkan peninsula in South-Eastern Europe is relatively homogeneous in terms of ethnicity and language. The Bulgarian language, a member of the South Slavic group of Indo-European languages, is seldom spoken outside Bulgaria and its currently diminishing population of 7.1 million. Consequently, the

1 For practical purposes, translations from Arabic have been left aside, although a separate study would probably show similar trends.

Bulgarian book market is limited, price sensitive, and the financial pressure on competing book publishers and sellers is strong.[2]

Under these circumstances it would be difficult to imagine that anything exciting is or has ever been happening in the even more restricted field of Bulgarian translations from Eastern, aka exotic, languages. As far as World Literature is concerned, Bulgaria appears as the backwaters of the periphery, or, more accurately, at the confluence of several peripheries (Moretti 2000, 56). Historically it has long constituted a periphery of the Christian world during the times of the Ottoman Empire, then a marginal zone of European capitalism until World War Two, while cultural interference was a collateral of the unflinching political loyalty to the USSR in the decades that followed. Centres may have shifted in time, but the Bulgarian circumstances have not, in the sense that there has always been a foreign model to look up to, external standards to measure oneself against, and a pervading sense of self-consciousness in presenting one's cultural achievements to the world. Scarcity of resources and linguistic restrictedness—in other words, the realities of life—would have predictably moderated the ambitions of those intent on opening new far-off horizons to the reading public, and made their efforts look heroic, isolated and unsustainable. Luckily, the narrative uncovered by this investigation proved to be more interesting, convoluted and revealing than the predictions.

Although translations from eastern languages had occasionally materialised on the Bulgarian market before 1950, the peak for most languages appears to be between the 1970s to the mid-1990s. The range of publications during that period is quite

---

2 In 2016 Bloomberg gave an estimate of the annual Bulgarian publishing market as 70 to 80 million BGN (35 to 80 million EUR) (https://www.bloombergtv.bg/svetat-e-biznes/2016-05-24/balgarski yat-knizhen-pazar-e-80-mln-lv-godishno). Data from the National Statistical Institute for 2017 indicate 7,991 new book titles released in almost 5 million printed copies. Out of these 2,658 were translations with 2,428,000 printed copies, which amounts to an average of 913 copies per edition (http://www.nsi.bg/sites/default/files/files/pressreleases/Pu blishing2017_ERAVU4K.pdf).

astonishing in terms of scope and numbers, an unlikely flourishing unseen before or since. This seems to be the time when, in Sarah Brouillette's terms (2007, 1), the material conditions of text-production, transmission and reception have been most favourable for this type of publication. In the following pages I will elaborate on these conditions. In order to explain this unparalleled efflorescence of literature in translation I will describe a set of circumstances which constitute the core of what Robert Darnton (1982) calls "the communication circuit" (68), namely the combination of intellectual influences, economic and social conjuncture and political sanctions. The second part of the chapter is devoted to describing the efflorescence itself: it sorts out the bibliographical data on Bulgarian translations from Eastern languages diachronically and according to the original language. It deals with numbers, identifies trends, and thus constitutes the factual basis of the narrative in the first part.

The Socio-Political Context

During most of the golden era of translations, politically Bulgaria was one of the so-called popular democracies constituting the former communist bloc. As one of the staunchest international allies of the USSR, it followed faithfully its example and leadership in all aspects of social and political life. The economy was entirely centralised and planned. Cultural contacts with the outside world were conceived within the framework of the great ideological divide between capitalism and the progressive world of "real" socialism. They were, consequently, closely supervised, both on the level of individuals and institutions. The access to information (including printed information) was a tool in the ideological fight and had to be filtered, as much as possible, both ways: on the one hand, the conviction of Bulgarian citizens that they were living in the best possible system had to be reinforced and preserved from any challenging doubt; on the other, the outside world should know about Bulgaria only what the ruling communist party would want it to know. This is the general context in which editorial policies were elaborated for the limited number of big state-owned publishing companies, such as Narodna

Kultura, Narodna Mladezh, Profizdat, Narodna Prosveta, Otechestven Front, and others. At the same time these companies were expected to turn out, at least, a nominal financial profit and thus to fulfil (as with every other industry) the five-year plans according to which the wheel of the economy was supposed to turn. Seen from today's perspective, the operation of the publishing and book-selling establishments of the communist era looks like some kind of wonderland which retains the social purpose of the activity (books are edited, printed and sold for a price, paid by customers/readers), but includes some strange underlying practices. These practices deviate from the usual financial logic and present challenges and tensions in unexpected places. As they constitute a part of the economic and social conjecture at the very centre of Danton's communications circuit, they need to be briefly delineated.

As in all the countries behind the iron curtain, publishing in Bulgaria was submitted to governmental approval through a centralized agency, created in 1954 as *Public Trust for Printed Works* (Държавно Търговско Обединение за Печатни Произведения) and restructured and renamed several times in the decades that followed. Its purpose was to receive all the requests from the publishing companies, to distribute accordingly the necessary supplies for the production of books (paper, ink, etc.) and to coordinate the editorial policies with the secretariat of the Central Committee of the Bulgarian Communist Party. Photocopying machines were rare. Such services were available to the general public only in small quantities in some of the most important libraries and under supervision. Typewriters could be acquired only by authorized institutions and were not available for sale to individuals. Imported books could be confiscated during customs checks at the border (and cause problems to their owner). Even ancient languages were not immune to suspicion: several Sanskrit books were confiscated from one of my informants upon her return from India. It was a precautionary measure: unable to understand the content, the authorities would not take the risk of letting in anything offensive to the government, which at that time was facing international criticism for its treatment of the Turkish minority.

Typically, if an editor wanted to publish a book (translated or not) a special form had to be filled in and submitted to the state agency. Filling in the form could be tricky: people could lose their jobs and forever ruin their careers for even daring to ask for authorization for the wrong book. Avoiding "aggravating the lion" was the guiding principle, as one editor of that time put it. Surprisingly, she added that this was not a big problem. In the 1970s, when the publishing of books in translation (mostly from Western European languages) intensified, the names of the forbidden authors were well-known to everyone in the business, even if such a list was never officially acknowledged. George Orwell's *1984*, for instance, was definitely on it, and so was the Quran, especially after the policy of forced assimilation towards the Turkish minority which brought about a massive emigration wave in the 1980s.[3] But the unspoken quality of the forbidden realm meant also that its boundaries could change in time, were anyone brave enough to test them.

Valentin Karamanchev (2016, 16–18), the head of the state agency for many years, recalls in his partially autobiographical book how Margaret Mitchell's *Gone with the Wind* came to see the light of day in Bulgarian. The combination of a charismatic "bourgeois" love story within the context of slavery had given the novel a very bad reputation with the communist politburo as racist propaganda. Sometimes, on closer examination, the bans on books could turn out to be, more than anything else, the unjustified result of personal idiosyncrasies. While defending the book on a committee against a strong opposition of high flying, but poorly educated, communist dignitaries, Karamanchev suddenly found an unexpected ally in the much-feared number two communist party official, Milko Balev, who

3 These events are officially referred to as the *Revival Process*: in 1984-1985 the members of the Turkish minority were forced to change their Arabic and Turkish names to Slavic ones. They were also banned from speaking Turkish in public and practicing Islam, or customs of Islamic origin. This period of repression continued until 1989.

happened to remember the novel fondly from having read it in prison during his turbulent youth. Once the boss had spoken, the (happy) fate of the classic book was sealed in an instant.

One of the reasons for Karamanchev's insistence on publishing *Gone with the Wind* was that he probably predicted a massive commercial success for the book. And herein lies another peculiarity of book circulation in a planned economy. The publishing executives were interested in selling out all their productions, which allowed them to fulfil their assigned plans, keep their jobs (more than anywhere else losing one's prestigious position in an authoritarian system is an irredeemable personal tragedy) and get bonuses for their employees. While a state-owned publisher could never go bankrupt in a planned economy, the editors-in-chief were held responsible for occasional poor sales figures.

In reality, that almost never happened. "Everything used to sell", I was told by Vera Gancheva, head of Narodna Kultura ("Popular Culture"), the biggest publisher of literature in translation in the 1970s and 1980s. Indeed, the bibliographical data systematically mentions the quantities of printed books for any given edition, and from today's perspective, they seem quite spectacular for such a small market. The 100,000 copies of the aforementioned first Bulgarian edition of *Gone with the Wind* sold out instantly. Little known Chinese novels, like *The Red Banner* by Lao She, published in 1984, would reach editions of over 10,000 copies – unimaginable figures even for bestsellers today. Even poetry would command figures around 10,000. Less wanted titles also found their way to potential readers through a system of donations (prisons and army libraries were the typical beneficiaries). Then, at the end of the five-year plan period, a few predictably very profitable publishing ventures (like *Gone with the Wind*) would seal the financial success of the industry in the eyes of the communist party leaders, ensuring the job stability of its bosses and the bonuses of its employees.

It was not just a case of a sellers' market. For books like Margaret Mitchell's there would be lines in front of the bookshops, people waiting for hours to be allowed to buy a limited number of books or taking advantage of a subscription system which gave them a first-served privilege. This hunger for books can be illustrated with an anecdote that an editor of that time shared. The new edition of a Balzac novel had just been released and the bookselling company had a work meeting with its regional representatives. The representative of Pernik literally burst into tears when she learned she would be allotted only 7,000 copies to distribute in her area. She obviously believed her sales results were being sabotaged on purpose. Pernik is a small blue-collar workers' town near Sofia. It would be a safe bet to say that in today's market a sale of 70 copies of anything from Balzac would be considered a success.

While the Bulgarian public in general were avid readers, there are more factors at play here than sheer intellectual curiosity. First of all, for most people, money was available while opportunities for spending it were relatively scarce. In the twisted rules of the planned economy, money was not the universal equivalent for goods and services the way it is in a free market. Basic necessities for living could be bought for money in shops, but for more sophisticated or bigger purchases like houses, cars, or traveling abroad, other proofs of entitlement were needed. Turning back to the situation in the publishing industry, the big publishers suffered no scarcity of cash, but they did not have the autonomy of even buying paper for a new edition without proper authorization from above, because paper was simply not available on the market.

A closed authoritarian society, offering limited prospects, tends to exacerbate the curiosity of its readers. People bought books with great eagerness, not only because the communist ideology imposed restrictions on information (thus boosting the interest for anything that may have filtered through) and because entertainment was rare, but also because, by and large, they could afford to do so. The printed books were not very high-quality editions, but were cheap and the high production quantities made them even cheaper.

Another possible line of explanation for the popularity of books would be to explore the sociological profile of the buyers. Starting in the 1950s, there was a massive movement of the population from rural communities to the cities. The communist regime opened the doors to higher education and positions in the administration to rural youths, who were often the first in their families to gain access to a university degree and a government job. After the purging of the old bourgeois establishment, there was a shortage of competent bureaucrats and educated civil servants. Preferences were given to those who had backgrounds in poor rural or worker families. As a result, the towns exploded with first generation city-dwellers, who still held to the traditional values and thought patterns of their upbringing, while at the same time striving for upward mobility in a society which, in spite of its basic ideological tenets, was far from classless.

In that context, culture was a cherished asset. Together with education, it was viewed as part of a world of sophistication inaccessible to the previous generations and a valued object of pride for families and individuals. It held social prestige. It was a sign of belonging to (or not being different from) the government executives and communist party officials, the diplomats, professors and writers who formed the upper cast of socialist privilege—the *nomenklatura*—who had access to what just money could not buy, like apartments, villas, western cars and special vacation resorts.

These phenomena can be interpreted through the lens of the concept of cultural capital as defined by Pierre Bourdieu (1986). In a system where economic capital is not available for appropriation, the race for cultural capital, in all of its states—embodied, objectified and institutionalized—is all the fiercer. While the horizon of opportunities for social growth of individuals was limited by the rigidity of a system where the state was the sole employer, Bulgarian society during the communist regime was nevertheless a relatively egalitarian one. Truly privileged as well as truly oppressed groups existed, but, for the great majority, in an environment where inherited property or money did not count for much, where education was free and books were cheap, the acquisition of cultural capital was a major field of competition. On a personal level it was an internalized value, a motive of pride. It was an important factor in group dynamics and hierarchies. By and large it commanded admiration and, if economic capital was inaccessible, it could still be converted into social capital and invested by its holders in building networks of "mutual acquaintance and recognition" (Bourdieu 1986, 56).

Educating the Reader

Direct or indirect translations from Chinese, Japanese, Hindi or any other "oriental" language, were practically non-existent until the second half of the 20th century. They started occasionally appearing in the 1950s, then the 1970s saw a turning point when the editorial policy towards translations was developed to a higher gear. This was due to a combination of factors.

More and more competent translators from eastern languages became available on the job market. Most of them were Moscow and Leningrad university graduates, and some were actively engaged in establishing relevant programs at Sofia University, which now had its own Centre for Eastern Languages and Cultures. Officially founded in 1985, the latter was gradually institutionalized as an educational hub for the so-called "rare" languages. Currently it offers courses and programs in Turkish, Arabic, Chinese, Japanese, Hindi, Urdu, Korean, Persian, Armenian, Vietnamese, Indonesian and Tibetan. The creation of such a centre, as everything else, could not have happened without political support. The official ideology encouraged the acquisition of modern languages. Such skills were in demand in the government units devoted to propaganda dissemination.

Meanwhile Leda Mileva, a famous writer and a diplomat, who represented Bulgaria at UNESCO from 1972 to 1978, was appointed as head of the Translators' Union, a powerful professional organization, and was determined to improve the scope and quality of the translations in print. She had a follower and supporter in Vera Gancheva, the aforementioned long-time head of the Narodna Kultura publishing house—the biggest publisher of translated literature. Ms Gancheva established in her institution the principle of always (or, at least, as much as possible) translating from the original language (and not through an intermediary language of translation, as had often been the practice so far). She is the source of most of the information presented in the following paragraphs, collected during three interviews conducted in the fall of 2017. This information was later confirmed by three editors who worked under her in the 1980s and are still active players in the publishing industry today.

The 1970s was a period of stability and relative prosperity. Lyudmila Zhivkova, the daughter of the general secretary of the Bulgarian Communist Party, headed the Committee for Art and Culture. She surrounded herself with intellectuals, supported their ideas and ensured access to generous funding. As a small country that had recently emerged from poverty, Bulgaria was striving for cultural recognition and Ms Zhivkova's position ensured that no expense would be spared in this effort.

Ms Gancheva and some of the editors who worked for her remember this period almost with elation, as a time when "everything was possible" (the phrase came up more than once in the interviews). As her efforts were in line with the general endeavour to elevate Bulgaria on the cultural scene, and thanks to protection from above, she enjoyed great freedom in taking editorial decisions and handling an almost unlimited budget, including in hard (i.e. western) currency. Editors travelled to international book fairs, and access to all the relevant information for their job was granted (travel abroad, whether for work or for pleasure, was a rare and exclusive privilege). Bulgarian translators from "rare" (in the official taxonomy) eastern languages would receive grants to work on their commissioned texts in the relevant country of origin. Thanks to an odd set of circumstances, this situation was (and still is) unparalleled in Bulgarian book history.

The people managing these resources had undertaken a task: to educate the Bulgarian reader, or in the terms of Ms Gancheva, to fill in the blank spots in their culture. This might seem a strange formulation, but it is quite symptomatic of the way the relation between texts, or works of art and their audience was conceived. The prestige of "culture" was such that once an artefact was introduced in the public sphere as cultural capital, open for appropriation (through the publication of a book), no other marketing effort was needed. The readers were targeted not as customers, but as people in need of an education. Crowd pleasers like *Gone with the Wind* were released occasionally, but in general pleasing the crowds was not a concern. The Bulgarian reader had to be on a par with the Polish reader, the French reader, the Soviet reader. Ms Gancheva was a woman on a mission. And it seems that, at least to some point, Bulgarian readers were willing to follow.

To this purpose the Translators' Union under Ms Mileva apparently elaborated, around 1979, painstakingly and in consultation with many specialists, a list of these blank spots as far as world literature was concerned. The list was to serve as a guiding plan for all the publishers in the years to come as to what books should be translated. As a corollary it also outlined a kind of historically located Bulgarian version of World Literature through the ideal of the "cultured" reader.

In spite of many efforts, I could not lay my hands on this list. The archive of the Translators' Union, after several moves from one location to another, was in a sad state of disarray and parts of it are presumed lost. A check in the National Archive was also of no help. Some of the people who worked around that time in Narodna Kultura seemed to remember that such a list existed, but no one had kept it in their possession. The people who were professionally active at that time are now deceased or long since retired. The investigation was not entirely fruitless though: it produced another list. Upstream of the Bulgarian idea of World Literature there was another set of books, created with the sanction of a prestigious international organisation.

The UNESCO list of World Literature

One of the former editors of Narodna Kultura, Ganka Petkova, while admitting she did not remember the Translators' Union list, suggested that it could have been inspired by a document published by UNESCO in the 1970s. A search in the digitalized archives of the organization confirmed this theory by yielding a document issued June 25, 1972, bearing the title *Tentative List of Representative Works of World Literature, Prepared with the Collaboration of Member States and the International Council for Philosophy and Humanistic Studies (ICPHS).*[4] The second page of the document specifies that the list be recommended for translations.

According to the introduction of the document it was painstakingly compiled during three years. Its purpose was twofold: on the one hand "to assemble an 'ideal library' reflecting as far as possible every work in the ancient and modern world which possesses an exemplary literary value"; on the other, "to propose to Member States a selection of literary works worthy of being translated". The list was established in consultation with the National Commissions of the organisation, which received an invitation to participate in 1968. In order to compensate for those who did not reply experts, selected in coordination with the ICPHS, were consulted.

The list follows an arrangement according to languages. Each author was deemed "representative" first of his language, then, when relevant, of his country. Most of the authors are contemporary, but several classical languages have been included as well, such as Acadian, classical Arabic, Egyptian, ancient Greek, classical Hebrew, Latin, Pali and classical Sanskrit. The National Commissions were asked to select a maximum of thirty authors. Most of them complied, but on some occasions (ancient Greek, modern Arabic, English, French, Spanish) this number was largely surpassed "on account of the exceptional wealth of certain literatures". Some pages appear to be missing—the languages following "Turkish" alphabetically do not show. Altogether the list includes approximately 1500 titles. The introduction ends with the following:

> It is to be hoped that this new contribution to the promotion of the international dissemination and the interpenetration of cultures will provide an opportunity for Member States to

4 https://unesdoc.unesco.org/ark:/48223/pf0000001229?posInSet =3&queryId=63ca94b6-0bb8-4ff5-8b5d-d474c64c0dd6

> complete this "ideal library" in their own languages according to national affinities and tastes.

While this document deserves a study in itself, what makes it particularly important for the history of Bulgarian translations is the strongly prescriptive interpretation it was given. According to Ms Petkova there was more to the UNESCO list than just a recommendation; it was perceived as a possible ranking basis. According to the number of titles present in any country's literary markets, a "cultural rating" would be established. The more the books from the list were made available through translation, the higher the position of the respective country. Hence Bulgaria's exceptionally ambitious translation program.

I could not get a direct confirmation that this is the way the UNESCO list was interpreted. Indirectly, however, several facts make it plausible. First of all, Leda Mileva came as head of the Translators' Union after eight years as the Bulgarian representative at UNESCO's headquarters. Her time as diplomat coincides with the publication of UNESCO's list. From a larger perspective, this chain of events would be symptomatic of the *zeitgeist*: from its eternally peripheral position Bulgaria was yearning for recognition. As a consequence, World Literature was shaped into a program. The UNESCO list was treated as a competition field in much the same way James English (2008) speaks of "the arts as international sport" (262). While Bulgarian citizens were vying for the acquisition, material and symbolic, of cultural capital, the same striving was reproduced in the cultural policy of their government.[5] Both inhabited a world where the perfect library and the perfect reader existed beyond doubt. The periphery does not question the target, set far away in the centre, but it will single-mindedly mobilise resources to outperform the other peripheries.

Looking back at this period, one striking feature is how stable and certain things seemed. The centralized communist order, with all

---

5 See the chapter by Yan Jia in the present volume for a similar account of the struggle for recognition of the People's Republic of China.

its faults and hypocrisies, had achieved a certain prosperity and managed to exude, by and large, a sense of permanence, of solidity. The future, collective and individual, had its limitations, but possessed a certainty beyond doubt. Whatever lay ahead had to be built on top of the already-existing, not by changing it, much less destroying it. Individuals had no choice but to embrace the state of affairs which gave them security in exchange for limitations in freedom and perspectives. That was a tolerable compromise for most. Rejecting it meant senselessly ruining your life and that of your family, pure and simple.

The Shift to Market Economy

In 1989 all that stability went up in smoke overnight. Todor Zhivkov, the secretary general of the communist party and head of state for 35 years, was ousted by his own politburo acolytes in an internal party coup. Soon, privatization started and private entrepreneurship was born. In a somewhat chaotic process, the big publishing houses (including Narodna Kultura) were dismantled into smaller private companies frequently headed by former editors or managers; often these companies were then divided even further. The number of registered publishers grew from 127 in 1985 to over 1600 in 1996. 70 percent of them published five books or less per year (Tsvetkova 2008, 21-22). A few, like Colibri, Bard and Ciela, have found their readers and still exist 25 years later, but most have disappeared. In recent years a consolidation trend is palpable throughout the publishing and bookselling industry, since it became painfully obvious that small publishers could not survive on their own in such a small market.

Still, for a while, editions of literature in translation, including those from eastern languages, continued with the same pace for a while throughout the 1990s. The newly formed private publishing houses released editions which they "inherited" from their predecessors of socialist times, with copyrights covered and ready for printing. Once this resource was exhausted, things became more difficult, sales numbers fell and fewer new titles were released.

The early 1990s, though, were a time of optimism and sheer intoxication with the seemingly limitless opportunities bestowed by freedom. Dimitar Tonin, whom I interviewed in the summer of 2017, was one of those optimists and an exemplary figure of a small publisher focused on Asian religions and cultures, very active in the 1990s and early 2000s. Having a strong personal interest in Buddhism, he created his publishing house, appropriately named Shambhala, shortly after the political changes. He started from scratch, without the benefit of any inheritance from the former state mastodons. Nevertheless, he was able to publish editions of Milarepa, Sakya Pandita, the *Dhammapada*, Shantideva etc., with sales numbers around 5,000 copies (up to 20,000 for the *Dhammapada* edition). Even so, he could never afford (as Narodna Kultura did) to commission translations from the original languages, which can be up to five times more expensive. Most of his books were translated from Russian or English.

Then the market shifted again, this time from the buyers' side. The game changed: the race for the appropriation of economic capital was open and, in the next 20 years, cultural capital suffered severe devaluation. The readers lost interest in being educated and their budget for books was diminished. Entertainment, a sphere almost completely ignored by the austere socialist publishing industry, entered the world of books. Other forms of leisure, unavailable before, appeared and started to compete for the money of the former eager readers, opening to the joys of consumerism. The New Age emerged on the literary market, and, according to Mr. Tonin, killed the interest in proper translations of eastern texts. The general level of interest in original texts fell dramatically, with customers favouring secondary, digested versions. Edition figures fell to between 300 and 500 copies and, consequently, costs per copy increased substantially. The editorial focus out of necessity shifted towards meditation guides and shamanic techniques.

If Shambhala is still present on the Bulgarian book market, it is mostly due to the resilience and fierce independence of Mr. Tonin himself. In the last ten years he has completely reinvented his editorial horizon and seems to have found his niche in off-the-beaten-track travel guides and books of Thracian history and religion. He is selling his old stock of eastern translations at a big discount through his Facebook page and e-versions of them at an even bigger discount.

At the opposite end of the spectrum, that of the current big players on the book market which emerged in the post-socialist circumstances, is Colibri, one of the three most successful private Bulgarian publishers of fiction in translation. I was able to interview Jechka Georgieva, one of the owners and editor-in-chief, who was part of the team around Vera Gancheva in Narodna Kultura. Colibri releases three to four new titles every week, of 300 to 1,000 copies each. The editors follow closely the global markets, with an eye on literary awards. Over the years, Colibri has gained an excellent reputation for their editorial choices, good quality print and high standards of translation. They cater to the tastes of educated readers who want access to the latest literary novelties. Their main challenge is to secure copyright for as many as possible of the best books internationally, and to stay financially afloat in a small and highly competitive market with many new releases and high production costs.

As expected, Ms Georgieva confirmed Colibri's obvious general lack of interest in direct translations from eastern languages, classical or modern. Only in Japanese authors, who enjoy a relatively constant circle of aficionados, is the additional investment considered worth the risk. Thus Haruki Murakami, as a rare exception, is systematically translated from Japanese these days, while Junichiro Tanizaki was translated from the English version. Even Man Booker Prize winner Eka Kurniawan was translated from English, and not from his native Indonesian. Whereas Narodna Kultura was striving to educate the reader through a "best of" selection from national literatures and Shambhala's policy followed the personal interests of its owner, Colibri tracks the international markets, book prizes and readers' tastes. Their perspective on world literature is best defined as global, with the value of the works assessed only on a world scale (English 2008, 304–05).

Translations from Eastern Languages

Before examining more closely what has been translated from each of the languages examined here, some explanation is needed about the general choices which were made, fully assumed by Ms Gancheva as far as Narodna Kultura is concerned. These remarks concern mostly the translations which appeared in the 1975–92 period, when availability of resources, linguistic competence and political will concurred and intensified the flow of publications.

While there was determination, as far as possible, to translate into Bulgarian from the language of the originals, Ms Gancheva chose not to aim for philologically accurate translations, or critical editions of pre-modern texts. In fact, the Bulgarian versions often took liberties with the original and the "rough" translation was reworked by a professional poet, or writer. This was the case, for instance, with the translation of the *Bhagavad-gita*. This reluctant cooperation created tensions with more academically-minded translators, but it was an understandable choice in light of the ambition to educate the reader, as mentioned above: if it was the general reader (and not the specialist) who was targeted, then the texts had to be easily understandable and accessible.

Thus, in spite of Ms Gancheva' s declared intentions, a few of the publications of Narodna Kultura were not translated from the original language and were, to some extent at least, the product of their Bulgarian authors' reimagining of the East. Perhaps the most notorious case was that of the poet Yordan Milev, who mastered only Russian, but produced translations from Arabic, Persian and Sanskrit. Paradoxically, these skilfully versified translations of Ferdowsi, Omar Khayyam, Saadi, Rumi and the *Panchatantra* today are even more popular on the market than the more accurate later versions.

Occasionally the integrity of the original text and the accuracy of the translation would be compromised by other considerations. Favouring the experience of the audience over the authenticity of the text is one thing, political censorship is another. Editors accepted the compromise to quietly eliminate politically incorrect passages in a translated text instead of abandoning the publication altogether. This is what happened with the translation of Kenneth Clark's *Civilisation,* which I read in Bulgarian before discovering, many years later, that the English original contained an additional paragraph, unkind to communist ideology. This practice permeated the sphere of publishing throughout the former communist bloc. Occasionally, the efforts to bring a text back on the track of political correctness could go to absurd lengths. One former editor of Narodna Kultura shared with me the following anecdote. An edition of a contemporary Vietnamese author was on its way. The translation was ready, an editor was working on it and (since she did not know Vietnamese) was comparing it with the Russian edition of the same author. Appalled at the discrepancies, she looked for an explanation. It turned out the Russian edition included a whole additional final chapter, which was missing in the Vietnamese original.

As shown in these examples, the political factor rarely intervened directly in the editing process, but when it did it trumped all others. Even if Ms Gancheva felt that "everything was possible", publications had to be authorized, the output was monitored and "mistakes" were being punished. It was common knowledge, and adapting to the unspoken rules was seen as common sense. By the 1970s editors had internalized censorship to the point of hardly being aware of it.

While eastern languages were deemed rather harmless and rarely captured the attention of the censors, in other ways politics still influenced the general picture. For instance, the prestigious World Classics series of Narodna Kultura included old Georgian, Uzbek and Kazakh texts, as well as a whole volume dedicated to the "poetry of the peoples of the Soviet Union", in an effort at cultural promotion (a poor compensation for colonial oppression).[6] Lastly, the data for all surveys comes from the database of the Bulgarian National Library.

---

6 Incidentally, neither of those three languages is included in the UNESCO list. This could be a sign that cultural promotion was allowed only "internally", within the territory of the brotherly popular democracies, but discouraged on the international cultural scene.

Translations from Chinese

These followed closely in intensity and themes the ups and downs of the complicated political history of relations with China. As early as the 1950s, between three and five titles appeared every year, mostly translated from Russian, or occasionally from French. The first direct Bulgarian translation from Chinese (Li Yingru's *Struggles in an Ancient City*), was published in 1952 by Bora Drumeva (later Belivanova). In general, the early translations feature modern short stories and novels with a strong social angle, Mao Tse Tung's speeches and writings in impressive numbers (typically 20,000 copies per edition), political treaties explaining China's position on Taiwan and Tibet, modern poetry, and speeches from congresses of the Chinese Communist Party. As early as 1967, translations from old Chinese appeared, as competent Bulgarian translators, mostly educated in the USSR, became available. Then, after the start of the political frictions and the Sino-Soviet split, for 15 years (1967 to 1983) the silence was almost complete. The veto was apparently lifted shortly before 1983. After that, the number of publications picked up again, and greatly intensified after 1990, when a program of Chinese studies was established in Sofia University. To the literary texts that had seen the light of day in Bulgarian were added many titles (up to 11 per year) related to martial arts, acupuncture, erotica, Chinese medicine, massage techniques, qigong (popular throughout the Cyrillic world as tsi gun) feng shui, falun gong, Confucianism, Chinese cuisine, etc. Predictably, these publications were seldom directly translated from the Chinese. During this most recent period three classical Chinese treatises conspicuously appear in many editions and in different translations: Sun Tzu's *Art of War* (nine editions), Laozi's *Tao Te Ching* (nine editions), and the *I Ching* or *Book of Changes* (four editions).

The public's interest in all aspects of Chinese culture has continued to grow in the last 20 years. It has considerably outgrown the categories of belles-lettres, classical or modern and is spreading to spheres as varied as calligraphy, meditation, divination, martial arts and psychology. The Chinese government through its spreading network of Confucius centres sustains this interest by sponsoring cultural initiatives, facilitating Chinese classes and providing scholarships for studying in China. First-rate literary translations, though appear rarely; they are usually done by university-level professionals.

Translations from Japanese

Translations from Japanese took a little longer to take off, but are currently flourishing. A couple of titles appeared in the 1950s and 1960s, translated from Russian versions. The first translation to be made explicitly from Japanese (as indicated on its first page) was published in 1977. In the 1970s and 1980s a small number of competent translators, usually Moscow or Leningrad University graduates, started working for Bulgarian publishers. The 1980s saw numerous excellent translations, all from Japanese, and all published by Narodna Kultura. Japanese Studies was established as a program in Sofia University in the 1990s. Then the pattern followed that of the evolution of translations from Chinese: a strong and stable interest from the general public, and many publications, mostly done from English versions. The thematic range comprises judo, martial arts, meditation, bushido, and yakudza. In contrast to the Chinese translation market, there is a manifest interest in modern Japanese literature, although, as mentioned previously, in most cases publishers are reluctant to take the financial risk of investing in direct translations from Japanese which will inevitably increase the production costs. Still, excellent translations of classical and modern texts, often sponsored through cultural funds, appear once in a while in the sphere of academic publishing.

Translations from Korean

Apart from some poetry and one North Korean drama, translated from Russian versions, nothing was published before the 1990s, with the exception of Kim Il-sung's speeches. Korean studies were developed in Bulgaria after the golden age of Narodna Kultura and thus did not benefit from the prime conditions for the production of translations. One or two titles per year (classical poetry, novels, and short stories) have been published since the beginning of the 21st century, about half of them directly from Korean thanks to the sponsorship of the Korea Foundation.

Translations from Sanskrit and Hindi

The World Classics series of Narodna Kultura features a translation from 1972 of excerpts from the *Mahabharata* and the *Ramayana*. Confusingly, the edition mixes two very different texts. While the *Mahabharata* excerpts are, indeed, taken from the classic Sanskrit epic, the *Ramayana* part features a much later reworking of the epic narrative, written by Tulsidas in avadhi (a dialect of old Hindi) in the late 16th century. While the translation was, indeed, made from the original languages (an Indian specialist, Sati Kumar, was involved), the historical and linguistic discrepancy passed apparently unnoticed. Narodna Kultura also published, in 1989, a translation of the *Bhagavad-gita*, and was able to provide the translator with a grant to work on it in India. A *Panchatantra* from 1981, also published by Narodna Kultura, is claimed to be a translation from Sanskrit, but is, in fact, a very free versified version of the Russian translation by the famous Bulgarian poet Yordan Milev, mentioned above. In the 1990s Plamen Gradinarov, a specialist of philosophical Sanskrit himself founded the Evrasia publishing house and tried to establish a series on Indian philosophy. As with Shambhala, the endeavour proved in time not to be commercially viable, but a few translations remain, of uneven quality, both from Sanskrit or English. In recent years a couple of titles have been translated directly from Sanskrit by university scholars and published through academic publishers and subsidized editions. The only translation from Hindi to Bulgarian before the political changes of 1989 was that of Premchand's *Godan*. Since then several novels and at least five collections of short stories have been translated and published in the last, thanks to certain pioneers' enthusiasm (V. Todorova-Marinova, N. Rozova, E. Konstantinova, V. Dimitrova and others) and subsidies (Rousseva-Sokolova 2010).

While a staggering number of commercially-motivated publications, culturally related to India (on yoga, spirituality, ayurvedic medicine, philosophy, astrology, etc.) have appeared since the 1990s, their original language was English and therefore they do not fall within the scope of this chapter.

Other Languages: Mongolian, Kazakh, Georgian, Uzbek, Vietnamese.

As mentioned above, these languages were promoted mostly for political reasons. A poem by the 12th-century Georgian author Shota Rustaveli, *The Knight in the Panther's Skin*, and 15th-century Alisher Navoi's poem *Hamsa* (in old Uzbek dialect) even made it into the World Classics series. While competent translators were available for Mongolian, all the other languages of the former Soviet Union member states were translated from Russian. Publications after 2000 are rare and subsidized.

Vietnamese is a strange case worth closing this brief survey with: the first collection of poems, translated from French appeared as early as 1939. Then nothing until 1993, when a tiny book of tales materialized. Close to nothing since then: a couple of publications promoting Vietnam, published by the Vietnamese embassy in Sofia and some short pieces in periodicals. The latest publication from 2016 is a translation from English of the teachings of Zen master and global spiritual leader Thich Nhat Hanh. The paradox is that there actually was a Vietnamese community living in Bulgaria throughout the 1980s. Following the signature of a bilateral agreement in the late 1970s around 15,000 Vietnamese workers came to work in Bulgaria in the industry and construction business, to study and to raise families. In other words, unlike many of the cultures mentioned here, Vietnam was accessible. Nevertheless, it somehow failed to impress the intellectual curiosity of Bulgarians and entered only very recently Sofia University as a field of study. Perhaps this very accessibility, yet the lack of social cachet of the Vietnamese immigrants, explains why Vietnamese literature never acquired the desirability of cultural capital. For Bulgarians at least, it fell short of being exotic.

If Goethe was able to contemplate the wide openness of World Literature with just a pinch of provincial anxiety, from the perspective of a Bulgarian the sensation would have been closer to a crushing sense of worthlessness. Attuned to their marginality, Bulgarian intellectuals have embraced the necessity of following the models imposed by different centres without challenging them. Self-assertion, as the example of the UNESCO list shows to some extent, translated into a competitiveness in fervour, a stronger desire to win the game without questioning the rules.

Reflecting a peripheral sphere of interest in a peripheral culture, the data about translations from eastern languages in Bulgarian, collected throughout this research, has appeared, at times, as a random accumulation of details. In such a small territory, things fall easily into the personal, the anecdotal, the circumstantial. The big picture gets fractured into singularities, into discrete facts and events too occasional to form a trend and too insignificant to be studied individually. If nothing else, this chapter is an attempt to posit connections between some of these dots and attribute meaning to some of the patterns observed.

Bibliography

Bourdieu, Pierre. 1986. "The Forms of Capital." In *Handbook of Theory and Research for the Sociology of Education*, edited by J. Richardson, 46–58. Westport: Greenwood.

Brouillette, Sarah. 2007. *Postcolonial Writers in the Global Literary Marketplace*. New York: Palgrave Macmillan.

Damrosch, David. 2003. *What is World Literature?* Princeton, NJ: Princeton University Press.

Darnton, Robert. 1982. "What Is the History of Books?" *Daedalus* 111 (3): 65–83.

English, James. 2008. *The Economy of Prestige: Prizes, Awards, and the Circulation of Cultural Value*. Cambridge, MA: Harvard University Press.

Karamanchev, Valentin. 2016. Караманчев Валентин, *Патила и страдалчества на книги и люде* [Toils and Miseries of Books and People]. Sofia: Sineva.

Moretti, Franco. 2000. "Conjectures on World Literature." *New Left Review* 1 (Jan–Feb): 54–68.

Rousseva-Sokolova Galina. 2010. "Behind and Beyond the Iron Curtain: Reception of Hindi Literature in Eastern and Central Europe." In *India in Translation through Hindi Literature*, edited by Maya Burger and Nicola Pozza, 235–47. Bern: Peter Lang.

Tentative List of Representative Works of World literature, Prepared with the Collaboration of Member States and the International Council for Philosophy and Humanistic Studies (ICPHS). 1973. UNESDOC Digital Library, document code: SHC/WS/236, SHC/WS/236 REV., https://unesdoc.unesco.org/ark:/48223/pf0000001229?posInSet=3&queryId=63ca94b6-0bb8-4ff5-8b5d-d474c64c0dd6.

Tsvetkova, Lyuba. 2008. Люба Цветкова. "Книгоиздаване и издателско-търговска билбиография от 1944 г. до първите години на преход към пазарно стопанство." [Publishing and Bibliography from 1944 to the Beginnings of the Market Economy] *Izdatel* 3–4: 18–22.

The Arabian Nights in Chinese and English Translations: Differing Patterns of Cultural Encounter and World Literature

Wen-chin Ouyang

Translation, Orientalism and World Literature

In the 1980s, a two-volume translation of *The Arabian Nights*, called *Tian Fang Ye Tan* (天方夜譚), appeared in Taipei. It was published by Guiguan Publishing Company (桂冠). The two "prefaces" preceding the translated tales are of interest. According to, Wu Qiancheng (吳潛誠) (1999), general editor of Guiguan's "world literature series" and a PhD in comparative literature, it is a literary masterpiece worthy of canonization world-wide (i–viii). The author of the "reader's guide", Su Qikang (蘇其康), associate professor of English literature at Zhongshan University, and also a PhD in comparative literature, asserts the same but makes an interesting observation. In comparison with a six-volume Chinese translation made from Richard Burton's English translation (1886) published in Beijing in 1982 (some say 1984), Su claims that the two-volume Taipei version is in effect an adaptation. Many stories are now very different from the "original" and in fact, the structure of the original is no longer recognizable. The frame-within-frame narrative structure of the original Arabic *Arabian Nights*, which is duplicated in Burton's English translation, has given way to discrete stories organized in a linear fashion but in no particular order (Su 1999, ix–xvii). Nevertheless, the two "prefaces" to the Taipiei Guiguan version assert that these distortions should not prevent readers from enjoying the stories, getting a flavour of the *Nights* as a work of literary art from the Middle East (referred to as *Tian Fang* in the title of Chinese translations) and learning about life in medieval Arabic-Islamic society.

The two "prefaces" to the Taipei translation hint at an interesting history of the Chinese translation, reception and assessment of *The 1001 Nights* that transcends political boundaries and, more important, the contemporary theoretical binary—of colonized and colonizer—in taking stock of, grappling with and coming to terms with cross-cultural encounters and exchanges in postcolonial studies and theories of world literature. This history, which has yet to be fully researched, mapped and written, opens up new vistas through which we may comprehend cross-cultural encounters and exchanges. It offers us an opportunity to reconsider not only "Orientalism" but also "World Literature". In the first instance, how would we retheorize Orientalism in a case where cultural encounter occurs outside the colonizer-colonized framework and is, more often than not in the contemporary context, mediated by a third party? Secondly, how would we theorize World Literature in which mediated translation is simultaneously a means of global circulation of literary works and a site of cross-cultural encounter and exchange? How would mediated translation refine and give nuance to our understanding of intercultural encounter that has thus far been narrowly located either in the dominant paradigm of western influence on the east, found in the pervasive discourses on modernity and modernization of the east, or in the marginalized attempts to address the instrumental role played by the Orient—the culture of the east in what Raymond Schwab (1984) calls the "Oriental Renaissance" in the west? In what ways can mediated translation help us reconsider the linear trajectory of world literature, in which Orientalism is implicated, from the national, always located in the east, to the international, forever located in the west and its capitals: London, New York and Paris?

The theoretical or analytical paradigms for the discussion of intercultural encounters I have mentioned above can be more specifically situated in the particular context of production of knowledge located in Middle Eastern Studies within the western academy, which has been dominated by the imitative or antagonistic reverberations of Edward Said's *Orientalism* (1978). Even translation has not escaped the hegemony of these paradigms. What gets chosen for translation or how a text is transformed during translation are theorized as implicating an Orientalist ideology operating behind the production of knowledge, whether one is engaged with the scrutiny of market forces driving what Bourdieu calls the "field of cultural production", or with the intricate processes of thinking and making language choices behind a translated text.

Such findings seem to confirm Said's thesis that in the west, the east is necessarily explicitly or implicitly represented as its other, subject to its will to power, and that any kind of representation the powerful makes of the powerless other, generally speaking, is frequently seen as a master-slave relationship. The translations of *The 1001 Nights* into English have not escaped this paradigm. Edward Said has a particular axe to grind with Edward Lane (1801–76) and Richard Burton (1821–90), whose English renditions of their respective *Arabian Nights* he sees as conforming to an Orientalist organization of knowledge, yet are reductive of the Orient, with their exoticizing and eroticizing of it fanning their own fantasy of mastery of their subject, or their other. The figures of Burton and Lane as Orientalists cast long shadows on Said's text, which is pervaded with references to their travels to the Orient, their role in cultural and academic Orientalism, and how their translations of *The Thousand and One Nights* played into the Orientalist agenda of European imperialism.

Cultural theories have made inroads into interrogating and subverting Said's paradigm, giving more complex and nuanced discussions of the relation between east and west.[1] However, they remain under the influence of, and haunted by the paradigmatic binaries that lie at the heart of Said's *Orientalism* and subsequent postcolonial theories and studies (Larzul 1996, 2004). The most pervasive theories of World Literature, intended to celebrate and

1 See, for example, Ballaster (2005); Brotton (1997) and (2002); Ganim (2005); Goody (1996); Jardine (1996); Jardine and Brotton (2000); Lewis (1996) and (2004); Lowe (1991); MacKenzie (1995); MacLean (2005); Melman (1992); Nash (2005); and Davis (2006).

encourage intercultural exchange between east and west in the west, are not immune to this "powerful west and powerless east" paradigm. The circulation of world literature through the means of translation is predetermined by the allure of the west, located in the metropolitan capitals of empire, on which the east casts its desiring eyes, with its various colonies competing for entry into the west. World literature, primarily an international canon of novels (understood as imitations of or derivations from the European novel), takes shape in the circulation of national literatures from the Third World to the First World, arriving successfully in London, New York or Paris (Moretti 2000, 2003, 2006; Damrosch 2003 and 2009; Casanova 2004).

Is there no way out of this intellectual impasse? Our personal experiences tell us that the ways in which we—intellectuals, scholars, academics, writers, artists, even hunters for the exotic, especially the multi-lingual and multi-cultural—respond to our cultural other(s) varyingly, contradictorily, complexly, are not always informed by our will to power in the same fashion. Whether we are powerful or powerless, we do not always desire to dominate the other; sometimes we even prefer to give in to the power, or allure, of the other even if the other is powerless. And then, how do we understand and define power? Rather than belabour these points I will pursue a line of inquiry that, I hope to show, is more productive for understanding and analyzing processes of cultural encounter and exchange and, more importantly, the attendant production and circulation of knowledge. I want to move away from the contentious and contested area of Middle Eastern studies, so caught up in preoccupations with power and power relations and shift focus to a site where the relationship between two different cultures is not so explicitly determined in terms of power. What lessons would we learn from another experience of intercultural encounter, that of the Middle East and China, two equally formidable empire complexes?

Mediated Translation and Global Circulation

World literature today provides an alternative to looking at diverse literary traditions together outside the politically charged influence studies that are inherent in comparative literature. Comparative literature has now moved away from influence studies to parallel studies that combine not only literary texts and traditions but also literature and the visual arts, music and cinema, opening up cultural exchange to disciplinary and medial encounters (e.g. literature and science, literature and the visual arts, literature and music, literature and cinema). World literature seems to restore the culturally downscaled encounters in comparative literature, but it does so by depoliticizing representations of cultural encounter accentuated in postcolonial studies, spearheaded by Said's *Orientalism*. By looking at modes of circulation and attendant modes of reading, world literature represents, nevertheless, a most welcome gesture. It acknowledges translation as a form of circulation that plays a role in the formation of an international canon.

The politics surrounding both translation and canon formation, nationally or internationally, and their attendant machinery, tend to be sidestepped, and even cultural encounters informing and underpinning the literary worlds (of world literature) often get brushed aside. If cultural encounter, which lies at the heart of both comparative literature and world literature, is rendered contentious by a hierarchy placing the west above the rest in the former, it is equally mismanaged in the latter by depoliticizing representations of cultural others and encounters with them. Nevertheless, world literature remains a potentially productive blueprint for a new comparative literature that reinstates comparative literary studies focused on cultural encounters. However, it will be necessary to re-politicize representations of cultural encounters, whether in the literary world (Hayot 2012) or outside in the machinery supporting, managing and promoting world literature, in order to think of translation beyond the transplanting of a literary work from one language into another. It needs to include circulation of a body of knowledge, such as Orientalism (Ouyang 2018), in the globalization of a literary work, and to consider circulation, here using the example of *The 1001 Nights*, as taking place along divergent but overlapping networks connected by multiple contact hubs.

The reception of the *Nights* in Chinese may not be a typical example of the encounter between Arabic and Chinese. Unlike pre-modern times, their relations are today mediated by Western Europe and North America. The popularity of *The 1001 Nights* in Europe prompted the Chinese to translate the stories but not until 1900, even though European (and especially English) translations of the *Nights* must have been available in China at the latest by 1870, when Kelly and Walsh, the first foreign bookshop, was founded in Shanghai. The Japanese, who translated the *Nights* into Japanese from as early as 1875, seemed to rely on Kelly and Walsh for their supply of European books. Tanizaki Jun'inchiro (1886–1965), one of the most celebrated Japanese novelists in the first half of the 20th century, refers to their role in making available English translations of the *Nights.* In the sixth chapter of *Tade kuu mushi* (1929; Some Perfect Nettles), the protagonist of his novel, Shiba Kaname,

> receives a complete set of Burton's editions as a gift from his friend Takanatsu, who has just returned from Shanghai. Takanatsu tells him how hard it was for him to get it there at *Kelly and Walsh* [. . .] and bring it back to Japan. (Sugita 2006, 138)

The implication of Europe in the spread, translation and reception of an Arabic work in Chinese is precisely why it is interesting, and hopefully edifying, to look at this encounter. It provides an alternative trajectory of circulation to that of the European translation and reception of *The 1001 Nights*. It also serves as a reminder of the multilingual and multicultural history of the mediated translation and reception of the *Nights* in Arabic.

Muḥammad Ibn Isḥaq Ibn al-Nadīm (d. 995 or 998) famously wrote of the Arabic *Thousand Nights* (*alf laylah*) as an Arabic translation of a storybook originally written in Persian known as *Hazār afsāneh*, or a thousand stories which, he explained, were fictional tales (*khurāfāt*) told at night (*asmār*). In the 10th century, and by the time he compiled the catalogue, *Fihrist*, of the extensive holdings in his bookshop in Baghdad, Arabic writers, whom he described as versed in the literary arts (*bulaghā'* and *fusahā'*), had already polished its language and begun to write in a similar vein. *Hazār afsāneh*, the first storybook ever, said to have been written for a Persian princess by the name of Humani, daughter of Bahman, begins with a king, who took a different woman every night and killed her at dawn, eventually marrying a princess (a daughter of one of the kings) by the name of Shahrazād, who was both intelligent and wise (*lahā ʿaql wa dirāyah*), and who started telling him stories at night but stopped in mid track at dawn. He stayed her execution so as to find out the ending of the story the following night. This went on for one thousand nights, until she bore him a child. When she confessed her machinations, the king, rather than punishing her for her deception, found himself in love with this wise woman and remained married to her. The king had a housekeeper (Qahrimānah) by the name of Dinārzād, who was in cahoots with Shahrazād.

Alexander the Great, Ibn al-Nadīm let it be known immediately, was in fact the first person ever (in history) who turned to storytelling at night during his military campaigns; among his entourage were clowns and storytellers, not for entertainment but for keeping vigil. Kings after him used *Hazār afsāneh* for similar purposes. The book contained less than 200 stories, for each would be told over a period of few nights. It was written in an "insipid" language (*ghathth bārid al-ḥadīth*) but this did not prevent literary figures such as Abū ʿAbdallāh Muḥammad b. ʿAbdūs al-Jahshiyārī (d. 942), the renowned 10th-century author of the *Book of Viziers and Secretaries*, from emulating its form and collecting Arabic, Persian and Greek stories in one book, albeit eschewing that night-within-and-into-night structure of storytelling. Each night would instead contain a self-sufficient story. Al-Jahshiyārī collected 480 stories or nights, and copied them by hand into around 50 folios, but he died before he could bring the number up to a full 1000.

Two other well-known works are mentioned in the same chapter (eight) and section (first of three) on nocturnal and fictional storytelling—*Sindbadnāmah* (aka The Seven Sages) and *Kalilah wa-Dimnah*—but discussion is deferred until the following paragraph on Indian storybooks (363–64). Though of Indian origin these two books were translated into Arabic from Persian by writers known for the beauty of their style, such as Ibn al-Muqaffaʿ (d. 759), whose Arabic renditions of pre-Islamic Persian works are today considered an integral, even indispensable part of the the classical Arabic literary tradition, or *Adab*. Ibn al-Muqaffaʿ's works, whether considered translations or adaptations, including the animal fables in *Kalīlah wa-Dimnah*, have become so assimilated into the fabric of the Arabic literary language that it is not possible to even think of Ibn al-Muqaffaʿ as a mere translator and his works "foreign" and as such non-canonical.

Ibn al-Nadīm's survey of translated storybooks drops hints of the divergent destinies of *The 1001 Nights* and *Kalīlah wa-Dimnah*. The anonymity of its translator and its "insipid" language seem to have relegated the former to the "popular" field of Arabic cultural production, together with the "epic cycles" (*sīrah*), while the latter, thanks to its famed translator and his "elegant" style, is elevated to "high" literature as the epitome of the "mirror for princes" genre. *The 1001 Nights*, despite its popularity even among the cultural elite of the Arabic-Islamic world, was of no literary consequence in Arabic until recently, after *The 1001 Nights* had acquired world literature status in Europe beginning in the 18th century, when Antoine Galland (1646–1715) translated, or rather adapted into French a body of stories from a 15th-century manuscript and other sources in two volumes (1704 and 1717). The *Arabian Nights* fever spread like wild fire, across Europe first, then around the world. *The 1001 Nights* in the state-of-the-art research is a shape-shifting chameleon that survives and thrives by globe trotting and crossing historical, geographical, cultural, linguistic, medial and generic boundaries. However, it remains without a definitive "original" text in any language.

The known "full" texts in Arabic, the Egyptian version published in Bulāq, Cairo in 1835 and the Indian version published in Calcutta, known as Macnagten or Calcutta II (1839–42), took shape in the aftermath of Galland's translation, developing from and expanding on his 15th-century manuscript by appending to it a variety of analogous manuscripts. The pre-modern global network of translation, adaptation and creation, from East and South Asia to the Mediterranean, that produced the textual network, or a body of overlapping texts written in "middle" Arabic, has yet to be mapped. Similarly, the post-Galland global proliferation of the "Oriental Tale", including *Aladdin* and *Ali Baba*, two "orphan tales" traceable neither to oral nor written Arabic origins, in literature, the visual arts, music, theatre and popular cultures across the six continents of the world, awaits full tracking. However, it is clear that *The 1001 Nights*, as a canonical work of world literature, exists only in the interstices of translation based on what we know, in fact, mainly mediated through Arabic first before the 10th century, followed by French in the 18th century, then by English, especially Burton, in the 19th century, which proliferated into other languages, including Chinese. The kernel of the Arabic full texts is possibly a body of tales purportedly translated from Persian, which may have been a Persian translation of a body of stories from multiple sources, such as Greek and Indian, onto which stories of all kinds and from all cultures are grafted throughout the ages. Galland's 15th-century manuscript is but one rendition of *The 1001 Nights*. Since the 18th century, European translations, including pseudo-translations and creations of oriental tales, have contributed to its making, even to the rise of its standing in Arabic literature.

The 1001 Nights in Chinese: Orientalism by Proxy?

As in the west, *The 1001 Nights*, famous and popular among the Chinese, is known as *Tian Fang Ye Tan* (天方夜譚) or *Yi Qian Ling Yi Ye* (一千零一夜), Chinese renditions of the *Arabian Nights* and *One Thousand and One Nights* respectively. It is primarily known as a collection of children's stories. In fact, an abridged version of *The 1001*

Nights was the first storybook I ever read when I was learning Chinese in Libya as a child. *Tian Fang* is the classical Chinese term for a region that is perhaps best conveyed by the medieval English term "Araby" (Metlizki 1977). *Ye Tan* means night talk, nothing like serious discussion but more like "table talk", or casual exchange of news and stories, or simply chatter. "Sindbad the Sailor" and "Aladdin and the Magic Lamp" are the two most memorable stories that I recall with fondness even today. When asked about *Tian Fang Ye Tan*, any Chinese person will immediately reply, "oh, yes, the famous children's stories from the Arab world". There are innumerable versions and editions of children's *Tian Fang Ye Tan*, all attributed to an anonymous "Arab" author, "*yi ming* 佚名", and they come in a plethora of shapes and sizes with little or next to no information on the sources and "authors"—compilers and translators—of the volumes. There is even less accounting for why some stories are chosen for inclusion and others are left out. *Yi Qian Ling Yi Ye* appears as titles of a number of collections of short stories in Taiwan, and *tian fang ye tan* stands for the fantastic in popular idiom.

The 1001 Nights found its way into Chinese as early as 1900, most likely through translations from European languages, especially Burton's English versions (1885–88). A Zhou Gueisheng (周桂笙) translated a selection of stories from the *Nights* in 1900, which he called *Yi Qian Ling Yi Ye* (Li 2000, 1.xix). During a search of the Chinese Union Library Catalogue, I also found a record of a four-volume translation by a Xi Rou (溪若) published in Shanghai in 1906. These and other translations, as well as adaptations from translations and adaptations from adaptations, all invariably given the titles *Tian Fang Ye Tan* or *Yi Qian Ling Yi Ye,* have been in continuous production up to the present.

There has been, it seems, a steady stream of *Arabian Nights* books in Chinese throughout the 20th and 21st centuries. *Tian Fang Ye Tan* is practically a literal translation of *Arabian Nights Entertainments*, including the archaic and exotic "twang", or slant Burton has given the *Nights* in his translation. This is not to say that the Chinese do not know of Antoine Galland, Edward Lane, Richard

Burton or John Payne (1842–1916)—these names are all mentioned in the different introductions to the various Chinese texts I currently have at my disposal. There is also the possibility of translating from Japanese translations, especially in Taiwan, a former Japanese colony, where early multi-volume Japanese translations (from as early as 1875) may have been known and available. At present, for one thing, more research is needed before any conclusion can be reached, and for another, what is available in the market never tallies with academic pronouncements. These are made mainly in introductions to various Chinese versions, written not by specialists in Arabic or Middle Eastern Studies but by comparative literature academics working primarily in the area of European literatures, clearly dominated by the anglophile, even when it comes to the transmission and dissemination of translations from the Arabic original.

In the 1930s, during the Chinese resistance to Japanese occupation, another stream of translations from the Arabic original, primarily of the Bulāq version, began to appear under the title *Yi Qian Ling Yi Ye*, a literal translation of the Arabic "one thousand and one nights". Two names emerge as heroes of such an enterprise. A Mr. Na Xun (納訓), apparently a Chinese Muslim, who made a five-volume translation in the 1930s known at the time as *Tian Fang Ye Tan*. In the 1950s a three-volume translation by the same Mr. Na appeared as *Yi Qian Ling Yi Ye*. Finally, a six-volume translation, a complete translation according to his Beijing publisher, appeared in 1982. This 1982 Beijing edition by Na Xun is the source text of the two-volume Taipei edition already mentioned, purportedly translated by a certain Zhong. Zhong, according to the "readers' guide" written by a Su Qikang, who at most edited Na's translation, restructured the work and reorganized the stories. Zhong's translation, however, has been very popular (Su 1999, xii) and has been in continuous demand since it first appeared in 1981. It is at least in its sixth reprint (1981, 1984, 1985, 1994, 1997 and 1999). And finally, a ten-volume translation of the Bulāq text was made by the now professor of Arabic at Beijing's Language Institute, Li Weizhong (李唯中), and published in Taipei in

2000. It was a limited edition and is now out of print. This translation is given the title of *Yi Qian Ling Yi Ye*.

From this very brief and sketchy overview, one may infer that Chinese translation of *The 1001 Nights* comes after and follows the trajectory of the European reception of the *Nights*, echoing its popularity, recent scholarship, academic priorities and intellectual agenda. From importing it as children's literature, then elevating it to a masterpiece of world literature, to an eventual insistence on identifying a single source text for translation despite awareness of the *Nights* as a cross-cultural composite work, it is finally used as a "text" to introduce the "marvellous" and "fantastic" world of Arabic-Islamic civilization in a "politically correct" global environment that insists on placing some emphasis on an education in non-western cultures and histories.[2]

In 2005, a travel book by Li Jing (李靜) and You Ziling (游紫玲) (Taipei: Jingfeng Wenhua) appeared under the title *Yi Qian Ling Yi Ye*, with the additional subtitle of *The Arabian Nights* in English. This book, pitched for the popular market, purports to take the reader on a tour, or "promenade", *san bu* (散步), of the civilization of "Araby" in the company of one of the "classics", "masterpieces", or even "scriptures", *jing dian* (經典), of the world. This book seems to go against the regular grain of books about the Arab world and Arabs in town. While it attempts to extol what it calls Arabic civilization, the knowledge it imparts is contradictory. It smacks of the kind of uncritical, popular Orientalism one finds often in American and British bookstores, where Arab(ic), Persian and Turkish cultures, not to mention others, are lumped together without distinction. And, at the end of the book, pages on belly dancing, customs of tea consumption, bread and Arab terrorism, all adorned with

2 I have not found any reference to *The 1001 Nights* as "adult" [pornographic] literature in Chinese. This does not necessarily mean there is no bifurcation of *The 1001 Nights* into "children's literature" and "adult literature," as in the Japanese case, but rather that at the present stage of my research I have not found similar evidence.

photographic clips, are added as a way of introducing the reader to the contemporary Arab world.

The illustrations accompanying the text are made up of Oriental and Orientalist materials haphazardly distributed across the visual landscape of the book usually without explanation. To put it simply, what one finds is a wholesale importation of kitch Orientalism or Orientalia fashionable in the west in the 19th century. The emphasis is on Araby's cultural difference from the Middle Kingdom, or China, even though this difference is never particularized; it belongs to the kind of fuzzy difference that also distinguishes the rest of the world, past and present, from China, from Chinese culture, or what one may call "self-defining othering". This comes across most strikingly in the illustrations found in the Chinese translations, the styles of which are invariably borrowed from a hodgepodge of Islamic, Biblical, Ancient Greek, Medieval European traditions of miniatures, and more often than not, from recent Japanese or European re-fabrications of these traditions.

But can we trust this contextual inference of what I call "Orientalism by proxy" as inherent in Chinese translation, both as a field of cultural production and as an instance of textual migration? By "Orientalism by proxy" I mean the migration of western Orientalism into the Chinese view of the Islamic Middle East, especially Araby, that defines the "civilized" self against an other that is both exoticized and eroticized, that fits into a stereotype of "the noble savage", "less civilized" or "religious" other (Larzul 2004); or alternatively that rationalizes cultural change, modernization in this case, by projecting the otherness of the past onto the "non-West" (Ganim 2005), or that opens up a cultural space for certain freedoms by deferring taboo issues to another site (Mack 1992). If I read into the publication of the Chinese translations of the *Nights*, in this case as a cultural field of production, the Orientalist impulses so familiar from Said's works and in the current frenetic Orientalism industry, would I find corroboration in the Chinese translations of *The 1001 Nights*, in the *Nights*' texts transformed during and through their journey into another culture, another language?

The translated texts, upon close scrutiny, tell a different story. I will demonstrate this by examining the Chinese translations of one story from *The 1001 Nights*, "Maʿrūf the Cobbler", but always in comparison with English translations, and use the lessons learned from this endeavour to rethink the theoretical and analytical underpinnings of Orientalism and World Literature. I move away from polarized positions towards Said's *Orientalism*: one put forward in postcolonial Middle Eastern studies informed by impulses for decolonization and an eagerness to condemn the western machinery of power and the "wrongs" it has done to and in the east (Kabbani 1986); and another found in their attendant responses, which point to the admiring intentions of the Orientalists, their positive attitude towards the east (Irwin 2006). I will instead take the Orientalism that is implicated in mediated translation, and consider it as a body of knowledge about the Orient, circulated globally along complex overlapping trajectories, in order to reorient world literature to the cultural encounter surrounding and within the literary world, and to move its circulation beyond a binary axis. I take a cue from Theo Hermans's notion of "thick translation" but tinker with his approach, focusing on translated texts rather than translators, and add to it Matthew Reynold's idea that "translation is creativity".

Translation as a Site of Thick Cultural Encounter

Theo Hermans (2003) argues for the injection of the notion of "thick translation" into the field of translation studies. He borrows the episteme "thick" from Clifford Geertz's term "thick description" and makes a case for translation as a cross-cultural encounter and translation studies as cross-cultural studies that must reflect the subject position of the translator; this includes the process through which one culture is habilitated into another in translation, and the context within which transfer of conceptual categories takes place across cultures. He gives as examples the discussions surrounding the English translations of Aristotle's *Poetics* and the Chinese *Book of Changes* and makes the following observation:

> The particular assumptions and presumptions informing domestic representations allow us to recognize—or to correlate—similarity in what is different and 'other', while at the same time they generate their own forms of dyslexia, enlarging certain aspects or kinds of similarity while creating blind spots elsewhere. (382)

Translation must accordingly be thought of as thick, as in "thick description" in cultural anthropology that no longer seeks accuracy—since that is impossible—but appreciation for both what is similar and what is different, and in what ways, from what angles, and in what respect, all in a self-conscious fashion. Hermans is here making a case for cross-cultural thick translation studies that will look at the act of translation in a variety of practices in different cultures, from a comparative perspective. This kind of translation studies:

> has the potential to bring about a double dislocation: of the foreign terms and concepts, which are probed by means of an alien methodology and vocabulary, and of the describer's own terminology, which must be wrenched out of shape in order to accommodate both alterity and similarity .(386)

I want to reverse the process Hermans proposes, and look at the translations of a text, each in its particular cultural, historical, linguistic, and subject-positioning context, and suggest that it would be equally fruitful to look at one moment of intercultural encounter in translation, locating it in the process of thick translation of which Hermans speaks. We will see translation as the liminal space where an intercultural encounter is negotiated in order to accommodate both alterity and similarity, each within a particular subjectified cultural, historical, epistemological and linguistic context. If we do, we will be able steer away from the binary so entrenched in discussions of cultural exchanges. Power has much to account for, but so do the following: how a subject positions herself vis-à-vis her own culture and the other, what language she speaks, how this language imprisons her in an epistemological framework, the historical circumstances she lives in, the field of cultural production she is engaged in, and what her agenda may be in terms of production of knowledge.

The Travels of "Maʿrūf the Cobbler"

I choose "Maʿrūf the Cobbler" for a number of reasons. The central motif of the story may serve as a metaphor for what I have been thinking of with regards to translation. When a text is translated from one language to another it migrates, leaving a home culture behind in order to find a new home in another culture, which entails living a new life. However, what is left behind, even when successful domestication into the new home occurs, can rear its ugly head and haunt the migrant. Maʿrūf runs away from his monstrosity of a wife, Fāṭimah al-ʿArrah, leaving her in Cairo, finds a new home in Ikhtiyān al-Khatan, marries the King's daughter and settles happily there, only to have his wife come after him. Put differently, a successfully translated text is often that which is domesticated into a new culture—that behaves like a native in a new language—while it retains traces from its past in another culture, another language.

More importantly, the two Chinese translations I have located for this story (Zhong 1999, 2.1223–89; Liu 2005, 518–40), what the *Nights* scholarship calls an "additional" or "orphan" story, found only in the Bulāq and Mcnagten texts, are purportedly from an original Arabic text, most likely the Bulāq edition (but the differences between Bulāq and Mcnagten are insignificant in this case). In addition to comparing Arabic and Chinese versions, I will also bring into the equation the available English translations (Burton 1886, 10.1–53; Dawood 1973, 372–404; Lyons 2008, 3.690–730), and see from a comparative perspective what actually goes on in the processes of translation. In particular I will examine the ways in which signs are structured similarly or differently in two or three distinct semiological systems that yield meanings the respective language users may comprehend within their particular linguistic culture (or culture of language use), which may in turn be simultaneously multiple in general (subject to heteroglossia) and individualized in particular (determined by the workings of the subject). I will tackle two areas of interest: one that is premised on, located in and expressive of difference, and the other of sameness.

In the first instance, how does a linguistic culture unfamiliar with monotheism convey the idea of one true God and the ways in which such an entity has structured a semiological system and spawned a tradition of storytelling informed by and steeped in a system of faith that has ramifications even in the minute belief in angels and genies? The idea of one omnipresent and omnipotent God, Allah, is perhaps less difficult a concept for audiences brought up in monotheism, such as Christians and Jews, to grasp than the Chinese readers of *The 1001 Nights*, for there is no equivalent monotheism in Chinese religions. The idea of one God may today be more readily comprehended by Chinese familiar with the monotheistic traditions—and most educated Chinese are—through translating "Allah" into "the True Lord" (*zhenzhu* 真主). However, how do Chinese and languages in general cope with signs that carry the weight of an entire cultural tradition constructed around this, let us say, mega-sign, which in turn structures into a worldview, and in an extremely intricate fashion, innumerable signs adopted and adapted from a variety of, let us say again, indigenous and foreign sources, only to spawn a new complex web of cultural traditions? In what ways do the two semiological systems embodied in the Chinese and English languages comprehend genies and their place, role and status in the Islamic worldview peculiar to Arabic vernacular fiction, a site on which pre-Islamic myths and traditions (including Biblical traditions), albeit transformed in Islam (Chraïbi 2005), feature prominently? Put differently, is it possible to make sense, fully, of the role the genie plays in informing the worldview, structure, narrative trajectory, and significance of an Arabic story in Chinese and English? In the second instance, where it is relatively safe to assume sameness in a number of cultures, such as social etiquette informing the conduct of men and women in society and structuring women-men relationships, is full equivalence possible? Or, in this particular story, does patriarchy manifest itself in the same manner across cultures, and does it offer identical representations of women?

Difference: Religious Worldview

"Maʿrūf the Cobbler" is, according to Peter D. Molan (1978), a morality tale with a mythic structure, "a ring of composition so typical of mythic lore" that it may be summarized as a tripartite flight-trial-return form (127). Maʿrūf, a poor but honourable cobbler, is unhappily married to a shrew, Fāṭimah al-ʿArrah. On a particularly bad day, he fails to bring her *kunāfah* pastry soaked in honey and she takes him to the local court, falsely accusing him of wife beating. Even though he is judged innocent, he is forced to sell his tools. Becoming even angrier, Fatimah files a further complaint with the governor. When Maʿrūf learns that the governor's agents, always harsh and violent in their dealings with the poor, are coming for him, he flees in terror. He arrives at the ruins of a mosque and starts weeping. A genie, disturbed by the noise, appears and upon hearing Maʿrūf's tale of woe takes him far away from his wife to a city called Ikhtiyān al-Khatan. There, the penniless and homeless Maʿrūf chances upon an older neighbour from Cairo. This old neighbour, now one of the rich merchants of Ikhtiyān al-Khatan, comes to Maʿrūf's aid. He advises Maʿrūf to pretend to be a rich merchant, to borrow money against a shipment of goods he would claim to be on its way, and to trade with the borrowed money. He even lends him a sum of money and goes so far as to fit him out with an appropriate suit and a mule and to introduce him to all the other merchants of the city. Maʿrūf, however, uses the money to help the poor of the city. Despite the grumblings of the merchants, who are now impatient to have their money back, Maʿrūf's reputation as a rich and generous man reaches the greedy king of Ikhtiyān al-Khatan. He marries his daughter to Maʿrūf, despite the objections of his vizier, who has designs on the princess and her father's kingdom.

Shortly after their marriage, the pressures on him to repay his debts and pay the princess's dowry to the king become unbearable, and Maʿrūf confides in his new wife. The princess lends him money and sends him into hiding, but tells the king that her husband has gone to meet his caravan. This time, Maʿrūf finds refuge with a farmer during his flight. When the farmer is away one day seeking food, he decides to help by ploughing the land. In a plot line smacking of

Aladdin and the Magic Lamp, Maʿrūf comes upon a subterranean vault divided into chambers filled with gold and precious stones. More importantly, he finds a seal ring engraved with mysterious talismans. He rubs it and a genie, Abū al-Saʿādāt, appears. The genie is the servant of the ring and the ring owner. Maʿrūf commands him to move the treasures to Ikhtiyān al-Khatan and is happily reunited with Princess Dunyā. His happiness is rudely interrupted by the scheming vizier, who gets him drunk one night, finds out his secret, steals his ring, banishes Maʿrūf and the king, and sets himself up to marry the princess and seize the kingdom. The princess pretends to agree to welcome the advances of the evil vizier, steals the ring from him through a ruse and brings home her father and husband. She keeps the ring until she dies. It is at this juncture, close to the end of the story, that Fāṭimah, his first wife, unfortunately finds her way to Maʿrūf, humbled by poverty and repentant. Too soft hearted to turn her way, Maʿrūf sets her up in her own palace. She proves ungrateful and tries to steal his ring. Maʿrūf's son happens to come by, sees her, and kills her. Happiness finally arrives for Maʿrūf. When he takes gifts to thank the farmer who helped him earlier in the story, he finds his beautiful daughter and marries her. In due time, he also finds a bride for his son, and everyone lives happily ever after.

The story, Molan argues, is a variant of the great "mono-myth" of the kind Joseph Campbell ([1949] 1973) studies in *The Hero with a Thousand Faces,* where he sums up in its tripartite structure—flight-trial-return—the quest of the riddle of life. Maʿrūf, faced with the culmination of evil in life (Fāṭimah, who symbolizes the eminence of death) flees, answering reluctantly the "call to adventure". He approaches the "threshold of adventure" when he arrives at the ruins of an old mosque. With the help of the genie, he arrives at Ikhtiyān al-Khatan, crossing the threshold into a supernatural world. Once magically settled, Maʿrūf is aided three times: by the merchant ʿAlī, by the princess, and by the supernatural being, Abū al-Saʿādāt. The aid in each case brings wealth, and in an increasing fashion. Each grant of aid, however, is a "test", or "trial", to see how Maʿrūf will handle something of great value. He fails to abide by "moderation in all things" each time, squandering his wealth away, not because the causes are wrong—aiding the poor is honourable—but because he is imprudently excessive. The supreme test comes when he obtains "the ultimate talisman", the magic ring. He is seduced into further excess—this time, drinking too much wine—and risks losing his wife and kingdom. "It is only here that Maʿrūf realizes his folly", Molan asserts,

> and learns his lesson. Here at the nadir of the mythological journey, Ma'rūf finally understands and receives his reward. He is reunited with the Princess and attains the prudent and proper use of the magic ring. It is now that his marriage, which had already taken place, becomes fruitfully consummated. (1978, 130)

For Molan, the fruitful consummation of the marriage represents the structurally necessary "sacred marriage" element of the schema [of a mythological journey]. The structurally necessary flight theme in the Maʿrūf tale, then, is represented by Maʿrūf's dual transformation into father and widower. Maʿrūf's son is the symbol of Maʿrūf's regeneration and this theme is further carried out as the tale progresses. The death of Princess Dunyā is the hero's return out of the underworld. His helper must be left behind, as he and his alter-ego son go forward. In our version, the world comes miraculously back to Maʿrūf with the reappearance of Fatimah. Thus, the threshold of the real world is recrossed; but it is a new Maʿrūf who faces the real world. He warns Fātimah that he is changed and will surely kill her if she crosses him. At first, he is cowed; but the world is unchanged, and she attempts to steal the ring, the symbol of Maʿrūf's new power and understanding—indeed, of his new life. But the world no longer has dominion over the new Maʿrūf. The terrors of death imminent in life are allayed symbolically in the slaying of Fātimah by Maʿrūf's new self—his son (1978, 131).

The "moral lesson" Molan speaks of is imparted through the structuration of the narrative in the form of a mythological journey as well as the saturation of the language of the story with Islamic symbols of loss as a result of excess. The main plot of "Maʿrūf the Cobbler" takes off from popular Arabic-Islamic lore with roots in the pre-Islamic past, the *asāṭīr al-awwalīn* (myths or legends of the ancients) that found their way into the Qurʾan and the *qiṣaṣ al-anbiyāʾ* (tales of the prophets) in both the Qurʾan and a multivalent body of storytelling outside the Qurʾan and the historical and exegetical tradition of *qiṣaṣ al-nabiyāʾ* (ʿAjīnah 1994, Kawwāz 2006, Tāj 2006). "Maʿrūf the Cobbler" combines elements from the legends of the pre-Islamic tribes of ʿĀd (mentioned alongside Thamūd and Pharaoh as Burton points out in a footnote) and "The Story of Solomon" from *Qiṣaṣ al-Anbiyāʾ*—his ring in particular. ʿĀd, a powerful tribe at the time of Noah and Hūd, was punished and made extinct for their treatment of the prophets, their tyranny and disregard for Allah's calls to faith (al-Ṭabarī 1989, 109, 118–31; Ibn Kathīr 1998, 93-106). The "city of many columns" (*iram dhāt al-ʿimād*) built by Shaddād Ibn ʿĀd, mentioned once in the Qurʾan, appears in the "tales of the prophets" (al-Kisāʾī 1998, 167–79; al-Thaʿlabī 1347 A.H., 99–102) and in *The 1001 Nights* in many guises; it is evocative of the vicissitudes of time and the fragility of life and used to extol patience and endurance. The splendour may remain, but life necessarily comes to an end (Hamori 1974). The real turning point in Maʿrūf's life occurs when he finds and takes control of "Solomon's ring", now poignantly attributed to Shaddād Ibn ʿĀd, perhaps as a double reminder of the necessity of virtue and, more importantly, that this is the Omnipotent God's command; for Solomon, with all his powers and mastery of the non-human world, including birds, animals, plants and genies, is like Shaddād Ibn ʿĀd, no longer with us.

There is an episode in the Arabic-Islamic Solomon legends that particularly resonates with "Maʿrūf the Cobbler". Solomon too loses his ring in which all his power resides for forty days, the duration of the transgression by one of his wives of the most sacred Islamic edict, to "worship no God but Allah". Jarādah, a new wife Solomon acquires after he conquers her idolater father, misses her father and asks to have some his clothes. She then uses them to make an effigy of her father, which she worships for 40 days. When Solomon finds out, he abstains from life and goes into the desert to worship God for 40 days. This, however, is not enough, and one day a recalcitrant genie steals his ring, which Solomon leaves with a trusted servant whenever he spends the night with a wife, in order not to taint it. Solomon is bereft of his ring, his power, for another 40 days, during which time the evil genie rules in his place and he wanders along the seashore like a madman, feeding on the fish he catches. Finally, the genie throws the ring into the sea and a fish swallows it. Solomon catches this very fish at the end of the 40-day period and when he cleans it, preparing to cook it for dinner he finds his ring in its belly (al-Ṭabarī, 1989, 371–75; al-Kisāʾī 1998, 356–57; al-Thaʿlabī 1347 A.H., 224–27). With the recovery of his ring, Solomon returns to power. Maʿrūf follows the same trajectory, albeit twice, in losing and recovering the magic ring. The culprits in the two stories are similarly punished by death.

Clearly, the symbolic weight of the two signs, references to Shaddād Ibn ʿĀd and Iram Dhāt al-ʿImād, and to Solomon and the temporary loss of his ring, cannot easily be conveyed in another language, a different semiological system uninformed by the web of signs (signifiers -> signifieds), or words that embody myths, spawned in the Arabic language. At the outset, the parodic effect of the name given to the servant of the ring, Abū al-Saʿādāt, or father of fortunes, is unavoidably lost not only in translation but also through transliteration. Burton's footnote, giving the name the meaning of "father of prosperities", comes closest to an awareness of its significance in the story; Abū al-Saʿādāt is indeed the father of Maʿrūf's good fortunes. Furthermore, even though the English language shares the Biblical tradition with Arabic, the symbolic systems of the same stories are not identical in Arabic and English. The absence of this equivalence is especially evident in the divergent translations of the various sub-species of the genies mentioned by Abū al-Saʿādāt in his significance-setting conversation with Maʿrūf. In one Chinese translation (Liu 2005), this key passage is omitted. As a result, the broader context of the story, which is fundamental to an understanding of the worldview framing the story I have already discussed above, is entirely lost.

"Genie", for example, is translated into *jing ling* (精靈) or *sheng ling* (生靈) in Chinese by Liu and Zhong respectively. *Jing ling* may sound like genie but is in reality a translation of "fairy", as in 'Tinker Bell" of *Peter Pan* fame, using two characters familiar to readers of Chinese stories—*jin* (精) meaning non-human creatures that can sometimes transmogrify into humans, and *ling* (靈) meaning a kind of knowledge that goes beyond reason and empiricism. In the other translation, the more popular Zhong Si version, the dialogue between Maʿrūf and the genie in which the latter tells Maʿrūf about who he is and where the treasures come from, is translated in full. However, it makes no sense of the world of genies in the "tales of the prophets" or *The 1001 Nights* to those who come from an Islamic cultural background or who are familiar with Arabic storytelling. This is how Abū al-Saʿādāt introduces himself to Maʿrūf in Zhong's Chinese (rendered into English):

> I am the king of gods (*shenwang* 神王) who protects the ring in your hand [. . .]. I rule over 72 tribes (*zhongzu* 種族), each tribe of 72 thousand tribesmen. Each tribesman rules over 1000 giants, and each giant over 1000 slaves, and each slave in turn rules over 1000 earth gods (*tudishen* 土地神).

I have quoted three terms in Chinese here because they have no correspondence in Arabic or English. I have translated *zhongzu* (種族) as tribe, which is only vaguely accurate. It is a term used in Chinese to refer to "nations" based on race. As for *shenwang* (神王) and *tudishen* (土地神), these two terms have one character in common, that is *sheng*, which means a kind god who can rank high or low as a member of the Chinese pantheon. It never denotes the omniscient, omnipresent monotheistic God who just is and rules supreme. *Shen* is, rather, in popular Chinese belief, a rank that a human can achieve by being virtuous in this life—and there are three systems of belief in Chinese: Buddhist, Daoist and, for the lack of a better word, popular. He is the "spirit" of someone who lives on after death in a kind of upper world and is given power, and at times armies, to help maintain justice in the human world. There is such a notion as "king of gods" in Chinese *shen* (神), which is usually juxtaposed to *gui* (鬼), a ghost, the spirit of an evil person condemned to live forever in the darkness of a nether world. *Tudishen* is a very low-ranking god given the task of protecting a small lot of land. Taipei is littered with temples erected for these local gods.

The Islamic lore of genies and their organization as parallel to humanity, most clearly spelt out in Solomon legends and reiterated in *The 100 Nights*, is domesticated into Chinese culture, becoming in the process integrated into the popular Chinese pantheon. This form of domestication by transforming an "alien" belief system into a "familiar" one makes sense especially if the translation is to be successful; for in this way the translation strikes a familiar chord with its audience even as it takes them on an adventure into a new world that is far from exotic but rather looks, feels and sounds quite familiar. Sameness is what makes difference palatable, edible and digestible. Does this explain Zhong Si's popularity? If this is what happens to difference, then what becomes of sameness? Let me now turn to my second example, which has to do with notions of womanhood.

Sameness: Social Etiquette

Maʿrūf's two homes are defined, one may argue, by his relationship with his two wives and the role they play in his life. His first wife, Fāṭimah al-ʿArrah, is ugly, nasty, crafty, dishonest, violent and a destroyer of men; his second wife, the princess of Ikhtiyān al-Khatan, is beautiful, intelligent, supportive and maker of kings. Maʿrūf's escape from Cairo is precipitated by Fātimah's nastiness. She even catches up with him after his second wife's death, when she tries to steal his ring and kill him. His second wife, Princess Dunyā, is her exact opposite. Once she is married, she becomes loyal to her husband. When she finds out the truth of his identity, she gives him money and sends him away so he may escape certain punishment. He understandably comes back to her when he finds Shaddād Ibn ʿĀd's treasures. When the "evil" vizier gets him drunk, steals his ring, sends him and later the king off to "nowhere", she pretends to want to marry him, then kicks him in the chest and face, takes away her husband's ring from the vizier, brings back her husband and farher, gives birth to a beautiful son, and is instrumental in Maʿrūf's inheriting kingship, all the while keeping the ring safe for her husband. These two "archetypal" women represent two sides of a coin that is womanhood and, in this particular case, physical beauty is synonymous with moral virtue.

Fāṭimah's nickname, al-ʿArrah, is a double-entendre. Read al-ʿArrah in the classical register, it means to be a shame or a disgrace, or to bring shame or disgrace; pronounced al-ʿUrrah, it then means mange or scabies or dung. She is described as *"fājirah sharrāniyyah qalīlat al-ḥayāʾ kathīrat al-fitan"* (Bulāq [1835] 1999, 6.653). Burton, Dawood and Lyons could not quite convey the implication and signification of these adjectives in their respective translations. Lyons translates these telling adjectives as: "His wife, Fatima, was an evil-minded, vicious and shameless intriguer who was nicknamed 'Dung'" (2008, 3.690). Dawood renders it blandly as, "He was married to a spiteful termagant called Fatimah, nicknamed by her neighbours 'the shrew' on account of her sour disposition and scolding tongue" (1973, 372). Burton comes closer in "and he had a wife called Fatimah, whom the folk had nicknamed 'the Dung'; for that she was a whorish, worthless wretch, scanty of shame and mickle of mischief" (1886, 10.1). There is a skewed focus on interiority in English translations. They give a sense that these adjectives describe the nature of Fāṭimah, thus defining her relationship with Maʿrūf, which is abuse on her part and fear on his. Lyons sees that:

> She dominated her husband, and every day she would hurl abuse and a thousand curses at him, while for his part he was afraid of her evil nature and of the harm that she might do him. He was a sensible man, anxious to protect his honour, but he was poor. (2008, 3.690)

In Dawood:

> She used her husband with heartless cruelty, cursing him a thousand times a day and making his life a burden and a torment. Maʿrūf was a sensitive man, jealous of his good name, and in time he grew to fear her malice and dread her fiery temper. (1973, 372)

And in Burton: "She ruled her spouse and abused him; and he feared her malice and dreaded her misdoings; for that he was a sensible man but poor-conditioned" (1886, 10.1).

These adjectives are best read not just as describing interiority but also as statements of exteriority, of her conduct in public that affects his relationship not only with her but also with society at large. He is, after all, a good, honourable man: *"li-annahu kāna rajulan ʿāqilan yastaḥī ʿalā ʿirdihi"* (because he was a man of reason who guarded his honour jealously), and therefore lets her be:

> *wa-kānat ḥākimah ʿalā zawjihā wa-fī-kull yawm tasubbuhu wa-talʿanuhu alf marrah wa-kāna yakhshā sharrahā wa-yakhāf min adhāhā* (She imposed her will on her husband. She cursed him every day a thousand times while he feared her evil [tongue] and was afraid of the harm she might do him). (Bulāq 1999, 6.653)

It is the fear of losing face, of being shamed, disgraced and dishonoured in public that makes him put up with her abuse at home. Once that is out of the bag, or when she shames him in public, he leaves. *Fājirah* must then be read as a synonym of *qalīlat al-ḥayāʾ*, as "mindless of public disgrace" and *sharrāniyyah* or *kathīrat al-fitan*, as causing public shame. They must be juxtaposed to his *ʿāqilan, yastaḥī ʿalā ʿirdihi*, which means not only that he is "jealous of his good name" (Dawood 1973, 372) as Dawood has it, but also that he refrains from conducting himself in any way that would bring dishonour upon himself or those around him. So, as Lyons's translation indicates ("He is a sensible man, anxious to protect his honour" [2008, 3.690]), honour is the crux of the matter, for it determines his standing in society and gives him power. His love for the princess then makes sense because she maintains his honour against all odds.

Her beauty is only ever described as "*jamīlah*" and "*dhāt ḥusn wa-jamāl*", terms that depict moral attributes and actions. Here, her actions speak for her moral beauty. When she finds out that Maʿrūf is a penniless cobbler living extravagantly as a wealthy merchant on borrowed money, including her father's, she helps him. She gives three reasons for this, rendered by Burton as: "thou art become my husband and I will never transgress against thee"; "it would be bruited among the folk that I married a man who was a liar, and impostor, and this would smirch mine honour"; and "Furthermore, and if he kill thee, most like he will require me to wed another, and to such thing I will never consent; no, not though I die" (Burton 1886, 10.24). These sentiments are repeated in Lyons as "but I have become your wife and I'm not going to neglect you"; "Then everybody would know that I married a fraud and I would be disgraced"; and "Also, if my father has you killed, he may try to marry me to another man and that is something I shall never accept, even if it costs my life" (Lyons 2008, 3.708). These explanations disappear in Dawood's translation:

> When she heard the cobbler's story, the Princess burst into a fit of laughter and said: "Truly, Ma'ruf, you are a subtle rogue! But what are we to do? What will my father say when he learns the truth? The Vizier has already sown suspicions in his mind. He will surely kill you, and I shall die of grief". (1973, 390)

These reasons are important because they mirror Maʿrūf's notions of honour and marriage as well as the ethical paradigm framing a woman's conduct as a member of society and especially as a wife. Loyalty to and support for a husband are wifely duties and of equal importance to maintaining his honour, and therefore, hers. While Zhong's translation (1999, 2.1254) comes very close to those of Lyons and Burton, Liu's Chinese translation sums this paradigm up in a four-character expression, *"fu qi yi chang* 夫妻一場" (2005, 528), which may be translated as "we have been husband and wife all this time", and which implies to any Chinese the duties expected of both husband and wife within the institution of marriage.

The addition of *"dwei wo qing shen yi zhong* 對我情深義重" ("you have been loving and loyal towards me") (Liu 2005, 528), confirms this further, that the responsibility must be mutual. That the princess is Maʿrūf's mirror ethically is accentuated in their juxtaposition to Fāṭimah al-ʿArrah, the transgressor of the ethical paradigm structuring marriage, or the husband and wife relationship not just between them but also in society. This understanding of marriage in Arabic-Islamic culture is easily translated into Chinese and requires no "domestication", for there is no paradigmatic difference between the two cultures at the ethical level and perhaps even in how ethics are bounded up in aesthetics. Fāṭimah's physical "ugliness", as juxtaposed to the Princess's "beauty", bespeaks her ethical depravity, and the inverse must be said of the Princess: that her physical beauty is a sign of her goodness. The "inadequacies" of, or "lapses" in English translations, in their turn towards interiority, even in Burton, show up the sameness between Arabic-Islamic and Chinese cultures where the "definition" of womanhood is at stake. However, is sameness total?

At the outset, sexuality, acknowledged in Lyons and Dawood and exaggerated in Burton, is completely expurgated in the two Chinese translations. There is no reference to sexuality, let alone sex. This may be part of the "orientalism by proxy" I spoke of earlier, but in reverse. As a masterpiece of world literature, it is given the status equal to a Chinese classic, which is viewed as too lofty for the kind of explicit references to sex so abundant in popular fiction and visual forms of expressions. There may be a cultural difference here too. The relative openness of Arabic "high" literature to treatment of sexuality and sex is not duplicated in Chinese culture. This flagrant omission is, however, less telling of cultural difference than the minute details of language that go towards bringing to life the two female protagonists of the story, into conjuring up in the mind of the reader the image of the two women, all fleshed out and in action. One instance of cultural difference may be located in the visual aesthetics encoded in language that in turn become verbal aesthetics, or, put differently, in the visualizing capacity of language regardless of the subject. In art, there can be beauty in the portrayal of what would conventionally be known as "ugly", whether we speak of works that use as their material word, image or sound. The aesthetics of the grotesque, for example, centre upon representations of the abnormal, the ugly. Let me turn to the ways in which Fāṭimah comes to life in Chinese. I will focus on the first paragraph of the story that offers characterization of both Maʿrūf and Fāṭimah and, more important, their relationship within the ethical framework of marriage I have already discussed.

In his translation of this paragraph, Liu's Maʿrūf is gentle, honest, and works hard every day to support his wife. He puts up with his wife because he does not want his problems to be known. Fāṭimah is, on the other hand, ill tempered, vain, greedy for a life of luxury, and loses her temper when she is dissatisfied. She quite often does not cook for her husband. Zhong's Maʿrūf is a humble man who knows his station in life. He is law-abiding and honest, reliant on hard work to make a living, and spends whatever he makes each day. Fāṭimah does not treat him like a human being. She not only nags him, but also makes him work on an empty stomach, caring not one bit about his health, when he does not make enough money (this is also reflected in Lyons). This kind of juxtaposition between Maʿrūf and Fāṭimah is not found in the Arabic original or English translations but makes perfect sense in Chinese. Maʿrūf does not deserve what he gets from Fāṭimah precisely because of his attributes. If he were vain, dishonest (but we know he can be dishonest) and lazy, he would have deserved someone like Fāṭimah as a wife. Fāṭimah is a "bad" wife because she is, in Arabic *"fājirah, sharrāniyyah, qalīlat al-ḥayāʾ kathīrat al-fitan"* and, above all, because she nags at home non-stop, does not treat him like a human being, and lets him go hungry. More important, she is vain. Vanity is the root of evil. It is unacceptable in a man, let alone a woman. A woman's vanity is her husband's downfall. However, these two characters are brought to life by the adjectives used to describe them and the adverbs applied to their actions, especially in Zhong's version. This first paragraph of the story conjures up in a few sentences the female-dominated relationships in Chinese fiction. The most famous couple is found in a famous 17th-century "low brow" novel known as *Marriage Destiny to Admonish the World* (*Xing Shi Yin Yuan* 醒世姻緣) and comprises Di Xich'en (狄希陳) and Xue Suchie (薛素姐). Suchie's antics, as detailed in the novel, deviate from the "norm" of behaviour expected of a proper Chinese woman, and as she grows more and more mad, her physical beauty deteriorates into ugliness.

Her abnormality starts before she is born. She is the reincarnation of a fox fairy seeking revenge upon her murderer, now reincarnated as Di Xich'en. The night before her wedding, she dreams that her heart has been ripped out and replaced by an evil one to better serve the purpose of vengeance. She shocks everyone during her wedding by bawling out the master of ceremonies. She then locks her husband out of the bridal chamber for three nights in a row, much to the distress of the bridegroom himself and the parents of both families. He finally uses trickery to consummate the marriage. Soon after the wedding, they get into a quarrel, which turns into a fight. Her husband grabs hold of a whip, which she immediately snatches from him. She then pushes him onto the floor with one hand, sits on his head, and gives him a full beating. She claws, slaps, clubs, and bites. On one occasion, she bites a piece of flesh almost completely off his arm. She interrogates and tortures her husband. At one point, she ties him to her bed and stabs him with two large needles. At another time, she jabs him with iron tongs. A third time she presses his fingers on heated pens. She uses him to feed the mosquitoes in her room. When he escapes to the capital and takes another wife, she dresses up a pet monkey in Di's clothes and clobbers it as if it were her husband. She sponsors a Buddhist ritual for the deceased for her living husband. She tries to use voodoo to murder him, too. She shows no respect for her parents and his. When she receives a beating from her mother-in-law, she sets their house on fire. She is responsible for the paralysis of both her mother-in-law and her own father, and eventually for the deaths of all her parents-in-law and parents. When her father-in-law takes in a new concubine, she tries to castrate him in order to prevent the birth of another heir. She uses the reverse sides of the portraits of her deceased in-laws as wallpaper for a shed (also in Chen 1993, 177-185).

Fāṭimah is equally evil and mad. Fāṭimah and Suchie are twins, but each brought up in a different culture—if I may use this analogy to speak of the ways in which cultural domestication takes place in the space of translation that necessarily situates itself in and takes its departure from the linguistic culture of the target language. A story comes to life in a new culture when it can seamlessly integrate into its linguistic culture, become a native sign in a semiological system premised on language and language use. Zhong's version is a good example of success in translation. "Maʿrūf the Cobbler" reads like a Chinese story that both engages with Chinese ethics and taps into Chinese aesthetics of representation. It evokes at the same a Chinese tradition of similar stories about shrews and their suffering husbands. This is achieved through the addition of small details that are irrelevant to the original audience but make perfect sense to the target audience. There is much difference in sameness.

Translation and Creativity in World Literature

Chinese translations of *The 1001 Nights*, as we have seen, are initially mediated by Burton, and informed by Orientalism, here understood as a body of knowledge about the Orient produced in the west, even when translators turned to the 19th-century Arabic full texts in the 20th century, for these texts were in part shaped by and in Orientalism. Orientalism here inhabits the literary worlds produced in translations, or more aptly, mediated translations, through which it is circulated around the globe as an inexorable part of *The 1001 Nights*. Both traverse linguistic, literary, cultural, and even religious boundaries along divergent routes, which are in turn connected by various networks overlapping at multiple temporal and spatial contact hubs. As such, *The 1001 Nights* conforms to but significantly goes beyond the horizon of expectation inherent in theories of world literature. It follows the proposed mode of circulation from one national field, Arabic in this case, to the international field, through translation into European languages here, but only in one instance closed in by a temporality located in the 18th and 19th centuries as well as a spatiality grounded in the binarization of Europe as world and Araby as its periphery.

However, opening up this narrow temporal and spatial framework of circulation to a broader canvas, and at the same time a more complex understanding of translation, rather than insisting on "untranslatability" (Apter 2013), brings into view a map of overlapping networks of circulation along the routes of which a literary work, chameleon-like, takes a different shape upon its arrival at each contact hub that serves as a center of world literature. Here, stories, not necessarily novels, also take shape in cultural encounters that necessarily inhabit their literary worlds. Orientalism, whether the kind of knowledge produced in the west about the east as defined by Said, or any body of knowledge produced about self and other in the processes of cultural encounter, remains inevitably an indelible thread in the fabric of world literature.

In the two Chinese translations of *The 1001 Nights* I have looked at, power plays little part in shaping the translated text. This applies equally to the English translations I have looked at. These English translations, to a great extent, reflect in their own ways the various stages of historical development of the west's views of the east through translations of *The 1001 Nights*, from Burton's highly exotic and erotic translation that paradoxically embodies Victorian morality, to Dawood's modern exclusive focus on interiority and Lyons's anti-Orientalism stance. All the translations seem to "struggle" with domesticating alien concepts and ideologies into a language that will be comprehended in terms of their "native" concepts and ideologies. Orientalism, as a theory interrogating the ways in which a culture comes to terms with an "other", can be refined to accommodate multiple patterns of cultural encounter if we re-examine each translation of *The 1001 Nights* as "thick translation".

Little research has been done on *The 1001 Nights* in Chinese, despite the historical relations between China and the world of Islam, and the popularity of the *Nights* among the Chinese reading public. The reasons are not immediately apparent. The reception of the *Nights* in Chinese is an interesting area of inquiry because it marks the beginning of a new way of cross-cultural interaction between China and the Middle East at the turn of the 20th century, this time mediated by a third party, certainly Europe and perhaps even Japan. At the same time, it points to translation as an important site of cultural encounter, of the migration of worldviews from one culture to another, here negotiated in language. However, the nature of the third-party mediation remains relatively unknown. Is there an "adult" (pornographic) tradition of *The 1001 Nights* in Chinese, as in English and Japanese, for example? This is one obvious question that does not yet have an answer. In addition, the sources and dates of Chinese translations cannot be pinned down. These all present challenges to the use of Chinese translations of *The 1001 Nights* in order to interrogate issues relevant to processes of cultural exchange. Is social etiquette picked up from Burton or the Bulāq text? Does a Chinese translation reflect developing modern sensibilities, which are glimpsed in a comparative look at Burton, Dawood and Lyons? And how important is class (whether that of the translator or the implied reader) in the final shape of translation? Looking after a husband's health through cooking is more likely to be a middle-class sentiment. Upper class Chinese women do not have to cook, since they have cooks and servants to take care of all their domestic chores.

This said, even a tentative comparative analysis of translations rendered in two different languages points to an area of distortion that occurs in one thick semiological system's attempt to comprehend, interpret, domesticate and express another culture, equally grounded in a thick system of thought and tradition of expression. This distortion may easily be located outside the dialectics of self and other that, informed by power, lead to misrepresentation. Cultural encounters must be grappled with from multiple perspectives and examined through a diverse body of sources. Terms like *Ah La Bo*, which recur in contemporary Chinese writings, are but one source of information. They demonstrate that the Chinese, like the rest of the world, know the Arab World as a "nation" occupying a finite parcel of land in the Middle East in the 20th century. This awareness of one of the contemporary Arab self-definitions does not necessarily exonerate the Chinese from misrepresentation (one may say a benign Orientalism in this case), for the Middle East remains a very vague "non-China" to the Chinese regardless of where they live (China, Taiwan, Hong Kong or the "diaspora"). The Chinese misrepresentation of the Arab world is clearly not driven by their will to dominate the Arabs. The question of representation and its attendant misrepresentation must remain open after *Orientalism*, for any theory of cross-cultural representation must take into consideration, in addition to discourse's relationship to power, the very structure of thought embedded in the language underpinning the discourse.

The singularity of each translation, whether into Chinese or English, points to another area of equal interest and importance. This is the creative mobilization of linguistic, literary and cultural tools accessible to each translator—in addition to his or her location in time and space, class, training, and attendant position towards and perspective of the cultural other—to fashion a "likeness", as Matthew Reynolds (2011, 2013) would say, that is necessarily grounded in a creative act of imagination and requiring interpretation and illustration of one language through another. The semantic and semiotic fields of each language are so wide-ranging that exact meaning always escapes capture. The ambiguity multiplies in translation between two languages. Translation is then, necessarily, a creative reckoning occurring in the liminal space between one language and another. It demands as well as produces creative understanding of one language and use of another.

This is true even, or especially, of successful "domestication" that seemingly transplants a "foreign" story seamlessly, even giving it roots in a "local" literary landscape, as we see in the Chinese translations of "Maʿrūf the Cobbler". Small details of each translation give this away, or reveal the creative impulse behind every step taken in translation, whether in the form of interpretation, illustration or paraphrasing, and disrupt any totalizing understanding of translation, whether this is Said's Orientalism or his detractors' anti-Orientalism. Diversity, of all kinds, in time and space, objectives, subject positions, linguistic abilities, literary and cultural backgrounds, and imaginative creativity must inform our understanding of the totality of the translations of *The 1001 Nights*, and more important, particularly in the context of theories of world literature, of *The 1001 Nights* as a literary work, by now a universally acknowledged canonical work of world literature, as existing only in mediated translation—translation here as understood by Reynolds—that has travelled around the world along multiple, overlapping networks of circulation.

Acknowledgements

A substantial part of this chapter was originally published in 2009 as "The Arabian Nights in English and Chinese Translations: Differing Patterns of Cultural Encounter" in *Les Mille et une nuits et le récit oriental: En Espagne et en Occident*, edited by Aboubakr Chraïbi et Carmen Ramirez, 371–400. Paris: L'Harmattan. The author is grateful to the editors for their permission to republish it in this extensively revised version.

Bibliography

ʿAjīnah, Muḥammad. 1994. *Mawsūʿat asātīr al-ʿarab ʿan al-jāhiliyyah wa-dalālatihā*. 2 vols. Beirut: Dār al-Fārābī.

Bulāq. [1835] 1999. *Alf laylah wa-laylah*. 6 volumes. 1999. Beirut: Dār Sādir.

Apter, Emily. 2013. *Against World Literature: On the Politics of Untranslatability*. London and New York: Verso.

Ballaster, Ros. 2005. *Fabulous Orients: Fictions of the East in England 1662–1785*. Oxford: Oxford University Press.

Brotton, Jerry. 1997. *Trading Territories: Mapping the Early Modern World*. London: Reaktion Books.

—. 2002. *The Renassiance Bazaar*. Oxford: Oxford University Press.

Burton, Richard. 1886. *The Book of The Thousand Nights and a Night*. 10 vols. London: The Burton Club.

Campbell, Joseph. [1949] 1973. *The Hero with a Thousand Faces*. Princeton, NJ: Princeton University Press.

Casanova, Pascale. 2004. *The World Republic of Letters*. Translated by M.B. DeBevoise. Cambridge, MA: Harvard University Press.

Chen, Fan Pen Li. 1993. "Suchieh: The Untamed Shrew of Hsing-shih yin-yuan." In *To Speak or Be Silent*, edited by Lina B. Ross, 177-185. New York: Chiron Publications.

Chraïbi, Aboubakr 2005. "Texts of the *Arabian Nights* and Ideological Variations." In *New Perspectives on The Arabian Nights: Ideological Variations and Narrative Horizons*, edited by Wen-chin Ouyang and Geert Jan van Gelder, 17–26. London: Routledge.

Damrosch, David. 2003. *What Is World Literature*? Princeton, NJ: Princeton University Press.

—. 2009. *How to Read World Literature*. Oxford: Wiley-Blackwell.

Davis, Natalie Zemon. 2006. *Trickster Travels: A 16th-Century Muslim between Worlds*. New York: Hill and Wang.

Dawood, N. J. 1973. *Tales from the* Thousand and One Nights. London: Penguin Books.

Ganim, John M. 2005. *Medievalism and Orientalism: Three Essays on Literature, Architecture and Cultural Identity.* Houndmills: Palgrave Macmillan.

Goody, Jack. 1996. *The East in the West.* Cambridge: Cambridge University Press.

Hamori, Andras. 1974. "An Allegory from the *Arabian Nights*: The City of Brass." In *On the Art of Medieval Arabic Literature,* 145–63. Princeton, NJ: Princeton University Press.

Hayot, Eric. 2012. *On Literary Worlds.* Oxford: Oxford University Press.

Hermans, Theo. 2003. "Cross-cultural Translation Studies as Thick Translation." *Bulletin of the School of Oriental and African Studies* 66 (3): 380–89.

Ibn Kathīr, Abū al-Fidā'. 1998. *Qiṣaṣ al-anbiyā',* In *Al-bidāyah wa-l-nihāyah,* edited by Ṣidqī Jamīl al-ʿAṭṭār, 93–106. Beirut: Dār al-Fikr.

Ibn al-Nadīm, Muḥammad Ibn Isḥaq. 1988. *Al-fihrist.* Edited by Riḍā al-Mazandarānī. Beirut: Dār al-Masīrah.

Irwin, Robert. 2006. *For Lust of Knowing: The Orientalists and their Enemies.* London: Allen Lane.

Jardine, Lisa. 1996. *Worldly Goods: A New History of the Renaissance.* London: Macmillan.

Jardine, Lisa, and Jerry Brotton. 2000. *Global Interests: Renaissance Art between East and West.* London: Reaktion Books.

Kabbani, Rana. [1986] 1994. *Imperial Fictions: Europe's Myths of Orient.* London: Pandora.

al-Kisā'ī, Abū Bakr Muḥammad Ibn 'Abdallāh. 1998. *Bad' al-khalq aw Qiṣaṣ al-anbiyā'.* Edited by al-Ṭāhir b. Sālimah. Tunis: Dār Nuqūsh ʿArabiyyah.

Larzul, Sylvette. 1996. *Les traductions françaises des Mille et une nuits: étude des versions Galland, Trébutien et Mardrus.* Paris: L'Harmattan.

—. 2004. "Les Mille et une nuits d'Antoine Galland: traduction, adaptation, creation." In *Les Mille et Une Nuits en partage,* edited by Aboubakr Chraïbi, 251–66. Paris: Sindbad Actes Sud.

Lewis, Reina. 1996. *Gendering Orientalism: Race, Femininity and Representation.* London: Routledge.

—. 2004. *Rethinking Orientalism: Women, Travel and the Ottoman Harem.* London and New York: I. B. Tauris.

Li, Jing and You Ziling. 2005. *Yi Qian Ling Yi Ye.* Taipei, Jingfeng Wenhua.

Li, Weizhong. 2000. "Introduction." In *Yi Qian Ling Yi Ye,* 1. xix–xxii. Taipei: Yuanliou.

Liu, Guangming. 2005. "Xiejiang Malufu." In *Tian Fang Ye Tan*, 518–40. Taipei: Shangzhou.

Lowe, Lisa. 1991. *Critical Terrains: French and British Orientalisms.* Ithaca, NY: Cornell University Press.

Lyons, Malcolm C. 2008. *The Arabian Nights: Tales of 1001 Nights.* 3 vols. London: Penguin.

Mack, Robert L. 1992. *Oriental Tales.* Oxford: Oxford University Press.

MacKenzie, J. M. 1995. *Orientalism: History, Theory and the Arts.* Manchester: Manchester University Press.

MacLean, Gerald. 2005. *Re-Orienting the Renaissance: Cultural Exchanges with the East.* Houndmills: Palgrave Macmillan.

Melman, Bille. 1992. *Women's Orients: English Women and the Middle East, 1718–1918.* Ann Arbor, MI: University of Michigan Press.

Metlizki, Dorothee. 1977. *The Matter of Araby in Medieval England.* New Haven, CT: Yale University Press.

Molan, Peter D. 1978. "Ma'ruf the Cobbler: The Mythic Structure of an *Arabian Nights* Tale." *Edebiyat* 3: 121–35.

Moretti, Franco. 2000. "Conjectures on World Literature." *New Left Review* 1 (January-February): 54–68.

—. 2003. "More Conjectures." *New Left Review* 20 (March-April): 73–81.

—. ed. 2006. *The Novel*, 2 vols. Princeton, NJ: Princeton University Press.

Nash, Geoffery. 2005. *From Empire to Orient: Travellers to the Middle East 1830–1926.* London and New York: I. B. Tauris.

Ouyang, Wen-chin. 2018. "Orientalism and World Literature: A Re-reading of Ṭāha Ḥusayn's Cosmopolitanism." *Journal of Arabic*

Literature (49): 125–52.

Reynolds, Matthew. 2011. *The Poetry of Translation*. Oxford: Oxford University Press.

—. 2013. *Likeness: Translation, Illustration, Interpretation*. Legenda Studies in Comparative Literature 30. Leeds: Modern Humanities Research Association and Maney Publishing.

Said, Edward. 1978. *Orientalism*. New York: Pantheon Books.

Schwab, Raymond. 1984. *The Oriental Renaissance: Europe's Discovery of India and the East*. New York: Columbia University Press.

Su, Qikang. 1999. "Gushi zhong de gushi—Tian Fang Ye Tan." In *Tian Fang Ye Tan*, ix–xvii. Taipei: Guiguan.

Sugita, Hideaki. 2006. "The *Arabian Nights* in Modern Japan: A Brief Historical Sketch." In *The Arabian Nights and Orientalism: Perspectives from East and West*, edited by Yuriko Yamanaka and Tetsuo Nishio, 116–53. London and New York: I. B. Tauris.

al-Ṭabarī, Abū Jaʿfar Muḥammad Ibn Jarīr. 1989. *Qiṣaṣ al-anbiyāʾ*, extracted from *Tārīkh al-rusul wa-al-mulūk* by Muṣṭafā ʿAbd al-Qādir, 109, 118–31. Beirut: Dār al-Fikr, 1989.

Tāj, ʿAbdallāh. 2006. *Maṣādir "alf laylah wa-laylah" al-ʿarabiyyah*. Sūsah: Dār al-Mīzān li-l-Nashr.

al-Thaʿlabī, Abū Isḥāq Aḥmad Ibn Muḥammad. 1347. A. H. [1928 AD]. *Qiṣaṣ al-anbiyāʾ al-musammā bi-al-ʿarāʾis al-majālis*, 99–102. Cairo: Dār al-Kutub al-ʿArabiyyah.

Wu, Qiancheng. 1999. "Guanlan huanqiu wenshue de qitsai kuangpu." In Zhong, *Tian Fang Ye Tan*, i-viii.

Zhong, Si. 1999. *Tian Fang Ye Tan*. Taipei: Guiguan.

Kuunmong in Translations: A Visual Linkage Between the Past and the Present

Yeogeun Kim

World literature existed before it was established as an academic discipline. Johann Wolfgang Goethe introduced the concept of *Weltliteratur* and emphasized to his confidant Johann Peter Eckermann, what could be shared in reading foreign literature. Goethe was struck by similarities between a Chinese novel he read in 1827, and his *Hermann and Dorothea*, as well as the novels of Samuel Richardson (Damrosch 2003, 11). *Kuunmong* (구운몽, 九雲夢, The Cloud Dream of the Nine, 1687–88), a Korean novel, can be considered in the context of world literature as it originated in the 17th century. This chapter, drawing on "critical world literature studies" as proposed by Stefan Helgesson and Pieter Vermeulen (2016), examines *Kuunmong* as a case study by investigating the "actuality" of how a text comes to be regarded as world literature. It probes the materiality of *Kuunmong*, as shaped by the respective, specific social contexts in which each translation was produced.

The initial justification for *Kuunmong*'s being considered as a text of world literature can be found in a work that emerged from its Chinese reception in the 19th-century: *Kuullu*. This Chinese rewriting of the Korean was in turn introduced to Koreans in an adapted Korean version entitled *Kuun'gi*. The circulation of *Kuunmong* beyond its national boundary was, therefore, possible because *Kuunmong* was written in Chinese as well as in Korean. The presence of two different language editions of *Kuunmong* is not exceptional. It was a common practice in the composition of Korean popular novels before the 20th century when the Korean readership was divided into two, often discrete but not necessarily exclusive, groups based on their ability to read either the Chinese or the Korean text.

In the early 20th century, *Kuunmong* began to circulate outside East Asia, as a number of foreign and domestic agents helped make it known to the west. Robert Danton (1982) states that the publisher has always been the major player in the making of a book (68), but in the *Kuunmong* publications translators were just as important, as Susan Bassnett argues (2016, 312). The first translation of the novel into English, made by Canadian missionary James Scarth Gale (1863–1937) during his stay in Seoul, was published in London in 1922. Gale's translation, as an illustrated text, exhibits the influence derived from the traditional reception of *Kuunmong*. The novel was not circulated as an illustrated text in the traditional East Asian region, but was significantly adapted into narrative paintings until the 20th century.

This chapter examines the stages that the 17th-century Korean novel *Kuunmong* went through to achieve its current status in terms of world literature. Gale's illustrations, including their subsequent use and modification in western-language translations as well as book cover designs will be analysed, and recent English and European-language translations of *Kuunmong* will be discussed in terms of the current environment in which the novel is situated. Recently the global landscape of Korean literature has been much changed due to the South Korean government's active attempts to promote its recognition amongst the global audience through institutional publicity. Although aiming to boost contemporary Korean literature, their efforts also extend to promoting *Kuunmong* as an example of traditional writing. This chapter, therefore, aims to evaluate the problematic "global literary marketplace" in relation to *Kuunmong* by focusing on the book's illustrations and cover designs.

The Composition of *Kuunmong*

Kuunmong was first written by Kim Manjung[1] 金萬重 (1637–1692) during his exile in Sŏnch'ŏn, P'yŏng'an province (located in present-

1 Kim is his surname because, in East Asia, surnames come first. This applies to all Korean, Chinese, and Japanese names in this article.

day North Korea) from the ninth lunar month of 1687 to the eighth lunar month of 1688. After that, it was repeatedly hand-copied by readers. In the late Chosŏn (1392–1910, the last dynasty of Korea), the prevailing method of circulating fiction was by hand-copying, because publishing was costly. Nevertheless, several decades after the author died, the *ŭlsa* (the 1725) edition of *Kuunmong* was published in the city of Naju, marking the first occasion when Korean fiction was commercially published. This confirms its popularity as a text that was in fact, widely read, from the king to low-born entertainers. From that time, the story went through multiple, successive translations and interpretations worldwide.

Whether the language of its first appearance was Korean or Chinese is still debated. Until the late 19th century, in Korea, popular novels were often written in literary Chinese as well as in vernacular Korean because most women were only able to read vernacular Korean. "Chinese" here means not modern Chinese, but Classical Chinese or literary Chinese, which like Latin in Europe, was a means of communicating and distributing knowledge among educated people in East Asia. In Korea, literary Chinese did not lose its role as the language for academic pursuits and political life for male Koreans educated in the Chinese classics until the late 19th century, when Korea was exposed to western influences introduced mainly via Japan. Until then it was thought right and proper that texts of public significance should be composed in Chinese. All educated Koreans were also given Chinese names, for instance, as seen in the author of *Kuunmong* as 金萬重. Novels originally written in Chinese were subsequently translated into Korean, often increasing their domestic popularity.

Storyline of *Kuunmong* Illustrated

Kuunmong is a love story concerning a noble man and eight women, set in 9th-century China. The hero, Sŏngjin, an aspiring Buddhist monk, encounters eight fairies and develops a desire for a successful life in the secular world. His desire is discovered. Because it is unacceptable for an ascetic monk to hold desires of any kind, his punishment is to be re-born as Soyu, son to a Confucian hermit. Luckily, Soyu achieves his worldly dream of becoming a high official and a military general and enjoys a happy life with eight beautiful women. All his success, however, is revealed as nothing more than a monk's dream. The story ends with Sŏngjin's abrupt awakening, his return to his monastery and his future as a renowned monk.

A quick Google search for *Kuunmong* shows that Kurodahan Press, a publisher based in Fukuoka, Japan, reprinted an English translation by James Scarth Gale in 2003. Kurodahan Press chose to reprint Gale's translation of 1922, because the translator was considered to appeal to the target audience. The translator, a Canadian who joined the American mission in Korea, adopted the writing style in which he had been trained at the University of Toronto. Also appealing was the cultural baggage of orientalism and colonialism during Japanese colonial rule in early 20th-century Korea. This added an eccentric character to Gale's translation in both the main text and the introduction by Elspet Keith Robertson.

Significantly, Gale's translation was published by the London-based publisher, Daniel O'Connor, and so entered the global market place. Effective promotion was the key to sales. Gale's *Kuunmong* was in the line-up of light reading materials advertised as books such as *Trivia: Or, The Art of Walking Streets in London* by John Gay. As *Kuunmong* was published in autumn, gift books for Christmas were also listed. In book publishing in the west, particularly for light reading materials including popular fiction, book illustrations and eye-catching front cover designs became increasingly important in the early 20th century. Gale aptly responded to the trend in the market and inserted illustrations into his translations. His text is the first illustrated version of *Kuunmong* carrying at least one illustration per chapter apart from the first and second chapters.

As complementary visual images facilitate greater accessibility than just the text alone, an illustrated text encourages reader engagement. Although Gale's illustrated *Kuunmong* does not reach that extensive level, the presence of illustrations in the text improves accessibility and may explain why several other reprints of Gale's English translation preceded Kurodahan's. In addition to the production of reprints, illustrations from the Gale text influenced both English and European language translations of *Kuunmong*, notably in English (2019 and 1974), Spanish (2006), Italian (2001), French (2004) and German (2011).

James Scarth Gale's Illustrations

Although Gale's translation was published by a British publisher, the style of illustration resounds with the traditional visual adaption of *Kuunmong* and exhibits an influence from Korean traditional illustrated books, for instance, the didactic book *Oryun haengsil-to* (Illustrated Guide to the Five Relations, 1787) by King Chŏngjo. The five relations were considered as fundamental human relations and became the focus of Confucian ethics in traditional Korea. *Oryun haengsil-to* is the culmination of a series of illustrated guide books reprinted and revised following its first version *Samgang haengsil-to* (Illustrated Guide to the Three Bonds) in 1434. Illustrated books of basic Confucian ethics, written in Chinese and Korean with illustrations targeting the illiterate, were intended to influence both the educated and uneducated. However, they were not only the most influential didactic texts but also prominent as a source of visual imagery because illustrated text was scarce before the 20th century in Korea. For example, 39 paintings[2] narrating *Kuunmong* adopted the composition style and major visual motifs from *Oryun haengsil-to*, regardless of the discrepancy in content and purpose. *Kuunmong* is a fictional story set in a variety of fantasy worlds, whereas *Oryun haengsil-to* was based on actual stories for moral education. Considering the limited availability of the illustrated text, it is not surprising that Gale's illustrations reflect *Kuunmong* paintings as well as *Oryun haengsil-to*.

For example, the description of gardens and buildings in Gale's illustrations demonstrates a similarity to *Kuunmong* paintings

---

2 Thirty-nine folding screens are reported by Kan Hoyun (2014, 119).

and *Oryun haengsil-to*. The domestic garden scene in Gale's illustrations features the banana tree despite its absence from textual description. For instance, both gardens in the residence of Chŏng Kyŏngp'ae family (a fairy reborn as a noble woman who the protagonist, Soyu, meets in his dream) and in the Princess Nanyang's residence (another fairy reborn as princess that Soyu meets in his dream) are depicted with this banana tree as seen in Image 1 and 2 respectively (from Chapters 4 and 11). The banana tree was a conventional image in the frequent description of gardens and buildings in Chinese vernacular illustrated novels which were then introduced to Korean paintings including *Kuunmong* paintings and *Oryun haengsil-to*. The story of Wang Pou, known for his filial piety, is an episode depicted in *Oryun haengsil-to*. Wang is from Wei (403–225 BCE), an ancient kingdom located in what is now Shanxi province, in north-central China. Despite its absence from textual description, a big subtropical banana tree with leaves flourishes to the left of Wang's house in the illustration (Image 3). The banana tree also appears in the *Kuunmong* painting at the Korean National Folk Museum (no. minsok 63586, ink and colours on paper, 391 × 136.5 cm). The fourth panel of this *Kuunmong* folding screen depicts the residence of Chŏng Kyŏngp'ae family (see image 4). Additionally, regardless of period and place in which an episode unfolds, buildings from the Yuan (1206–1368) and Ming periods (1368–1644) were frequently depicted in *Kuunmong* paintings and *Oryun haengsil-to*. The architectural style of Wang Pou's house and buildings displayed in traditional *Kuunmong* paintings is also translated into Gale's illustrations of the residences of Chŏng Kyŏngp'ae and Princess Nanyang.

The immediate influences on Gale's illustrations come from *Kuunmong* paintings and *Oryun haengsil-to*, but relate further back to the origin of book illustration in Korea, *Samgang haengsil-to* (1443). Unlike *Kuunmong* paintings and *Oryun haengsil-to* where one scene is depicted per panel (paintings) or per page (*Oryun haengsil-to*), Gale often arranged two half-folio scenes for a single illustration. This style was initially present in *Samgang haengsil-to*, which was modelled on the 15th-century Ming Chinese books of *shuochang cihua* (ballad-narrative) performance (Ko 2006, 162). Since the period of Six Dynasties (220–589) in China, image and text have been composed to share the same page, usually with illustration above and text below. The new style entered the picture in the 15th century, featuring a full-page presentation of the image, and thus accommodating more than one action, mostly two, that occur in different points of narrative time. Each action was marked by thin lines of hills, clouds or buildings. Similarly, more than half of Gale's illustrations clearly exhibit two main events representing the corresponding chapter, for instance chapters 4–5, 7–9, 11–13 and 16, with the exception of several illustrations, including the first, that are placed as the frontispiece next to the title page. The first illustration depicts the very moment that triggers the conflict of desire, leading to the development of the entire story, a scene in which all the main characters, that is, Sŏngjin and the eight fairies, meet each other for the first time at the bridge. The importance of this bridge scene demands full-page presentation, and it was the most frequently depicted scene in *Kuunmong* paintings.

All of Gale's illustrations, framed in a rectangular form, carry Chinese calligraphy outlining the chapter in a phrase inside or outside the image, in addition to English translations of the Chinese phrase added below the image. In the first illustration, four Chinese characters, in a style of calligraphy, are inserted in the upper part of the image, and below the image box is an English translation of the phrase "The Fairies on the Bridge" (Image 5). Apart from this first illustration, all other calligraphies are separately presented above the image. All illustrations are inserted into the book on a thicker piece of paper than that used for other pages. The reverse side of each image is empty, lacking any text, indicating that each piece of illustration was printed separately from the text and then combined into the book.

The whole set of illustrations with hand-written Chinese characters was found in the Gale Papers, a collection of Gale's manuscripts together with miscellaneous materials stored at the Thomas Fisher Rare Book Library at the University of Toronto. This may suggest that illustrations were printed in advance in Korea where Gale resided before he added, or had his acquaintances add, Chinese calligraphy to the illustrations. In the process, calligraphy came to be written into the first illustration, a relatively uncluttered image to serve as a frontispiece. The cramped composition of in-text illustrations, most of which results from the design for fitting two distinct scenes to one image, hardly secures room for Chinese characters. These illustrations with calligraphy, then, may have been sent to the publisher in London to be added to the English text printed there.

Gale's translation carries 16 illustrations altogether. The first, the bridge scene, appears on the page to the left of the title page, i.e., a frontispiece (Image 5). This illustration directly presents the main event in chapter one but also is representative of the entire story as discussed above. Chapters 1 and 2 have no illustrations, whereas Chapter 11 has two. The subsequent reprints and English (2019 and 1974) and European language translations reproduced these 16 illustrations entirely or selectively, sometimes with modifications. Prior to the elaboration of Gale's influence on other publications of *Kuunmong* translations, the social context in which English and European language translations and publications of *Kuunmong* were funded in particular by South Korean agency will be explained. The section that follows helps to situate these translations in relation to institutional publicity in the global literary marketplace.

Efforts to Promote Korean Literature Globally

In this section, efforts made by the South Korean government to promote Korean literature including *Kuunmong* on the stage of world literature will be discussed. The focus of this investigation is on projects by the Literature Translation Institute of Korea (LTI Korea). The Literature Translation Institute of Korea is one of several similar national organizations[3] established by the South Korean government.

3 For example, the National Gugak (Korean Traditional Music) Center, National Institute of Korean Language, National Theater of Korea, National Folk Museum of Korea, National Library of Korea, National Museum of Korea, The National Academy of Arts of the Republic of Korea,

The institution was established in March 2001, through a merger of the Korean Literature Translation Fund and the Korea Arts & Culture Service overseas translation project. Their website shows that the institute has its own library where translations of Korean literature are presented alongside original works.[4]

As can be inferred from its name, the mission of LTI Korea is to improve awareness about Korean literature worldwide. LTI Korea explicitly indicates its role as "executing the intention" of the Korean government to "make Korean literature and culture known outside of Korea in order to contribute to the formation of world literature".[5] Korean literature, as defined and envisioned by the government, includes all literature produced in the Korean peninsula or by Koreans before 1953 when Korea was divided into North Korea and South Korea, but subsequently it includes only literature produced in South Korea or by South Koreans. To achieve its goal of globalising Korean literature, LTI Korea early on emphasised support for translators. Besides financial support, in July 2002 it started short-term training programs, then in 2015 expanded these into a two-year funded education program run by the Translation Academy (established in 2008) aimed at helping students "sharpen their skills through a systematic curriculum".[6] The student body mostly consists of foreigners, but sometimes includes Koreans as well. The programs articulate the intention of LTI Korea to increase the number of qualified translators.

The two-year program takes students from five western languages: English, French, German, Spanish, and Russian, on courses like Translation of Korean Literary Texts, Study of Translation Styles,

---

Korea National University of Arts, KTV, Korean Culture and Information Service, and National Museum of Modern and Contemporary Art, Korea

4 The LTI library collection will be discussed in detail later in relation to *Kuunmong*.

5 The quotation is my translation from the history section at the LTI Korea website. https://www.ltikorea.or.kr/history/history.do. In the English version of the website, this section is missing.

6 From the English version of the LTI website. https://www.ltikorea.or.kr/en/tranacademy.do

Korean Literature, Korean Culture, and Korean Language. The Korean language course is only for non-Koreans. However, there are in fact other programs run by the Academy, which are less densely organised, such as the two-year Special Course that consists of two-hour weekly meetings and requires an independent translation of at least one short story and one workshop with a writer per term. Offering bi-weekly seminars, the Translation Atelier is a practical program open only for LTI translation course graduates who have an individual translation project to pursue. Over 1,000 graduates have completed the Academy courses since 2008.[7]

LTI Korea also holds various projects to promote Korean literature including translation awards, support for translators and publishers, and translation workshops. Since 2014, translation workshops, funded by LTI Korea, have been held frequently in European universities including Universidad de Málaga in Spain (four times, 2015-2018); Sapienza Università di Roma and Università degli studi di Napoli L'Orientalein in Italy (four times, 2014-2015 and 2017-2018); Institut national des langues et civilisations orientales in France (three times, 2014–2016); and МГУ имени М.В.Ломоносова (Moscow State University) and Санкт-Петербургский государственный университет (St Petersburg University) in Russia (three times, 2015, 2016, and 2018). Three English language workshops were held in the UK (2015–2016) and the USA (2015), but only one in China (2017), Mongol (2018), and Brazil (2018). In these workshops, contemporary Korean novels and poems are translated. The complete list of workshops funded by LTI Korea from 2014 to 2018 is as follows.[8]

7 For more details see the program section https://www.ltikorea.or.kr/en/tranacademy/regular.do

8 The table was adopted and translated from https://www.ltikorea.or.kr/overseauni/overseauni.do

Year	Language	Country	Institution
2014	French	France	Institut national des langues et civilisations orientales
	Italian	Italy	Sapienza Università di Roma
	Swedish	Sweden	Stockholms Universitet
2015	English	USA	University of Arizona
	English	UK	British Centre for Literary Translation
	French	France	Institut national des langues et civilisations orientales
	Spanish	Spain	Universidad de Málaga
	Russian	Russia	МГУ имени М.В.Ломоносова
	Italian	Italy	Sapienza Università di Roma
2016	English	UK	British Centre for Literary Translation
	French	France	Institut national des langues et civilisations orientales
	German	Germany	Ruhr Universität Bochum
	Spanish	Spain	Universidad de Málaga
	Russian	Russia	Санкт-Петербургский государственный университет
2017	German	Austria	Universität Wien
	Spanish	Spain	Universidad de Málaga
	Italian	Italy	Sapienza Università di Roma
	Chinese	China	Shandong Daxue 山东大学 (Sandong University)
2018	Spanish	Spain	Universidad de Málaga
	Russian	Russia	Санкт-Петербургский государственный университет
	Italian	Italy	Università degli studi di Napoli L'Orientalein
	Portuguese	Brazil	Universidade de São Paulo
	Danish	Denmark	Københavns Universitet
	Mongolian	Mongol	Хүмүүнлэгийн ухааны их сургууль (University of the Humanities)
	Bulgarian	Bulgaria	Софийски университет (Sofia University)

The majority of translations of Korean modern literature are the indirect or direct result of LTI-led translation projects in various ways: namely, translation academy programs and overseas translation workshops. More direct support of the translation and publication of Korean literature is made by offering translation grants and publication grants, currently four times a year. The LTI Korea report also mentions flexibility for funding and the time line for translations of Korean classics. For instance, a new English translation of *Kuunmong* submitted to the final list in 2006, was considered. As the reports on translation support up to 2017 show, contemporary

Korean novels outweigh other genres by over 50 per cent (828 out of 1,508 in total), but 9 per cent (136 out of 1,508) were Korean classics including classical literature. The full list of translation grants is below.[9]

Year	Total in Year		Genres					Total
	languages	total	contemporary			children	Humanities and social science (classics)	
			novels	poetry	others			
2001–2005	25	255	145	58	8	-	49 (41)	255
2006	20	69	29	11	-	1	28 (14)	69
2007	17	98	58	14	-	-	26 (9)	98
2008	14	41	26	6	-	-	9 (2)	41
2009	16	80	44	10	1	16	9 (2)	80
2010	13	110	54	13	3	18	22 (5)	110
2011	14	105	57	8	-	22	18 (2)	105
2012	14	90	57	4	-	10	19 (1)	90
2013	17	82	44	14	-	6	18 (3)	82
2014	21	108	64	15	1	5	23 (5)	108
2015	17	142	82	23	1	4	32 (8)	142
2016	22	182	80	21	1	13	67 (32)	182
2017	23	146	88	21	5	3	29 (12)	146
Total	37	1,508	828	213	20	98	349 (136)	1,508

The publication grant was initially made to support overseas publishers who wish to publish LTI Korea funded-translations, but since 2014, it has been offered to overseas publishers who plan to both translate and publish Korean works. In this case, translation as well as publication support will be provided. The amount of the grant varies, but publication support is approximately five million KRW, for instance, for a novel. LTI Korea emphasises fast and efficient procedures, possible when translation and publication are undertaken by the same publisher, stating "this streamlined process reflects the needs of overseas publishers".[10] This change indicates that

9 The table was translated from https://www.ltikorea.or.kr/transtatic.do
10 For more details, see https://www.ltikorea.or.kr/en/transsupouben.do

since 2014, translation and publication grants have been made available only to support translated works to be published by overseas publishers. Some translations, such as the English translation of *Kuunmong* by Richard Rutt and Kim Chong-un, published in Korea, were not successful. This translation is currently out of print and not available at Amazon. The demands of the global marketplace led to LTI Korea's strategic decision to favour overseas rather than domestic publishers. The full list of publication grants is given below.[11]

11 The table was translated from https://www.ltikorea.or.kr/overseapubsta.do

Year	Total in Year		Genres					Total
	languages	total	contemporary			children	humanities and social science (classics)	
			novels	poetry	others			
2001–2005	19	202	103	53	7	1	38	202
2006	18	62	33	15	2	-	12	62
2007	16	49	22	10	5	-	12	49
2008	16	94	33	48	-	-	13	94
2009	15	75	32	24	-	-	19	75
2010	15	53	26	9	4	-	14	53
2011	15	54	31	9	1	1	12	54
2012	14	55	34	11	-	3	7	55
2013	14	74	60	5	-	2	7	74
2014	18	142	97	13	-	11	21	142
2015	14	94	53	16	1	3	21	94
2016	18	152	80	16	2	5	49	152
2017	27	140	73	22	2	5	38	140
2018 (up to 2nd quarter)	18	63	34	13	2	8	6	150
Total	38	1,309	692	258	24	37	265	1,309

Similar to the report of translation grants above, 50 per cent, (or 692 out of 1,309 in total) of the support was given to contemporary Korean novels, but Korean classics, including classical literature, were also funded for publishing, although the exact percentage is not listed in the table. The fact that translation and publication support for Korean classical literature was granted indicates that recent translations of Korean classical literature are situated not-so-differently from contemporary Korean literature in relation to promotions initiated by LTI Korea, although early translations were made before the institute was established. Additionally, since 2010, the institute inaugurated its own designation list of books for translation in parallel to supporting books proposed by translators and publishers. Until 2015, 1,074 books in total were selected. Although not explicit in the tables above, among the list of books designated for translation support in 2015 (as stated in LTI Korea's 2015 annual report) were 41 books collected from classics, and *Kuunmong* was one of those.

Kuunmong Translations

The current activities of LTI Korea by no means excludes translations of one particular Korean classical novel, *Kuunmong*. First, LTI Korea's promotional effort will be discussed as demonstrated in the on-line and off-line presence of *Kuunmong* translations at the LTI Korea library. Then, evidence for direct support for translation and publication of *Kuunmong* by the institute will be provided. *Kuunmong* is well known and has been well-researched, because there are many translations in existence. Perhaps only one classical work, *Ch'unhyang chŏn,* [12] outweighs *Kuunmong* in terms of popularity. The oldest translations of *Kuunmong* along with *Ch'unhyang chŏn* are available on-line at the LTI Korea website. Under the "Archive" menu on the

---

12 *Ch'unhyang chŏn* is usually translated as the *Tale of Ch'unhyang*. Ch'unhyang and Yi Mongnyong fall in love; soon after that, however, unfavourable circumstances separate them. Yi eventually comes back to Ch'unhyang as a successful man to marry Ch'unhyang.

English version of the site are e-books and Korean short stories. E-books are suitable for browsing publications either in Korean or in English, and *Kuunmong* and *Ch'unhyang chŏn* are represented in the "Digital Library of Korean Classics" category under e-books. The majority of the Korean classics listed are Korean folk tales. For *Kuunmong*, James Scarth Gale's (1922) English translation, *The Cloud Dream of the Dream, A Korean Novel: A Story of the Times of the Tangs of China about 840 A.D.* features, and for *Ch'unhyang chŏn*, *Printemps Parfumé* (1892) by J. H. Rosny is represented. The website category "Korean Short Stories" is the section for reading contemporary Korean literature in English.[13] "Hŭkpaek sajinsa 흑백사진사 (Black and White Photographer)", authored by Han Yujoo 한유주 and translated by Janet Hong, found under the menu "Korean Short Stories", for example, is a kind of experimental short story.[14]

The LTI off-line collection of *Kuunmong* translations consists of 23 texts, of which 18 are translated into foreign languages. The remaining five texts are modern Korean translations including one for elementary students. There are also three Korean publications related to *Kuunmong*: a collection of *Kuunmong* manuscripts, one scholarly interpretation of *Kuunmong*, and one rewriting by the Korean novelist Ch'oe Inhun 최인훈 (1936–). The six English translations, of which three are James Scarth Gale's 1922 translation, outnumber those in any other language. The strong presence of Gale translation exhibited in its reprints will be discussed in detail later. The remaining three editions differ from Gale's. "A Nine Cloud Dream" by Richard Rutt and Kim Chong-un is one of the stories in *Virtuous Women: Three Classic Korean Novels, A Nine Cloud Dream, Queen Inhyŏn, Ch'un-hyang* (Kim 1974). *The Nine Cloud Dream: A Korean Classic* (Kim 1975a) was translated by the Creative Writing Group in the Department of English Language and Literature, in the prestigious private Ewha Womans University in Seoul. Only these two English translations of *Kuunmong* (Kim 1974 and Kim 1975a) were published originally in Korea,

13 For more details, see https://www.ltikorea.or.kr/en/e_essay.do
14 The short story *Hŭkpaek sajinsa* can be read from https://issuu.com/ltilibrary/docs/_korean_short_stories_han__yujoo__b

whereas all other foreign language translations were published by overseas publishers. Just recently, another English translation, *The Nine Cloud Dream* (Kim 2019), by Heiz Insu Fenkl was published by Penguin Classics in the USA.

Besides English translations, ten other foreign language translations are available at the library: in Russian, Czech, German, Romanian, Italian, French, Spanish, Polish, Japanese and Arabic. All the foreign language translations of *Kuunmong* available in the LTI library are listed in the table below.[15]

Year	Language	Translator	Title[16]	Publisher	format
1961	Russian	А. Артемьев-ой and Г. Рачкова	*Облачный сон девяти*	Государственн-ое издательство художественн-ой литературы	print
1974	English	Richard Rutt and Kim Chong-un	"A Nine Cloud Dream" in *Virtuous Women: Three Classic Korean Novels, A Nine Cloud Dream, Queen Inhyŏn, Ch'un-hyang*	The Royal Asiatic Society, Korea Branch	print
1975	English	the Creative Writing Group	*The Nine Cloud Dream: A Korean Classic*	Ewha Womans University	print
1975	Japanese	Kō Sōkei	*Kyūunmu*	Kōrai Shorin	print
1990	Japanese	Kōno Eiji	"Kuunmon"[17] in	Daisan bunmeisha	print

15 See more details here: http://library.ltikorea.or.kr/bibliography?keys=%EA%B5%AC%EC%9A%B4%EB%AA%BD&search-button=Search&sort_by=field_language_value&sort_order=DESC&items_per_page=10&page=2.

16 The full title is shown on the title page when applicable.

17 Eiji respected the Korean pronunciation Kuunmong and approximated it with Japanese, instead of replacing it with the Japanese pronunciation Kyūunmu.

			Hankoku koten bungakusen		
1992	Czech	Miriam Löwenstei-nová	*Sen devíti z obláků*	Reflex	print
2001	Italian	Maurizio Riotto	*Il sogno delle nove nuvole: romanzo coreano del XVII secolo*	Sellerio	print
2003	English	James Scarth Gale	*Kuunmong: The Cloud Dream of the Nine, a Korean Novel: A Story of the Times of the Tangs of China about 840 AD*	Kurodahan Press	Reprint of 1922 with new intro-duction
2004	English	James Scarth Gale	*The Cloud Dream of the Nine*	Kessinger Publishing	Reprint of 1922
2004	French	John et Geneviève T. Park	*Le Songe Des Neuf Nuages: Roman du XVIIe Siècle*	Maisonneuve & Larose	print
2006	Spanish	Na Song-Joo and Javier Cortines	*El sueño de las nueve nubes*	Hiperión	print
2007	Polish	Oh Kyong-Geun and Tomasz Andrzej Lisowski	*Sen ulotny jak obłok*	Officina Tum	print
2009	English	James Scarth Gale	*The Cloud Dream of the Nine, a Korean Novel: A Story of the Times of the Tangs of China about 840 A.D. (1922)*	Cornell University Library	Reprint as an exact scanned copy of 1922
2009	Romanian	Oum Tae Hyun and	*Visul învolburat al*	Pararela 45	print

		Eliana Cristina Ionoaia	*celor nouă*		
2010	Russian	Аделаида Федоровна Троцевич and Adelaida Fedorovna Trocevič	*Сон в заоблачных высях*	Гиперион	print
2011	German	Huwe Albrecht	*Wolkenträu-me: ein klassischer Roman aus dem Korea des 17. Jahrhunderts*	EOS	print
2012	Arabic	Walaa Maged Mohamed Kourashy	*Arabic حلم السحاب (hulm alsahab)*[18]	Animar for Literature and Arts	print
2017	English	James Scarth Gale	*The Cloud Dream of the Nine, a Korean Novel: A Story of the Times of the Tangs of China about 840 A.D.*	LTI Korea	e-book of 1922
2019	English	Heinz Insu Fenkl	*The Nine Cloud Dream*	Penguin Classics	print

The list shows that the number of new translations has greatly increased since 2001, the year when LTI Korea was established. This is particularly true of translations into European languages. Before 2001, there were English, Russian, Czech, and Japanese translations. The scope and depth of Russian scholarship of Korean classical literature have placed it ahead of any other country—a phenomenon that may reflect its close ties with North Korea's since the time of the Soviet Union. However, history goes further back to before Korea was divided into two countries. St Petersburg University has been the centre of Korean studies in the country since the Korean language was first taught by Kim Pyŏng'ok in 1896.

18 My transliteration added.

Recent translations contrast with earlier English translations of *Kuunmong* published before 1975, by James Scarth Gale, Richard Rutt and Kim Chong-un, and students at the Ewha Womans University. These early translators into English, of both foreign missionaries and Koreans, had extensive experience of living in Korea unlike recent foreign translators listed in the table above. Their translations were occasioned by the translators' personal interest in traditional Korean literature that had developed from their experience of Korean culture, by contrast to the indirect exposure to Korean literature of recent translators for academic or non-academic reasons. In 1888, Gale was appointed a missionary of Toronto University's YMCA and was sent to Korea, where he lived for 40 years until departing for England in 1927. Rutt served as an Anglican missionary from 1954 to 1974 in South Korea.

The LTI Korea library collections of *Kuunmong* translations tend to focus on western languages, and are lacking Chinese translations and are relatively incomplete in Japanese translations. The oldest Japanese translation was made by Chōsen Kenkyūkai 朝鮮研究会 (Chosŏn Research Society) in 1914, and it may reflect Japanese imperial interest in Korea as a Japanese colony at the time, for it is not displayed in the library. Two different types of Chinese text for *Kuunmong* have been published: the original Chinese edition of *Kuunmong*, either in literary Chinese characters or printed in simplified modern Chinese characters, by contrast to modern Chinese translations from the literary Chinese text. *Kuunmong*, published by Shanghai Guji chubanshe in 1994 retained the original literary Chinese but in 2014 was printed in simplified Chinese characters with modern paragraphing and reader-friendly punctuation. This may be because *Kuunmong*, written in literary Chinese, is as readable as any other traditional text produced in China for a Chinese audience. *Kuunmong* in this group is sometimes annotated, a common practice with Chinese classical texts, as, for example, in the text by Wang Wenyuan 王文元 (2010). However, Yang Erning 楊爾寧 in Taiwan translated *Kuunmong* into modern Chinese (2015). None of these is available in the LTI library collection of *Kuunmong*. This may be in line with the Translation Academy's policy of offering regular programs only in western languages and the high frequency of translation workshops held in European educational institutions.

Similarly, LTI Korea's emphasis on western languages is also evident in their direct financial support for the production and publication of *Kuunmong* translations. The Spanish translation, *El sueño de las nueve nubes* by Na Song-Joo and Javier Cortines, was funded in 2003. The Polish translation *Sen ulotny jak obłok* by Oh Kyong-Geun and Tomasz Andrzej Lisowski received the translation grant in 2005 and was published by Officina Tum in 2007 with the publication grant. The Rumanian translation, *Visul învolburat al celor nouă* by Oum Tae Hyun and Eliana Cristina Ionoaia, was funded for translation in 2006 and for publication by Pararela 45 in 2009. A new English translation, *The Nine Cloud Dream* by Heinz Insu Fenkl, was also a recipient of the translation grant in 2006. The reason for the selection, as the LTI Korea on-line news of September 6, 2006 states, is because Gale's 1922 translation was by then out of date, so new translations were required. Rutt and Kim's 1974 English translation was not considered in their statement.

A Russian translation *Сон в заоблачных высях* by Аделаида Федоровна Троцевич and Adelaida Fedorovna Trocevič was published by Гиперион in 2010, the result of a contract that LTI Korea made for publication of ten Korean classics with the publisher Гиперион (Giperion) in 2007. Гиперион, established in 1995, is an international publisher based in St Petersburg with overseas branches in USA, Japan, Germany, France and Israel. This project aimed to rekindle the life of Korean classics that were translated by professors at St Petersburg University but had gone out of print. Professor Adelaida Fedorovna Trocevič was the chief editor for revisions of Russian translations and completed the series in 2016. At the celebration on November 29, the editor Trocevič and the publisher Гиперион were lauded with the prize of achievement by LTI Korea. The German translation, *Wolkenträume: ein klassischer Roman aus dem Korea des 17 Jahrhunderts* by Huwe Albrecht, was published by EOS with the publication grant in 2011. Exceptionally, the Vietnamese translation of *Kuunmong,* CỬU VÂN MỘNG: Giấc Mơ Chín Tầng Mây by Jeon Hye Kyung and Ly Xuan Chung, was funded in 2006. The reason for the selection was that *Kuunmong* is on the list of 100 classics suggested for translation, in addition to the good quality of the translation.

Most LTI Korea grant recipients are academics, which may make for better institutional publicity and recognition of translated works, particularly when translators are based in overseas universities and use translations for their teaching. Heinz Insu Fenkl, who does English translations, is an Associate Professor of English at SUNY New Paltz, where he currently teaches creative writing in addition to courses on Asian and Asian American literature and film. Huwe Albrecht, who does German translation, teaches Korean studies at the University of Bonn. Na Song-Joo, for Spanish translation, is a professor at Hankuk University of Foreign Studies. Oum Tae Hyun, who translates into Rumanian, teaches Rumanian at Hankuk University of Foreign Studies; Eliana Cristina Ionoaia, who is a doctoral student at the University of Bucharest, also translates into Rumanian. Vietnamese translation is undertaken by Jeon Hye Kyung, Professor of Vietnamese Language at Hankuk University of Foreign Studies, and Ly Xuan Chung conducts research on North Eastern Asia at the social science research institute in Vietnam.

The ways in which *Kuunmong* as a sample of Korean classical literature is treated in relation to world literature has been discussed with a focus on various projects led by LTI Korea representing the South Korean government's efforts. LTI Korea tends to focus on western language translations of Korean literature including *Kuunmong* and their publications in major western markets. This may reflect their institutional attempt to make *Kuunmong*, a work from a minor culture, smoothly advance into the major culture. This background knowledge helps us understand how translations of *Kuunmong* come into the global market in a particular form. Remarkably, the majority of European language translations were made possible by direct financial support from LTI Korea. The new English and Western European language translations, in particular, adopted Gale's illustrations to the text or for the book cover. The re-use of Gale's illustrations reveals the marketing strategy for the sale of *Kuunmong* as one that targets English and Western European language-speaking readers, by promoting a traditional image of Korea or East Asia in general. This tendency echoes the earlier marketing strategy for Gale's translation that used exoticism to appeal to the early 20th-century British audience. Further discussion of the relation between these recent translations and Gale's illustrations will follow.

Adoptions of Gale's Illustrations

Two new English and four Western European language translations adopted Gale's illustrations, either in their entirety or selectively. Regardless of how many of Gale's illustrations were recycled, or how often, Chinese calligraphy is almost invisible. Even the first illustration containing calligraphy inside is no exception in this consideration. Fenkl's new English translation, which adopted all of Gale's illustrations, is unique in reproducing the original frontispiece containing calligraphy. However, no English caption was provided for the calligraphy, and the Chinese characters seem to have been treated only as images rather than writing. Not only is calligraphy visible, but Fenkl notably added one new illustration in the Gale style, as chapter two alone lacked an illustration when the original frontispiece was relegated to chapter one. All sixteen illustrations of Gale's and Fenkl's single addition, enlarged to fit to the page, were presented with no English captions. The front cover carries another version of the bridge scene—the scene already presented in the frontispiece. This way, the traditional image of the book was intensified.

Spanish translations, *El sueño de las nueve nubes* (2006) and the Italian translation *Il sogno delle nove nuvole: romanzo coreano del XVII secolo* (2001), carry replicas of Gale's illustrations for most chapters, except the frontispiece. These replicas, enlarged to fit to the page, were presented with Spanish or Italian captions instead of the English ones. All the Western European translations adopting Gale's illustrations provide captions below, while omitting the Chinese calligraphy. The bridge scene, where the protagonist Sŏngjin meets eight fairies, is missing. This is in contrast to Gale's translation in which this scene is immediately visible once the book is opened, ensuring its significance. The image may have been omitted because it contains calligraphy inside the image box. For all other illustrations that were carried over to Spanish and Italian translation, the calligraphy is separate from the image so that it is easily removable.

The French translation, *Le Songe Des Neuf Nuages: Roman du XVIIe Siècle* (2004), devised a different approach to Gale's illustrations. Four illustrations in total, including the frontispiece, are similarly enlarged to fit to the page with French captions, but they are imitations of Gale's images, rather than replicas. Calligraphy can be easily left out in the process. This way of rendering, in particular, allows ease for "calligraphy-free" reproduction of the frontispiece where calligraphy was originally embedded inside the image. The imitations are sometimes intended to be misleading. For instance, in the bridge scene, Sŏngjin looks like a European monk with his hat not separate from, but instead connected to his lengthy robe. In Gale's unerring illustration, Sŏngjin's pointed hat is not attached to his outfit the way in which it is usually worn by a travelling Buddhist monk in traditional Korea.

Gale's Illustration, produced in the style of traditional Korean paintings, may still be considered enchanting by 21st-century readers, but calligraphy may be considered too esoteric for a contemporary novel. Earlier, in Rutt and Kim's English translation (1974) were replicated four of Gale's illustrations with calligraphies. With the exception of the first illustration of both Fenkl's translation and the Kurodahan reprint, however, more recently, only the Cornell scanned copy (2009) presents Chinese calligraphy in all illustrations—these show no modification of Gale's.

Additionally, the front cover for the Spanish translation (Image 6) is taken directly from one of the illustrations in Gale's translation: that in Chapter 8, "Chin See's Fear: Cloudlet Says Farewell" (Chin See and Cloudlet are two of the story's women characters). Also, the German translation *Wolkenträume: ein klassischer Roman aus dem Korea des 17. Jahrhunderts*, carries no full scene of any Gale's illustrations but adopts visual excerpts depicting the protagonist and his woman in the style of Gale's illustration for the front cover (Image 7). The German front cover will be discussed in detail below in comparison to other front cover designs. The overt indication of a foreign classical novel's cultural identity is not the only available option for marketing. Sometimes it may be better not to be culturally specific and entirely neutral. Apart from Gale's illustrations, nevertheless, in the new English and European language translations, traditional images from Korea or East Asia are not rarely visible on the front cover. The various types of front cover design of the *Kuunmong* translations, including traditional images, are discussed below.

Front Cover Images in *Kuunmong* Translations

Aside from the direct influence of Gale's illustrations witnessed in the Spanish translation of *Kuunmong*, there are three different types of book cover imagery: directly or indirectly related to the novel or traditional imagery; not attached to a specific national culture; or mixed with contemporary popular culture. The first group, constituting the majority, includes Rutt and Kim's English translation, Fenkl's English translation, the Kurodahan reprint, the Italian translation, the e-book of Gale's translation by LTI Korea, the Chinese translation (2014), and the Russian translation (2010). The second group features French translation. The third group comprises German translation. Each different style of image accentuates culturally specific elements, promotes a non-human but common appeal, or utilises contemporary pop icons.

Rutt and Kim's English translation "A Nine Cloud Dream" is one of the stories in *Virtuous Women: Three Classic Korean Novels, A Nine Cloud Dream, Queen Inhyŏn, Ch'un-hyang*. The front cover (Image 8), among three entries, adopted one of the most popular images from the *Kuunmong* story. The first encounter of the monk Sŏngjin and the eight fairy maidens was most frequently painted in *Kuunmong* images that circulated in traditional Korea. The scene was adopted from one of the *Kuunmong* folding screens at the Han'guk Chasu Museum (embroidery, ten panels, 34.0 x 140.0 cm) [19] in Seoul that was produced in 19th-century Korea. While no bridge is depicted, there is, in general, minimal rendering of the background. This non-descriptive background contrasts with the elaborate description of all nine characters in the scene.

Fenkl's translation also takes this scene for the front cover (Image 9), which was rendered by book artist FeiFei Ruan. The bridge, made of wood, is a very sketchy depiction compared to the traditional majestic stone bridge (See Gale's illustration for instance, Image 5). Additionally, instead of the actual meeting, the moment the eight fairies fly up into the sky to disappear from Sŏngjin at the end of their brief encounter is visualised. Sŏngjin is walking on the bridge, while all enlarged eight fairies dominate the image. Their individual faces, hairdos and necklaces, along with distinct hand gestures, are decidedly much more elaborate than those of the protagonist, who is marginalised both in scale and detail. Magnified bold delineation of the upper bodies of the fairies enables a sensual delivery of the monk Sŏngjin's inappropriate desire for women. Their enchanting beauty is amplified by blow-up portraiture, where they are looking at the protagonist below in a tantalising gaze with almost closed slanting eyes. Because of the way this composition features a sense of great gravity in the upper two-thirds of the scene, the image seems likely to turn over at any moment. This way, the bridge scene is rendered incomparably active, as opposed to the rather static style of Gale's illustration and other similar traditional *Kuunmong* paintings. This is the most dynamic and sensuous depiction of the bridge scene ever created. The sensual image of eight fairies may be strategically presented to target a wider readership, regardless of their cultural literacy or taste related to *Kuunmong* as a 17th-century Korean classical novel. The title gives no indication of the novel's provenance.

The front cover of the Kurodahan reprint of Gale's translation (Image 10) takes a painting from "Examples of One Hundred Painting Styles" by Japanese artist Kano Shōun (1617–1702). The Kano school

19 Hereafter referred to as the Chasu screen A.

in Japan painted in the Chinese style—specifically that of Tang China—during the period in which the *Kuunmong* story is set. This Japanese painting exhibits similarity to the scene of Chŏng Kyŏngp'ae's family residence in chapter 4, one of four illustrations embedded in the French translation, where the protagonist, disguised as a Taoist priestess, is visiting Chŏng Kyŏngp'ae, his future wife, and playing on the harp. The title on the front cover of the Kurodahan reprint excludes the background of the narrative, i.e. Tang China, but this style of imagery may function as a visual reference to Tang China.

The front cover image of the Italian translation (Image 11), where all of Gale's illustrations except the frontispiece were transferred, presents nine characters of *Kuunmong* but in the form of a stylized Buddhist painting commonly found in monasteries. Sŏngjin is elevated to the Buddha surrounded by eight Bodhisattvas, echoing the end of the narrative. Sŏngjin, enlightened and awakened from his dream, returned to the monastery and became a renowned monk, and was then considered a de facto Buddha. The eight Bodhisattvas refer to eight fairies, who returned together with Sŏngjin and became devoted to Buddhism. This imagery is related to the story but, as a stylised Buddhist painting, exhibits little linkage to Gale's illustrations and other traditional *Kuunmong* paintings.

The e-book version of Gale's translation published by LTI Korea features another *Kuunmong* folding screen at the Han'guk Chasu Museum (embroidery, ten panels, 37.0 x 167.0 cm, 19th century)[20] (Image 12). It is a ten-panel embroidery screen whereas most *Kuunmong* screens were painted in colour either on silk or paper. Being embroidery, it was expensive and probably in the possession of the royal household or noble family. Embroidery screens were only allowed for the upper class due to the anti-sumptuous-consumption policy throughout the Chosŏn era (Kim, Chŏng, Chŏng and Han 2016, 91) in which this screen was produced. Chasu screen B is much more elaborate and of better quality than Chasu screen A. The narrative order of the traditional Korean folding

20 Hereafter referred to as the Chasu screen B.

screen was arranged from right to left. The first three panels of ten occupying the upper half of the front cover present, starting from right to left, three rendezvous scenes of Ka Ch'unun, Chin Ch'aebong, and Kye Sŏmwŏl (three of the eight women characters in the narrative), followed by family reunion and the bridge scenes. The use of high-quality traditional *Kuunmong* imagery confers suitable elegance upon *Kuunmong* as a classic, befitting the status currently granted to this novel in Korea as well as for some foreign readerships.

The Chinese translation (2014) also used the Chasu screen B for the front cover (Image 13), as well as on the title page (Image 14). Seven panels from the second to the eighth are reproduced with the ninth and tenth cut out at the shoulder of the book and the first panel folded inside to be invisible. The bridge scene is placed in the middle of this arrangement. The same seven panels again appear on the title page with only the central panel of the bridge scene maintaining the original saturation while the colours of the remaining six, three on each side, are bleached out. The bridge scene is highlighted not only by orientation but also in intensity. The bridge scene of a different folk-style painting, added to the dust jacket, is partially placed at the bottom left under the title on the front cover (Image 15) and again appears in its entirety on the page next to the copyright information (Image 16). This way the bridge scene is visually emphasised. Sharing all the same features with the folk-style bridge scene, another scene featuring Chin Ch'aebong (one of the women characters) follows at the back of the title page (Image 17).

The Chasu screen B was arguably used in the palace where folding screens narrating Chinese stories, such as Guo Ziyi's (697–781), famous for his prosperous life in all aspects, were popular among the 19th-century Korean royal household. In this screen, administered by professional court artists, proper delivery of the background of the story is measured out. It is not an accurate representation of Tang China, however, but of Ming China from which the convention of narrative imagery for *Kuunmong* paintings derived, as discussed above. This means that Chinese style imagery such as the

Chasu screen B may appeal to cultivated Chinese readers who are familiar with traditional Chinese narrative paintings.

The Russian translation (Image 18) promotes the image of traditional Korea that is not related to *Kuunmong*. It features a fragment from a folk painting entitled *Ch'ŏnggŭm sangryŏn* 聽琴賞蓮 (Listen to the Tune of Kayagŭm and Enjoy the View of Lotus in the Pond; ink and colours on paper, 28.2 × 35.6 cm, Image 19) by Korean artist Sin Yunbok 申潤福 (1758–?), who is known for his sensual images of heterosexual love. The scene is contained in an album of 30 scenes, stored at Kansong Museum in Seoul, that depict pleasure activities and the romantic relationships of men of yangban (ruling class) with mostly female entertainers. Taken from the painting *Ch'ŏnggŭm sangryŏn* but with the background bleached, this presents a man of yangban hugging from behind a woman who is most likely a female entertainer. The depiction of intimate relationships with anyone other than female entertainers was taboo in 18th-century Korea. This depiction of the romantic couple's physical intimacy is only loosely related to the story.

In contrast, although the French translation carries four of Gale's illustrations in the text, the front cover (Image 20) features a cloudy blue sky. The other extreme of marketing *Kuunmong* is to put forward a modern, fancy, great look, as opposed to an "oriental" image of Korea in particular or East Asia more broadly. In-text illustrations are not readily accessible to potential readers. The front cover is where the first crucial impression is made upon those who lack any background knowledge of *Kuunmong*.

Maximizing contemporary and classical appeal, a German translation (Image 7) of this 17th-century Korean love story features James Bond on the front cover. Bond stands by a white Aston Martin sports car and greets Soyu, the personification of the monk's desire and the hero of the Korean love story, who appears as a general riding a white horse, the pre-modern equivalent to Bond's Aston Martin. Two elegant women, one in a European and the other in a Chinese dress, are approaching in the background. The juxtaposition of European and East Asian couples might be appropriate, as the story possesses elements common to both Korean and European popular romance. As a love story, *Kuunmong* shares elements of popular culture that may well be timeless: a hero who enjoys the greatest success in his career, in addition to a perfect married life with no less than eight women. German readers may encounter *Kuunmong* as a novelty, an addition to their reading of popular literature.

Conclusion: *Kuunmong* in the Global Literary Marketplace

Comparative research on translations of a single story contributes to a better understanding of the requirements and conditions which allow a book to make its way into the foreign market in the context of world literature. *Kuunmong*, as well known to any Korean as *Hamlet* is to an English audience, is regarded by Korean readers as a time-tested and proven classic, but successful marketing for foreign readerships may require different approaches and considerations rendering it as either a classic or a popular novel, and this may be reflected in the rendering of in-text illustrations and front cover designs. Gale's original illustrations drew heavily on traditional images of Korean book illustrations and *Kuunmong* paintings. Various ways of recycling Gale's illustrations in the new English versions and several Western European language translations further demonstrate the persistence of the traditional, perhaps more rightly "oriental", eccentricity associated with the marketing strategy of a foreign tale produced in a remote time and place. This excentricisation of the *Kuunmong* text resounds with Graham Huggan's (2001) argument in his extensive exploration of the commodification of the "exoticized" margins. However, *Kuunmong* may have not engaged in a form of what Huggan calls "strategic exoticism" or "staged marginality" (77, 87) to resist Eurocentric values; nevertheless, adoption of the strategy featuring exotic imagery has contributed to the success of *Kuunmong* in becoming a work of world literature. Analysis of the book cover designs additionally reveals the complexity of literary global markets. On the grounds of the translation business of Korean literature, the role of LTI Korea is well exemplified in the case of *Kuunmong* translations. LTI Korea promotes Korean literature by engaging in various projects with a focus on translations that aim for institutional publicity such as academic endorsements and global recognition by resorting to academic translators and overseas major book markets targeting European languages and English-speaking audiences.

Bibliography

Bassnett, Susan. 2016. "The Figure of the Translator." *Journal of World Literature* 1 (3): 299–315.

Bourdieu, Pierre. 1986. "The Forms of Capital." In *Handbook of Theory and Research for the Sociology of Education*, edited by J. G. Richardson, 46–58. New York: Greenwood Press.

Brouillette, Sarah. 2007. *Postcolonial Writers in the Global Literary Marketplace*. New York: Palgrave Macmillan.

Damrosch, David. 2003. *What Is World Literature?* Princeton, N.J.; Oxford: Princeton University Press.

Darnton, Robert. 1982. "What Is the History of Books?" *Daedalus* 111 (3): 65-83.

Han, Yujoo. 2015. "Hŭkpaek sajinsa 흑백사진사." In *Korean Short Stories in Translation*, edited by LTI Korea library. Translated by Janet Hong. Seoul: LTI Korea. https://issuu.com/ltilibrary/docs/_korean_short_stories_han__yujoo__b

Helgesson, Stefan, and Pieter Vermeulen. 2016. "Introduction: World Literature in the Making." In *Institutions of World Literature: Writing, Translation, Markets*, edited by Stefan Helgesson and Pieter Vermeulen, 1–20. London: Routledge.

Huggan, Graham. 2001. *The Postcolonial Exotic: Marketing the Margins*. London: Routledge.

Kan, Hoyun. 2014. *Kŭrim kwa sosŏl i mannassŭl ttae: han'gŭk kososŏl t'ŭkkang*. Seoul: Saemunsa.

Kim, Manjung. 1922. *The Cloud Dream of the Nine, a Korean Novel: A Story of the Times of the Tangs of China about 840 A.D.* Translated by James S. Gale. London: D. O'Connor.

—. 1914. *Kyūunmu*. Translated by Chōsen Kenkyūkai. Seoul: Chōsen Kenkyūkai.

—. [1922] 1950. *The Cloud Dream of the Nine, a Korean Novel: A Story of the Times of the Tangs of China about 840 A.D.* Translated by James S. Gale. Boston: Maynard & Company.

—. 1961. *Облачный сон девяти*. Translated by А. Артемьевой and Г.

Рачкова. Moscow: Государственное издательство художественной литературы.

—. 1974. "A Nine Cloud Dream." In *Virtuous Women: Three Classic Korean Novels, A Nine Cloud Dream, Queen Inhyŏn, Ch'un-hyang*, translated by Richard Rutt and Kim Chong-un, 1–178. Seoul: The Royal Asiatic Society, Korea Branch.

—. 1975a. *The Nine Cloud Dream: A Korean Classic.* Translated by Creative Writing Group. Seoul: Ewha Womans University.

—. 1975b. *Kankoku koten bungaku senshū.* Translated by Hong Sanggyu. Tokyo: Kōrai Shorin.

—. [1961] 1982. *Облачный сон девяти.* Translated by А. Артемьевой and Г. Рачкова. Moscow: Художественнаая литература.

—. 1990. "Kūunmon." In *Kankoku koten bungakusen*, edited by Kono Eiji, 167–220. Tokyo: Daisan bunmeisha.

—. 1992. *Sen DEVÍTI z oblaků.* Translated by Miriam Löwensteinová. Praha: Reflex.

—. 1994. *Jiuyunmeng*. Shanghai: Shanghai Guji chubanshe.

—. 2001. *Il sogno delle nove nuvole: Romanzo coreano del XVII secolo.* Translated by Maurizio Riotto. Palermo: Sellerio.

—. [1922] 2003. *Kuunmong: The Cloud Dream of the Nine.* Translated by James Scarth Gale. Fukuoka: Kurodahan Press.

—. [1922] 2004. *The Cloud Dream of the Nine*. Translated by James Scarth Gale. Whitefish: Kessinger Publishing.

—. 2004. *Le songe des neuf nuages: Roman du XVIIe siècle.* Translated by John Geneviève T. Park. Paris: Maisonneuve & Larose.

—. 2006. *El sueño de las nueve nubes.* Translated by Na Song-Joo and Javier Cortines. Madrid: Hiperión.

—. 2007a. *Sen ulotny jak oblok.* Translated by Oh Kyong-Geun and Tomasz Andrzej Lisowski. Gniezno: Officina Tum.

—. 2007b. *CỬU VÂN MỘNG: Giấc Mơ Chín Tầng Mây.* Translated by Jeon Hye Kyung and Ly Xuan Chung. Vietnam: Viện Nghiên cứu Văn hoá; Nhà xuất bản Khoa học xã hội.

—. 2009. *Visul învolburat al celor nouă.* Translated by Tae Hyun Oum and Elina Christina Lonoaia. Piteşti: Pararela 45.

—. [1922] 2009. *The Cloud Dream of the Nine, a Korean Novel: A Story of the Times of the Tangs of China About 840 A.D.* Translated by James Scarth Gale. Ithaca, NY: Cornell University Library.

—. 2010a. *Сон в зАоблачных высях.* Translated by Аделаида Федоровна Троцевич and Adelaida Fedorovna Trocevič. Санкт-Петербург: Гиперион.

—. 2010b. *Jiuyunmeng.* Annotated by Wang Wenyuan. Shanghai: Fudan daxue chubanshe.

—. 2011. *Wolkenträume: ein klassischer Roman aus dem Korea des 17.* Jahrhunderts. Translated by Albrecht Huwe. ankt Ottilien: EOS.

—. 2012. سحاب حلم. Translated by Walaa Maged Mohamed Kourashy. Cairo: Animar for Literature and Arts.

—. 2013. *Skydrømmen.* Translated by Jarne Byhre. Oslo: SOLUM.

—. 2014. *Jiuyunmeng.* Shanghai: Shanghai Guji chubanshe.

—. 2015. *Jiuyunmeng.* Translated by Yang Erning. Taipei: Junshi wenhua.

—. 2019. *The Nine Cloud Dream.* Translated by Heinz Insu Fenkl. New York: Penguin Classics.

Kim, T'aeja, Chŏng Hyeran, Chŏng Yŏngyang, and Han Chŏngyŏp. 2016. *(Susil kwa maŭm i hamkkye han) Han'guk ŭi chasu ŏje wa onŭl.* Páju: Mijinsa.

Ko, Yŏnhŭi. 2006. "17·18 segi, Chungguk ŭi p'anhwa sŏjŏk yut'ong i Chosŏn hoehwasa e mich'in yŏnghyang – sansu p'yohyŏn mit hwajo p'yohyŏn ŭl chungsim ŭro." In Hong Sŏnp'yo, Nam Chŏnghŭi, Chŏng Sŏnhŭi, Ko Yŏnhŭi, Ch'a Mihŭi, Kang Yŏngsim, Han Chagyŏng, and Yun Taesik, *17·18 segi Chosŏn ŭi oeguk sŏjŏk suyong kwa toksŏ munhwa*, 147-178. Seoul: Hyean.

LTI Korea library, ed. 2015. *Korean Short Stories in Translation.* Seoul: LTI Korea library. https://www.ltikorea.or.kr/en/e_essay.do

Smith, Margaret M., John Newel Lewis, and Ronald R. McCarty. "Book Illustration." Published online: 2003. (updated and revised, 20 January 2016; updated bibliography, May 26, 2010; updated and revised, July 15, 2008) https://doi.org/10.1093/gao/978 1884446054.article.T009989

Appendix

Image 1: Gale's illustrations to Chapter 4. (Kim 1922)

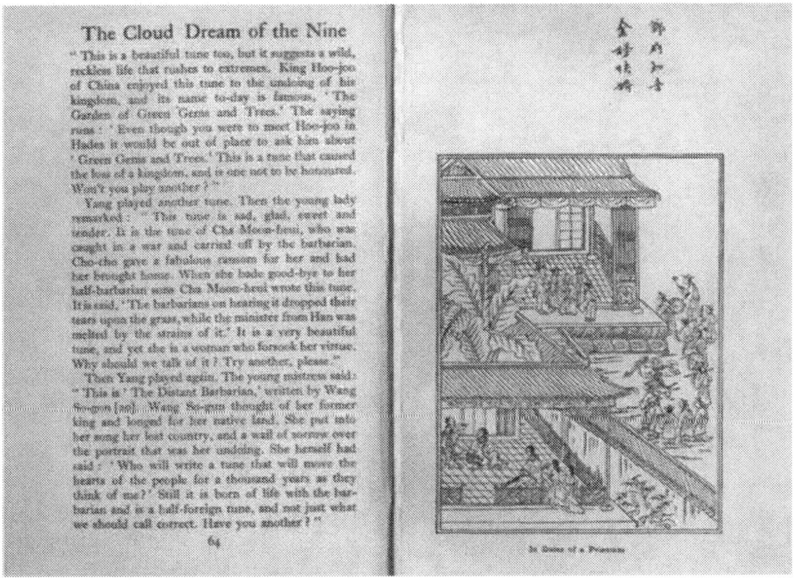

The Cloud Dream of the Nine

"This is a beautiful tune too, but it suggests a wild, reckless life that rushes to extremes. King Hoo-joo of China enjoyed this tune to the undoing of his kingdom, and its name to-day is famous, 'The Garden of Green Gems and Trees.' The saying runs: 'Even though you were to meet Hoo-joo in Hades it would be out of place to ask him about 'Green Gems and Trees.' This is a tune that caused the loss of a kingdom, and is one not to be honoured. Won't you play another?"

Yang played another tune. Then the young lady remarked: "This tune is sad, glad, sweet and tender. It is the tune of Cha Moon-heui, who was caught in a war and carried off by the barbarian. Cho-cho gave a fabulous ransom for her and had her brought home. When she bade good-bye to her half-barbarian sons Cha Moon-heui wrote this tune. It is said, 'The barbarians on hearing it dropped their tears upon the grass, while the minister from Han was melted by the strains of it.' It is a very beautiful tune, and yet she is a woman who forsook her virtue. Why should we talk of it? Try another, please."

Then Yang played again. The young mistress said: "This is 'The Distant Barbarian,' written by Wang So-goon [20]. Wang So-goon thought of her former king and longed for her native land. She put into her song her lost country, and a wail of sorrow over the portrait that was her undoing. She herself had said: 'Who will write a tune that will move the hearts of the people for a thousand years as they think of me?' Still it is born of life with the barbarian and is a half-foreign tune, and not just what we should call correct. Have you another?"

64

Image 2: Gale's Illustrations to Chapter 11. (Kim 1922)

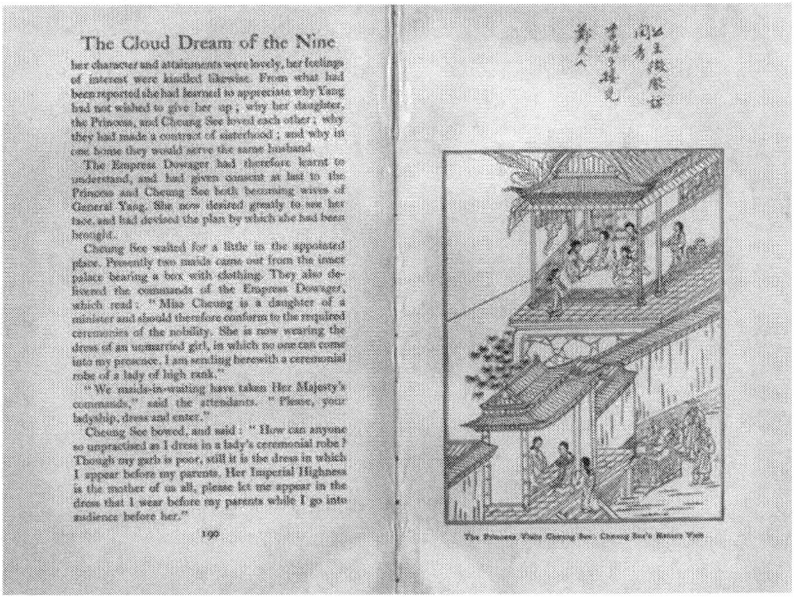

The Cloud Dream of the Nine

her character and attainments were lovely, her feelings of interest were kindled likewise. From what had been reported she had learned to appreciate why Yang had not wished to give her up; why her daughter, the Princess, and Cheung See loved each other; why they had made a contract of sisterhood; and why in one home they would serve the same husband.

The Empress Dowager had therefore learnt to understand, and had given consent at last to the Princess and Cheung See both becoming wives of General Yang. She now desired greatly to see her face, and had devised the plan by which she had been brought.

Cheung See waited for a little in the appointed place. Presently two maids came out from the inner palace bearing a box with clothing. They also delivered the commands of the Empress Dowager, which read: "Miss Cheung is a daughter of a minister and should therefore conform to the required ceremonies of the nobility. She is now wearing the dress of an unmarried girl, in which no one can come into my presence. I am sending herewith a ceremonial robe of a lady of high rank."

"We maids-in-waiting have taken Her Majesty's commands," said the attendants. "Please, your ladyship, dress and enter."

Cheung See bowed, and said: "How can anyone so unpractised as I dress in a lady's ceremonial robe? Though my garb is poor, still it is the dress in which I appear before my parents. Her Imperial Highness is the mother of us all, please let me appear in the dress that I wear before my parents while I go into audience before her."

190

Image 3: Wang Pou's story from *Oryun haengsil-to* (reprint of 1797)[1]

21 Printed in 1850. Catalogue number at National Library (Seoul, Korea): han kojo 57-ka 686

Image 4: Fourth panel of *Kuunmong* folding screen at the National Folk Museum (no. minsok 63586, ink and colours on paper, 391 x 136.5 cm, 19th century)

Image 5: Frontispiece and title page of Gale's English translation (Kim 1922)

THE CLOUD DREAM OF THE NINE ❧ *A KOREAN NOVEL*: A STORY OF THE TIMES OF THE TANGS OF CHINA ABOUT 840 A.D. BY KIM MAN-CHOONG (1617 - 1682 A.D.) PRESIDENT OF THE CONFUCIAN COLLEGE ❧ ❧ TRANSLATED BY *JAMES S. GALE* 30 YEARS RESIDENT IN KOREA WITH AN INTRODUCTION BY ELSPET KEITH ROBERTSON SCOTT AND SIXTEEN ILLUSTRATIONS

PUBLISHED BY DANIEL O'CONNOR LONDON: 90 GREAT RUSSELL STREET, W.C.1 ❧ ❧ ❧ MCMXXII

Image 6: Front cover of Spanish translation by Na Song-Joo and Havier Cortines (Kim 2006)

Image 7: Front cover of German translation by Huwe Albrecht (Kim 2011)

Image 8: Front cover of English translation by Richard Rutt and Kim Chong-un (Kim 1974)

Image 9: Front cover of English translation by Heinz Insu Fenkl (Kim 2019)

Image 10: Front cover of Kurodahan reprint of James Scarth Gale's English translation (Kim [1922] 2003)

Image 11: Front cover of Italian translation by Maurizio Riotto (Kim 2001)

Image 12: Front cover of E-book of James Scarth Gale's English translation by LTI Korea (Kim [1922] 2017)

Image 13: Front cover of Chinese *Kuunmong* published by Shanghai Guji chubanshe (Kim 2014)

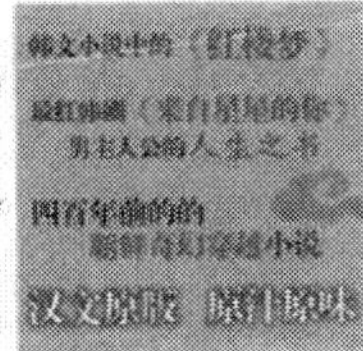

Image 14: Title page of Chinese *Kuunmong* published by Shanghai Guji chubanshe (Kim 2014)

Image 15: Bridge scene of a different folk-style painting partially added to the dust jacket of Chinese *Kuunmong* published by Shanghai Guji chubanshe (Kim 2014)

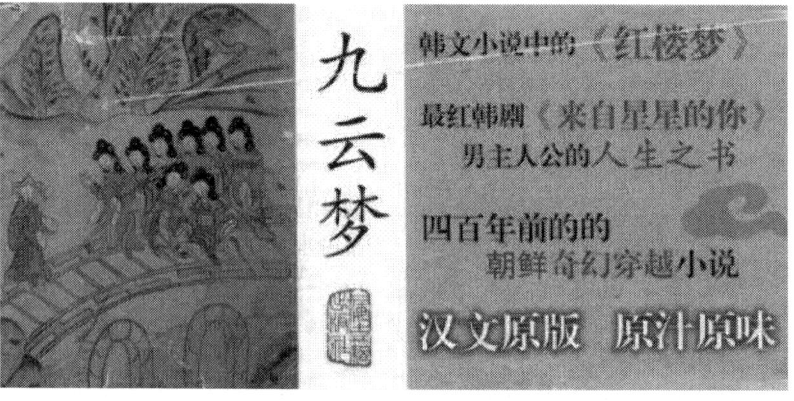

Image 16: Bridge scene of a different folk-style painting added to the page next to copyright information of Chinese *Kuunmong* published by Shanghai Guji chubanshe (Kim 2014)

Image 17: A folk-style Chin Ch'aebong scene of Chinese *Kuunmong* published by Shanghai Guji chubanshe (Kim 2014)

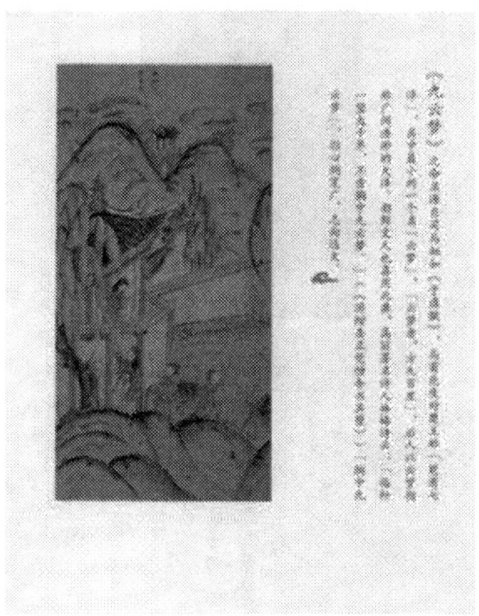

Image 18: Front cover of Russian translation by Аделаида Федоровна Троцевич and Adelaida Fedorovna Trocevič (Kim 2010a)

Image 19: A folk painting entitled *Ch'ŏnggŭm sangryŏn* 聽琴賞蓮 (listen to the tune of kayagŭm and enjoy the view of lotus in the pond, ink and colours on paper, 28.2 x 35.6 cm) by Korean artist Sin Yunbok 申潤福 (1758–?) at Kansong Museum

Image 20: Front cover of French translation by John Geneviève T. Park (Kim 2004)

Afterword

Elleke Boehmer and Matthew Reynolds

World Literature in Motion, a remarkable collection of essays, considers from a range of different perspectives the extent to which literature, specifically here world literature—its production, appearance, content, visibility—is shaped by and contingent upon its situatedness, its at once global and local positions. Each essay explores that situatedness in various inventive and always persuasive ways. From many different angles the contributors point out that how we read and value world literary texts depends upon the constant interaction of a variety of cultural brokers and mediators—publishers, editors, translators, printers, booksellers, literary prize judges—who are moreover globally distributed, as they show. An impressively broad range of these different players feature in the book, and their involvements are minutely observed, always with recourse to a rich international array of archives and sources.

Taken together, the essays testify to the profit that "grounded" (as the editors have it) book-historical and more generally textually materialist approaches can bring to postcolonial and world literature studies. The focus of each essay is that synergetic moment when we look at the book or magazine, or hear the radio programme, not only as a text on which to comment critically, but also as an object of material culture. Here we are reminded that the literary is never a settled value, or set of things, but a shifting field in which the texts and their evaluation are constantly on the move, globally in this case—a field that therefore requires us restlessly to query our understanding of the literary status quo.

Such insights are perhaps especially acute in postcolonial and world literature studies, as the essays all in their different ways suggest. First, as McDonald and Kelly have already pointed out in the Foreword, these studies are intensely concerned with books as objects simultaneously determined by external and internal forces, including by transnational and translational processes. Second, postcolonial and world literature studies feature objects of knowledge that bring together academic and commercial interests in striking ways. These objects are often seen as exotic, other or different, and hence have commercial value as marketable commodities, as we see in several of the essays. Yet they are also interesting to researchers for the discussions they facilitate on, for example, boundary crossing, intercultural relationship, and hybrid cultural production. They invite an intermingling of "commercial" and "academic" interests.

World Literature in Motion represents an important contribution to what the editors Flair Donglai Shi and Gareth Guangming Tan call critical world literature studies, a sociological approach to world literature texts as "interrelated [sets] of social phenomena", first outlined in the work of Stefan Helgesson and Pieter Vermeulen. Shi's introduction offers an authoritative, balanced outline and guide to this emergent, rapidly shifting field, observing the vigorous challenge it mounts vis-à-vis the sometimes-overlapping fields of comparative and postcolonial literary studies, and tracing the constant repositioning of the field that these critical manoeuvres bring about.

The editors' hope is, first, that the collection's "emphasis on the agency of the primary data and contexts in question" creates a "flexible and holistic" critical approach, and, second, that this might help offset the sense of "fragmented territorialisation in the ever-expanding field of World Literature". Throughout, the essays work to complicate "our understanding of how literary centres and margins work in practice", and question the paradigms of singular centres, unbudging peripheries, and the set of power relations between them that underpin the Moretti and Wallerstein accounts of world literature and its systems. As comparatists, the writers of this afterword applaud the editors' hope, and delight in the book's appearance. We hugely admire the careful attention to archival evidence that all the contributors have demonstrated, and the extremely hard work that has gone into the making of their essays.

The final important section on translations "beyond the anglophone, that is, between different languages that are not English (or at least between different contexts where English is not the primary linguistic medium)" lays down important standards and guidelines for both the world literature and the postcolonial fields. In both, English is too often taken as an easily accessible, transparent envelope to literary writing, with the result that generally, and within these fields themselves, linguistic diversity and especially minor language writings are too often under threat. Refreshingly, we see here instead how translation activities and book industries operate across a very diverse range of languages, and in regions like East Asia, the Middle East, or Eastern Europe and Africa where circulation is not necessarily mediated by postcolonial conditions, or not as those conditions have conventionally been defined. Translation emerges as transmission, not only across language-difference, but through the varied resistances of institutions, circumstances and individuals, and among localities and particular social practices and textures, such as ideas of etiquette and elements of folklore. As Wen-Chin Ouyang says, we "see translation as the 'liminal' space where an intercultural encounter is negotiated in order to accommodate both alterity and similarity, each within a particular subjectified cultural, historical, epistemological and linguistic context".

However, as we read through the collection, whether from the beginning, or following different themes, interesting group conversations emerge between many of the chapters. All are concerned in one way or another with the power relations through which the postcolonial marketplace and the spaces of world literature overlap, with the combined forces of commerce and politics that impinge on the decisions of editors and book prize committees, and with the processes through which books are shaped by certain ideological developments yet not wholly determined by them either. Literary production, the contributors find, comprises a spaghetti network of myriad different pathways of mediation and interaction, involving giant players like UNESCO and Penguin Random House, and singular, grounded yet still always influential actors such as broadcasters, translators, censors, and playwrights. The qualities of different media and forms are shown to matter: the ability of radio to create intimacy across distance, or of a magazine to curate a diverse selection of texts so as to create relations between them. A question of genre can close or open a pathway to circulation (only if a book was defined as a novel could it be eligible for the Booker Prize). Small contingencies have far-reaching consequences. Would *Gone with the Wind* have been translated in communist Bulgaria if a powerful party official had not happened to enjoy reading it in prison? Would the Man Asian Literary Prize have folded had its judges leaked more, or given more exciting press conferences?

This volume which studies so many means by which world literatures—or worlds of literature —are created is itself one of those means. It is itself both local and global: it has a point of origin in Oxford, and exhibits what is in some respects an Oxford emphasis on textual materiality and the study of institutions; but it is published in Germany, distributed in the UK and the US, written by a diverse group of contributors, and brings a wide range of texts together, connecting also to a great variety of locations. As the Introduction notes, this critical work is therefore a "highlighted continuation" of its subject, intervening in, and altering, the field that it describes. Texts such as *Closed Doors* and *Plucked in a Far Off Land* by the Cypriot writers Costas Montis and Taner Baybars—even though they were written in or have been translated into English—have barely circulated beyond Cyprus until their discussion in this volume, through which their participation in one always situated and partial construction of world literature is asserted. Just like the Chinese journal *Yiwen/Shijie wenxue*, then, this volume offers a "configuration of world literature" that is valuably non-hierarchical and counter-hegemonic, a multi-perspectival challenge to what Flair Donglai Shi's Introduction nicely calls "the haughty modifier that is '(the) world'".

Notes on the Contributors

Meleesha Bardolia is a PhD candidate in English Literature at the University of Melbourne. Her research interests include post-Mabo Australian literature and post-apartheid South African literature and the relationship between law and literature. She holds an MSt in World Literatures in English from the University of Oxford. Meleesha is also a filmmaker and her work has screened at various international film festivals including the 64th Melbourne International Film Festival, NYC PictureStart Film Festival and the Anthology Film Archives in Manhattan.

Elleke Boehmer is Professor of World Literature in English, in the English Faculty at the University of Oxford, and Director of The Oxford Life Writing Centre at Wolfson College. She is a foundational figure in the field of colonial and postcolonial literary studies, and her monographs include *Colonial and Postcolonial Literature* (1995, 2005), *Empire, the National and the Postcolonial* (2002), and the biography *Nelson Mandela* (2008). *Indian Arrivals 1870-1915: Networks of British Empire* (2015) was the winner of the biennial ESSE prize 2015-16. Her novel *The Shouting in the Dark* was published in the UK, South Africa and Australia, and won the Olive Schreiner Prize in 2018. She is also the General Editor of the Oxford Studies in Postcolonial Literatures Series and served as a Man Booker International judge 2013-15.

Rivkah Brown is a freelance print and audio journalist based in London. Her writing has been published in *The Financial Times, The Economist, The New Statesman, The Guardian, Ha'aretz, The Independent, The Baffler* and *The London Review of Books Blog*. Her podcasts, for *UnHerd* and *The Inkling Magazine*, have been listened to by tens of thousands of people. She completed her MSt in World Literatures in English at the University of Oxford with the help of an Ertegun Graduate Scholarship in the Humanities and holds a BA in English from the University of Cambridge.

Lubabah Chowdhury is a PhD candidate in English at Brown University. Her research interests include Caribbean women's literature in the 20th century, Third World and radical Black feminisms and representations of Afro-Asian relations in literature. Her work has been published in *de genere: Journal of Literary, Postcolonial and Gender Studies* and is forthcoming in *The Journal of Commonwealth and Postcolonial Studies*. She was a Visiting Research Student at King's College, London for the 2019-2020 academic year.

Katelyn Edwards is a Project Engineer for EWI, a development firm representing the Southeastern United States. She holds a Master of Studies in World Literatures in English from the University of Oxford, where she received the 2016 Marion Butler Prize, awarded to the master's thesis with the highest mark in Oxford's postgraduate English Department. Her research interests include the socio-political space of literary production and the intersections of literary institutions and questions of the book. Her current development projects include the renovation of the historic Armature Works Building in Tampa, Florida.

Sana Goyal is a PhD candidate at SOAS, University of London, researching contemporary African literature and literary prize culture. She is a book critic and has contributed to *Vogue India, Mint Lounge, Scroll.in, Huffington Post India, The Cardiff Review, Africa in Words*, and *Los Angeles Review of Books*. She was the Reviews Editor of issue three of CHASE's peer-reviewed postgraduate journal, *Brief Encounters*. Between January 2019 and 2020, she was on a CHASE-funded editorial placement at *Wasafiri* magazine. She is at home in London and Mumbai.

Yan JIA (贾岩) is Assistant Professor of Hindi and Indian literature in the Department of South Asian Studies at Peking University. He holds a PhD in Cultural, Literary and Postcolonial Studies from SOAS, University of London. His research interests include modern Hindi literature, post-1950 literary relations between China and India, and comparative/world literature.

Michelle Kelly is a Departmental Lecturer in World Literature in English at the Faculty of English Language and Literature, University of Oxford. Her research focuses on South African and world literature, on the intersections between law and literature, literature and other art forms, and material cultures. She is completing a monograph on J. M. Coetzee and confession, and co-editing a book, *Prison Writing and the Literary World*, focusing on the institutions through which prison writing emerges and circulates.

Yeogeun Sue Kim (김여근) is a DPhil candidate in Oriental Studies at the University of Oxford. Her thesis explores translations and adaptations of classical Korean fiction: *A Dream of the Nine Clouds* (구운몽, 九雲夢) and *The Tale of ChunHyang* (춘향전, 春香傳). Her research interests include reception theory, media studies, and visual culture. As a visual artist, she also founded a program on art and environment and taught at Chungbuk National University in Korea.

Peter D. McDonald is Professor of English and Related Literature at the University of Oxford and a Fellow of St Hugh's College. He writes on literature, the modern state and the freedom of expression; the history of writing systems, cultural institutions and publishing; multilingualism, translation and interculturality; and on the limits of literary criticism. His main publications include *British Literary Culture and Publishing Practice, 1888-1914* (1997), *The Literature Police: Apartheid Censorship and its Cultural Consequences* (2009), and *Artefacts of Writing: Ideas of the State and Communities of Letters from Matthew Arnold to Xu Bing* (2017).

Daniele Nunziata is a Lecturer in English at St Anne's College, University of Oxford. His primary research concerns postcolonial literature from the Eastern Mediterranean (the Middle East) with a focus on literary portrayals of Cyprus in travel writing before and after its independence from the British Empire. Central to this is the need to address the island's historical and contemporaneous relationship with imperialism, nationalism, and partition, asking questions about the language and literary form used by postcolonial Cypriot writers.

His other publications concern this context and other aspects of postcolonial, comparative, and world literature studies. This ranges from 19th-century Orientalist women's writing on Cyprus and its implications for the concept of auto-exoticism; to mid-20th-century translations and transcriptions of oral narratives across the African continent by the OUP and how it complicates our ideas about the British publishing industry's relationship with orature and cultural capital.

Wen-chin Ouyang (歐陽文津 وين - جين أويان), FBA, is Professor of Arabic and Comparative Literature at SOAS, University of London. She is the author of *Literary Criticism in Medieval Arabic-Islamic Culture: The Making of a Tradition* (1997), *Poetics of Love in the Arabic Novel* (2012), and *Politics of Nostalgia in the Arabic Novel* (2013). She has also published widely on *The Thousand and One Nights*, often in comparison with classical and modern Arabic narrative traditions, European and Hollywood cinema, magic realism, and Chinese storytelling. She is Editor-in-Chief of *Middle Eastern Literatures* and a member of the editorial board of Bulletin of SOAS. She founded and co-edits *Edinburgh Studies in Classical Arabic Literature*. A native speaker of Arabic and Chinese, she has been working towards Arabic-Chinese comparative literary and cultural studies, including Silk Road Studies.

Matthew Reynolds is Professor of English and Comparative Criticism at Oxford where he chairs the research program Oxford Comparative Criticism and Translation (OCCT). Recent publications include *Translation: A Very Short Introduction* (2016), *The Poetry of Translation: From Chaucer & Petrarch to Homer & Logue* (2011), *Likenesses: Translation, Illustration, Interpretation* (2013). With OCCT colleagues, he has also co-edited *Comparative Criticism: Histories and Methods* (a special issue of *Comparative Critical Studies*, 2015) and *Minding Borders: Resilient Divisions in Literature, the Body and the Academy* (2016). Current projects include *Prismatic Translation*—an investigation of the uses of multiple translations—and *Translationality: Literature Across Languages.* He serves as the general editor of the book series Transcript (Legenda) and Honorary Secretary of the British Comparative Literature Association.

Rashi Rohatgi is Associate Professor of English at Nord University. Her 2014 monograph, *Fighting Cane and Canon: Abhimanyu Unnuth and the Case of World Literature in Mauritius*, includes the first English translation of Unnuth's poetry, and she is currently translating his seminal novel *Lal Pasina*. Her research foci are world literature, diaspora culture, and international pedagogy, with recent work addressing Indian Ocean and Scandinavian literatures and the teaching of comparative literature. She has served as Reviews Editor for the African literature site *Africa in Words* and as Fiction Editor for the literary journal *Boston Accent Lit*, where she convened the Accent Prize.

Galina Rousseva-Sokolova is currently Associate Professor at Sofia University (Bulgaria) and Jindal Global University (India), teaching courses in Indian literature, cultural studies and comparative religions. With a PhD from the École Pratique des Hautes Études (Paris), her field of expertise is pre-modern Indian vernacular literature, on which she has numerous scholarly publications and translations in English, French and Bulgarian.

Flair Donglai Shi (施东来) is a DPhil candidate in English at the University of Oxford. His thesis focuses on the Yellow Peril as a traveling discourse in modern Anglophone and Sinophone literatures. His research areas include literary feminism and queer studies, critical race studies, and comparative Chinese and Sinophone literatures. His articles have been published in many academic journals including *Women: A Cultural Review*, *Comparative Literature & World Literature*, *CLEAR (Chinese Literature: Essays, Articles, and Reviews)*, and *Comparative Critical Studies*.

Lucy Steeds is a writer and researcher based in London. She holds an MSt in World Literatures in English from the University of Oxford. Her current work examines the legacies of colonialism and in particular the intersections of literature and technology in colonial and postcolonial contexts, through the Internet, new media, and most significantly, radio. She has also written about technology and censorship in Hong Kong and mainland China, as well as the role of radio in colonial India and the Caribbean diaspora. She has been an active contributor to Oxford's Race and Resistance research network and continues to explore the ways in which technology and literature inform discussions of orality, resistance, and identity.

Gareth Guangming Tan (陈光明) is a Policy Research Analyst at the Singapore Institute of International Affairs (SIIA). Gareth's work centres on the ASEAN region, and his research focuses specifically on the politics and international relations of Myanmar, Malaysia and Indonesia. His output at the SIIA consists of special reports, chairman's notes and other materials, which have been circulated to the SIIA's corporate members. His articles have been featured in *the Straits Times* and *Asian Geographic Magazine*. Prior to signing on with the SIIA, Gareth was a Research Assistant in the Lee Kuan Yew School of Public Policy's Asia Competitiveness Institute, where he worked on national and sub-national economic research and business case studies. Gareth holds a Masters in World Literatures from the University of Oxford, and a BA (English) from the University of York in the United Kingdom.

Carmen Thong is pursuing a PhD in English at Stanford University as a Knight-Hennessy Scholar. She graduated with a BA (Hons) in English Literature from the University of Warwick, and an MSt World Literatures in English from the University of Oxford. She also worked in B2B Strategy and as a Management Associate with a telco in Malaysia after receiving a full undergraduate scholarship from the company.

Acknowledgement

This book project would not have been possible without the generous academic and editorial support offered by our series editors, Professor Janet Wilson (Northampton) and Dr. Christopher Ringrose (Monash). As first-time editors, we would like to express our utmost gratefulness towards them. We must also thank all of our contributors for their patience and understanding. They always gave us their full trust even when the publishing process suffered from unexpected delays.

As mentioned in the Foreword, this project was first conceptualised with the guidance and encouragement of our mentors in the Master of Studies in World Literatures in English program at Oxford University in 2015. As students who benefited greatly from the program, we must thank Professor Elleke Boehmer, Professor Peter D. McDonald, Dr. Sowon Park, and Dr. Michelle Kelly for exposing us to diverse perspectives and approaches in the fields of book history, postcolonial studies, and world literature. We hope that this edited volume will honour their hard work and reflect the transformative effects the program has had on the intellectual trajectories of their students. During our time at Oxford, the Oxford Comparative Criticism and Translation (OCCT) research centre had been a valuable intellectual space to debate issues in world literature and comparative studies, and we are grateful for the opportunities OCCT gave us to connect with many of our contributors based outside of Oxford.

During the long process of putting together this volume, numerous friends and colleagues have kindly read parts of the manuscript and offered helpful advice on the theoretical and argumentative weaknesses they found in many places. For the time they have spared to help with this project, we are indebted to Dr. Xiaofan Amy Li (UCL), Dr. Jinyi Chu (Yale), Dr. Yan Jia (PKU), Dr. Sam Perks (NTU), Roweena Yip (NUS), Po-hsi Chen (Yale), Yan Chen (Oxford), Hyei Jin Kim (Oxford), and Sherry Yuwei Lu (Cambridge). We would also like to thank the dedicated editorial help offered by

ibidem Press, especially Valerie Lange and Jana Dävers, who always replied to our emails and requests in the timeliest fashion.

Finally, since Flair is based in Oxford and Gareth in Singapore (2016–2020), much of the work on this edited volume was done through online communications, and we would like to express our individual appreciation of the help we received from our respective institutions throughout the years. Flair is much obliged for the academic and emotional support offered by his PhD supervisors, Professor Matthew Reynolds and Professor Margaret Hillenbrand. This edited volume had indeed been a big bittersweet distraction for Flair during his time in Oxford, and he would not have been able to finish it without both supervisors believing in him and ensuring that he could do this while working on his thesis. Gareth would like to thank his colleagues at the Asia Competitiveness Institute and Singapore Institute of International Affairs for supporting his continued participation in this project. He would also like to thank Roweena Yip for her academic and emotional support during crunch periods associated with this project.

***ibidem**.eu*